Reverse Symbolism
Dictionary : Symbols
Listed by Subject

Reverse Symbolism Dictionary : Symbols Listed by Subject

compiled by
STEVEN OLDERR

McFarland & Company, Inc., Publishers
Jefferson, North Carolina, and London

British Library Cataloguing-in-Publication data are available

Library of Congress Cataloguing-in-Publication Data

Olderr, Steven.
  Reverse symbolism dictionary : symbols listed by subject / by
Steven Olderr.
    p. cm.
  Includes bibliographical references.
  ISBN 0-89950-561-9 (lib. bdg. : 50# alk. paper) ∞
    1. Symbolism—Dictionaries. 2. Emblems—Dictionaries. I. Title.
CB475.O37 1992
302.2'22—dc20   AUG 1 6 1993   90-53517
                                                        CIP

Manufactured in the United States of America

McFarland & Company, Inc., Publishers
  Box 611, Jefferson, North Carolina 28640

For William H. Whitaker

Foreword

This is a reverse dictionary of symbols: the thing or idea to be symbolized is listed first, followed by a list of symbols. The work is based upon my book, *Symbolism: A Comprehensive Dictionary* (published by McFarland in 1986), but is far from simply a reconfiguration of the information in that work. While the two books are complementary, it is not necessary to have one to make sense of the other. That book is for the person seeking to learn the meaning of a symbol that has already been used elsewhere. This book is designed for the person looking for a symbol to use in his own creation.

Terms

The technical terms of symbolism are inexact. Attribute fades off into emblem, emblem onto association, and so forth. Some items are clearly attributes, some are clearly emblems, some are both, some are not exactly either. The definitions that follow are about as close as one can come. They are presented not as iron-clad rules, but as guidelines to aid understanding.

- **allusion**   a reference to an historical person or event, or an artistic or literary work. To have an "albatross around one's neck" is an allusion to Coleridge's poem "The Rime of the Ancient Mariner."

- **association**   something linked in memory or imagination, or by correlation or analogy with an object, idea, person, or event. The letter "A" is associated with beginning.

- **attribute**   an object closely connected with or belonging to a specific person, office, or event. The keys to heaven are an attribute of St. Paul.

- **emblem**   an object or representation of an object suggesting another object or person. Three feathers are an emblem of the Prince of Wales and Wales itself.

- **symbol** something which is itself, yet stands for, suggests, or means something else by reason of relationship or convention. A dove is a symbol of peace.

Allusions, associations, attributes, and emblems are all considered symbols, but not all symbols are one of these.

Further Information

As with its precursor, this work brings together more items than any other single source. Fortunately, most of the symbols are obvious in origin and use. To explain everything contained herein would require a much larger, much more expensive book. Unfortunately, explanatory information on symbolism is often scattered or so detailed that it is only of interest to scholars.

In many cases, brief explanations can be culled from standard encyclopedias, biographical dictionaries, and common reference works such as *The Reader's Encyclopedia*, or *Butler's Lives of the Saints*.

Background information cannot necessarily be found in works on symbolism; nevertheless, the following works may also be useful:

Cirlot, J. E. *A Dictionary of Symbols*, 2d ed. Philosophical Library, 1971. 419pp., illus.

> Trending into the scholarly. Very good as far as it goes, but some entries are discussed and never defined, and the scope of the entries does not always cover the range of use to which a symbol may have been put. Nevertheless, there is probably more general background material here than anywhere else. Includes a 40 page introduction on the use and interpretation of symbols.

Cooper, J. C. *An Illustrated Encyclopedia of Traditional Symbols*. Thames and Hudson, 1978. 207pp., illus.

> Less detailed than the Cirlot book, but more entries and broader in scope.

DeBles, Arthur. *How to Distinguish the Saints in Art by Their Costumes, Symbols, and Attributes*. Art Culture Publications, 1925. 168pp., illus.

> Very good information in a very narrow area.

deVries, Ad. *Dictionary of Symbols and Imagery*. North-Holland, 1974. 515pp.

> A general dictionary that shows what else a particular symbol is used for, but offers no explanations of why.

Ferguson, George. *Signs and Symbols in Christian Art*. Oxford University Press, 1959. 123pp., illus.

An excellent book dealing especially with Renaissance Christian art. Individual articles are not comprehensive, however, and the index must be used to gather complete information.

Hall, James. *Dictionary of Subjects and Symbols in Art.* Harper, 1974. 345pp.
A very good source for art symbols.

Olderr, Steven. *Symbolism: A Comprehensive Dictionary.* McFarland, 1986. 159pp.
The best single source to find out what else a particular symbol is used for, although it offers few explanations of why. The present *Reverse Symbolism Dictionary* is keyed to this earlier work.

Don't be discouraged if your local library does not have these particular works; they may have others, and your librarian will be able to get a great deal of information from general reference books.

Reverse Symbolism Dictionary

A

A *association:* one

Aaron *associations:* golden calf; priests with censers, the ground opening at their feet • *attributes:* almond; breastplate; censer; flowering almond; flowering rod or wand; golden bells on the hem of a garment; rod with snake (Aaron and Moses before Pharaoh; the miracles of Aaron and Moses); triple tiara

abandon *see* **wantonness**

abandonment willow • *flower language:* creeping willow; garden anemone; laburnum; willow • *see also* **forsakenness**

abbesses *attribute:* crozier with a white banner or veil

abbots *attributes:* crozier; crozier with a white banner or veil; white miter (now worn by bishops, but formerly worn also by cardinals and abbots—an abbot's miter was usually unadorned)

Abel *association:* lamb on an altar as a sacrifice • *attributes:* shepherd's crook, especially when shown with a lamb; staff

Abel and Cain *see* **Cain and Abel**

abeyance *see* **latency**

abnegation *see* **self-denial**

abnormality blot; dwarf; renaming; stain; trapezium (in comparison with a trapezoid, it shows an even greater degree of abnormality and irregularity); trapezoid; twisting • *associations:* eight (corresponds to violent passions, abnormal tendencies); jester; left side • *see also* **irregularity**

abomination *see* **disgust**

abortion nutmeg

Abraham *associations:* brazier with wood and knife (Abraham and Isaac);

faggots formed in a cross • *attributes:* knife and a starry blue shield; knife, especially a sacrificial knife; shofar

absence broom placed by the door of a cottage (the woman of the house is not at home) • *flower language:* wormwood; cochorus (impatient of absence); wormwood; zinnia (thoughts of absent friends)

absolute zero *see* **zero**

absolution *see* **confession and absolution; forgiveness**

absolutism czar; emperor

abstinence purple • *Judaism:* acacia (sexual abstinence) • *see also* **chastity**

Abstinence personified *attribute:* palm tree

abstraction desert (the realm of abstraction, truth, purity, ascetic spirituality, spirituality in general, and holiness); snow-covered mountain (abstract thought); sphere

absurdity *see* **folly**

abundance beehive; chrysanthemum; clover; coconut; cornucopia; feather; fig; flour (abundant life); fruit (abundance, spiritual abundance); gladiolus; grain; horn [animal]; lionheaded ox (abundance and earthly power); milk and/or honey; mustard [plant]; palm tree; plow; St. Julian; sheaf; sycamore; summer; wheat • *China:* wild bear (the wealth of the forest) • *Norse mythology:* golden hair • *see also* **fruitfulness; plenty; prosperity**

Abundance personified Ceres with a cornucopia, sickle, or wreath of corn (the earth's abundance personified) • *attributes:* cornucopia; globe; rudder; palm tree

1

abuse *flower language:* crocus, saffron (do not abuse)

abyss deepness; ocean

Academy personified *attribute:* myrtle

accommodating disposition *flower language:* valerian

accounting tapster (a falsifier of accounts)

accusation Astaroth

achievement architectural column (especially free standing columns); coronation; gold rose (absolute achievement); mountain peak; symmetry; tripod (achievement in song or dance) • *associations:* three; four (tangible achievement); ten (spiritual achievement) • *kabala:* nine (associated with spiritual achievement)

Achilles infant held by his ankle over a river; chariot with a body dragging behind (the victory of Achilles over Hector)

acknowledgment lavender plant • *flower language:* Canterbury bell; flax (I am sensible of your kindness)

acquiescence *see* **defeat; passivity; submission; surrender**

acquisition *association:* W • *heraldry:* snail (acquired possessions to be preserved and expanded)

acquittal *Greece:* white stone (a vote for acquittal)

Actaeon a hunter turning into a stag, or observing a nude woman

action arm; bow with arrows (action as a means of effecting the will); bugle, trumpet (call to action); diamond key (the power to act); falcon (evil thought or action); ford, fording (marks a decisive stage in action, development, etc.); hunter (action for its own sake); Mars; sails, spurs (stimulus to action); sieve (self-knowledge through action); sulfur (desire for positive action); torch (the active, positive power of nature); woodpecker (perserverant action) • *associations:* eight (the perfect blending of action and reaction, knowledge and love, conscious and unconscious); G; the right side; seven (willful and unexpected action) • *heraldry:* eagle (a man of action); horse (readiness for action) • *kabala:* three

active principle one; tarot cards I to XI; a triangle with the apex up

activity arm (generally, the position of the arm shows the activity, e.g., offering, worshipping, inviting, etc.); beehive; lark; Leah (the active life); orchestra (the cooperation of the discrete toward a given end, activity of the corporate whole); pheasant; rooster; Saturn [god]; teeth (expression of activity, especially sexual activity); thyme • *associations:* L; three • *flower language:* thyme

actors *association:* Pluto [planet]

Adam the angel Jophiel holding a flaming sword or wheel (the expulsion of Adam and Eve from Garden of Eden); Christ child holding an apple (Christ as the new Adam; Christ as the redeemer of man from Original Sin holding the Fruit of Salvation); gardener; hermaphrodite (Adam before Eve was created out of him); skull and crossbones at the foot of the Cross (refers to the legend that the cross of Jesus rested on the bones of Adam) • *attributes:* bunch of keys; skull • *attributes of Adam after the Fall:* hoe; mattock; shovel

adaptation and coordination Temperance [tarot]

adaptability ash tree; chameleon; mercury [element]; trout • *Christianity:* gourd • *see also* **versatility**

administration Judgment [tarot] (active administration of the law); rochet (loving administration); sword (administration of justice) • *China:* unicorn (wise administration of government); wild pear tree (wise administration)

admiration *see* **respect**

admission white stone (admission to a theater)

admonition *see* **warning**

Adonis infant in a tree trunk; hunter restrained by nude woman; woman whose arms are sprouting myrrh branches with nymphs nearby holding a baby (birth of Adonis) • *associations:* anemone [flower]; plants • *attributes:* flute; grain

adoration daisy; frankincense; hand held flat on the heart • *flower language:* cacalia (adulation); dwarf sunflower • *see also* **love; worship**

adornment tattoo

Adrian, St. soldier with an anvil • *attributes:* anvil; lion; sword with anvil

adroitness *see* **finesse**

adulation *see* **adoration**

adultery bush (a spot for lurking, ambush, spying, illicit love); centaur (the sin of adultery); heart pierced with an arrow with a woman's head shown on the heart (sin against the 7th Commandment, i.e., Thou shalt not commit adultery); lamprey, alone or entwined with a snake • *ancient Britain:* stork • *associations:* scarlet letter A; yellow • *see also* **cuckolding**

Adultery personified *attribute:* rooster

adulthood trousers

Advent *associations:* lily of the valley; purple; violet [color]

adventure boat; gull; journey (adventure; the desire for adventure); kite [toy]; ocean; riding, especially on an animal; road; sails; ship; Ulysses • *association:* W (adventurousness)

adversaries *see* **enemies**

adversity cabin; hyacinth [flower] (resistance to adversity); snowdrop (friendship in adversity) • *association:* D • *Christianity:* oak (endurance against adversity) • *flower language:* camomile (love in adversity; energy in adversity); evergreen thorn (solace in adversity); spruce pine (hope in adversity); xeranthemum (cheerfulness under adversity) • *see also* **negativity**

advice ear; whispering • *flower language:* rhubarb

Aeetes *attribute:* scepter of ivory

Aeneas younger man with an older man on his shoulders

affection amaranth; animal fat; born on a Friday, worthily given (or, loving and giving); bouquet (sweet thoughts; declaration of affection; a tribute); cat's eye [gemstone] (platonic affection); embrace; garnet (deep affection); intestines; ivy (undying affection); kissing; licking; opal (protection from evil affections); partridge, sorrel, stork (parental affection); pear; stroking; tree; turquoise [gemstone] (sincere affection); turtledove; vine; woodcock; wormwood • *association:* O [letter]; *China:* peony; *flower language:* garden or double daisy (I share your affection); gillyflower (bonds of affection); gorse (enduring affection); green locust tree (affection beyond the grave); honeysuckle (generous and devoted affection); jonquil (desire for a return

of affection); pink convolvulus (worth sustained by judicious and tender affection); sorrel (especially parental affection); tuberose received from the hands of a lady (mutual affection) • *heraldry:* dog; dolphin • *see also* **attachment; friendship; love**

Affection personified *attributes:* dock [plant]; lizard; pear

affliction bitter herbs; broken stone; corrosion; rat (infirmity and death); rust; sackcloth, especially with ashes; sea of flames; thorn • *flower language:* aloe • *Judaism:* matzo • *see also* **disease; pestilence; plague; sickness**

affluence *see* **riches**

affront *see* **humiliation**

Africa personified *attributes:* coral necklace; cornucopia (occasionally); elephant, or just an elephant's head; lion; scorpion; serpent

Afro-Americans *association:* watermelon (usually used in a pejorative sense)

afterlife Egypt (concern with life after death) • *Greece:* asphodel (association)

afternoon autumn

afterthought *flower language:* China aster; Michaelmas daisy; starwort

Agatha of Sicily, St. *attributes:* breasts in a plate; lamb; shears; pincers; veil

age ass (a man 80 to 90 years of age); bat [animal] (a woman 80 to 90 years of age); beard; billy goat (a boy 10 to 20 years of age); bull (a man 20 to 30 years of age); calf (a boy up to 20 years of age); cat (a man 70 to 80 years of age); dog (a man 60 to 70 years of age); dove (a girl 10 to 20 years of age); fox (a man 40 to 50 years of age); goose (a woman 50 to 60 years of age); hen (a woman 40 to 50 years of age); lion (a man 30 to 40 years of age); magpie (a woman 20 to 30 years of age); one hundred and ten (the perfect age to die); peahen (a woman 30 to 40 years of age); puppy (a boy up to 10 years of age); quail (a girl up to 10 years of age); rust; twenty-one (coming of age); vulture (a woman 60 to 70 years of age); wolf (a man 50 to 60 years of age) • *associations:* 18, 21 (coming of age) • *flower language:* guelder rose; snowball [flower]

aged ass (a man between 80 and 90 years of age); autumn; bat [animal] (a woman between 80 and 90 years of age); buzzard; cat (a man between 70 and 80 years of age); chair; crab tree (old, foolish, and cowardly people); cress; December; dog (a man 60 to 70 years of age); ember; lizard (disrespect for elders); reptile; scarecrow; vulture (a woman 60 to 70 years of age); water cress • *associations:* December; evening; hawthorn trained over a bench to make a bower (old men); north; winter; yellow leaf • *attributes:* crutch; gray beard; gray hair; spectacles [eyeglasses]; skull (Old Age personified); staff; walking cane • *China:* crane [bird] • *emblem:* crutch (those who care for the aged) • *flower language:* American starwort (cheerfulness in old age); tree of life • *see also* **longevity; maturity**

agents *see* **messengers**

aggressiveness banners in superfluous numbers (aggressive militarism); right hand; spider

agility *see* **nimbleness**

agitation drunkenness (religious frenzy) • *flower language:* moving plant; quaking grass; quamoclit; sainfoin; shaking sainfoin • *see also* **excitement**

Agnes, St. *attributes:* being bound to a stake; crown of olive branches; fire; lamb; long flowing hair; olive branch; sword

agony *see* **suffering**

agreements knot • *flower language:* broken straw (renunciation of an agreement); corn straw [maize]; phlox (unanimity) • *see also* **concord; contracts; covenants; harmony**

agriculture Abel, Cain (primitive agriculture); cattle in a pasture; Ceres; harrow [tool]; hoe; Issachar; ox; plow; Saturn [god]; sheaf; sickle; swastika; water buffalo; wheat with grapes • *China:* ox • *emblem:* corn [maize] • *see also* **farmers; harvest; sowing**

Agriculture personified *attributes:* grain

Agrippina the Elder urn held by woman with boat

Agrippine sibyl *attribute:* whip

Aidan, St. *attribute:* stag

aid *see* **help**

air bird; children playing with toy windmills (allegory of air); eagle; fan (celestial air); feather; Quetzel (Aztec and Mayan god of air); swinging (purification by air); wind (air in its violent and active aspect) • *emblem:* full sails • *see also* **wind**

Air personified anvil tied to the feet of a woman (Juno as Air personified) • *attributes:* bird (attribute of Juno personifying air); chameleon

alacrity *see* **promptness**

alarm *see* **fear; horror; warning**

alchemist old man with a bellows at a furnace • *attributes:* black castle; crucible; forge; hourglass

alchemy *association:* tremella nestoe • *emblem:* winged dragon

alcoholism pink elephant (popular symbol for delirium tremens)

alder tree *Celtic association:* F

alehouses *see* **taverns**

alertness *see* **wakefulness; watchfulness**

Alexander the Great coronation of a young woman by a soldier (the soldier is Alexander the Great) • *association:* rope binding a chariot, tied with the Gordian knot

Alexis, St. occasionally represented as a ragged pilgrim • *attribute:* bowl

Alfred, St. *attribute:* harp

All Saints Day *association:* red

allegiance broken straw (renunciation of allegiance); hand clasped between two others; sword held with the hilt upward; tattoo (declaration of allegiance; mystic allegiance) • *see also* **loyalty**

allegorical figures *occasional attribute:* polygonal nimbus

alliance hands clasped in a handshake

allurement fleece (alluring desire); merman, mermaid (fatal allurement); pipe [music]; spikenard • *see also* **attraction; seduction; temptation**

almoner *attribute:* purse

Alpheus *attribute:* urn, especially when lying on its side

altar sanctuary lamp, vigil candle (when lit, denotes the presence of the host at the altar in Catholic and Anglican churches); table

alter ego shadow

alteration *see* **change**

Amarillis and Mirtillo coronation of a youth by a maiden, or vice versa, in a pastoral setting

ambiguity jerkin [ambiguity of thought]; mask

ambition airplane; giraffe; herb (primitive desires and ambitions aroused by the senses); hollyhock; ivy; ladder; lion; orange [color]; spider • *association:* club suit [playing cards] • *flower language:* hollyhock (especially female ambition); mountain laurel • *heraldry:* orange [color] (worldly ambition)

ambivalence amphisbaena (an ambivalent situation; the anguish caused by an ambivalent situation); Death [tarot]; duality; twilight; *associations:* six; W (wavering emotions)

Ambrose, St. *attributes:* beehive (especially when pictured with two scourges); book with a pen on a writing table; bull; dove; Gregorian music written on a scroll; ox; scourge, whip (usually with three knots, sometimes two scourges with a beehive); writing pen; writing table with pen and books

amelioration *flower language:* milkvetch

America *emblem:* American Indians (early America)

America personified *attributes:* bow and arrows; caiman; crown of feathers; severed head pierced by an arrow

amiability *see* **friendliness**

amicability *see* **friendliness**

amnesty white • *see also* **truth**

amniotic waters *association:* ocean

Amon *emblem:* papyrus

amorousness *see* **love**

Amos *attributes:* shepherd's crook; staff

Amphitrite *attribute:* trident (occasionally)

amulets *see* **charms [amulets]**

amusement playing cards; popinjay • *flower language:* bladder nut • *see also* **play; sports**

Anael *associations:* three; five • *kabala:* eight (association)

Anake *attribute:* hammer

anarchy the Furies; red flag; torch • *see also* **chaos**

Anat *attribute:* ostrich feathers

ancestors doll; warrior • *heraldry:* Melusina, mermaid, merman (seafaring ancestors)

anchorites *see* **hermits**

Andrew, St. aged saint with an X-shaped cross praying before an image of the Virgin and Christ child; man being scourged; man with a fish in his hand • *associations:* people climbing up ladders set against a house; X • *attributes:* boathook with an X-shaped cross; book with a scroll or a tall cross; fishnet; spear with a V-shaped frame; St. Andrew's cross; two fish crossed

Andrew Corsini, St. bishop with the Virgin Mary appearing to him in a vision

androgyny fir; fleur-di-lys; hermaphrodite (androgynous self-creation); lute; mast on a ship; pyramid; round tower surmounted by a crescent; shovel; six-pointed star (also the androgynous nature of the deity); swan; Tiresias; tortoise; turtle; violin • *association:* Y

Andromeda man chained to a rock, attacked by a monster

Angela Merici, St. *associations:* cloak; ladder

Angelica, St. soldier with a dragon

angels plumed serpent (angel of dawn); seven trumpets (the seven archangels) • *associations:* nine (the nine choirs of angels); seventy-two; shooting star; trumpet (particularly the archangel Gabriel); twelve (the twelve legions of angels); wings • *attribute:* wings • *Christianity:* two (angels at the tomb of Christ) • *see also* **cherubim; powers [angels]; principalities [angels]; putti; seraphs; thrones [angels]; virtues [angels]** and names of particular angels, such as **Anael, Lumiel, Uriel,** etc.

anger ants in swarms; burning, peony (anger; indignation); carbuncle [gemstone] (especially when related to the eyes); devil with a red face; ember; furze; Judgment [tarot] (hotheadedness); nostrils, stomach (seat of anger); porcupine (blind anger); Satan; spleen (seat of the emotions of sexual passion, mirth, impetuosity, capriciousness, melancholy, but especially anger); Taurus (anger that is slow to come, but then unleashed in fury); turkey (senseless anger) • *associations:* purple-red; red • *flower language:* barberry; citron (ill-natured beauty); fumitory; whin • *see also* **bitterness; fury; resentment; temper; wrath**

anguish *see* **suffering**

anima damsel; Eurydice (the poet's anima escaping); princess; sleeping beauty; succubus; woman • *attribute:* palm tree

animality *see* **brutishness**

animals brooch in the shape of an animal endows the wearer with characteristics of that animal; Friday (according to the Bible, land beasts man were created on a Friday); oyster (lowest form of animal life); red flower (animal life); reptile (an infernal animal); tail (indicator of an animal's mood); Thursday (according to the Bible, sea beasts and birds were created on Thursday) • *low animals:* cloven feet (attribute of unclean animals); dog; dogfish (the lowest form of fish); buzzard; flea; goat (a low animal because it is dirty, but sometimes considered a sacred animal because in its natural state it lives in high places); hiding under a rock (association); kite; oyster (the lowest form of animal life); pigeon; rate; snake; swine; worm • *sacred animals:* cat (Egypt); cow (India); dove; eagle, goat (a sacred animal because it lives in high places in its natural state, but sometimes considered a low animal because it is dirty); Phoenix • *see also* **brutishness**

animosity *see* **hate**

ankles *attribute:* Uranus [planet]

Anne, St. *attributes:* book; door; green mantle [clothing]; red

annihilation *see* **defeat**

announcement gong

annoyance fly [insect]; gnat; hands on hips; mosquito; nettle; pigeon (modern use); rubbing [motion]; thorn

Annunciation *see* **Virgin Mary**

anointing balm; chrism; olive branch; oil

Ansanus, St. soldier with palm and banner of the Resurrection • *attributes:* baptismal cup; bunch of dates; cauldron of boiling oil; white banner with red cross

answer *flower language:* woodbine [monthly honeysuckle] (I will not answer hastily)

antagonism *see* **anger; hate**

Anthony of Padua, St. monk restoring a youth's severed leg • *attributes:* book pierced by a sword; Christ child; crucifix, especially with an unclothed Christ; fire; fish; flaming heart; flowering cross; infant in a cradle; kneeling ass; lily; money chest containing a heart

Anthony the Great, St. man with flames underfoot; monk; praying desert hermit having a monstrous or erotic vision • *association:* centaur; lion scratching out graves in the desert • *attributes:* aspergillum; blue theta on the shoulder; crutch, especially with a bell on it; fire; raven with a loaf of bread; staff with a tau cross on the end; swine

anti-hero Punch and Judy (the anti-hero overcoming learning, domesticity, death, and the Devil)

Antichrist Babylon; basilisk; leopard

anticipation *see* **expectation**

antidote rue [plant] (antidote for madness and poison) • *flower language:* white poppy

Antipas, St. *attribute:* brass ox

antithesis and thesis *see* **thesis and antithesis**

Anubis *attributes:* caduceus; shepherd's crook

anxiety broom [for sweeping] (the power to do away with worry and trouble); mosquito; quivering; smelling; sweat; zigzag • *flower language:* Christmas rose (tranquillize my anxiety); golden marigold (uneasiness); red columbine (anxious and waiting) • *see also* **fear**

apathy *see* **indifference; passivity; stoicism; stolidity**

apes *association:* banana

aphrodisiac ants; asparagus; camphor (an anti-aphrodisiac); chocolate; dove meat; duck meat; nettles; nutmeg; oysters; periwinkle; potatoes; pepper; radishes; tusks

Aphrodite *associations:* copper; eagle • *attributes:* conch shell; cypress; octopus; violet hair; wings • *emblems:* gull; star of the sea (usually seven-pointed); swan (usually white)

apocalypse angel with a key descending into a pit with a dragon; angel with flaming pillars for legs; book with seals upon it laying in the lap of Christ; dragon being thrown into a pit by an angel; eagle's scream; eclipse of the sun (omen of the end of the world); four horsemen, especially when charging; horse with a sword coming from its mouth; scroll or book being eaten by St. John; seven falling stars; sickle, especially when held by Christ enthroned with angels about • *associations:* birch;

six hundred and sixty-six (also applied to Martin Luther and other Protestants, and Adolf Hitler)

Apollo Bacchus (antithesis of Apollo); man shooting python with arrows • *associations:* maiden with upraised arms sprouting branches; ring finger; sparrowhawk; Sunday • *attributes:* amber [gemstone]; bow and arrows; chariot drawn by four horses; cicada; cow; crane [bird]; crow; crown of laurel; cypress; flute; globe; goose; griffin; horse; lute (occasionally); lyre; nimbus; sapphire; shepherd's crook; silver bow [archery]; sun; swan; viol; wolf • *emblems:* laurel; raven

Apollonia, St. *attributes:* forceps holding a tooth; garment of palm leaves

apostasy idol

apostles *see* **Jesus Christ**

appeal *see* **prayer; supplication**

appeasement *see* **placation**

appetite herb (appetizer); Reynard the Fox (carnal appetite); thirst (blind appetite for life) • *Greece:* parsley (worn on the head, it was thought to increase cheerfulness and appetite) • *see also* **eating; gluttony; hunger**

apple quince (in hotter countries, may be used as the fruit of the Tree of Knowledge and may partake of other symbolism of the apple)

appointment *see* **meeting**

appreciation *see* **gratitude**

apprehension *see* **anxiety**

apprentices green knight • *attributes:* piece of chalk or charcoal • *see also* **neophytes**

approval almond (seeking divine favor or approval); thumb held up; forefinger and thumb forming a circle; nodding the head; smile

April *associations:* Aphrodite; cherry blossom; cuckoo; hyacinth [flower]; rook [bird] • *birthstone:* diamond

aptitude *see* **skill**

Aquarius *associations:* cherry tree; daffodil; garnet; N; peach tree; platinum; R; Saturn [planet]; Uranus [planet]; violet [color] • *attributes:* aquamarine [gemstone]; pitcher [vessel]; turquoise [gemstone]; vase • *emblems:* pot (usually earthen); two wavy lines

Aquila [constellation] *association:* eagle

Arabian countries *emblem:* scimitar

Arachne woman at loom with spider's web; woman turning into a spider; woman weaving watched by the goddess Minerva • *association:* spider ophrys

arcana *see* **esoterica**

archangels seven trumpets (the seven archangels)

archbishops *attribute:* crozier terminating with a cross that has two horizontal pieces

archers *flower language:* German iris

Archimedes soldier slaying a sage (death of Archimedes)

architecture compasses [dividers]

archivists *heraldry:* cup

ardor *see* **love; zeal**

Ares *see* **Mars [god]**

argument *see* **discord; dissension; quarreling**

Argus *attribute:* shepherd's crook

Aries *associations:* A; bloodstone; brilliant red; E; east; geranium; honeysuckle; iron; jasper (especially red jasper); Mars [planet]; Q; ram [sheep]; spring [season]; thorn • *attribute:* aquamarine [gemstone]

Arion man with a lyre and/or crown of laurel, riding a dolphin; *attribute:* viol

aristocracy *see* **nobility**

Aristotle and Campaspe old man on all fours, bridled and ridden by a woman

Arithmetic personified *attributes:* abacus; rule [measuring]; tablet with a stylus

Ark of the Covenant ciborium (especially when supported by pillars as a canopy over an altar) • *associations:* acacia, shittim (both reputed to be the wood the Ark was made of)

Armida *attribute:* chariot drawn by horses • *Armida and Rinaldo:* nymphs bathing observed by soldiers; soldier holding a mirror for his mistress; soldier sleeping beside a pillar with a woman kneeling beside him; two lovers in a mirror

Armistice Day *association:* poppy

armor steel

army *see* **the military; warriors**

arrogance hands on hips; sneering; turkey

art acanthus (also love of art); lark (natural art); palette; swan song (tragic art) • *association:* six

Artemesia *attributes:* funeral urn; goblet; moon; woman drinking from a cup

Artemis *see* **Diana**

artfulness *heraldry:* ant

Arthur, King *attributes:* grail; round table; three crowns

artifice acanthus • *flower language:* acanthus; clematis

artificiality cube (suggests an artificial or constructed object)

artisans brooch (may indicate the wearer's trade)

artists *attributes:* compasses [dividers] (especially in renaissance or baroque portrait painting); laurel (in portraiture, it implies the subject was a literary or artistic figure); Prometheus (the artist)

artlessness *see* **ingenuousness**

arts and crafts *association:* Venus [planet]

the arts *associations:* blue stockings (attribute of a woman having intellectual or literary interests); curly hair (one who follows the arts or has a facility with foreign languages); nine (fine arts) • *flower language:* laurel

Asaph, St. *attribute:* bishop's miter on a scroll

Asariel *association:* eighteen

asbestos *association:* Mars

ascension column [architectural] (the upward impulse); obelisk; rope; stairs; thread; tower; tree • *association:* fifteen • *see also* **elevation; Jesus Christ**

asceticism camel; cincture; cutting of the hair; desert; gray; hermit; hood; tonsure

Asclepius *association:* crow • *attributes:* caduceus; dog; moon; serpent; staff

Asher *association:* cornucopia • *attributes:* animal horn; palm tree

ashes cremation (return to ashes) • *association:* gray

Asia personified *attributes:* camel; censer; crown of flowers; jewels; palm tree; tiger

asp *flower language:* lavender (the asp that killed Cleopatra)

aspiration bird; deer; dove; gothic arch; hill; ibis; journey; knock, knocking; mast; obelisk; penance (aspiration which implies discontent with the worldly conditions to which one is bound for a time); Phaeton (aspiration

beyond abilities); pigeon; pyramid; rosary (the futility of aspiration); the soul; spine; spire; stairs; tall tree; triangle with apex up (the aspiration of all things toward unity); wings • *flower language:* daily rose (I aspire to your smile); mountain pink • *heraldry:* poplar • *Judaism:* five (ancient association); frog (a lower order aspiring to become higher) • *see also* **desire; hope; longing; wishing; yearning** • *aspiration of the soul:* deer (especially a jumping deer); hart (especially when jumping, or drinking from a stream); stag; thrush; tower • *association:* Neptune [planet]

assassins *attribute:* dagger

assault *see* **attack**

assertiveness flag (self-assertion); mace [weapon] (the subjective assertive tendency in man) • *association:* eight (self-assertion and material success)

asses *association:* long ears

assignation *see* **meeting**

assimilation devouring (assimilation of the powers of that which is eaten); digestion (especially spiritual assimilation)

assistance *see* **help**

Assyria bee

astrology armillary; compasses [dividers] • *emblem:* winged dragon

astronomy seven stringed lyre (the seven planets known to the ancients) • *attributes:* armillary; celestial globe; compasses [dividers]; quadrant [astronomical device]; quadriga; sextant

astuteness *see* **cleverness; intellect; sagacity; wit**

asylum *flower language:* juniper

Atalanta *attribute:* quiver of ivory

Athanasius, St. *attributes:* book between two Doric columns; sailboat or ship on the Nile

Athena lark (a disguise for Athena) • *associations:* crane [bird]; goat • *attributes:* clockwise spiral; crown of violets (occasionally); helmet; wings • *emblems:* gull; olive branch or tree

Athens, Greece *emblem:* Athena

Atlantic Ocean anchor (as a 19th century sailor's tattoo: service in the Atlantic)

atonement *see* **expiation**

Atonement, Day of [Yom Kippur] bull with censer • *association:* eight

Atropos *attribute:* shears
attachment ivy • *flower language:* Indian jasmine (I attach myself to you); mourning bride (unfortunate attachment); thornless rose (early attachment) • *see also* **affection; friendship; love**
attack hail (attack by an enemy) • *heraldry:* wolf (caution in attack)
attention seeking hand raised over the head
Attis *attribute:* grain
attraction dimple (attribute of attractive children and maidens); lodestone; siren [mythology] • *flower language:* garden ranunculus (you are rich in attraction); Japan rose (beauty is your only attraction)
auction red flag
audacity *flower language:* larch
augurs *see* **foretokens and signs**
augury *see* **divination; foretokens and signs**
August *associations:* harvest, harvesting • *birthstone:* peridot; sardonyx • *China:* pear blossoms (emblem)
Augustine of Hippo, St. *attributes:* Bible opened to Romans 13; child; dove; heart, often flaming and transfixed with one or two arrows; inkhorn; one or two arrows piercing the breast (occasionally); writing pen
Aurora *attributes:* chariot drawn by four horses; cicada; flower; necklace; torch
austerity Lent; sloe; thistle; thorn • *flower language:* common thistle
Australia *emblems:* emu; kangaroo; mimosa
authenticity ring; seal [stamp]
authority angel with a scepter (divine authority); balcony; birch rod (school authority); bishop (religious authority); cushion; castle; cathedra; chain; chair; chariot; crozier; desk; empty chair (absence of authority); eyes; face; fasces (controlled power resulting in authority); fire; flaming sword (divine authority); hand (authority, usually the authority of the father, emperor, deity, etc.); head; key; mace [weapon] (especially the authority of the state); marble; palace; parasol; ring (delegation of authority); romanesque arch; rudder; scepter; south (to face south was to speak with the authority of the gods; spiral; staff, wand (authority;

official authority); sun; sword; throne; violet [color]; wand; wings • *associations:* blue and red (authority and love, respectively—often used for the color of God's clothes); club suit [playing cards]; Germany (subservience to authority) • *China:* eagle; five-clawed dragon (imperial authority); four-clawed dragon (authority lower than that of the emperor; parasol; ring • *heraldry:* sun
authorization seal [stamp]
authors *see* **literature; writers**
autonomy clock (related to the magical creation of beings that pursue their own autonomous existence); tarot cards I to XI (the autonomous) • *see also* **freedom; independence**
autumn afternoon; apple (but also a herald of spring); brown; copper; counterclockwise swastika; deer; evening; flock of geese; frost; gentian; grain; pomegranate; poppy; press [tool]; scythe; setting of the Pleiades; sheaf with a sickle; vine; west; west wind • *associations:* E (autumnal equinox); gnat; October; ring finger (autumn; autumnal equinox) • *China:* chrysanthemum; *Greece:* hare (emblem)
Autumn personified *attributes:* cornucopia; vine
avarice coin, coins; hyena; itchy palm [hand]; Jew; leech; Mammon; merchant; mole [animal]; purse; rake [tool]; spider; weasel; whale; wolf • *Christianity:* billy goat • *flower language:* buttercup (desire for riches); scarlet auricula • *see also* **greed; money**
Avarice personified *attributes:* blindfold; golden apples, golden balls (associated with the harpies that accompany Avarice personified); owl; harpy blindfolded; mole [animal]; money bag; monkey; purse; toad used as a steed; wolf
Ave Maria *emblem:* A.M.
aversion *see* **disdain; disgust; displeasure; hate; rejection**
avoidance closed eyes
awakening almond; amazement (part of the process of spiritual awakening); deluge (awakening of the mind from ignorance and error); ibis (spiritual awakening); Judgment [tarot]

B

Baal *attribute:* footstool
babbling *see* **chatter**
babies *see* **infancy**
Babylon golden city; golden eagle
Bacchae *attribute:* tambourine
Bacchus infant fed by a satyr; infant in the arms of Mercury; *associations:* awl root; centaur; goat; ivy; tambourine (Bacchanalian worship) • *attributes:* chariot drawn by centaurs, goats, leopards or tigers; crown of vine; dove; goat; grapes; leopards; pipe [musical]; red eyes; satyr; thyrsus; wine; winnow
Bacchus, St. soldier • *attribute:* palm tree
bachelors *see* **single men**
the back *attribute:* Venus [planet]
bad habits handcuffs
bad luck *see* **misfortune**
bad news mushroom
bad shot with a weapon tailor
bailiff *heraldry:* cup
Balaam *association:* ass
balance chrysalis; equinox (the point of balance and change reached within the soul's development when a new process is started); flower; High Priestess [tarot] (a balance between initiative and resistance); judge (restorer of natural balance); Justice [tarot] (balance of opposites); pendulum (balance of judgment); see-saw; Sun [tarot] (balance of the conscious and unconscious, the spiritual and physical); tide (balance of nature); weaving as a feminine activity (balance and order in nature); Wheel of Fortune [tarot]; yoke • *associations:* eleven; O [letter]; six; two • *kabala:* eight • *see also* **equilibrium**
baldness eagle
Baldric, St. *attribute:* falcon
Balthazar *attribute:* casket of myrrh
bane *flower language:* white poppy (you

are my bane and antidote)
bankers *attributes:* gold bottle; purse
banking *emblem:* money chest with metal bands
bankruptcy green bonnet (attribute of a bankrupt person); loss (spiritual bankruptcy)
banquets *see* **feasts**
bantering *flower language:* southernwood • *see also* **talk**
baptism ark; centaur on a font (the overcoming of original sin by baptism); chrism; eagle; eight-pointed star; fish, especially three fish, or two fish crossed; fleur-di-lys (purification by baptism); font; Gabriel Hounds (the lost souls of unbaptized infants); hyssop; Noah's ark; octagon; Red Sea; salamander; shell dripping with water; two stags drinking; water; well • *associations:* crystal; eight
Barbara, St. *attributes:* cannon; chalice with a wafer; palm tree; peacock or peacock feather; tower (usually with three windows)
barbarianism north; reading the Gospel from the north end of a church (desire to convert barbarians)
barbers *attributes:* basin, or basin and ewer together; scissors • *emblems:* red and white striped pole; red, white, and blue striped pole (often used in the United States); *heraldry:* scissors
Barnabas, St. *attributes:* Bible opened to the Gospel of St. Matthew; lance; stone
barrenness bush; chaff; closed door; devastation (barrenness and unproductiveness of the spirit); lemon; sand; • *associations:* brown; gray • *see also* **desolation; sterility**
barriers closed door or gate • *association:* D (material barriers)
Bartholomew, St. *attributes:* Bible open to the Gospel of St. Matthew;

book with a flaying knife; cross with an empty skin; death by flaying; fig; knife, especially three flaying knives; scimitar

baseness American Indians (the darker side of the personality; the instincts of natural men); brass (when compared to gold or silver); chaff; cremation (destruction of what is base to make way for what is superior); dog; horse (the baser forces in man); husk; intestines; lead [metal]; liver (the baser part of the personality); monkey; Pan (baseness of involutive life); panther skin (the overcoming of base desires); red knight (the ability to overcome baseness and all trials through sacrifice); sewer [drain]; shadow (base or evil side of the body); six-pointed star (the upper and lower worlds); swine (baseness; the transmutation of the higher into the lower); Vulcan (the creative mind which has been captured by the lower qualities); wallowing (baseness; depravity); weeds; worm • *flower language:* dodder • *see also* **animals; brutishness; desires; force; lowliness**

Baseness personified *attribute:* hoopoe

bashfulness *see* **shyness**

basis *see* **foundation**

Bath, Order of the red ribbon

bathroom crescent moon on an outhouse door (use reserved for females); sun on an outhouse door (use reserved for males)

battle *see* **war**

Baucis *association:* linden

Bavo, St. man carrying a large stone; man praying in a tree, or in front of a tree; soldier with a falcon on his wrist, he may also have a stone in his hand

bay [plant] *association:* laurel

bearer horseman (bearer of immortality or prophecy)

Beast of the Apocalypse six hundred and sixty-six (also applied to Martin Luther and other Protestants, and Adolf Hitler)

Beast of the Second Coming androsphinx [lion's body with human head and hands]

beating *see* **whipping**

beauty Adonis, Endymion (youthful beauty); amaryllis; camellia japonica (pure beauty; exotic, seductive beauty); cedar; candlestick (beauty of ripe age); cherry blossom (spiritual beauty); china, jasmine (delicate beauty); coot; cowslip (comeliness; divine beauty); doll, nymph (beauty with no feelings); elm; Eve; fir (regal beauty); flower; gillyflower (natural beauty); lamp; lotus blossom; Lovers [tarot] (moral beauty); magnolia; marble (cold beauty); marigold (beauty; comeliness); olive tree or branch; orchid; park; pheasant; quince (scornful beauty); rose [flower]; rose quartz (enhancer of inner and outer beauty); ruby; silk; son; stag; summer (beauty anticipating decline); swan; tiger; tower • *associations:* born on a Monday, fair of face; L; six; twelve; Venus [planet] (love of beauty) • *China:* kingfisher; orchid; peacock; pearl; pheasant (occasionally, beauty and good fortune) • *feminine beauty:* cherry blossom; crab apple blossom, magnolia blossom (China); lily (queenly beauty); magnolia (feminine beauty and sweetness); panther (in heraldry: a beautiful woman, tender, but fierce in defense of her children) • *flower language:* alyssum (worth beyond beauty); azalea, camellia japonica (fragile and ephemeral beauty); burgundy rose (unconscious beauty); calla aethiopica (magnificent beauty); China Rose, damask rose (beauty always new); chrysanthemum (regal beauty); citron (ill-natured beauty); clematis, kennedia (mental beauty); corn marigold (comeliness); flower-of-an-hour, hibiscus, Venetian mallow (delicate beauty); French honeysuckle (rustic beauty); full red rose; glory flower (glorious beauty); garden wallflower, gillyflower, ten-week stock (lasting beauty); Japan rose (beauty is your only attraction); laburnum (pensive beauty); lady slippers (capricious beauty); night-blooming cereus (transitory beauty); orchid (a belle); particolored daisy; red-leaved rose (beauty and good fortune); red rosebud (you are young and beautiful); rose; thrift, throatwort (neglected beauty); trillium (modest beauty); unique rose (call me not beautiful); variegated tulip (beautiful eyes) • *heraldry:* emerald; green; oak; rose [flower] *short-lived beauty:* bough bearing fruit or blooms; cherry blossom; daffodil; garland; glass *see also* **loveliness**

Beauty [Comeliness] personified *attribute:* wagtail

Becket, Thomas *see* **Thomas a Becket, St.**

bed *association:* sheet

Bede, St. *attribute:* pitcher with rays above it

beer *associations:* Germans, Germany (beer drinking); hops; mugwort

beggar *attributes:* bowl; crutch; tabor; tin cup

beginners *see* **neophytes**

beginning A; apple; April; birch; catastrophe (the beginning of a transformation); child; compasses [dividers] (the beginning of all things); dawn; door; finger snapping (beginning or end of a cycle); infant; maiden (any new start, such as spring, dawn, etc.); Moon [tarot] (regression to make a new start); prophet; morning; mustard seed (great growth from a small beginning); spring [season]; sunrise; womb • *associations:* black (the germinal stage of a process); crow; Leo (the spiritual beginnings of man); ten; thirteen • *beginning and end:* alpha and omega; ashes, dust, sarcophagus (an ending that is also a beginning); snapping of the fingers (the beginning or end or a cycle, process, or idea); tetractys • *associations:* Aries (the beginning or end of a cycle or process); three (the beginning, middle, and end)

behavior apron (purity of life and conduct); caduceus (good conduct); compasses [dividers], square (right conduct); globe amaranth (decorum); Justice [tarot] (strict and correct behavior); silk (bonds of social behavior) • *association:* one thousand, one hundred [1,100]

being *see* **existence**

belief beheading (ideas, opinions, beliefs, or institutions at the end of their cycle); changing clothes, lowered mast (a change in beliefs or opinions); city (the beliefs of the society of which it is a part; manifestation of a particular discipline or principle); cloak, clothes (mental covering, often revealing the wearer's principles of action, opinions, prejudices, associations, mental state,

beliefs, profession, etc.); hemlock (punishment for unpopular beliefs); mast; toe (a person's way of life) • *Christianity:* light • *flower language:* passion flower • *heraldry:* angel; vine • *see also* **ideas; opinions; thoughts**

believers and nonbelievers wheat with tares (believers and nonbelievers, respectively, in the church, who will be separated out at Judgment Day)

Belisarius blind and begging soldier

belle [woman] *flower language:* orchid

Bellerophon horseman on winged horse

Bellona *attributes:* gadfly [insect]; scourge [whip]

beloved one gazelle; rose [flower]

Benedict, St. *attributes:* aspergillum; axe; blackbird; broken cup or glass, sometimes with wine running from it; broken sieve; dove; drinking vessel with snake in it; ladder; loaf of bread, especially with a snake emerging from it; raven with a loaf of bread; white miter (occasionally)

benediction gold rose (papal benediction)

beneficence *see* **benevolence**

benevolence albatross [beneficent nature]; alms box; buckle (the good will and protection of Isis); child (beneficent change); crane [bird] (good life and works); elf (light colored elves are generally favorable to man); elm tree with vine; feeding (dispensing goodness to the mind and soul); flowing or full robe; hand that is open; holly; mallow; maniple; mistletoe; open purse (Christian benevolence); orange [color]; plumed serpent; strawberry; three feathers (good thought, word and deed); valerian; water lily; woodcock • *associations:* Jupiter [planet]; yellow • *China:* dragon (attribute of beneficent deities); mani (benefaction) • *Christianity:* flower (result of charity and other good works); strawberries with other fruit (good works of the righteous); white bird • *Egypt:* lizard • *flower language:* calycanthus; marjoram; marsh mallow; potato • *Greece:* asp • *see also* **benignity; charity; generosity; goodness**

Benevolence personified *attributes:* hyacinth [flower]; mallow

benignity cherry (sweetness of character derived from good works); white

fleecy clouds; wings • *flower language:* white mullein (good nature)
Benignity personified woman expressing milk from her breasts
Benjamin, Tribe of *association:* wolf with lion • *attribute:* amber [gemstone]
bereavement *see* **mourning**
Bernard, St. praying saint before an image of vision of the crucified Christ, with Christ reaching down to him • *attributes:* beehive; book; cross with instruments of the passion; crozier; demon in chains; dragon underfoot; nails [for wood]; writing pen
Bernardino of Siena, St. *attributes:* dove hovering around a man's ear; heart; heart or the letters IHS on a tablet or sun; three miters on the ground; white beard
betrayal being thrown from a rock (punishment for traitors); bird; cloud; dagger (weapon of traitors or assassins); nightingale; one thousand, one hundred [1,100]; rat (informant); rope; St. Peter; silver as payment, particularly 30 pieces of silver (the betrayal of Jesus by Judas) • *associations:* thirteen; yellow • *Christianity:* club [bat] • *flower language:* Judas tree; white catchfly (betrayed) • *see also* **abandonment; disloyalty; treachery; treason**
betrothal red carnation • *association:* ring finger • *see also* **courtship; marriage**
betterment *see* **improvement**
betting *see* **gambling**
Bible book; double headed lectern (the Old and New Testaments); elm (the strength derived by the devout from their faith in Scripture); lighthouse; miter lappets [fanons] (the letter and the spirit of the Old and New Testaments); open book; scroll (Scripture); Solomon's seal
Bible. New Testament *associations:* double-headed lectern (the Epistles and the Gospels); south (the New Testament, particularly the Epistles); twelve, especially twelve scrolls (the Epistles)
Bible. Old Testament flaming sword; harp (the Psalms); scroll with sheaf of wheat (Old Testament pentecost) • *association:* fifteen (the gradual psalms) • *attributes:* miter [hat] (Old Testament priesthood); scroll

(authors of the Old Testament); turban (Old Testament figures) • *Old Testament worship:* laver of brass; tabernacle in a tent; table with shewbread
Bible. Old Testament personified synagogue
bigotry lobster; wax seal [stamp] (narrowmindedness) • *see also* **prejudice**
binary functions *see* **opposites**
binding *see* **bonding; bonds**
biological objects *association:* oval shape (biological and natural objects)
birds dove, eagle (spiritual birds); pigeon (in modern urban use, a low bird) • *association:* Thursday (according to the Bible, sea beasts and birds were created on a Thursday)
birth brick; five-petalled lotus; flower; fountain; Judgment [tarot] (the mystery of birth in death); knock, knocking; mandorla (birth into the next world); ostrich egg, pelican (virgin birth); rattle; scissors; spark (the spiritual principle giving birth to each individual); stork; tetractys (birth, growth, and death); unicorn (high birth); urn with a lid on it (the state of supreme enlightenment which triumphs over birth and death) • *associations:* Born on a Sunday, you'll never want (or, lucky and happy, good and gay); Born on a Monday, fair in the face, (or, full in the face); Born on a Tuesday, full of grace (or, full of God's grace; or, solemn and sad); Born on a Wednesday, sour and sad (or, full of woe; or, merry and glad); Born on a Thursday, merry and glad (or, has far to go; or, inclined to thieving); Born on a Friday, worthily given (or, is loving and giving; or, free and giving); Born on a Saturday work hard for your living; right side; shell (virgin birth); thirteen; Virgo (birth of a demigod) • *see also* **childbirth**
birthstones *January:* garnet • *February:* amethyst • *March:* aquamarine, bloodstone • *April:* diamond • *May:* emerald • *June:* alexandrite, pearl • *July:* ruby, star ruby • *August:* peridot, sardonyx; *September:* sapphire, star sapphire • *October:* aquamarine (occasionally), opal, tourmaline • *November:* topaz • *December:* turquoise, zircon
bishops *attributes:* amethyst [gemstone]; cathedra; church model being

carried (a particular model being carried may indicate that the person was its founder or first bishop); epigonation (Eastern Orthodox bishops); gloves; lapis lazuli (part of a bishop's ring); mace (battle weapon of medieval bishops); purple biretta; purple mantelleta (worn by bishops as a sign of limited authority or jurisdiction); violet or purple cassock; white miter (now worn by bishops, but formerly worn also by cardinals and abbots--an abbot's miter was usually unadorned) • *see also* **archbishops; cardinals [clergy]**

Biton chariot drawn by two youths (Cleobis and Biton are the youths)

bitterness aloe; dandelion; gall (also the bitterness of injustice); olive; rhubarb; rue [plant]; wormwood (bitter labor); wormwood and gall • *flower language:* aloe • *Judaism:* chicory, dandelion, eryngium, horseradish, maror, mint, sorrel (the bitterness of bondage) • *see also* **anger; resentment; sourness**

black ace of spades; pitch [tar] • *China:* associated with even numbers

black magic *see* **magic**

blacksmiths *association:* miner • *attributes:* forge; hammer • *emblem:* horseshoe

blackthorn *association:* sloe

Blaise, St. *attributes:* crossed candles, or candles in an iron comb; iron wool carding comb; taper [wick]

blamelessness *see* **innocence**

blandness white

blasphemy the letter B as a brand; tongue

blessedness cherry in Christ's hand (the delight of the blessed); mandorla (perfect blessedness)

blessing cup; dew (divine blessing); gourd; hand raised with first two fingers extended; hand raised with palm outward; hands clasped beneath the hand of God (the blessing of marriage by the church); hands laid on the head; rainbow; sun • *heraldry:* hands; purse (a liberal blessing) • *Judaism:* hands upraised with middle and ring finger separated (Jewish blessing)

blindness blindfold, mole eyes (intellectual and spiritual blindness); hood (spiritual blindness) • *attributes:* bandaged eyes; cane (especially a

white cane); dark glasses; harp (associated with blindness in conjunction with cunning or aristocracy); mole [animal]; owl eyes; snow; staff; stone; tin cup (impoverished blindness)

bliss birds drinking from a vase (eternal bliss); Cockaigne (ridicule of poetic bliss or wishful thinking); fruit, lily, lute (heavenly bliss); myrrh • *see also* **ecstasy; happiness; joy; love**

bloating *see* **swelling**

blockade idol (fixed ideas which bar the way to truth)

blood acacia gum (menstrual blood); carbuncle [gemstone]; coral [sea coral]; grapes (also the blood of Christ); lion; overturned cup spilling wine (the spilling of blood); red flower; red knight; sap; wine (blood; the blood of Christ) • *associations:* D; red

bloodletting pouring out wine (bloodletting in a ritual sacrifice) • *association:* saucer

bloodshed aurora borealis (omen of bloodshed)

bloodstone *association:* Mars

bloodthirstiness ferret; tiger; weasel

blue *associations:* four (bright blue); six (light blue) • *kabala:* eight (silvery blue)

bluntness *flower language:* borage

blushes *flower language:* damask rose (a maid's blushing); marjoram

boastfulness spread-eagle body position • *flower language:* hydrangea

Boaz and Jachin two pillars shown apart

body boat (the human body); caduceus (health of the body and spirit); clothes; devouring (dissolution of the body after death); east (the right half of the body); garment; house (the parts correspond to the body: attic = mind, basement = unconscious, kitchen = place of transmutation, windows and doors = body openings, etc.); kidneys (bodily constitution); reins (relationship of the body and soul); room [chamber] (privacy of mind and body); Sphinx (pleasures of the body); steed; tabernacle; thigh (dynamic support of the body); tomb (the body and its fleshly desires); World [tarot] • *associations:* nine (the three worlds: corporal, intellectual, and spiritual); red (the body of man) • *body and soul:* bite (the seal of the spirit upon the flesh);

crossroads (intersection of body and soul); duality (the physical and spiritual nature of all things; empty vase (the body separated from the soul); green (victory of the spirit over the flesh); helmet (protection of the soul from the assaults of passions and desires); reins (relationship of the body and soul); shadow (the evil or base side of the body; existence between body and soul) • *see also* **soul**

Bohemian-Americans *emblem:* mushroom

bohemianism actor, artist, musician, tinker (people conceived of as living outside the conventions of society)

boisterousness Hercules (in Elizabethan times: a ridiculous, brawny, boisterous tyrant)

boldness brass; larch; oxlip [plant]; sea lion; sparrow; young man • *flower language:* larch; pink • *see also* **bravery**

Bonapartists *emblem:* violet [flower]

Bonaventura, St. *attributes:* angel bearing a sacramental wafer; book; cardinal's hat lying on the ground or in a tree; chalice; ciborium; communion cup with a wafer; cross with a chalice

bondage cage; chain; collar [for restraint]; cord; eating the food of another world binds one to that world; Egypt; iron; knot; rope; seaweed (bondslaves); string • *Judaism:* chicory, dandelion, eryngium, horseradish, maror, mint, sorrel (the bitterness of bondage) • *see also* **imprisonment**

bonds bracelet, necklace (cosmic and social bonds; erotic bond, especially when worn by a woman); necktie (social bonds); ring; sharing food (bonding); silk (social bonds); slapping hands with someone, spitting (binding to a bet or contract) • *flower language:* convolvulus; gillyflower (bonds of affection); guelder rose; snowball; tendrils

Boniface, St. bishop with his foot on a fallen oak • *attributes:* axe; book pierced by a sword; cauldron; raven; scourge [whip]; sword

books eyeglasses (bookishness) • *association:* beech (formerly used to make covers)

boorishness *see* **crudity**

bootlicking *see* **subservience**

booty *see* **plunder; treasure**

Boreas old man with serpent tails for feet; old man with wings carrying off naked girl • *attribute:* horse

boredom Hermit [tarot]; moss; whistling • *flower language:* mosses gathered together (ennui) • *see also* **monotony**

bounty *see* **abundance; plenty; prosperity**

bourgeoisie maple (bourgeois earthly happiness) • *association:* geranium • *see also* **middle classes**

boxers *attribute:* rawhide gloves (ancient times)

Boy Scouts *attributes:* campaign hat; knee socks; neckerchief; shorts • *emblem:* fleur-de-lys

boys calf (a boy of up to 20 years of age); billy goat (a boy 10 to 20 years of age); puppy (a boy up to 10 years of age) • *see also* **the male; men; youth**

bragging dog; Hector; neighing • *association:* Spain

brain anvil; belly (the antithesis of the brain or spirit); forge • *association:* P • *see also* **mind**

bravery Amazon [mythological woman]; bear; boar; chrysalis; club [bat] (intrepidness); Diomedes; eagle; gall; leopard; lion; oak leaf; ox; panther; soldier; sparrowhawk (brave warrior); steering oar (the skill, knowledge, and/ or bravery of the wielder); tamed tiger (strength and valor in the fight against evil); thyme; wolf; wreath • *China:* leopard; panther • *flower language:* French willow (bravery and humanity); oak leaf • *heraldry:* bull; lion; ox; rhinoceros (one who does not seek combat, but will defend to the death if attacked) • *see also* **boldness; courage; pugnacity**

brawn Hercules (in Elizabethan times, a ridiculous, brawny, boisterous tyrant; whale (brawn without intellect)

bread manna (bread of life); wheat (bread of the eucharist)

break *see* **rupture**

breasts figs (breasts; sex in general; when opened, a fig is a symbol of the vagina)

breath nostrils (seat of the breath of life); sails (creative breath); spiral • *association:* three hundred (breath of God)

Brennus soldier throwing his sword onto a scale pan

brevity Sparta (brevity of speech) • *see also* **transitoriness**

bribery capon (a bribe for judges); coins; gilded hand; hand with money; hand with palm upward; itchy palm of the hand; silver as payment; silver weapons
brides heifer • *attributes:* myrtle wreath; white gown • *Judaism:* long flowing hair • *Middle Ages:* green stockings (worn at weddings by an older unmarried sister of the bride) • *see also* **marriage**
bridge between heaven and earth *see* **heaven and earth**
Bridget, St. pilgrim • *attribute:* crozier (occasionally)
brilliance comet (a brilliant, but short-lived career); diamond [gemstone] • *China:* silver • *flower language:* aconite-leaved crowfoot (luster); damask rose (brilliant complexion); Indian cress; ranunculus (I am dazzled by your charms)
brimstone *association:* Mars
the British *see* **the English**
Bronze Age *association:* Neptune [planet]
Bronze Age personified *attribute:* spear
brotherly love *see* **love**
browsing cow; rabbit; sheep
Brunhilde *attribute:* circle or wheel of fire
Bruno, St. saint praying in the desert or the wilderness • *attribute:* chalice
brutality club [bat]; iron hand; sow (brutalization); Strength [tarot] (the triumph of intelligence over brutality); tiger • *see also* **cruelty; ferocity; violence**
brutishness boar (low animal nature); buffalo (untamed nature; base forces); centaur (the complete domination of a being by baser forces; brute force; the superior force of the instincts); steed (the animal in man);

tail (animal power) • *see also* **animals; baseness**
Buddha bamboo; bo tree • *attribute:* orange [color] • *China:* knot (emblem)
Buddhism *association:* saffron
buffoons *see* **fools**
building trades *association:* square [tool] (the building trades in general, carpentry in particular) • *see also* **construction**
bulkiness *association:* Jupiter [planet] • *flower language:* gourd; pumpkin; watermelon
bumpkin jay
burden bundle; millstone; yoke
bureaucracy beehive • *emblems:* paper; red tape
burial bandages (the winding sheet of the tomb); cave; cradle (coffin); devouring; earth [soil] (the great sepulcher); gingerbread (burial offering); unlighted candle (burial of an excommunicated person) • *associations:* comb; elm (cemeteries); jar; linen, wool (burial shroud) • *flower language:* persimmon (bury me amid nature's joys) • *see also* **embalming; funeral; the grave**
buried treasure chest [packing trunk] • *association:* hazel wand (said to find water, buried treasure, murderers, thieves)
burning spearmint (burning love) • *flower language:* fleur-di-lys (flame; I burn)
burning bush of Moses acacia; shittim
burnt offerings *Judaism:* shank bone, burnt eggs (a reminder of burnt offerings and the ancient glory of the Temple)
business *see* **commerce**
Byzantine empire double-headed eagle (the union of the Roman and Byzantine empires)

C

caddishness one thousand, one hundred [1,100]
Cadmus pitcher overturned shown

with a corpse entwined by a serpent; sower of dragon's teeth • *association:* dragon's teeth

caduceus hazel wand; three-pronged fork

Caesar's government rudder with a caduceus and cornucopia

Cain *attributes:* knotted club; ox goad; plow; yoke • *Cain and Abel:* jawbone of an ass (the slaying of Abel by Cain); two altars

calamities *see* **disasters**

Caleb *attribute:* grapes

call *see* **summons**

Calliope *attributes:* crown of laurel held in the hand; scroll; tablet with a stylus; trumpet

Callisto and Diana goddess accusing pregnant nymph (Diana and Callisto, respectively)

calmness *see* **tranquillity**

calumny *flower language:* hellebore; madder • *see also* **humiliation; slander**

Calumny personified woman with a torch dragging a youth before a judge (the woman is Calumny)

Calvary cross on three steps (finished redemption: the steps represent faith, hope, and love)

calves and knees *association:* Saturn [planet]

Campaspe *see* **Aristotle and Campaspe**

Canaan grapes borne on a staff by two men (entry into Canaan); milk and honey

Canada *emblems:* beaver (formerly an emblem of Germany); maple leaf

Cancer [zodiac] *associations:* acanthus; anemone [flower]; chrysoprase (occasionally); eagle; H; Monday; moon; ice blue; pearl; rubber tree; ruby; S; silver; sixty-nine; violet [color]; yellow-orange • *emblems:* crab; sixty-nine (especially when it is turned on its side)

Candlemas *association:* snowdrop

candor bare breasts; removing a glove, especially the right • *associations:* blue; right side • *see also* **frankness; honesty; truthfulness**

cannibals *cartoon attribute:* large kettle

Cape Horn tattoo of a full-rigged sailing ship (attribute of a 19th century sailor who had sailed around Cape Horn)

capriciousness carnation; nanny goat; wind • *flower language:* lady slippers, musk rose (capricious beauty) • *heraldry:* carnation • *see also* **impul-**siveness; unpredictability

Capricorn *associations:* baboon; black; dark blue; December; hyacinth [flower]; ivy; J; Jupiter [planet]; lead [metal]; P; pansy; pine; ruby (occasionally); Saturday; turquoise; violet blue; zircon • *emblem:* goat with a spiral tail

captives *see* **prisoners**

cardinal virtues *Christian association:* four (the four cardinal virtues)

cardinals [clergy] *attributes:* gloves; miter (especially red: formerly white, but these were also worn by bishops and abbots as well); mule (mount of a cardinal); red cassock; red hat; red mantelleta (worn as a sign of limited jurisdiction or authority); sapphire ring

care acanthus (solicitude about lowly things); bread (care and nurture); bridle (worldly interests and cares); coltsfoot (maternal care); elephant; fiddle, fiddler (freedom from care); hen with chicks (maternal care; the solicitude of Christ); hill (place of freedom from care); hoopoe (parental care); milk, mother (nurture); mist; scorpion (defensive stewardship)

Care personified *attribute:* greyhound

carefulness *see* **caution**

carelessness grasshopper (carefree life); lark (recklessness); weeds • *association:* three • *flower language:* almond (thoughtlessness) • *see also* **folly; indifference**

carnality *see* **worldliness**

Carnea *attribute:* hawthorn

Carolingians *heraldry:* bee

carpenters *attributes:* axe; hammer; hatchet; square [tool] (the building trades in general, carpentry in particular)

carrion eagle, fox, hyena (eaters of carrion)

Carthage *emblem:* horse's head

Cassiel *associations:* fifteen; twenty-one

castigation *see* **criticism; punishment**

castles *heraldry:* beaver (skill, especially in castle building)

Castor *attribute:* horse • *Castor and Pollux:* Gemini; two infants hatched from eggs; two soldiers with two maidens on horseback

castration amputation; blindness (euphemism); capon (eunuch); circumcision, cutting off a finger (ritual or sublimated castration); devouring, loss of teeth (fear of castration); felling a tree; loss of teeth; reaping; sickle (instrument of castration); transvestitism (overcoming a castration anxiety)

catacombs altar shaped as a tomb (reminiscent of the early church when the eucharist was celebrated in the catacombs)

catalyst farmer (the catalyst of the forces of regeneration and salvation in harmony with nature) • *associations:* E; three

catastrophes see **disasters**

catechumens deer (a Christian catechumen searching after truth)

Catherine of Alexandria, St. *attributes:* crown; garment of leaves, usually palm leaves; lamb; sword; wedding ring; wheel with knives or spikes in it, which may be broken

Catherine of Siena, St. *attributes:* chrism; cross with a heart or lily; crown of thorns; demon underfoot; dove; rosary (occasionally); stigmata; wedding ring

Catholicism *emblems:* red rooster; red weather cock (occasionally); rosary

cattle goat (the poor man's cow)

cauldron of plenty urn • *association:* U

causation Wheel of Fortune [tarot] (the law of cause and effect) • *association:* A

caution castle (an embattled spiritual power ever on watch); elephant; hermit crab; Hermit [tarot] (meticulousness); rubbing the fingertips; tortoise • *association:* Saturn [planet] • *heraldry:* wolf (caution in attack) • see also **precaution; providence**

cavalry *emblem:* bugle

caves hollow [topography] (abstract form of a cave)

Cecilia, St. *attributes:* cauldron of boiling oil; crown or garland of red and white roses; harp; musical instruments; music written on a scroll; organ [instrument]; three wounds on the neck

celebrations see **festivities; rejoicing**

celibacy bluebottle; willow; bachelor's buttons • see also **chastity**

cemeteries see **burial; the grave**

center family (qualities in close connection with one another and with a common center); marrow (center of

being); navel; point • see also **middle; mystic center**

Cephalus and Procris hunter grieving over a woman shot by an arrow (the hunter is Cephalus, the woman is Procris)

Ceres Ceres with a chariot drawn by dragons, or with a torch (the search for Proserpine) • *associations:* copper; plant [botany] • *attributes:* ant; chariot drawn by dragons; cherry; cornucopia; crown of corn; fruit in a cornucopia; grain; purple foot; serpent; sickle (occasionally); scythe (occasionally); sow [swine]; torch; wheat

chairmen *attribute:* gavel

chalice tulip (chalice of the eucharist)

challenge eagle's scream; gauntlet; hands on hips; rooster (defiance); woman with breasts thrust forward • *heraldry:* gauntlet (challenge and readiness for combat) • *challenge to a duel:* grouse feather in a hat; slap in the face with a glove; throwing down a gauntlet

Chamael *attribute:* staff with cup

chamberlains *heraldry:* key

chance bouncing ball; dice; loom; wings • see also **fate**

Chance personified *attribute:* rudder

Chancellor, Lord *emblem:* woolsack [United Kingdom]

change bridge (also the desire for change); changing clothes (changing personalities, roles, opinions, loyalties, beliefs, etc.); child (sign of impending beneficent change); cicada (metamorphosis); clouds; door; earthquake (a sudden change in a process); equinox (the point of balance and change reached within the soul's development when a new process is started); fan; fracture, fragmentation (the disabling or changing of whatever the broken object symbolizes); intersection (the point at which change is sought or induced); journey (desire for change); latch, especially on a door (ability to resist change); lowered mast (change in belief or opinions); Phoenix [bird] (power to overcome change); stranger (mutation; possibility of unforeseen change); turning of the tide, swinging (life's changing fortunes); wallowing (a sacrificial act to encourage change) • *associations:* five; M; one; T; W • *flower language:* pimpernel • *heraldry:*

crescent • *see also* **transformation; transition; transmutation**

changeability chameleon; dock [plant]; Helen of Troy; moon; Proteus; seesaw; wheel; woman (the changing and intuitive) • *association:* five • *flower language:* rye grass • *see also* **inconstancy**

changelessness *see* **constancy; intransigence; steadfastness**

chanting wood pigeon (monotonous chanting)

Chanukkah *see* **Hanukkah**

chaos black (primordial chaos); carnival, orgy, saturnalia (invocation of chaos); circumference (viewed from without, the circumference is the defense of the conscious world against the unconscious or chaos; darkness (primeval chaos); deepness; desert (especially a vast and unknown desert); dragon; evening (return to chaos); golden egg (the sun, laid on waters of Chaos by the primeval goose); horse (the blind forces of primeval chaos); leviathan (waters of chaos); lobster; music, necklace (order from chaos); noise; nothingness; orgasm (a voluntary return to primordial chaos from which life proceeds); ostrich (a monster of chaos); slime (substance of chaos); tamed tiger (the defense of order against chaos); tortoise (chaos with the hope of renewal of life); World [tarot] (perfection as the end of creation out of chaos) • *see also* **anarchy; disorder**

Chaos personified Demogorgon

character borage (the whole plant symbolizes roughness of character); cherry (sweetness of character derived from good works); crest (indicative of the predominating characteristic of its owner); eyes (the abode of intellectual character); face (mirror—sometimes false—of a man's character); forehead (reflection of character or feelings); garment (reflection of character); plane tree (strength of character) • *associations:* E (intellectual character); index finger; M (strength of character) • *heraldry:* fess

Chariot [tarot] *association:* G

charisma *associations:* K; Q; Uranus [planet]

charity alms box: basket; beauty; bowl; breasts; carbuncle [gemstone];

chasuble (Christian charity); circle or wheel of fire; coins at the feet of an old man; cross with anchor and heart (faith, hope, and charity, respectively); feather; flame; grapes; green; Hanged Man [tarot] (power derived from charity, wisdom, and other higher virtues); hind [deer]; lamp; light; loaf of bread (charity to the poor); manger (charity arising from humility); olive branch; open money bags; plane tree (charity; charity of Jesus Christ); purse (especially when open); ruby; saffron; sheep; summer; sword and children; three feathers passing through a ring (faith, hope, and charity); tulip; water lily; wild grapes; woman placing a coin in a chest (the widow's mite) • *associations:* red; seven • *Christianity:* flower (the result of charity and other good works) • *flower language:* turnip • *heraldry:* dolphin • *see also* **benevolence; generosity**

Charity personified *attributes:* cornucopia; flame on the head; flaming heart; fruit in a bowl; vase with flame coming from its mouth; woman nursing a child (especially more than one child); woman with a flame in her hand; woman with a hand on her heart

Charlemagne *attribute:* cloak lined with ermine

Charles Borromeo, St. praying saint surrounded by angels • *attributes:* crucifix; Eucharist; rope around the neck

charm Amphion • *association:* U • *flower language:* musk rose cluster • *heraldry:* linden (often only the leaf is represented); rose [flower]

charms [amulets] *for animal powers:* brooch in the shape of an animal endows the wearer with the powers of that animal) • *for appetite:* parsley worn on the head • *for cheerfulness:* parsley worn on the head • *for courage:* bloodstone • *for enhancement of beauty:* rose quartz (inner and outer beauty) • *for fertility:* effigy • *for faithfulness in love:* opal • *for good luck:* coin; earring; four leaf clover; horseshoe with the ends up; rabbit's foot; six-pointed star; verbena • *for health:* Solomon's seal • *for placating gods:* effigy • *for presence of mind:* bloodstone • *for protection:* pierced ears (blood sacrifice for the protection of a child); silver (in China, silver is only for the protection of a child); verbena • *for protection from acts of passion:* white heather • *for protection from colds:* garlic • *for protection from death:* beryl; rattle • *for protection from defilement:* bamboo (China) • *for protection from disease:* agate; amber [gemstone] • *for protection from drowning:* gold earring • *for protection from drunkenness:* radish • *for protection from evil:* amber [gemstone]; camphor; candle; cherry tree; effigy; fireworks; gold beads; incense; iron nails; juniper; onion; onyx; opal; pungent smell; rattle; sea coral; touching or knocking on wood; two fish; waving a banner; white rooster (China) • *for protection from evil spirits:* garlic; obelisk; onion; pungent smell • *for protection from eye ailments:* beryl • *for protection from fainting:* beryl • *for protection from fire:* pearl (China); red rooster (China); swastika over a door • *for protection from flies:* fly painted on a picture (in 15th and 16th century Europe, a fly painted on a picture was a charm to prevent real flies from landing in fresh paint) • *for protection from plague:* acorn; garlic • *for protection from poisoning:* radish • *for protection from seasickness:* beryl • *for protection from snakes:* agate; garlic • *for protection from sorcery:* pentagram • *for protection from the evil eye:* blue beads; cosmetics; garlic; gold beads; hand with fingers extended (especially the index and little finger) • *for protection from throat ailments:* beryl • *for protection from vampires:* garlic • *for protection from witches:* birch; rowan (but also used by them) • *for protection of innocence:* opal • *for rain:* jar

charms [attractions] *flower language:* Asiatic ranunculus (your charms are resplendent); mignonette (your qualities surpass your charms); peach blossom (your qualities, like your charms, are unequalled); ranunculus (I am dazzled by your charms; you are radiant with charms); spindle tree (your charms are engraved in my heart); thorn apple (deceitful charms)

Charon *attributes:* blue boat; ferry; red eyes

chastisement *see* **punishment**

chastity amethyst; bar on a female

symbol (circle, oval, etc.); bee; camphor; cincture; circle or wheel of fire; closed book; clouds; crescent moon; elephant; emerald (victory over the flesh); ermine; gardenia; honey; ice, icicle (feminine chastity); kingfisher (connubial chastity); laurel; lily; moon; myrrh; nun; nymph (guardian of chastity); orange [fruit]; Phoenix [bird]; plum blossoms; poppy; salamander; scepter (the power of chastity); sieve; silver; snow; stag; steel; stork; thorn (the road to chastity); two edged sword lying between a sleeping man and a sleeping woman; unicorn (feminine chastity); veil (especially white); violet [flower]; white dove with changeable tints (chastity fighting and surmounting the passions of life); white rose (chaste love) • *association:* blue • *Christianity:* alb; chestnut (triumph over the temptations of the flesh); elephant (priestly chastity); emerald [gemstone]; hare at the feet of the Virgin Mary; lapis lazuli; three knots in a monk's girdle [cincture] (the vows of poverty, chastity, and obedience); tortoise • *flower language:* chaste tree; orange blossoms • *heraldry:* blue; elephant; harp; silver • *see also* **celibacy**

Chastity personified maiden with upraised arms sprouting branches • *attributes:* boar underfoot; chariot drawn by unicorns; dove (especially two); ermine; palm tree; Phoenix [bird] (especially on a shield); sieve; unicorn; veil

chatter brook; chirping cricket; chough; cicada; crow; duck; grasshopper (meaningless chatter); hen; magpie; parrot; sieve (small talk); sparrow; swallow [bird] • *flower language:* abecedary (volubility) • *see also* **gossip**

cheapness tin • *see also* **miserliness**

cheating buttered hay

cheerfulness crocus; elephant with its trunk held up; globe amaranth • *flower language:* American starwort (cheerfulness in old age); buttercup; Chinese chrysanthemum, xeranthemum (cheerfulness under adversity); correopsis (always cheerful); pimpernel • *Greece:* parsley (when worn on the head, it was thought to increase cheerfulness and appetite) • *see also* **happiness**

chemists unicorn (trademark of chemists or druggists, signifying the purity of their goods)

cherubim angel with a book; angel's head with wings; red or golden yellow angel; winged wheel • *association:* Ark of the Covenant • *attributes:* flaming sword (the cherubim protecting the Garden of Eden); topaz • *see also* **angels**

childbirth alcove; bed; cradle; dittany; straw girdle [cincture] (an aid to childbirth); tunnel (birth trauma) • *association:* three • *emblems:* dittany (emblem of Juno as Lucina, "the bringer of light," who took responsibility for mothers and babies during childbirth) • *flower language:* dittany of Crete • *see also* **birth** (for characteristics associated with the days of birth)

childhood ball, toy (childhood play); fairyland (escape or regression to childhood); morning; pimpernel

childishness calf • *flower language:* buttercup; kingcup

children branch [plant]; nightjar (the soul of an unbaptized child); satyr (child of the Devil); seed; silver (charm to protect children from evil); string of beads • *associations:* O [letter]; three • *attribute:* dimple (attractive children) • *China:* lotus; silver (charm to prevent evil to children) • *heraldry:* panther (a beautiful woman, normally tender, but fierce in defense of her children) • *see also* **boys; girls; infancy**

China dragon tattoo (attribute of a 19th century sailor who had been to China) • *emblems:* chrysanthemum; dragon; jade

chivalry armor; cherry tree; knight • *flower language:* great yellow daffodil; helmet flower; monkshood • *heraldry:* daffodil; falcon • *see also* **gallantry; gentility**

Chloe *attribute:* syrinx

choice crossroads; fir; Fool [tarot] (a choice of vital importance); fork in a road or path; intersection; Lovers [tarot] (the right choice); rule [measuring]; seesaw; winnow; winnowing

choirs of angels *association:* nine (the nine choirs of angels)

Choler personified *attributes:* flame; lion; sword

the chosen hoe (election of the chosen)

Christ *see* **Jesus Christ**

the Christian personified *attribute:* pheasant

Christianity armor, oak (Christian resistance to evil); Bible (Protestantism in particular, Christianity in general); cherry in Christ's hand (the delight of the blessed); church procession (Christians going forth to work in the world); cross; crown (Christian reward); fish; flaming sword with a shield, white horse (Christian conquest); grasshopper or locust [insect] held by Jesus Christ (the conversion of the nations to Christianity); hyacinth [gemstone], flaming heart (Christian love); Jesus Christ; leaven (Christian influence); orb with a cross on it (Christian dominion of the world); pheasant; plowman (the Christian community); plantain (food of the multitude seeking Christian growth or salvation); potter's wheel (divine influence on Christian life); open purse (Christian benevolence); reading the Gospel from the north end of the church (the desire to convert the barbarians); rock (Christian steadfastness); rooster; stairs (Christian pilgrimage); swan (Christian retirement); tamed falcon (a gentile convert); torch (Christian witness) • *Christian enlightenment:* dove on the shoulder of a saint (divine enlightenment); eagle (Mary leading people to true light); cross with an orb or globe (the gradual enlightenment of the world) • *heraldry:* fish • *see also* **the church**

Christians beaver (in early Christianity, the Christian who makes sacrifices for the sake of his soul); birds feeding on grapes (the faithful gathering sustenance from Christ, usually through the eucharist); birds in a vine (Christian souls abiding with Christ); bulrushes (the humble faithful who abide with Christ); curlew (the good Christian); deer (a Christian searching after truth); eagle (a Christian soul strengthened by grace); griffin (those who oppress Christians); hare (those who put their faith in Christ); hart (faithful Christians partaking the waters of life); hart being hunted (persecution of Christians); heron (the

Christian who turns away from false doctrine); Job (the faithful Christian); lotus; salamander (the Christian who resists temptation through grace); stag (the Christian longing for God); stag being hunted (persecution of Christians); tamed falcon (a gentile convert to Christianity); vine with branches (Christians and Christ); workers in a vineyard (the work of good Christians for the Lord) • *attributes:* myrtle (gentile converts to Christianity); sword (martyrs) • *emblem:* ass (early Judaic Christians)

Christina, St. arrow held by a maiden with a millstone

Christmas *associations:* comet; holly; mistletoe; poinsettia; red and green together; shepherd's crook

Christopher, St. giant with a child on his shoulders • *attributes:* Christ child; lantern; mermaid, merman; staff made of a palm tree; torrent

Chrysostom, St. *see* **John Chrysostom, St.**

Chtonius *attribute:* moon

the church ark (the covenant God made with Noah and the church); beehive; boxwood (grace of the church); bride; bride and groom together (the church and Christ, respectively); cassock (devotion to God and the church); Ceres (used in the Middle Ages); city on a hill (the prominence and stability of the church); dolphin; drag net; Esther (the church of the gentiles); flock (the church congregation); gold and silver dove with many wings; flowers in a field (the Virgin Mary and the church); Greek cross; harbor; High Priestess [tarot]; house on a rock [the church securely founded on the rock of faith); ivory tower; Jerusalem; jester (church critic); Jesus Christ; key of gold (material power of the church); key of gold and key of silver (the power of the church to bind and to loose); lamb with a nimbus on top of a hill (the church with Christ as the head—four streams on the hill represent the Gospels); lamb with a white flag that has a cross on it (the body of Christ, that is, the church—a cruciform flagstaff indicates the way Christ redeemed man); man preaching from the stern of a ship (St. Peter leading the

church); matron; mill; moon (the church reflecting the light of Christ, however, when the sun and moon are together, it can mean the church and the synagogue, respectively); moorings; mustard [plant]; net; Noah's Ark; olive tree or branch; organ [instrument] (praise of God from the church); partridge (may also mean the Devil, however); peacock (the ever-vigilant church); pomegranate; priest; quatrefoil (the four Greek or four Latin doctors of the church); Reynard the fox; rock; sailboat; seven golden candlesticks, or seven-branched menorah (the seven early Christian churches of Asia Minor); ship; ship on a stormy sea (the church surviving heresy, schism, and persecution); soil; square (firmness of the church); temple on a hill; tree; twelve men rowing a ship (the apostles moving the church); two eyes, one opened and one closed (the church and synagogue, respectively); vineyard; wheat and tares (the church on earth) • *association:* twelve; *Church Militant:* chancel (passage from this world into eternal into eternal life, or from the Church Militant to the Church Triumphant); communion rail (the separation between the Church Militant and the Church Triumphant); forty (association); processional cross (the Church Militant); rood beam (the necessity of the cross of Calvary in passing from the Church Militant to the Church Triumphant) • *Church Triumphant:* chancel (passage from this world into eternal life, or from the Church Militant to the Church Triumphant); communion rail (the separation between the Church Militant and the Church Triumphant); rood beam (the necessity of the cross of Calvary in passing from the Church Militant to the Church Triumphant) • *persecution of the church:* burning bush (the church being persecuted but not perishing); Hagar (the church in bondage); harbor; hare being hunted (persecution of the church); ship on a stormy sea (the church surviving heresy, schism, and persecution) • *see also* **Christianity; Jesus Christ**

the Church personified *attributes:* key; shield

Cimerian sibyl [Cimeriana] *attribute:* horn of milk
Cimon and Pero woman nursing an old man
Cincinnatus plowman approached by Roman soldiers and offered a sword (the plowman is Cincinnatus)
Cinderella *attributes:* bellows; carriage made of a pumpkin; glass slipper
Circe *association:* swine in a palace • *attributes:* magic wand; swine
circle rosary (circle of perfection) • *association:* ring
circumcision Abraham's seal; eight; knife
circus *associations:* elephant; seal [animal] • *emblem:* calliope
cities *heraldry:* dolphin (coastal cities)
cities personified matron • *attribute:* turreted mural crown
claims *see* **pretension**
clairvoyance eyes in odd places of the body; horse (sometimes credited with clairvoyance); jasper • *see also* **extrasensory perception**
Clare of Assisi, St. *association:* nuns watching soldiers scaling city walls • *attributes:* cross with monstrance; crozier; garment of palm leaves; lily; pyx bearing the Host
clarity black and white together; diamond [gemstone]; nose; onyx
class distinction dung (an equalizer of the various classes); dust (the great equalizer)
Claudia model of a ship in the hand of a woman; woman pulling a boat upstream
clay *China:* odd numbers (association)
cleanliness basin, or basin and ewer together; broom [for sweeping]; cat; hyssop; lynx; sixpence; white gloves; whistling • *flower language:* broom (neatness) • *heraldry:* ermine • *see also* **fastidiousness**
cleansing *see* **purification**
clearness *see* **clarity**
Clement of Rome, St. *attributes:* anchor; fountain; lamb
Cleobis and Biton chariot drawn by two youths (the youths are Cleobis and Biton)
Cleopatra asp (Cleopatra's suicide); woman with a serpent to her breast • *attribute:* pearl • *association:* purple

sails (Cleopatra's barge); *flower language:* lavender (associated with the asp that killed Cleopatra)
clergy belfry (religiosity undone by clerical weakness) • *association:* black • *attribute:* turned collar • *see also* **bishops; cardinals [clergy]; deacons; monks; nuns; priests**
Cletis *association:* silver foot
cleverness ass; dock [plant]; lamprey; mouse; Ulysses • *flower language:* pencilled geranium; white pink • *heraldry:* ant; helmet surmounted by a wolf's head (courage and astuteness) • *see also* **cunning; intellect; sagacity; wit**
Clio *attributes:* book; crown of laurel; scroll; swan; tablet with a stylus; trumpet
clitoris man in a boat; pearl (Victorian euphemism)
Cloelia woman on horseback, sometimes nude
Clorinda and Tancred female soldier dying, comforted by a male soldier; soldier pouring water on a dying woman from his helmet
closing *see* **completion; ending**
clothing *China:* kingfisher (gaudy raiment)
Clotho *attributes:* distaff (attribute of the Fates, especially Clotho); spindle
clouds falcon; sheep; white feathers; winged elephant • *association:* gray; mist; white
Clovis dove carrying an ampulla (the baptism of Clovis)
clumsiness badger • *association:* left side; thumb • *see also* **crudity**
cocaine snow
Cocles, Horatius soldier fighting enemy on a bridge
coffins *see* **burial**
cohesion burr; necktie; rock; stone; string (cohesion of all things)
coldheartedness eyebrows set far apart; fish • *flower language:* angus castus; chaste tree; hortensia; hydrangea; lettuce • *see also* **hardheartedness**
coldness December; frog; ice; marble (cold beauty); moon; north; north wind; owl; reptile (cold bloodedness); snow covered mountain (cold reason); winter • *associations:* blue; eight; four; seven • *China:* even numbers (association) • *United States:* brass monkey • *see also* **coolness; frigidity**

colds [disease] garlic (protection from colds)

Colette, St. *attribute:* lamb

collectors polyp

colonizers *emblem:* fern

combat *see* **war**

combination Temperance [tarot] (successful combination)

comedians *attributes:* white nose (in the Chinese theater) • *see also* **fools; jesters**

comedy mask with a smile; sock [stocking]

comeliness *see* **beauty**

comfort blanket; cushion; east wind (comforter); harbor; nest; pillow; warmth (especially maternal comfort) • *association:* six (material comforts) • *China:* mulberry tree (comforts of home) • *flower language:* pear tree; scarlet geranium • *see also* **ease**

coming of age *association:* eighteen (occasional modern use); twenty-one (traditional)

command finger snapping (peremptory command); index finger; scepter (military command); club suit [tarot] (power of command) • *heraldry:* purple; red

Commandments, Ten *association:* ten

commemoration poppy (commemoration of the dead on Armistice Day— now Veteran's Day in the United States)

commerce caduceus (commerce and industry); coins; dolphin with a trident (freedom of commerce); factory chimney • *associations:* diamond suit [playing cards]; O [letter] • *see also* **merchants**

Commerce personified *attribute:* stork

common ground *heraldry:* hoe (a right to part of the common ground)

common people *see* **lower classes**

common sense Punch and Judy (contagious humor and common sense overcoming all obstacles)

commonness coot (a common or stupid fellow); copper (metal of the common people); potato

commonweal *see* **community spirit**

communication closed room with windows (lack of communication, but with the possibility of communication); closed room without windows (no possibility of communication);

drum (communication, especially of word or tradition); epileptic seizure (communication with deities or spirits); intersection; letter [epistle]; mountain (place of communication with deities or spirits); railroad train; Saturn [god]; sigma, sigmoid, stairs (communication between worlds); window • *associations:* Libra; Mercury [planet]

communion *see* **eucharist**

communism *emblems:* hammer and sickle; red flag; red dawn (Chinese communism)

community anthill; plowman (the Christian community)

community spirit ant • *heraldry:* fess (someone willing to work for the common good)

companionship *see* **friendship**

compass [direction] four pillars (the four points of the compass)

compassion columbine (in Elizabethan times); elder tree; intestines; lion; stomach; vulture • *association:* three (concern for others) • *flower language:* allspice; elder tree • *kabala:* three hundred • *see also* **consolation; kindness; mercy; pity; sympathy**

complacence folded hands

complaining carp; nudity (protest) • *association:* Ireland (querulousness)

complaisance *see* **agreeability**

complementary functions *see* **opposites**

completeness *see* **wholeness**

completion ebb tide; feast (a completed period or stage of development); rose [flower]; west; wheel; World [tarot] (the final blending of personal consciousness with universal completion) • *associations:* eleven (surfeit of completion and perfection); nine; thirty-three • *kabala:* four • *see also* **ending; wholeness**

complexion peaches and cream (beautiful complexion) • *flower language:* damask rose (brilliant complexion)

complexity spiral; wheels within wheels

compliments *see* **praise**

composure *see* **poise**

compulsion *see* **force**

comprehension *see* **understanding**

concealment cloak; clothes; curtain; darkness; helmet with the visor down (hidden or suspect thoughts); night; robe • *association:* gray

conceit Aeolian harp; ass; goose; jackdaw; lapwing (a stupid fellow who thinks he knows better than his elders); stork

concentration carnival, saturnalia (the desire to concentrate all the possibilities of existence in a given period of time) • *association:* four; M

conception *see* **impregnation; Virgin Mary**

concern *see* **anxiety; compassion**

concord caduceus in a woman's hand; embrace; hands clasped in a handshake; longevity (concord with God); lyre; milk; olive branch or tree; pomegranate • *flower language:* lote tree • *heraldry:* hands • *see also* **agreements; harmony; peace**

Concord personified *attributes:* bundle of arrows; cornucopia; fasces; olive branch; sheaf of grain; two doves facing each other

concubines *see* **courtesans; mistresses; prostitutes**

conduct *see* **behavior**

conductor *see* **guide**

confectioners *attribute:* bottle of colored liquid

conference sitting; table

confession crossed keys, amethyst (confession and absolution); pillow (mute audience of confession) • *see also* **forgiveness**

confidence chrysoprase; falcon; fern; House of God [tarot] (the dangerous consequences of over-confidence); ship • *flower language:* hepatica; flowering reed (confidence in heaven); fuchsia (confiding love); lilac polyanthus; liverwort • *self-confidence:* Aeolian harp; carbuncle [gemstone]; opal (charm for self-confidence and hope); rooster • *see also* **faith; trust**

Confidence personified woman with a boat in her hand (Claudia personifying Confidence or Trust)

confinement prison; stocks (for restraint) • *see also* **bondage; imprisonment**

confirmation [religion] chrism; hands laid on the head; white dress

conflict chess; feathered serpent with horns (opposite forces in conflict); lapwing (a stupid conceited fellow who thinks he knows better than his elders,

hence, conflict of generations); leper (the lower mind troubled with conflicting emotions, desires, and ideas); weapons • *associations:* eleven; seven; three (resolution of conflict) • *flower language:* licorice (I declare against you); rocket • *see also* **discord**

Confucius *emblem:* plum tree

confusion honeycomb; leper (the lower mind troubled with confused ideas); Tower of Babel (confusion of speech); zigzag • *association:* seventy-two • *flower language:* love-in-a-mist (perplexity)

congregation [church] flock of sheep

congruence *see* **harmony**

conjugality *see* **marriage**

conjunction altar; child (conjunction of the conscious and unconscious); church; crossroads; temple (intersection of any binary form: space and time; body and spirit, heaven and earth, etc.); flaming hearth (conjunction of the masculine fire and the feminine hearth); peace (conjunction of the higher and lower planes); prince waking a sleeping princess; sword (conjunction of the physical and spiritual) • *see also* **connection; opposites**

conjuring *see* **magic**

connection fossil (a linkage between two worlds); golden chain (the spirit binding earth to heaven); hole, mirror (the passage between worlds or existences); king and queen together; rope, thread (the connection between planes of existence); tree (connection of heaven, earth, and the underworld) • *association:* eight • *connection of heaven and earth:* beanstalk; bridge; center; column [architectural]; cross; hanging bell; harp; ladder; mast; Milky Way; mountain; pillar; rainbow; scepter; sigma; sigmoid; smell; spire; stairs; tower; weaving • *see also* **communication; conjunction**

conquest chariot; flaming sword with a shield (Christian conquest); golden fleece, occasionally white fleece (conquest of the impossible); grass (acquisition of territory by conquest); steel (all-conquering spirit); white knight (the one chosen to conquer) • *see also* **defeat; subjugation; victory**

conscience cheverel; deafness (inability to hear the voice of the conscience or spirit); drowning (being overwhelmed by the conscience); goat (repression of one's conscience); Mercury [god]; sapphire; silver (clear conscience); tower; voice; whip; wineskin (heavy conscience); worm; wound • *associations:* ocean; Neptune [planet] (cosmic conscience)

conscious attic; drowning (being overwhelmed by the conscious); father; front; garden; Gorgon (a condition beyond the endurance of the conscious mind); island (consciousness and will as refuge from the unconscious; the synthesis of consciousness and will); men; reflection of a lake or pool; tarot cards I to XI; warrior (latent force in the personality ready to aid the conscious) • *association:* right hand • *conscious and unconscious:* child (conjunction of the conscious and unconscious); circumference (viewed from without: the circumference is the defense of the conscious against the unconscious, or chaos); dawn (the unconscious broadening into consciousness); eight (associated with perfect blending of the conscious and unconscious, knowledge and love, action and reaction, etc.); H (associated with union of the conscious and unconscious); ford, ice (the dividing line between two levels such as the conscious and unconscious, sleeping and waking, time and eternity, etc.); gorge [topography] (that part of the conscious through which parts of the unconscious may be glimpsed); king and queen, marriage (the union of the conscious and unconscious); snail (the self: the shell represents the conscious, the soft inner part the unconscious or personality); Sun [tarot] (balance between the conscious and unconscious); World [tarot] (the merging of the subconscious and the super-conscious with the conscious) • *conscious threatened by the unconscious:* erupting volcano (the sudden attack of the unconscious on the conscious); fighting a monster (fighting to free the conscious from the unconscious); fingers; locomotive; men-eating monster; nightmare; quicksand • *see also* **preconscious; subconscious;** **superconscious; unconscious**

consciousness dawn (the unconscious broadening into consciousness); ford, ice (the dividing line between two states such as consciousness and unconsciousness, sleeping and waking, etc.); island (consciousness and will as a refuge from the unconscious; the synthesis of consciousness and will); Judgment [tarot] (personal consciousness starting to blend with the universal); king that is old (collective consciousness); king, Virgo (supreme consciousness); Magic [tarot]; mirror; plow (man's earthly consciousness); pool [water] (universal consciousness); prophet (dawning of a higher consciousness); reflection; Saturn [god]; ship; warrior (forces of consciousness warring within the personality); watchtower; window; World [tarot] (cosmic consciousness; the final blending of personal consciousness with universal completion) • *association:* four (the functional aspects of consciousness: thinking, feeling, sensation, and intuition) • *self-consciousness:* mirror; Narcissus [mythology]; reflection in water

consecration ampulla; ciborium; eagle and globe or orb (consecration of power); oil; seven (sword held with hilt upward) • *emblem:* two wheeled plow

consequence reaping

conservation of earth's resources tree, whale (modern times) • *association:* green

conservatism rock • *associations:* brown; Saturn [planet]

consideration *flower language:* single aster (I will think of it); white clover (think of me)

consolation balsam; breasts; cup; fountain; poppy; vinegar (final consolation); wren • *flower language:* evergreen thorn (solace in adversity); red or corn poppy; snowdrop • *see also* **compassion; sympathy**

constancy balances; bamboo; black; blue; bluebell; carbuncle [gemstone]; chrysanthemum; dove; fir; forget-me-not; goose; hill; iron; marigold; myrtle; Phoenix [bird]; Pole Star; rock; square [shape]; stars; stocks [for restraint]; sword hanging overhead (constant threat); tulip; turtle dove; violet [flower and color]; yew • *Christianity:*

diamond [gemstone] • *flower language:* blue hyacinth; bluebell; cedar of Lebanon; pyramidal bellflower • *heraldry:* cube; dove (loving constancy); ivy (constant love); lozenge [shape]; salamander; tree (constancy in faith) • *see also* **faithfulness; intransigence; loyalty; stability; steadfastness**

Constancy personified *attributes:* brazier; pillar; spear with a pillar; sword and pillar

constipation prune (suggestive of constipation, both physical and mental)

construction cornerstone (a remnant of the foundation sacrifice, originally a child was used, later, small animals • *association:* scaffold • *heraldry:* beaver (skill, especially in castle building) • *see also* **building trades**

consul *Rome:* scepter tipped with eagle (attribute)

consummation burial (consummation, in its various senses); coronation

contact abandonment (loss of contact with God or nature); bare feet (direct contact with Mother Earth, holy or saintly persons are often portrayed with bare feet) • *flower language:* burdock, red balsam (touch me not)

containment *see* **female principle**

contemplation bo tree; Buddha; copestone; eagle; feather; fishing; harp; hermit; looking into water; Mercury [god] (intellectual contemplation); monk; nun; old man; Rachel (the contemplative life) • *association:* blue (especially divine contemplation) • *Christianity:* lion • *heraldry:* lyre • *Judaism:* hare • *see also* **introspection; meditation; pensiveness; reflection; thought**

contempt aloe; dog (from the Middle Ages onward, also used as a symbol of loyalty); middle finger upraised; nuditas temporalis (contempt for worldly things); scorpion; thumb in the mouth or between closed fingers; thumb to the nose, or biting the thumb; worm • *Bible:* dog (an object of contempt, but in Christianity from the Middle Ages onward, a symbol of loyalty • *see* **happiness**

contests blue ribbon (first place); red ribbon (second place)

continence bee; cincture; Hanged Man [tarot]

continents five circles intertwined (the continents of Asia, Europe, America, Africa, Australia) • *see also* **Africa; America; Asia; Australia; Europe**

continuity banana, banana tree (continuing life); bracelet; distaff (the continuity of creation); ring; Ouroboros (continuity of life); rosary (perpetual continuity); scales on mermaids, dragons, the Devil (the past continuing in the present; the inferior continuing in the superior); spider (continuous sacrifice)

contracts ring; scroll; slapping each other's palms or spitting (binding to a bet or contract) • *flower language:* broken straw (rupture of a contract) • *see also* **agreements; covenants**

contraction Wheel of Fortune [tarot] (the equilibrium of the contrary forces of expansion and contraction)

contrariness bird cage (man's contrariness) • *association:* Ireland (querulousness)

contrition *see* **remorse**

control billows, drunkenness (loss of control); chains (legal control); Chariot [tarot] (self-control); king (control; self-control); rudder; skidding (loss of control of the id by the ego and superego); steed (control of baser forces) • *see also* **regulation**

conversation two millstones (mutual converse of human society)

conversion *see* **Christianity**

conviviality drunkenness; inn; ivy wreath; pine cone; table; tapster (false geniality) • *see also* **fellowship; friendliness; hospitality**

coolness *association:* blue • *heraldry:* bat [animal] (coolness in the time of danger) • *see also* **frigidity; poise**

cooperation beehive; orchestra (cooperation of the discrete toward a given end) • *associations:* B; K; T; two

coordination Temperance [tarot] (coordination and adaptation)

copulation *see* **sex**

coquetry cat; convolvulus; dandelion; fan [handheld]; giraffe; handkerchief • *flower language:* dame violet, queen's rocket (you are the queen of coquettes); day lily; spurge laurel; three-colored convolvulus

cordiality *see* **friendliness**

correction *see* **punishment**

corruption Bacchus; incest (corruption of the natural order); leaven (increasing corruption); moth; oil (preservation against corruption); pond; sepulcher; siren [mythology] (corrupt imagination); sty [animal pen]; swine (corruption in general, also the plunge into moral corruption); thaw; Vulcan (a weak, materialistic, and corrupt soul); wolf

Cosmas and Damian, Saints twins • *attributes:* lancet; mortar and pestle; ointment; patient with one white leg and one black leg; surgical instruments

cosmos light (cosmic energy); Ouroboros (cosmic unity); plants [biology] (the healthy growth of plants indicates cosmic, spiritual, and material fecundity); pool [water] (cosmic knowledge); scales [biology] (cosmic inferiority); swastika with straight ends in a circle or triangle (cosmic harmony); thunder (cosmic disturbance); tree (the life of the cosmos); zither • *associations:* O [letter]; one; seven; zither • *cosmic forces:* flock (the disordered or semi-ordered forces of the cosmos, often with a negative connotation); gargoyle; griffin (the relationship between psychic energy and cosmic forces); flock (the disordered or semi-ordered forces of the cosmos, often with a negative connotation); harpy (evil harmonies of cosmic forces); lyre or onion (harmony of cosmic forces); ox; phallus (propagation of cosmic forces)

counterpoise *see* **balance**

countries *see* **nations**

country life *see* **rusticity**

courage agate; Ajax; ass; bloodstone (charm for presence of mind and courage); blue; boar; breastplate; breasts thrust forward; bulldog; carp; cricket [insect]; daffodil; dog; helmet; hummingbird; lion; mantis; mockingbird; mutilation (proof of courage); Nike; oak; olive (courageous love and faith); quail; red; Sparta; spine; stomach (seat of courage); sturgeon; thyme; tiger; tourmaline; weasel • *association:* seven • *China:* amber [gemstone]; quail • *flower language:* black poplar • *heraldry:* cat; daffodil; elephant; ermine; greyhound; griffin; helmet surmounted by a wolf's head (courage supplanted by astuteness); lance; lion; raven; red;

serpent; squirrel; swallow [bird]; unicorn • *see also* **bravery; pugnacity**

courtesans *attributes:* braids (note that this is also the attribute of a young girl); exposed breasts • *see also* **concubines; mistresses; prostitutes**

courtliness *see* **chivalry; gallantry**

courtship gloves and ring (traditional courting gifts); linnet; spring [season] • *see also* **betrothal; love; lovers; suitors**

covenants ark, Ark of the Covenant, Noah's ark, rainbow (God's covenant with Noah and mankind); blood • *association:* phallus • *associations:* acacia, shittim (Ark of the Covenant) • *see also* **contracts**

cowardice chicken; crab tree (old, foolish, cowardly people); dove; goose; hare; hind [deer]; hyena; jackal; kite [bird]; knight pursued by a hare; ostrich; tailor; white feathers; wolf • *associations:* white; yellow • *see also* **fear; horror; terror**

cowboys *attributes:* bandanna; lasso; spurs

cows goat (the poor man's cow)

cradle boat (the womb or the cradle rediscovered); Mount Ararat (the second cradle of mankind)

craft *see* **cunning**

crafts *associations:* Athena (spinning, weaving, and other women's crafts); Venus [planet] (the arts and crafts)

craftsmen *attributes:* apron; brooch (may indicate the wearer's trade)

creation air; alpha and omega, Phoenix [bird], scarab (creation and destruction); anvil, double-headed eagle, light, lotus, spire (creative power); aquatic plants, ocean (primordial creation); bird; chaos, inability to speak, night (incipient creation); churning; clockwise spiral; compasses [dividers], dancing (the act of creation); crow; dawn; Death [tarot]; distaff (the continuity of creation); dove flying over water (especially when the dove has a three-rayed nimbus); egg; field (physical creation); fire; furnace, volcano (creative fire); Gemini (creative and created nature); golden egg (the sun, laid on the waters of chaos by the primeval goose); goose, pole, storm (creative energy); Demogorgon (the creative spirit); Gordian knot, labyrinth (the loss of the spirit in the process of creation and the need to find it again); Gorgon (the infinite forms in which creation is manifested); gourd (creative power of nature); hammer; lake (source of creative power); lotus, octopus, web (unfolding of creation); meteorite (heavenly creative fire); mouth (creation; the creative word); oar (creative thought); pyramid (the whole work of creation); river (the creative power of time and nature); sails (creative breath); scepter (the creative power of the word); scissors; Sophia (the creative spirit of God); the soul (the creative part of mankind); sowing; sphere (creative motion); spinning of thread; stone (the first solid form of creation); storm; thunderbolt (supreme creative fire); sun (creative light); twelve pillars; vine (unfailing source of natural creation); weaving (especially as a feminine activity); World [tarot] (the totality of the manifest world as a reflection of permanent creative activity; perfection as the end of creation out of chaos) • *associations:* blacksmith; book; clock (the magical creation of beings that pursue their own autonomous existence); forty-two (creative generation); frog; heart suit [playing cards] (the creative world); Mars (the idea that there is no creation without sacrifice); red (creative power); seven; seven-branched menorah (the six days of creation, with the center light as the sabbath); six, six-pointed star (the six actual days of creation according to the Bible); Taurus • *Biblical creation:* Sunday (light); Monday (division of waters); Tuesday (dry land, pastures, trees); Wednesday (heavenly bodies); Thursday (sea beasts, birds); Friday (land beasts, man and woman); Saturday (rest) • *Egypt:* mace [weapon] (the creative word) • *Near East:* egg • *self-creation:* birch; hermaphrodite (androgynous self-creation); scarab

creativity bee; dove on one's shoulder (creative imagination); north wind; Gemini (creative and created nature); the soul (man's creative part); Vulcan (the creative mind which has been captured by lower qualities) • *associations:* A; Aries • *see also* **imagination**

the creator carpenter; father; fire; giant bird; Leviathan (rebellion

against the Creator); potter; rock; spider; tailor; trident (the male as creator) • *association:* one • *emblems:* ram [sheep]; six-pointed star; stone; sun • *see also* **deities; God**

credulity *see* **fools**

crime prison • *flower language:* tamarisk

Crime personified *attribute:* tamarisk

criminals black flag (execution of a criminal); hanging [execution] (death of a common criminal—nobles and the rich were beheaded) • *association:* orange [color] (used in the ancient East) • *see also* **thieves**

cripples man carrying a bed (Christ's healing of the paralytic) • *attribute:* cane [for walking]; wheelchair • *emblem:* crutch (those who care for the aged or crippled)

crippling *see* **disabling**

criticism axe (the critical faculty); flak; hedgehog (the critical aspect that destroys error); jester (a critic of church and establishment practices) • *association:* forty (castigation) • *flower language:* cucumber

Croesus *association:* fourteen

Cronus *attributes:* scythe; sickle

crook [staff] *association:* P

crosses marriage on a Thursday is associated with crosses (i.e. religion) • *see also* **Jesus Christ**

crowds *Judaism:* one hundred and twenty people (a large crowd)

crown World [tarot] (the final crown of the initiate)

crown of thorns *see* **Jesus Christ**

crows jackdaw (shares the unfavorable symbolism of kites and crows)

crucible oven

crucifixion cross • *see also* **Jesus Christ**

crudity *see* **rudeness**

cruelty basilisk; bear; cage; cat; iron; kite [bird]; lamia; leopard; mantis (cruelty and greed disguised by a hypocritical attitude of prayer or religiosity); nettle; orange [color] that is impure; ostrich; polyp; second toe longer than the first toe (sign of a cruel husband); steel; stepmother; thin lips; tiger; tooth; vulture (ruthlessness); wolf • *associations:* eight, one (ruthlessness); *flower language:* nettle • *Old Testament:*

goat • *see also* **brutality; ferocity; meanness; viciousness**
crusaders *attribute in art:* crossed legs, right over left • *heraldry:* crescent (high honors, especially in the Crusades); moor's head (service in the Crusades)
Crusades sword
cry siren [mechanical device] (cry of terror or alarm)
cuckold Vulcan; wood pigeon • *attributes:* bugle; cap (used to hide the horns of a cuckold); horns
cuckolding cistern (a wife who must be guarded to be kept pure); cuckoo (cuckolder); fishing; middle finger upraised • *see also* **adultery**
culmination *see* **completion**
cults hand on the mouth (member of a secret cult)
culture rhinoceros • *associations:* J; nine; seven • *China:* bamboo • *Rome:* Greece (the highest culture)
Cumean sibyl [Cumana] woman with cupped hands before Apollo • *attributes:* bowl; cradle; manger
Cunegunda, St. *attribute:* heated plow
cunning ape; blackbird; camel; cat; chimera; cicada; crow; dog; ferret; fox; hedgehog; hippopotamus; Justice [tarot]; lapwing; leopard; Mephistopheles; net; octopus; soil; partridge; polyp; Reynard the fox; spider; tiger; whale; wolf; worm • *China:* fox; serpent; white face (in Chinese theater, a cunning but dignified man) • *heraldry:* bat [animal]; cat; elephant; fox (strategic cunning); leopard; martlet; wolf (martial cunning) • *see also* **cleverness**
Cunning personified *attribute:* poppy
Cup [tarot] *association:* U
cup-bearer *heraldry:* cup (holder of the honorary title of royal cup-bearer or meat carver)
Cupid naked infant with wings; naked maiden with a lamp, standing over a sleeping god (Psyche standing over Cupid) • *associations:* goat; goose; heart pierced with an arrow; wings • *attributes:* blindfold; bow and arrows; cat; chariot drawn by four white horses (attribute of Cupid personifying Love); chariot drawn by goats; dart; globe (occasionally); torch • *emblem:* heart [organ]
cure balm; sulfur and eggs (cure for unrequited love) • *flower language:*

balm of Gilead
curiosity bow with arrows (penetrating inquisitiveness); crane [bird]; ear; ferret (curiosity about hidden things); fishing (curiosity about the unconscious); hare; hound; nose; sycamore; tailor (sexual curiosity) • *association:* P • *flower language:* sycamore • *see also* **investigation; searching**
curses *see* **magic spells**
Curtius, Marcus soldier on horseback, leaping into a pit
customs *see* **traditions**
Cyanus *association:* cornflower (Cyanus was turned into a cornflower by Flora)
Cybele *attributes:* bunch of keys; chariot drawn by lions; crescent and seven-pointed star; globe; lion; mountains, red heather and bees together; scepter; seven-pointed star; sow [swine]; turreted mural crown
cycles agriculture (cyclic existence); beheading, catastrophe, corpse, deluge, dusk, sunset (end of a cycle); bracelet, circle, ring (eternally repeated cycle); clock; disguise (entrance into a new stage of life); finger snapping (beginning or end of a cycle); earth [soil] (the cycle of existence as a symbol of man's life); fish with a bird's head--usually a swallow's (bringer of cyclic regeneration); moon; Phoenix [bird] (a cycle of destruction and re-creation); procession; seven-pointed star (cyclic progression); sewing; sunrise (start of a cycle); Temperance [tarot] • *associations:* Aries, S (start of a cycle); Pisces, ninety, seven (end of a cycle); two
Cyclops one-eyed giant
Cygnus youth changed into a swan
cynicism Mephistopheles
Cyprian, St. *attribute:* double-headed axe
Cyprus *associations:* Aphrodite; copper
Cyril of Alexandria, St. *attributes:* scroll with the word "Theotokos"; writing pen
Cyril of Jerusalem, St. *attribute:* purse
Cyrus the Great woman placing a severed head in an urn (Tomyris, Queen of Scythia, with the head of Cyrus the Great) • *association:* message discovered in a hare's body
Czechoslovakian-Americans *emblem:* mushroom

D

Daedalus *see* **Dedalus**

Dafilo and Granido kneeling youth offering a shell as a cup to a maiden

daintiness lily of the valley

dalliance amethyst (usually deep love, but sometimes dalliance); eagle; king; primrose

Damian and Cosmas, Saints *see* **Cosmas and Damian, Saints**

the damned *Christianity:* billy goat

Damocles *association:* sword hanging overhead

Dan, Tribe of *emblem:* serpent

dancing cymbal (especially two cymbals); daffodil; flute; tripod (achievement in song or dance) • *association:* waves [water] • *flower language:* ivy geranium (I engage you for the next dance)

danger dagger; dolphin; forest; gorge [topography]; heron (danger overcome); lion (danger of being devoured by the unconscious); Medusa (the dangerous woman); nettle; quicksand; rattlesnake; reef (danger of the unconscious); serpent; shark; sneezing on a Monday (omen of danger); spider (especially a black widow or tarantula); sword hanging overhead; sweating image (dangerous passage); wasp (petty danger) • *association:* eleven • *China:* swallow's nest • *flower language:* Carolina rose (love is dangerous); rhododendron; rose bay [oleander]; rose bay (beware of excess); tuberose (dangerous pleasures) • *heraldry:* bat [animal] (coolness in the time of danger); ship (succor in extremity) • *see also* **threat; warning**

Daniel *attributes:* lion; ram [sheep] with four horns

Dante *attribute:* crown of laurel

Daphne maiden with laurel sprouting from her arms • *attribute:* sunflower

Daphnis *attribute:* syrinx

daring *see* **bravery**

darkness Africa; American Indian, savage (the darker side of the personality); blindness; chimera; counterclockwise swastika; dragon; leopard (dark force); Negro (child of darkness; the darker side of the personality); night; nightshade; noon (the opposite of darkness); owl; russet [cloth] (love of darkness and lies); Russia; scroll in the hands of a patriarch (the darkness faith was enveloped in before Christ); slug [animal] (the tendency of darkness to move toward light); smoke (mental darkness); stable (realm of darkness from which light emerges); west; winter; wolf • *flower language:* enchanter's nightshade (dark thoughts)

daughters *flower language:* cinquefoil (beloved daughter)

David *association:* five; six-pointed star [the star of David] • *attributes:* bell; crown and scepter; five stones and a sling; Goliath's severed head; harp, especially when with a lion; horn of oil; lion; man wrestling with a lion; shepherd's crook; staff; turreted castle

David, St. *attributes:* dove; fountain; leek; mountain

dawn child; crane [bird]; dancing peahen; dog; east; ibis; incense; lark; maiden; prophet (dawning of a higher consciousness); plumed serpent (angel of dawn); raven; rook [bird]; russet [cloth]; thunderbolt; white horse; white rooster • *associations:* Aphrodite; Aries; dew; red (dawn deities); red cow • *emblem:* hind [deer] • *see also* **sunrise**

Dawn personified *attributes:* cicada; russet mantle [clothing]

day eagle; sundial (daytime, as opposed to the hourglass which indicates night); twilight (threshold of day and night) • *associations:* light blue; radiance (daylight in both its good and bad senses); two (day and night)

deacons *attributes:* dalmatic (although bishops and abbots may wear it under a chasuble); maniple, tunicle (used at a high mass by subdeacons); stole [religious garment] worn on the left shoulder and across the breast

dead burial (honoring the dead); aloe (purification of the dead); barnacle goose (the unhallowed soul of a dead person); dog (companion of the dead); dolphin, Mercury [god], shepherd (conductor of the souls of the dead); empty chair; firefly (a spirit or ghost of the dead, especially a dead warrior); poppy (commemoration of the dead on Armistice Day, which is now Veteran's Day in the United States); skull (the worldly survival of the dead); hollow [topography], interior of a mountain (occasionally), moon, pyramid (abode of the dead) • *associations:* dolphin (related to death and homage to the dead); nudity • *attributes:* crown (martyrs); white fillet (attribute of the dead in the Elysian fields) • *early art:* clean shaven persons were dead, the living were shown bearded • *Egypt:* ellipse (the world of the dead) • *flower language:* rosemary (remembrance of the dead) • *Greece:* asphodel; red food (food of the dead)

deans [clergy] *attribute:* black cassock with red piping

death abandonment; ace of spades; almond; apple; ashes (death; death of the body); asphodel; autumn; azalea (fatal gifts); balances (death; life and death); bandages (the winding sheet of the tomb); banner with cross held by a lamb (Christ's victory over death); banshee (messenger of death); baptism (death of the old, resurrection of the new); basilisk; bat [animal]; bay wreath; bee; being bound to a stake (death of a fertility king); beheading (a noble death); bell; beetle; beryl, rattle (charm against death); black angel; black bull; black cat; black flag; black horse; black ox; black rooster; black scarf; black veil; blot; bone; bonfire; bow [archery]; bramble; briars; broken stone, or pillar; broken handcuffs (death and sin overcome); burnt stick or wood (death and wisdom); buzzard; carrion; casket; centaur; center (going through death to eternity); cinquefoil [plant]; closed eyes; clouds; coffin; coldness; counterclockwise spiral or swastika; crab; crocus; crow; crown (victory over death; attribute of a martyr); crown of periwinkle; cutting reins; cypress; cypress and marigolds (death and despair, respectively); daffodil; daisy (the silence of death); dead leaves; deadly nightshade [belladonna]; Death [tarot] (death of

the old self, but not necessarily the person); devouring (dissolution of the body after death, fear of death); door; dove issuing from one's mouth (the soul escaping after death); dropping a curtain; dusk; dust; earth [soil] (the end of material life); ebony; elder tree; falcon; father; Egypt (concern with life after death); fern leaf (victory over death); fig; fillet; five-petalled lotus; flower, ocean, vegetation growing in cycles (death and regeneration); frost; gate; gibbet; tickling (a disgraceful death); gourd; granite; handcuffs (death; sin); handful of earth (death and mortality); hands laid on the head; hands raised and open; hanging [execution] (an ignominious death; death of a common criminal); harp (longing for death); harpist, musician (fascination with death); hawthorn; hazel; headless horseman; hemlock; Hesperides; hood; hourglass; ice; invisibility; island; ivy; jackal; Judgment [tarot] (the mystery of birth in death); kicking over a full bucket; kite [bird]; knife; knocking; lake (the transition between life and death, often in a destructive sense); laurel; lead [metal]; loss; maggot; marble; mermaid; merman; mole [animal]; moon; muffled drum; Narcissus (death of youth); net; nettle; night; nightshade; noose (death by hanging); ocean (mediator between life and death); one hundred and ten (a perfect age to die); one way road; orchard; overturned cup spilling wine; owl; ox skull (but when adorned and shown with horns: immortality); parsley; Phoenix [bird] (power to overcome death); poppy; primrose; pyramid; rat (infirmity and death); ratsbane (lechery causing disease and death); raven; reaper (death deity); reaping; red hand (threat of death); returning to one's birthplace or homeland (dying in the positive sense of reintegration with the spirit of God); rider on a pale horse; rowan; sarcophagus (the earth as the beginning and end of material life); scissors; scythe; sepulchre; serpent; severed head (life of the soul after death); sheaf with a sickle; sheet; shroud; sickle; siren [mythology] (death bearer; death wish); Sirius; skeleton; skull; skull with a cross (meditation on the eternal life that comes after death);

snow; spade [shovel]; spikenard; spiral (the mystery of life and death); spread-eagle body position; stain; starling (life in death); stick; sting; Styx; sunset; swan song; swastika with curved ends within a circle or triangle; sword; tetractys (birth, growth, and death); thief; thumb down; trumpet; twin serpents; uraeus (power over life and death); urn; urn with a lid on it (the supreme enlightenment which triumphs over birth and death); valley; vampire; violet [flower]; vulture; waves [water] (death and maternity); west (to turn west is to prepare for death); west wind; white flag with a red cross (victory over death); white flower; willow wreath; winding sheet; winter (death; involutive death with the promise of rebirth); withered plant; withered tree; wolfsbane (deadliness); worm; wren; yew • *associations:* animal skin (death and regeneration); basil (Middle East); birch; black; bull; dark complexion; field; fountain; dolphin (death; homage to the dead); hen; horse; L (violent death); left hand; left side; M [tarot]; middle finger; myrtle; pinching; red and black (life and death, respectively); Rome (heroic death); seventy; thirteen; toadstool; yellow (death and decay) • *China:* five bats [animals] (the blessings of longevity, wealth, health, virtue, and a natural death) • *Egypt:* baboon; crocodile • *emblems:* the Grim Reaper; skull and crossbones • *flower language:* asphodel (my regrets follow you to the grave); basil; bouquet (we die together); currants (thy frown will kill me); dried white rose (death is preferable to loss); gum cistus (I die tomorrow); hemlock (you will be my death) • *Greece:* bronze gong (sounded at the death of a king) • *omens:* aurora borealis, eclipse of the sun (death of a king or leader); bird tapping at a window or flying into a house; black hand or spot; caladrius turning away from a sick person; chirping cricket; earthquake (divine death); Gabriel hounds; golden plover song; spilling a cup of wine; vulture; washing in a stream • *still life painting:* coins (the power and possessions that death takes away); crown, scepter (the earthly power that death takes away); purse (possessions that death takes away) • *see also* **destruction; mortality; murder**

Death personified old man or old woman, especially 90 to 100 years old; reaper; skeleton • *attributes:* chariot drawn by two oxen (usually black); horse with three legs (in time of pestilence); old man or old woman, usually 90 to 100 years old); scythe; toad (especially when shown with a skull and crossbones); two-pronged fork

debauchery bacchante (a woman given to debauchery and sin); Bacchus; dice • *associations:* blue eyes with dark rings around them (Elizabethan times); red eyes • *see also* **degeneration; lasciviousness**

debilitation cancer [disease] (a debilitating situation)

Deborah *attributes:* crown and scepter

debtors scourge [whip] (Roman punishment for debtors)

decay Aquarius (the dissolution or decomposition of the world of phenomena); autumn (incipient decay); Caliban; cancer [disease], gangrene, rotting (decay; spiritual decay); copper; counterclockwise swastika; Death [tarot]; dust; left hand; leprosy (spiritual decay caused by lack of moral progress); maggot; mold; moth; mouse; rat; ruins; slime; spider web); summer (beauty anticipating decline) • *associations:* dirty yellow; green • *still life painting:* flower, especially with dewdrops • *see also* **degeneration; destruction; disintegration; stagnation**

deceit apple; bird cage; brook; buttered hay; Circe (feminine wiles); clothes; cosmetics; cuckoo; duck; embrace; eyebrows that meet; fishhook; flower; fly [insect]; hairy arms (Jacob's deception of Isaac); honey; ivory gate (entrance to deceptive dreams); lapwing; Liguria; lynx; nightingale (the Devil's deceit); ocher; partridge; siren [mythology] (deceptive or empty attraction); stilts; sugar; tiger; whale; wolf; wooden horse • *associations:* seven; two; yellow • *flower language:* dogsbane; jasmine; thorn apple (deceitful charms); Venus flytrap; white, or winter cherry • *see also* **dissimulation; falsity; fraud; treachery**

Deceit personified serpent with a woman's head • *attribute:* mask

December goat with a spiral tail • *birthstones:* turquoise; zircon • *China:* poppy (association)

decency *see* **goodness**

deception *see* **deceit**

decision Hanged Man [tarot] (a suspended decision); scissors (spiritual decision)

declaration *flower language:* tansy (I declare against you)

decline *see* **decay; degeneration**

decomposition *see* **decay**

decorum *see* **behavior**

decrease counterclockwise spiral • *flower language:* yellow sweet brier (decrease of love)

Dedalus carpenter; carpenter building a wooden cow (Dedalus working for Pasiphae); man and youth flying together (Dedalus and his son Icarus); man making wings

dedication [setting apart for divine use] chrism; holy water; oil; olive branch; tonsure (dedication to divine service) • *association:* red

defamation *see* **calumny**

defeat ashes; bird of prey flying from left to right before a battle (omen of defeat); black stone; broken arch, mast, stone, or pillar; elephant with trunk drooping; hands loose at the sides; lemon; lowering or striking a flag; lowering or striking sails; mace [weapon], nothingness (annihilation); skunk (complete defeat); surrender of a handful of grass; throwing a towel into a boxing ring • *association:* Pisces • *see also* **ruination; subjugation; submission; surrender**

defect abortion (defect in the soul or spirit); blot; maiming (defect or weakness in the soul, revenge for maiming shows some vestige of moral strength remains); stain • *flower language:* henbane • *see also* **imperfection**

defenders of the faith *association:* south wall of a church

defense arm; circle or wheel of fire (inviolability); drawbridge; eyebrows; fist (deterrent capability); gate; griffin or tornado (invincibility); hedgehog (strong defense); horn [anima]; scales [biology]; scorpion (defensive stewardship); shield (also defense of the spirit); soldier; tamed tiger (defense of order against chaos); wall • *association:* M (indomitability) • *heraldry:* fox

(sagacity or wit used in one's own defense); helmet (surety in defense); rhinoceros (one who does not seek combat, but will defend to the death if attacked); sword; tortoise (invulnerability) • *self-defense:* armor; buckle; hedgehog; raised arms • *see also* **impregnability; protection**

defenselessness *see* **helplessness**

defiance *see* **challenge**

defilement *China:* bamboo (charm to protect from defilement)

degeneration adultery (forsaking a higher life for a lower one); claw (degenerate sexuality); dismemberment; dispersal; divorce for the purpose of marrying another (leaving a higher nature for lower desire); herd that is disorderly; multiple heads (fragmentation, however, it can sometimes indicate a positive intensification) • *see also* **debauchery; decay; disintegration**

degradation *see* **humiliation**

deities *see* **gods**

dejection *see* **despair; despondency**

delay Hanged Man [tarot] (a suspended decision); wall • *flower language:* eupatorium; flax-leaved goldilocks (tardiness)

delegation ring (delegation of authority)

deliberation *heraldry:* snail

delicacy almond; dew • *flower language:* bluebottle; centaury; corn bottle

delicacy *see also* **fragility**

delight *see* **joy**

Delilah *attributes:* scissors

delirium tremens pink elephant

deliverance *see* **salvation**

della Gherardesca, Ugolina old man dying in prison with dead children

Delphic sibyl [Delphica] *attribute:* crown of thorns

the deluge ark; dove with ark; dove with olive branch; Noah's ark; rainbow and ark; water • *association:* forty

delusions House of God [tarot] (megalomania); Satan • *association:* fourteen • *see also* **falsity**

demand hand held out palm up (demand for possession, bribe, or payment)

dematerialization Death [tarot]

Demeter *see* **Ceres**

Demetrius, St. soldier standing with sword, shield, or lance

demigods *association:* Virgo (birth of a demigod)

demiurge crow (a demiurgic power); playwright; prince; sorcerer (the evil demiurge); Vulcan

Democratic Party [United States] *emblem:* donkey

demons crossroads (meeting place of demons, witches, etc.); Demogorgon (an underground demon); demon emerging from a victim's mouth (exorcism); eagle shown as a bird of prey (the demon that ravages souls); epileptic seizure (demonic possession); iron key (keeps demons and witches from entering keyholes); keyhole (place for the entry of demons, witches, etc.); python; red eyes (demonic fury); west (abode of demons) • *association:* hedgehog (demonic possession) • *attribute:* red hair • *China:* willow (power over demons) • *see also* **devils; monsters; Satan**

denial abortion (denial of nature); St. Peter • *self-denial:* amethyst; bull; Hanged Man [tarot]; midnight • *see also* **refusal**

Denis, St. *attribute:* severed head that is held under the arm

Denmark *emblems:* kettle drum; raven

density lead [metal] (gravity and density, especially in a spiritual sense)

dentists *attribute:* forceps holding a tooth

departure gate (departure from this world); shadow (a departed soul) • *flower language:* sweet pea

dependability bricks; chrysanthemum; romanesque arch • *association:* Taurus • *see also* **stability; trustworthiness**

dependence ivy; knot, plait (interdependence); tarot cards XII to XXII • *heraldry:* swallow [bird]

depersonalization cosmetics; hood

depravity *see* **baseness**

depression *see* **despair; despondency**

deprivation *see* **poverty**

depth abyss

derisiveness *see* **mockery**

descent *flower language:* Jacob's ladder (come down)

desert cactus

desertion columbine

desire Bacchus (the uninhibited unleashing of desire); bottomless pit or well (insatiable desire); Circe (desire leading to good or evil); drugs; fleece (alluring desire); goat's milk; helmet (protection of the soul from the assaults of passions and desires); itching (desire in general, but especially sexual desire); knight (the spirit controlling the instincts and desires); lily; prison (the early state of the soul in which the spirit is in bondage to the lower instincts and desires); siren [mechanical] (desire leading to self-destruction); sulfur (desire for positive action); swan song (desire, desire leading to self-destruction); swine (desire that seeks sustenance in matter rather than spirit); wind; woman as captive (higher nature held by latent desire) • *associations:* ocean, quivering (sexual desire) • *China:* wolf (cupidity) • *Christianity:* sycamore (cupidity) • *flower language:* four leaf clover (be mine); jonquil (desire; from the 19th century on—I desire a return of affection); mezerion (desire to please); touch-me-not (impatient desire) • *sexual desire:* bull, hound, lion (male sexual desire); cow, lioness (female sexual desire); ibis; itching (desire in general, but especially sexual desire); monkey; pin; sting • *see also* **aspiration; longing; lust; passion; yearning**

desires Amazon [mythology] (the higher emotions that oppose the desires); apple, fruit (earthly desires); cattle; Devil [tarot] (instincts and desires); fornication (the primacy of base desires); fox (base desires); goat; harpy (unregulated desires to promote their own ends); herb (primitive desires aroused by the senses); keel (lower instincts and desires); panther skin (the overcoming of base desires); prison (the early state of the soul in which the spirit is in bondage to the lower instincts and desires); savage; tiger (violent desires); tomb (the body and its fleshly desires) • *association:* base metals

desolation absence of sedge; bat [animal]; bittern; cormorant; ocean (unbounded desolation); owl; sitting on the ground; spider web; vulture • *see also* **barrenness; despair**

despair black; black poplar; carrion; marigolds; marigolds and cypress (despair and death, respectively); owl;

rags; rope; spider (despair and hope); web • *flower language:* jasmine; marigolds; yew • *see also* **despondency; melancholy**

Despair personified hanging man; woman killing herself with a sword • *attribute:* marigolds

desperation willow • *association:* orange [color] that is impure

despicability *see* **animals; baseness; dishonor**

despondency ivy • *associations:* blue; brown; gray • *flower language:* humble plant; lichen • *see also* **despair; melancholy**

despotism *see* **tyranny**

destiny linen; mother; stars; thread; web • *associations:* sixty; three • *kabala:* sixty • *obstruction of destiny:* quicksand; reef • *see also* **fate; fortune; Wheel of Fortune**

destruction alpha and omega (creation and destruction); battering ram; belt, sword (destruction of the physical); cannon; club [bat] (victory through destruction); corrosion; counterclockwise spiral; Death [tarot]; deluge, Phoenix [bird] (destruction and regeneration); desert animals (destruction and evil); devouring; dismemberment; dispersal; fire; hail; fracture, fragmentation (destruction and disintegration of the spirit); Furies (guilt turned to destruction); locusts, serpents (forces of destruction); hammer; harpoon; leopard; mace [weapon] (annihilation as opposed to simple victory); magpie (destruction of vermin); Mars; mole [animal]; moth; mouse; mouth (destruction as in devouring); north wind; rat; rust; Saturn [god] (destructive time); scissors; sponge (obliteration); threshing; tornado; trident; volcano (destruction; divine destruction); whirlwind; wind; wine press; worm (insidious destruction) • *association:* Pluto [planet] • *flower language:* basil (death and destruction, especially in the Middle East where it is planted in graveyards) • *self-destruction:* eight (association); enemies (the forces threatening a person from within); Furies (guilt turned upon itself to the destruction of the guilty); Phrygian cap; siren [mythology] or swan song (desire leading to self-destruction) • *see also* **death;**

desolation; ruination

detachment Hanged Man [tarot], hood (detachment from materialism)

detention petrification (detention of moral progress) • *see also* **confinement; imprisonment**

deterioration *see* **degeneration**

determination *China:* iron • *heraldry:* millstone

deterrence *see* **defense**

development conch shell (the spiritual and natural means of development rendered active); corn [maize] (development of a potentiality); corset (society hampering the development of a psyche); fairy (personification of a stage in the development of the spirit); feast (a completed period or stage of development); ford, fording (marks a decisive stage in action, development, etc.); traveller (someone engaged in personal development, especially spiritual or religious) • *heraldry:* tortoise (glorious development of family) • *see also* **growth**

deviation twisting

Devil *see* **Satan**

devils *associations:* black; brass (occasionally); brimstone [sulfur]; darkness; fifteen; fire; impure orange [color]; red; red and black • *attributes:* barbed or pointed tail; bat [animal]; cloven feet; horns; horse with three legs; owl; pitchfork; red beard; red clothing; red garters; scaly skin; trident; wings of skin; wart • *see also* **demons**

Devil personified salamander (but may also be Jesus Christ as the king of fire)

devotion alexandrite (undying devotion); Artemesia (a widow's devotion to her husband's memory); breasts; heart pierced with an arrow (deep devotion); heliotrope [gemstone]; orb with a spread eagle; rosary; soldier (devotion to a cause); stag; sunflower; wisteria (the gentleness and devotion of womanhood) • *associations:* blue; cube; T • *flower language:* American cowslip (you are my angel, my divinity); arbor vitae (live for me); cedar leaf (I live for thee); cornflower (devotion to an inferior); heliotrope; honeysuckle (generous and devoted affection); Peruvian heliotrope • *heraldry:* cube; marigold; pelican, usually with wings spread (filial devotion) • *see also* **faith**

devouring destruction; lion (the danger of being devoured by the unconscious); sinking in mud or quicksand; Saturn [god] (destructive and devouring time)

devoutness see **piety**

Dialectics personified attribute: scorpion

Diana goddess accusing pregnant nymph (Diana and Callisto, respectively); huntress; may be shown as one of three faces in the moon (the other two would be Kore and Hecate) • associations: crane [bird]; fawn; grotto; hart; Monday • attributes: bow and arrows; chariot drawn by one white horse and one black horse; chariot drawn by stags; crescent moon; dog; golden bow [archery]; guinea hen; hind [deer]; lance; leopard; necklace; shield; stag; white flower; wings

dichotomy twilight

Dido association: death on a funeral pyre

dieting celery; lettuce; radish

difference Temperance [tarot] (that which is always different yet always the same)

difficulty see **trouble**

diffidence see **shyness**

digestion association: Q (digestive organs); China: dove, pigeon (good digestion)

dignity almuce; cathedra (episcopal dignity); canopy, lion (royal dignity); cloak (superior dignity); dahlia (the dignity of the lower or middle class); diamond [gemstone] (dignity and wealth, especially royal); elephant (puissant dignity); diamond [shape] (royal dignity and wealth); elm; epigonation; globe (imperial dignity); gold chain; horn [animal]; onyx; ostrich feathers (knightly dignity); parasol; ruby; skullcap; stole [religious garment] (priestly dignity and power); swan; zodiac (dignity of labor) • association: purple • China: parasol; peacock; white face (a dignified but treacherous or cunning man) • Egypt: leopard (the dignity of the high priest) • emblem: two- wheeled plow (royal dignity) • flower language: clove; laurel-leaved magnolia; hundred-leaved rose (dignity of the mind) • heraldry: angel; cherub; ermine; gold; purple; seraph; swan with a crown on

its neck • Middle East: camel

diligence bee; hare (diligent service); hoe; plow; swallow [bird]; Trojan • heraldry: hands • see also **industry**

Diligence personified attribute: thyme

Diogenes old man with a lamp • attributes: bowl; lamp; lantern • emblem: Hermit [tarot]

Dionysus calf (the young Dionysus); Judgment (dionysian ecstasy) • association: date tree; goose • attributes: flute; horse; magpie; moon; myrtle; staff; swine; white bull • emblem: panther

deoxyribonucleic acid [DNA] double spiral

depililatory resin

diploma sheepskin

diplomacy association: two

direction index finger; star, stars; toe; wand

dirtiness see **filth; impurity**

Dis association: cypress

disability see **handicap**

disabling amputation of the thumbs and great toes (incapacitation of a warrior); fracture, fragmentation (the disabling or altering of whatever the broken object symbolizes)

disagreeability dancing (release from disagreeable circumstances)

disagreement flower language: broken corn straw • see also **discord**

disappearance Death [tarot] (dematerialization)

disappointment quince • flower language: Carolina syringa; fish geranium (disappointed expectation); kabala: ninety • see also **frustration**

disapproval thumb down

disarmament removing a glove, especially the right glove (disarming oneself before a superior)

disasters China: red clouds (calamity and warfare) • kabala: seventy • omens of disaster: aurora borealis; "blood" on the moon; screech or squinch owl; remora

Disaster personified thief (natural disaster)

discernment key of silver; sword suit [tarot] • see **judgment; taste**

disciples see **Jesus Christ**

discipline gavel; scourge [whip]; sheaf; yoke • associations: eight; four; L; ninety (divine discontent); Saturn [planet] • see also **order**

discomfort boil [sore]; burr

discontent penance (aspiration which implies discontent with the worldly conditions to which one is bound for a time) • *association:* ninety (divine discontent)

discord apple, especially a golden apple; blackthorn; broken corn straw (disagreement); harlequin (discordant elements in life); lute with a broken string; scorpion (discord and mischief); sword • *see also* **conflict; dissension; quarreling**

discouragement *see* **despair; despondency**

discovery light • *flower language:* maiden blush rose (if you love me you will find it out) • *heraldry:* foot (discovery of an important track or fact that brings lasting merit)

the discrete marriage (urge of the discrete to unite); orchestra (the co-operation of the discrete to a given end)

discretion key; lance; lemon • *association:* gray • *flower language:* lemon blossoms; maidenhair fern • *see also* **judgment**

Discretion personified *attribute:* camel

discrimination smelling • *association:* eight

disdain finger snapping; person kicking a globe (disdain for the world); quince (scornful beauty); rue [plant]; spitting • *flower language:* ficoides (your looks freeze me); rue; yellow carnation; yellow narcissus • *see also* **rejection**

disease agate, garlic (protection against contagious disease); amber [gemstone] (protection against disease); arrow; fly [insect]; louse [insect]; rat; ratsbane (lechery causing disease and death); yellow flag • *association:* red • *see also* **affliction; pestilence; plague; sickness**

disentanglement cabbage

disfavor *see* **displeasure**

disgrace *see* **humiliation**

disguise gypsum; scarecrow (disguise to avoid facing reality) • *flower language:* stramonium

disgust excrement; stomach (seat of disgust); swine (abomination) • *flower language:* frog ophrys • *see also* **aversion; displeasure**

disharmony disease (natural or spiritual disorder or disharmony); multicolored garment; pain (mental or spiritual disharmony)

dishonesty index finger as long as the middle finger

dishonor cowherd (honored in Greece, but dishonored in Britain, Egypt, and elsewhere); goat; stain

disintegration broken stone (psychic disintegration); dismemberment or dispersal (disintegration, especially mental); disorderly herd (disintegration; degeneration; regression; loss of unity); dust; fracture or fragmentation (destruction and disintegration of the spirit); multiplicity; stars • *association:* two • *see also* **decay; degeneration; dissociation**

disloyalty cosmetics; partridge (disloyalty to one's own kind) • *see also* **betrayal; treachery; treason; unfaithfulness**

dismay *see* **disgust; displeasure**

dismemberment broken stone; broken necklace with scattered beads (psychic dismemberment); dispersal

Disobedience personified *attribute:* peacock

disorder abortion (defect in the soul or spirit); ache, pain (mental or spiritual disorder); blindfold (mental or spiritual blindness); blindness (the mind not awakened by the spirit; lack of spiritual perception); boil [disease] (a psychological affliction or spiritual shortcoming); Caliban; cancer [disease]; captive (the spirit held latent); darkness (spiritual darkness); deafness (inability to hear the voice of the conscience or the spirit); devastation (barrenness and unproductiveness of the spirit); Devil [tarot]; disease (natural or spiritual disorder or disharmony); drought (an inert spiritual condition); entombment (detention of the spirit in the world); fracture, fragmentation (destruction or disintegration of the spirit); gangrene; Gordian knot, labyrinth (remoteness from one's spirit and from God); hood (spiritual blindness); Icarus (intellect rebelling against the spirit); insanity (a disordered condition in the soul); lameness; leprosy; (rotting of the spirit due to a lack of moral progress); loss (spiritual bankruptcy); Mephistopheles (the negative aspect of the psychic function which has broken away from the spirit to acquire independence); mole eyes (intellectual and spiritual blindness); rotting; sick king (sterility of the spirit); thorn (materialism killing spirituality) weeds • *association:* brown (spiritual death and degradation) • *see also* **chaos**

the disparate Wheel of Fortune [tarot] (intermingling of the disparate)

dispersal waving a banner (dispersal of evil spirits)

displeasure crow; disease (divine displeasure); gnat (the forces of dissatisfaction); hands raised and open (dismay); thumb down • *China:* imperfect ring (the emperor is displeased) • *flower language:* currants (thy frown will kill me) • *see also* **aversion; disgust; gloom**

disposition crooked fingers (sign of a crabbed disposition) • *flower language:* rye grass (changeable disposition); valerian (accommodating disposition) • *see also* **emotions; feelings; mood; temper**

disquietude *see* **anxiety**

disrespect *see* **mockery**

disruption storm (psychic disruption)

dissatisfaction *see* **displeasure; gloom**

dissembling *see* **dissimulation**

dissemination sowing

dissension broken straw; dragon's teeth (the seeds of dissension); Lovers [tarot] (antagonism); rhubarb (argument) •*flower language:* Pride of China • *see also* **discord; quarreling**

dissimulation crocodile; daisy; Eve; fennel; Helen; magpie; mask; moonlight, rose-colored spectacles (distorted truth); opossum • *flower language:* manchineal tree (duplicity) • *see also* **deceit; falsity; hypocrisy; intrigue; treachery**

Dissimulation personified *attributes:* magpie; monkey

dissociation ghost; invisibility • *see also* **disintegration; dissolution**

dissolution Aquarius (the dissolution or decomposition of the world of phenomena); devouring (dissolution of the body after death); digestion; gray horse; nymph; swarms of insects; thaw (dissolution of the flesh) • *see also* **disintegration; dissociation**

distance *see* **remoteness**

distinction carnelian; ostrich feathers; ribbon; sash [clothing]; skullcap; woodpecker • *flower language:* cardinal flower • *heraldry:* peacock (distinction and power); oak leaves (military power) • *see also* **eminence; honor; merit**

distraction lantern; rabbit; sulfur

distress flag flown upside down; hands raised and open; nettle

distrust *flower language:* cyclamen; lavender

Distrust personified *emblem:* French lavender [plant]

disturbance *see* **trouble**

disuse rust

diuretic dandelion

diversion hyacinth [flower]

diversity multicolored garment (diverse knowledge or possibilities); necklace (unification of diversity) • *see also* **variety**

dividing line bridge; ford, fording; gate; ice

divination barley; dice; dove; eagle carrying a victim (augury); fountain; tooth; tortoise • *associations:* fingertips; little finger; Monday (works of divination) • *see also* **foretokens and signs**

divinity arrow (the light of divine power); bo tree, crystal ball (divine law; divine light); brass (in the Middle Ages, the divinity of Christ); breath (the divine element in man); earthquake, thunderbolt (divine intervention); flaming pillar or tree trunk (divine light); Gordian knot, Solomon's knot (divine inscrutability); jasmine (divine hope); king (divine right); light (divine revelation); linen (divine truth); lute (divine praise); mace [weapon] (divine office); musician (harmony with the divine); Pandora, Pandora's box (rebellion against divine order); Pasiphae (the deliberate flouting of divine law and divine order); potter's wheel (the Christian's life shaped by divine influence); sapphire (divine truth); scroll on a gravestone (divine revelation; in Judaism, divine presence); seamless garment (the divinity of Jesus Christ); seed (divine instruction); tablet [for writing] (divine order; divine revelation); tonsure (divine service); rainbow (divine pardon and reconciliation); unguent (divine love and truth); wings (divine mission) • *associations:* four (usually a "human" number, but may also be associated with divinity; divine equilibrium, especially in Christianity); gold; ninety (divine discontent) radiance; wings • *attributes:* aureole (divinity: normally only used for members of the Trinity, occasionally for the Virgin Mary); • *divine inspiration:* dove on the shoulder of an Apostle; eagle (the inspiration of the Gospels); flame on the head; flaming mountain; lark (inspired visionary); lizard; white rose (inspired wisdom) • *divine messenger:* angel; cherub; dove; eagle; Elijah (messenger of the Messianic Age); Gabriel (messenger of the Day of Judgment); goat; Mercury [god]; raven; seraph; stag; tide; white bird; wings (attribute) • *divine wisdom:* aspalathus (the wisdom of the Lord); bright yellow, orange-yellow (associated with divine wisdom or goodness); butter (divine love and wisdom); flaming pillar or tree trunk (the God of light and wisdom); galbanum; gold; hearing (reception of divine wisdom); linen; pentagon (heavenly wisdom); tree (wisdom, sometimes divine) • *emblem:* parasol • *heraldry:* star (divine grace) • *see also* **God**

DNA double spiral

docility lamb; parrot; robin (tameness) • *flower language:* bulrush; rush

Docility personified *attribute:* parrot

doctors *see* **physicians**

doctors of the church quatrefoil (can stand for either the four Greek or the four Latin doctors of the church) • *attributes:* book; writing pen

doctrine wolf (false doctrine)

documents scroll (especially a legal document)

dog bite *association:* dog hair (said to cure dog bite)

domesticity cat; flax (domestic industry); mouse; swallow [bird] • *flower language:* houseleek (domestic economy); sage (domestic virtues)

domestics *see* **servants**

domination broom [for sweeping]; dragonfly (male domination); Emperor [tarot]; Empress [tarot] (dominance by persuasion); matron (domineering mother); monsters carried in a procession (indicates they are dominated);

square (tense domination); whip • *associations:* one; sun

Dominic, St. praying saint before Saints Peter and Paul and receiving staff and book • *attributes:* dog with flaming torch in its mouth; halo; lily; rosary; star on the forehead

Dominicans black and white dogs together

dominion *see* **sovereignty**

Don Quixote knight charging a windmill

Donatian, St. *attribute:* wheel with candles in rim

Donatus of Arezzo, St. *attribute:* broken chalice

doom cancer (impending doom)

door *see* **entrance**

dormancy sleeping beauty (dormant female sexuality; dormant memories in the unconscious)

Dorothea of Cappadocia, St. woman holding a torch being tied to a stake • *attribute:* basket of flowers and fruit (often roses and apples); crown of roses; three apples, often with three roses

dotage grasshopper

double vision *association:* four

doubt *see* **skepticism; uncertainty**

drabness *see* **dreariness**

Dracula, Count *attributes:* bat [animal]; black cape; fangs

dragon *association:* octopus

drama buskin (especially tragedy); mask with a frown (tragedy); mask with a smile (comedy)

dreams bubble; lotus; meadow (dreaminess); onyx (protects against nightmares); sleep (giver of prophetic dreams); Tower of Babel (an impractical dream); waves [water] • *entrance to dreams:* horn gate (entrance to prophetic dreams); ivory gate (entrance to deceptive dreams) • *flower language:* osmunda

dreariness Russia • *associations:* black; brown; gray • *see also* **misery**

drinking beer (originally the drink of the gods, now the drink of the lower classes); tinkers (impressive drinkers); wine (drink of the gods and of the upper classes; a spiritual drink) • *associations:* Germany (beer drinking); Ireland (whisky drinking); Netherlands; scarlet (steady drinking) • *see also* **drunkenness**

dross *see* **impurity**

drought brass; chimera; comet (omen of drought); dust

Drought personified thief

drowning gold earring (protection from drowning for sailors); rags thrown in the water (substitute for drowning)

drudgery ditch digging; hobby horse (drudge); house cleaning; loading trucks

druggists *attribute:* jar of colored water • *emblem:* unicorn (trademark signifying the purity of their goods)

Druids *associations:* four leaf clover; mistletoe; verbena; yew • *emblem:* oak

drunkenness centaur; radish (thought to prevent drunkenness); wheelbarrow • *flower language:* vine • *see also* **drinking; intemperance; intoxication**

Drusiana and St. John woman rising from coffin

dryness biscuit; potsherd

duality *see* **opposites**

dueling grouse feather in a hat, slap in the face with a glove, or throwing down a gauntlet (challenge to a duel) •

heraldry: grouse [bird] (a forbearer who fought a gallant duel, or was a great hunter)

dukes *heraldry:* ram [sheep]

dullness brown; capon (a dull fool); gray; meatloaf; potato

dupes *see* **fools**

duplicity *see* **dissimulation**

durability chestnut (obstinate durability); dogwood; iron; marble; mule; oak; rock • *flower language:* dogwood • *heraldry:* ash tree (toughness) • *lack of durability:* paper; tin • *Middle Ages:* brass • *see also* **endurance**

duration *flower language:* cornel tree; dogwood

duty chimere (dutiful perseverance) • *China:* pigeon (impartial filial duty) • *flower language:* lint (I feel all my obligations)

dwarves *association:* long ears

dying *see* **death**

dynamism ocean (dynamic force); Virgo (supreme dynamic consciousness) • *association:* three (moral and spiritual dynamism)

dynasty *association:* twenty

E

eagerness *flower language:* ivy sprig with tendrils

earliness *early attachment:* thornless rose (flower language) • *early death:* Adonis [mythology]; anemone [flower] • *early morning:* spring [season] (association)

ears *association:* F (corresponds to the ears and the heart)

earth altar (the intersection of heaven and earth); angel (spiritual influences acting upon the earth); anvil; ball; closet; cube; elephant; footstool; fruit (earthly desires); globe; god naked to the waist (the top half represents the sky, the clothed bottom half represent the earth); lance (an earthly weapon as opposed to the spiritual implications of the sword); lion; oval; plow (man's earthly consciousness); pomegranate

(rejuvenation of the earth); Proserpine; russet [cloth]; sarcophagus (the earth as the beginning and end of material life); smoke (futility of earthly existence); skull (the transitory nature of earthly life; the useless nature of earthly things); son (earthly spirit); square canopy; square [shape] (earthly existence); table; tortoise; tree (the fecundity of the earth); turquoise [gemstone] (earth and water); wheat (bounty of the earth) • *associations:* black; brown; C; cow; even numbers (earthly things); four (four corners of the earth); ocher; yellow • *Chinese associations:* even numbers; yellow • *earth goddesses:* abyss, well (access to earth goddesses); bare feet (direct contact with Mother Earth); goose; woman nursing more that one child • *earth goddess attributes:* cornucopia; grapes with wheat lion; scorpion; serpent; spindle; turreted mural crown; wheat with grapes • *earth gods:* abyss, well (access to earth gods) • *see also* **heaven and earth; world**

earthquake comet (omen)

ease cat; clover • *China:* chrysanthemum (life of ease) • *see also* **comfort**

east *see* **Orient**

East India Company *heraldry:* moor's head (service in the Crusades, or the East India Company)

Easter bursting pomegranate; butterfly; peacock; Phoenix [bird] • *emblems:* chick; hare; lily; rabbit

eating leprosy (punishment for eating tabooed food) • *see also* **appetite; food; gluttony; hunger**

eavesdropping *see* **spying**

ebb and flow of fortune tide

ebullience yeast

eccentricity *see* **oddity**

echo *association:* two

eclipse *ancient Greece:* a bronze gong was sounded at the eclipse of the moon

economy *association:* ring finger • *flower language:* houseleek (domestic economy) • *see also* **frugality**

ecstasy angelica; Judgment [tarot] (Dionysian ecstasy); tears [weeping] (ecstasy of joy); tabret (ecstasy of victory; religious ecstasy); thyrsus; timbrel (religious ecstasy); wind (inducer of ecstasy) • *associations:* toadstool (ecstatic visions); white • *see also* **bliss; happiness; joy** • *erotic ecstasy:* eating a fig; floating (especially female ecstasy); honey; nightingale

Eden, Garden of Euphrates River (the fourth river of the Garden of Eden); flaming sword (attribute of the cherubim protecting the Garden of Eden, and also of the archangel Jophiel driving Adam and Eve from the Garden) • *see also* **paradise**

Edmund, St. *attributes:* sword; three arrows

education cherry tree; key • *association:* six • *China:* purple (associated with an educated person) • *flower language:* cherry tree • *see also* **teaching**

effeminacy chicken; Endymion (man trespassing into woman's realm); water fly (an effeminate homosexual) • *association:* pink [color] • *see also* **homosexuality**

efflorescence rolled papyrus

effort *see* **striving**

ego horseman (the ego trying to control the id); mirror • *association:* P • *see also* **personality**

egoism cuckoo; dog; Narcissus; rooster; sage [herb] • *associations:* gray; impure orange [color] • *flower language:* narcissus, especially poet's narcissus • *see also* **selfishness**

Egypt fly [insect]; golden eagle; iron furnace (Egypt as a place of bondage and oppression); mummy (ancient Egypt); sword (10th plague of Egypt); pyramid and star, Sphinx (the flight into Egypt; Israel in Egypt) • *associations:* fez; ten (the ten plagues of Egypt); white garment • *emblems:* crescent; lily (the upper kingdom of Egypt); pyramid; red crown and papyrus (the lower kingdom of Egypt); Sphinx; white crown and flowering rush (the upper kingdom of Egypt)

eight eighty (multiplies the values of the number eight) • *associations:* H; Q (primarily associated with the number eight, but sometimes with the numbers one and seven); Uranus [planet]; Z

Eighth Commandment heart pierced with an arrow with a coin on the heart (sin against the 8th Commandment: Thou shalt not steal)

El [god] *attributes:* footstool

elasticity cheverel

elders lizard (disrespect for elders) • *association:* twenty-four (the Four and Twenty Elders)

election fir (the elect who are in heaven); hoe (election of the chosen); pitcher [vessel]

electricity amber [gemstone]; zigzag

elegance carriage [vehicle]; dahlia; elm (stateliness); goat (inelegance); greyhound; hind [deer]; jasmine; king; ruby [gemstone]; white gloves • *flower language:* locust tree; pink acacia; pomegranate flower by itself (mature elegance); rose acacia; white acacia; yellow acacia (elegance and grace) • *see also* **dignity; gracefulness; poise**

elements *association:* four (the four elements, earth, air, fire, and water)

elevation ascending (a raise in value or worth); cedar; eagle; fir; dolphin (the highest order of fish); helmet (lofty thoughts); legs; Moon [tarot] (the upward progress of man); mountain (loftiness of spirit); musician (the mind that foster higher emotions); myrrh; nun; palm tree; peace (union or conjunction of the higher and lower planes); sibyl (the intuiting of higher truth); six-pointed star (the upper and lower worlds); tower; two feathers; wax; winged sandals (lofty thoughts); wings • *associations:* right side • *heraldry:* gauntlet (elevation and reward); gold (elevation of the mind); harp • *see also* **ascension**

Elijah *association:* fiery chariot • *attributes:* mantle [clothing]; loaf of bread carried by a raven; scroll and red vestment; sword • *Judaism:* glass of wine (set out on Seder nights for Elijah, messenger of the Messianic Age); opened door on Seder night (to allow the entrance of Elijah, announcing the Messianic Age)

elimination *associations:* Pluto (elimination or destruction); X

Elisha *association:* double-headed eagle • *attributes:* mantle [clothing]; two-headed dove

elixir of life milk

Elizabeth of Hungary, St. woman giving money away • *attributes:* beggar; flowers; roses in the lap or apron; three crowns

Eloi, St. blacksmith shoeing a horse, having first removed its leg • *attributes:* anvil; horse with its leg removed for shoeing; tongs

eloquence agate; Balder; bee; brass; caduceus; Calliope; chrysoprase; giraffe; goose; honey (also religious eloquence); iris [flower]; leech (grandiloquence); Nestor; pebble; silver; tongue; tulip; water lily; willow • *association:* lips • *flower language:* lagerstraemia; lotus • *heraldry:* merman; mermaid • *see also* **talk**

Eloquence personified Mercury [god] • *attributes:* parrot; pearl

elusiveness foxfire; grail; golden fleece; white fleece (occasionally)

Elysian Fields white fillet (attribute of the dead in the Elysian Fields)

emasculation spaniel

embalming *associations:* aloe; myrrh; resin • *see also* **burial**

embarrassment *flower language:* love-in-a-puzzle

Emerantiana, St. *attribute*s: stones on a book

emergence mud (emergence of matter); snail (emergence of sexual power)

eminence *China:* sturgeon (literary eminence) • *heraldry:* centaur (eminence in battle) • *see also* **distinction**

Emmaus pilgrim (Jesus Christ at Emmaus)

emotions Amazon [mythological woman] (the higher emotions which oppose the desires); cattle; city (lack of emotional, spiritual, or natural contact); divorce (the apparent or delusive separation of emotion from reason); drunkenness (revelation of inner thoughts and feelings); echo, mirror (reflection of one's inner self, feelings, or emotions); Eve (emotionality); grain (cultivated higher emotions in the soul); heart suit [playing cards]; Helen (the instinctive and emotional aspects of woman); husband and wife (mind and emotion, respectively); leper (the lower mind troubled with conflicting emotions, desires, and confused ideas); musician (the mind that fosters higher emotions); neck, virgin (purified emotions); Negro (the emotional and primitive self); perfume; relief that is more than sufficient (the powerful surge of an idea or emotion in all its nascent strength); spleen (seat of the emotions, sexual passion, mirth, impetuosity, capriciousness, melancholy, and especially anger); Trojan (lower emotions); very long legs (stirring emotions); whirlpool • *associations:* B; brown (Victorian lack of emotion or spirituality); moon; pink [color]; Venus [planet] (sexual emotions); two; W (wavering emotions) • *flower language:* purple lilac • *see also* **disposition; feelings; mood; passions**

Emperor [tarot] *association:* Hercules

emperors crown of laurel (attribute of Roman emperors); nimbus (attribute of deified Roman emperors) • *China:* five clawed dragon (imperial authority); imperfect ring (the emperor is displeased); jade (emblem); perfect ring (the emperor is pleased); yellow (associated with imperial power and both the emperor and his son) • *see also* **kings**

emptiness bubble (emptiness of material existence or personality; lack of substance); overturned bowl or pitcher (the emptiness of worldly things, especially in a still life painting) • see also **hollowness**

enchantment Circe; forest; quicksand • *Elizabethan England:* Bermuda • *flower language:* verbena • see also **magic; magic spells; sorcery; witchcraft**

enclosure see **female principle**

encouragement flagellation (encouragement against spiritual laxity or inertia); goldenrod

endearment calf • see also **love; praise**

endeavor see **work**

ending beheading; catastrophe; corpse; death; Death [tarot] (death of the old self, but not necessarily physical death); deluge; dropping a curtain; dusk; earth [soil] (the end of material life); ebb tide; finger snapping (the end of a cycle, process, or idea); inverted torch on a tombstone (end of a family line); sunset • *associations:* Aries (the beginning or end of a cycle or process); ninety; Pisces; seven (the end of a cycle) • *end of a cycle:* beheading; catastrophe; corpse; deluge; dusk; finger snapping; sunset • *beginning and end:* alpha and omega; ashes, dust, sarcophagus (an ending that is also a beginning); tetractys • see also **apocalypse; completion; finality**

endlessness see **eternity; the infinite**

endurance bricks; bronze; camel; carnation; carp; evergreen; fern; flint; lupin; maniple; oak; pine; Prometheus (magnanimous endurance of unwarranted suffering); pyramid; rock; salamander (enduring and triumphant faith); sand; Saturn [god]; stomach; Trojan; willow • *associations:* eight; orange [color]; Taurus • *China:* tortoise • *flower language:* gorse (enduring affection); marigold (endurance in love, especially of women) • *heraldry:* orange [color]; ostrich (often with a horseshoe in its mouth) • see also **durability; perseverance; persistence**

enemies dog (prowling enemies); dragon; hail (assault of an enemy) • *flower language:* grass-leaved goose foot (I declare against you—usually the stems alone are presented)

energy beans; carbuncle [gemstone]; carp; clubs [playing cards]; coal [mineral] (repressed energy; the negative side of energy); dynamo; Emperor [tarot]; fountain (spiritual energy); goose, pole (creative energy); griffin (the relationship between psychic energy and cosmic force); hair, especially dark hair; hippopotamus (strength and vigor); king (energy and power); legs; light (cosmic energy); mast; Mercury [god] (intellectual energy); metal (energy solidified); muscular and/or hairy man (energetic and strong mentality); rain (an increase in spiritual energy); serpent (generative energy); speed; thighs (sexual vigor); tiger; triskele; vein (vital male energy) • *associations:* E; orange [color] (vigor); ring finger; scarlet • *flower language:* camomile (energy in adversity) • *heraldry:* cat (indefatigability); Pegasus (energy leading to honor) • *kabala:* three • see also **force; libido; power; vitality**

enforcement teeth (means of enforcement)

engagement see **betrothal**

engineering beaver

England *emblem:* lion

English *attributes:* derby hat; scarlet coat (British soldiers); scepter tipped with a dove, scepter tipped with an orb and cross (English kings); tea; umbrella

enhancement see **improvement**

enigmas key; sphinx

enjoyment see **pleasure**

enlargement see **expansion; growth**

enlightenment baboon; crown, especially a jewelled crown; fire (spiritual enlightenment and zeal); griffin with a ball underfoot (enlightenment protecting wisdom); shining face; torch; two griffins (enlightenment and wisdom); urn with a lid on it (the state of supreme enlightenment) • *Christian enlightenment:* dove on the shoulder of a saint (divine enlightenment); eagle (Mary leading people to true light); cross with an orb or globe (the gradual enlightenment of the world)

enmity see **hate**

ennui see **boredom**

Enoch two pillars of Enoch (the brick pillar is proof against fires; the stone pillar is proof against water)

enslavement see **slavery**

entanglement bramble; comb; cabbage (disentanglement); knot; net;

rope; stocks [for restraint]; web • *see also* **entrapment**

entering *see* **entrance**

enterprise *see* **adventure; ambition**

enthrallment *see* **imprisonment**

enthusiasm lemon • *flower language:* lemon (zest); schinus (religious enthusiasm)

entrance Cancer [zodiac] (the threshold through which the soul enters upon its incarnation); disguise (entrance into a new stage of life); hill (entrance to Valhalla); keyhole (entrance of demons, witches, etc.); mouth; oak; river (entrance to the underworld); tattoo (rite of entry) • *associations:* N; St. Peter (holds the keys to heaven's gate) • *entrance to another world:* alcove; crystal ball; door; gate; key; mirror • *entrance to dreams:* horn gate (entrance to prophetic dreams); ivory gate (entrance to deceptive dreams) • *entrance to heaven:* door; gate, especially of pearl or gold; gold key (key to heaven's gate); iron key (locks heaven's gate); rood screen; Solomon's seal (key to the kingdom of heaven); two brass mountains • *entrance to Hell or the underworld:* brass gate; descending stairs; the open jaws of a whale; river • *see also* **threshold**

entrapment entanglement (being caught in the universe and being unable to escape by any means); net; web • *see also* **entanglement**

entreaty *see* **supplication**

enuresis *Elizabethan times:* dandelion

envy bramble; dog; jaundice; Leviathan; manger; nettle; pale face (an envious and untrustworthy man); raspberry; spider • *Christianity:* dragon • *flower language:* crowsbill • *see also* **jealousy**

Envy personified woman gnawing on a heart • *attributes:* dog (occasionally); greyhound; scorpion; squill; squinting

ephermerality garland (ephemeral beauty); mushroom • *association:* even numbers

Ephraim, Tribe of *attributes:* grapes

Epiphany five-pointed star; golden casket; three caskets

episcopacy *see* **bishops**

Epistles [New Testament] *see* **Bible. New Testament. Epistles**

equality balances [scales]; chess (the sexes meeting on equal terms); dust (the great equalizer); level [tool]; round table; swallow [bird] • *association:* blue (fairness) • *Judaism:* tallith (when worn by the entire congregation in a synagogue: a sign that all men are equal before God) • *see also* **impartiality**

equilibrium caduceus (moral equilibrium); Libra (moral and psychic equilibrium); Lovers [tarot] (antagonistic by complementary forces creating an equilibrium); onion (the cosmos in equilibrium); symmetry (supreme equipoise); throne; two dolphins swimming in the same direction • *associations:* four (divine equilibrium, especially in Christianity) six; two • *see also* **balance**

equinoxes *associations:* E; ring finger (autumnal equinox); furze, index finger (spring equinox)

equipoise *see* **equilibrium**

equity square [shape] • *association:* D • *heraldry:* dice

Equity personified *attributes:* swallow [bird]

equivocation mask; relief lacking in force

Erasmus, St. bishop holding a model of a ship • *attribute:* nails [for wood] protruding from the fingers

Erato *attributes:* lyre; putto; swan (occasionally); tambourine (occasionally); triangle [musical instrument] (occasionally); viol

Erichthonius serpent with an infant in a basket

Ermina female soldier with shepherds and basketmakers; maid cutting her hair with a sword

Eros *see* **Cupid**

eroticism eating a fig (erotic ecstasy); flute (a phallic and lascivious instrument; erotic anguish or joy); mare (erotic madness); necklace (an erotic bond, especially on females); Phrygia (eroticism in a superior form); Phrygian cap (obsessive eroticism) • *ancient times:* white bird • *associations:* five; fifteen • *see also* **sex**

error black; black horse; blindness; darkness; deluge (awakening of the mind from ignorance and error); dirtiness (the accumulation of error, prejudice, and sin); goat's milk; Gordian knot; hedgehog (the critical aspect that destroys error); labyrinth; leopard (the

opinionated lower mind full of errors that are mingled with the truth); Moon [tarot]; thorn • *Christianity:* dragon • *flower language:* bee ophrys; cardamine (paternal error); fly orchis
Error personified *attributes:* dragon
Erythraean sibyl [Erythraea] *attributes:* animal horn; lily
Esau *attribute:* bow and arrows
escape carnival, saturnalia (the desperate quest for a way out of time); dancing (the desire for escape); death (escape from unendurable tension); drugs, drunkenness (escape from reality); fairyland (escape or regression to childhood); flying; Hanged Man [tarot] (a flight to overcome evil); flying; lobster; nightingale (poetic ecstasy or escape); orgy (escape from time to pre-time); south (direction of escape); thread (escape from the material world to the spiritual); triangle with the apex up (the urge to escape from this world to the Origin) • *flower language:* pennyroyal (flee)
esoterica pearl (esoteric wisdom) • *association:* Y (the search for mystic or esoteric wisdom) • *see also* **knowledge; wisdom**
the establishment jester (a critic of Church and establishment practices); Pentagon [building] (the United States military establishment)
esteem *see* **respect**
estrangement *flower language:* lotus flower alone (estranged love)
eternity ball; bird drinking from a vase (eternal bliss); bracelet; circle; center (going through death to eternity); condor; elephant; evergreens; ford (the dividing line between two states, such as time and eternity); fossil; globe; hill; lantern (transitory life in the face of the eternal); marble; metal; oak; Ouroboros (time and eternity); Phoenix [bird] (eternity; eternal youth); poinsettia; pyramid (eternal light); ring; rosary (perpetual continuity); rose window; salt; scarab; serpent in a circle, biting its tail; seaweed (the eternal); Shangri-la (eternal youth); Strength [tarot] (power through conscious awareness of eternity); swan; wreath • *associations:* blue; child (the eternal); eight; mandorla (perpetual sacrifice and regeneration); O [letter]; ocean; one thousand; zero • *China:* jade; knot

(the "mystic" or endless knot); ring • *Christianity:* hand raised with the first two fingers extended; oak • *eternal life:* butterfly; chancel arch (passage from this world into eternal life); crown; dove with olive branch; egg surrounded by serpent (the eternal germ of life encircled by creative wisdom); flowing fountain; harbor; holly; monolith; obelisk; peacock; seaweed; skull and crossbones (meditation on the eternal life that comes after death); tree; wine (youth and eternal life)
Eternity personified *attributes:* chariot drawn by angels
ether *association:* zero
eucharist altar; altar shaped like a tomb (reminiscent of the early church where the eucharist was celebrated in the catacombs); bell (the coming of Christ during the eucharist); birds feeding on grapes (the faithful gathering sustenance from the blood of Christ); biscuit (the host, distributed without love); bread (especially with a chalice); chalice; chasuble (celebration of the eucharist); ciborium; communion cup with a wafer; cruet; cup; dove drinking from a cup or eating bread (the soul being fed by the eucharist); dove on a pyx (reservation of the sacrament); goblet; grain (especially when shown with grapes); grapes with wheat or bread; honey; manna; monstrance; ostentorium; paten; pelican; stole [religious garment] when worn crossed; tabernacle; table; tulip (chalice of the eucharist); vine with wheat; wheat (bread of the eucharist); wafer (the host of the eucharist); wine
Euclid *attribute:* compasses [dividers]
eunuch *see* **castration**
Euphemia, St. sword piercing a woman's bosom with a lion present • *attributes:* bear; garment of palm leaves; lily; lion; saw [tool]
Europa maiden abducted by a white bull to the sea (Zeus raping Europa)
Europe *association:* straight sword • *attribute:* blue eyes (northern Europeans)
Europe personified *attributes:* cornucopia; horse; scepter
European sibyl [Europeana] *attribute:* sword
Eurydice serpent entwined around a

woman's arm or leg • *attributes:* crown of violets; violet hair

Eustace, St. soldier with a stag • *attributes:* brass bull; horse; stag with a crucifix between its antlers

Euterpe *attributes:* crown of flowers; pipe; trumpet (occasionally)

evanescence *see* **transitoriness**

evangelists four fountains (the four evangelists); four urns with water flowing from them (the four evangelists and the four Gospels) • *associations:* four; tetramorph • *attributes:* inkhorn (St. Matthew and other evangelists, but often the inkhorn is held by an angel in the latter cases); scroll (sometimes the apostles, but usually the evangelists) • *see also* **Jesus Christ; Luke, St., John, St.; Mark, St.; Matthew, St.**

evasiveness Proteus

Eve *attributes:* distaff, spindle (after expulsion from Eden); sheep • *Virgin Mary as the second Eve:* orb with a snake around it at the feet of the Virgin Mary; Virgin Mary holding an apple

evening *see* **night**

everything *flower language:* rose in a tuft of grass (there is everything)

evil ablution (purification, especially of subjective and inner evils); acacia thorn (the divine power to repel evil); adder (hidden evil); Alastor (man's inner evil driving him to sin); amphibian; asperges (expulsion of evil); basilisk; bear; black castle (abode of Pluto or an evil power); black robe (sinisterness); blackbird; bondage (immobilization through sin or evil); chimera (complex evil); crocodile; cockle; crossroads (meeting place of evil beings); darkness; dart (evil words); desert animals (evil and the forces of destruction); devil; dragon; excrement; extra fingers (occasionally); falcon (an evil person); feather (the purification of evil); frog; Gabriel hounds; gargoyle (evil forces made to serve good; evil spirits or passions; scarecrows for evil spirits); giant (impending evil); goat; goblet; gorge (evil forces); Hanged Man [tarot] (a flight to overcome evil); harpy (evil; evil harmonies of cosmic forces); hemlock; holy water (expulsion of evil); hornet; Hydra (multifarious evil); hyena; index finger (delivery from evil); lamia

(evil woman); lamprey; lizard (the power of evil); Mars (objective evil); moon (potential evil); mouse; mud; Neptune [god] (the regressive and evil side of the unconscious); night; night air; Pegasus (innate capacity for changing evil into good); pine pitch; rat; raven; Satan; Saturn [god] (subjective evil); satyr; scar (a remnant of mutilation, usually with sinister connotation); scorpion; serpent (the evil inherent in worldly things; the evil side of nature); shadow (the evil or base side of the physical body); shark; sleep (susceptibility to evil); slime; smoke; sorcerer (evil demiurge); sow (swine) (the fecundity of evil); tamed tiger (strength and valor in the fight against evil); troll (mythic being); tusk (spiritual power overcoming ignorance and evil); viper (evil genius); volcano; vulture; wasp; west (abode of evil); wind (evil powers); wineskin (evil mindedness); wolf (the principle of evil) • *associations:* black; black horse (steed of a villain); dark complexion (attribute of a villain); eighteen (in the Old Testament, an evil number, but in Christianity a number of great reward); indigo; multiple eyes (usually); seventy-two • *China:* black; serpent • *Christianity:* Antichrist (evil adversary of the soul); armor (the Christian faith as protection against evil); chimera (the spirit of evil); cockle (evil invading the good field of the church); gargoyle on the outside of a church (evil passion driven out of man by the Gospel); hawk (the evil mind of the sinner); serpent at the foot of the cross (Jesus overcoming the evil that leads man into sin) • *Egypt:* cockle • *evil eye, protection against:* blue beads; gold beads; garlic; index and little finger raised • *evil souls:* larvae (Rome) • *evil spirits:* Alastor (an evil spirit that haunts a family); Demogorgon; demon; epileptic seizure (possession by evil spirits); gargoyle; toad • *evil spirits, protection against:* onion; onyx; purgative (drives out evil spirits) • *omens of evil:* being pricked on the finger by a needle; burning or tingling ears, especially the right ear (someone is speaking evil of you); comet; crow (usually); dark clouds; east wind; dark clouds, storm clouds; heart missing from a sacrificial animal; lapwing; letter [epistle]; meteor (usually); nightjar; one eye (extra human effort devoted to one aim, usually evil); picture falling off the wall for no apparent reason; pointing; raven; red sky at morning; ruby changing color (mischief); screech or squinch owl; sneezing (everywhere but Greece or Rome); sneeze on a Sunday, for safety seek, the Devil will have you the whole of the week; storm clouds; two; vulture • *protection from evil:* amber [gemstone]; amulet; armor; bell (exorcism of evil); camphor; candle; cherry tree; effigy; fern; fireworks; gargoyle; gold beads; incense; iron nails; juniper; obelisk; onion; onyx; opal (prevents evil affections); piercing the ears of children (blood sacrifice to protect them); pungent smell; purgative; rattle; sea coral; touching or knocking on wood; silver (china, for children); two fish; waving a banner; white rooster (china) • *see also* **good and evil; sin; sinners; villainy; wickedness**

Evil personified   the Devil; Leviathan • *attribute:* long nails [anatomy]

evolution   clockwise spiral; Death [tarot] (the progress of evolution); fossil; journey; light; lotus; Negro (the soul before entering on the path of spiritual evolution); orb with wings; orderly herd (coordinated desires and emotions working for the evolution of the soul); sword; Temperance [tarot] (perpetual evolutive movement from the past to a golden future); turtle (natural evolution, not spiritual); Wheel of Fortune [tarot] (truth and spiritual evolution attained on earth); whirlwind (universal evolution); wings (the possibility of spiritual evolution) • *associations:* right side; the last six signs of the zodiac (Libra, Scorpio, Sagittarius, Capricorn, Aquarius, Pisces) • *evolution and involution:* eagle devouring a lion (victory of the evolutive over the involutive); two dolphins swimming in opposite directions • *spiritual evolution:* lotus; Negro (the soul before entering on the path of spiritual evolution); orb with wings; pilgrimage (the process of spiritual evolution); search for treasure (the search for spiritual evolution); sword; wings (the possibility of spiritual evolution); World [tarot] (truth and spiritual evolution

attained on earth) • *see also* **germination; growth**

exaggeration   spread-eagle body position

exaltation   decoration; palm tree; throne; victorious lion (exaltation of virility) • *see also* **honor; praise**

examinations   *China:* sturgeon (scholarly excellence, particularly in examinations)

example   Hanged Man [tarot] • *heraldry:* sun (magnificent example)

exasperation *see* **annoyance**

excellence   flour (the finest extract of something, as opposed to bran); flower (the finest product); Parnassus • *China:* jade; sturgeon (scholarly excellence, particularly in examinations) • *flower language:* red camellia japonica (unpretending excellence); strawberry (perfect excellence); Venice sumac (intellectual excellence) • *heraldry:* gold • *see also* **perfection; superiority**

excess   oats (youthful excess) • *association:* eleven (surfeit of completion and perfection) • *flower language:* saffron (beware of excess)

excitement   fever; pin (often sexual excitement); quivering (sexual excitement); very long legs (love of excitement) • *association:* E • *see also* **agitation**

exclusiveness   nightingale

excommunication   burial with an unlighted candle (an excommunicated person); two keys crossed (excommunication and restoration)

excrement   mud

executions   axe; black flag (the execution of criminals); cord; hatchet; rope • *associations:* beheading (typical execution for upper class prisoners); gallows (typical execution for lower class criminals, especially thieves); neck • *heraldry:* sword

executioners   *attributes:* black hood; yellow (Spanish Inquisition)

exhaustion *see* **fatigue**

exhibitionism   seal [animal]

exhilaration   helmet with a strange crest (restless exhilaration)

exhile   *association:* Pisces

existence   ant (the fragility and impotence of existence); bottomless cask (the apparent futility of earthly existence); carnival, saturnalia (the desire to concentrate all the possibilities of existence in a given period of time); circle (never ending existence); clock (cyclic existence of man, the seasons, etc.); cross (the suffering of existence); Death [tarot] (dematerialization); marrow (center of being); shadow (existence between soul and body); knot (an individual's existence); ship (living to transcend existence); twilight (perfection of a new state of being); voice (immaterial existence) • *associations:* clock (the magical creation of beings that pursue their own autonomous existence); N (physical existence); one; square [shape] (earthly existence) • *cyclic existence:* agriculture; earth [soil] (the cycle of existence as a symbol of man's life) • *material existence:* eating; hare; turtle

existentialism octopus; Saturn [god] (man as an existential being)

exit *see* **passage**

exorcism demon emerging from a victim's mouth • *associations:* aspergillum: aspergillum; bell • *see also* **possession**

exoticism sandalwood; Siamese cat; tea

expansion *associations:* fifty (expansion to infinity); Jupiter [planet]; Wheel of Fortune [tarot] (the equilibrium of the contrary forces of expansion and contraction) • *heraldry:* snail (acquisitions to be preserved and enlarged) • *see also* **growth; increase**

expectation anemone [flower]; bride; bridegroom; gooseberry; tickling • *associations:* forty; green • *flower language:* anemone; celandine (expectation of joys to come); fish geranium (disappointed expectation); zephyr

expeditions *heraldry:* ship (veteran of sea expeditions)

experience hold of a ship (experience on the lower plane); road • *association:* five (new experience)

experiment guinea pig; kite [toy] • *kabala:* six

expiation black knight; blood on a doorpost; cross, especially a Latin cross; cutting off a finger; Hercules (expiation of sins through heroic striving and heroism); incense; mistletoe; scapegoat (vicarious atonement); veil • *associations:* blue; forty; forty-two • *see also* **Atonement, Day of**

exploration sea serpent (formerly used on maps for unexplored waters); submarine boat (the means of exploring the unconscious) • *association:* ocean

expression file [rasp] (refined ideas or expressions); teeth (expression of activity, especially sexual activity)

expulsion closed gate or door

exquisiteness mimosa

extent *flower language:* gourd

extermination *see* **death**

extract flour (the finest extract of something, as opposed to bran)

extrasensory perception deafness, dumbness [inability to speak] (sometimes an indication that a person has a compensatory sixth sense) • *association:* Neptune [planet] • *see also* **clairvoyance**

extravagance poppy; silk; tulip • *flower language:* daphne odora (painting the lily); scarlet poppy (fantastic extravagance)

extremes Icarus (the danger of going to extremes)

extroversion *association:* right side

exuberance yeast

eyes beryl (charm against eye diseases); sun (the eye of God); window • *association:* crystal • *flower language:* variegated tulip (beautiful eyes); scarlet lychnis (sunbeaming eyes) • *see also* **sight**

Ezekiel wheel with eyes on the rim (Ezekiel's vision) • *emblems:* closed gate; turreted gate

F

F *association:* six
Fabricus Luscinus *association:* ele-

phant in a net
face Monday's child is fair in the face

(or, full in the face); Born on a Monday, fair of face
facility *see* **skill**
facts leaves (true facts) • *heraldry:* foot (the discovery of an important track or fact which gains lasting merit)
failure ashes; elephant with drooping trunk; lemon; loss of hair; loss of teeth (also fear of failure); zero • *associations:* F (failure, especially in education); forty-two (being cut off halfway to perfection); Pisces
fainting opal (charm against fainting)
fairies beetle • *associations:* blackberry; forest (home of fairies); mushroom; pinching; sweet brier • *attributes:* broom [for sweeping] (well-meaning fairies); blue eyes (good fairies); cloak trimmed with crimson feathers; lack of footprints; pointed ears
fairness *see* **equality; impartiality**
faith broken pillar (broken faith); cedar (steadfast faith); church; crayfish (loss of faith); crozier; cypress (occasionally the righteous man who preserves his faith); diamond [gemstone] (invulnerable faith); eagle; elm (the strength derived by the devout from their faith in scripture); feather; fish; hyacinth [flower]; kingfisher (connubial faith); mustard [plant] (especially the seed); oak; olive tree or branch (courageous faith and love); pearl; Phoenix [bird]; salamander (enduring and triumphant faith); sheep (the faithful); shield; silver; staff; yew • *associations:* blue; gold (the triumphant glory of faith); white • *Christianity:* birds feeding on grapes (the faithful gathering sustenance from the blood of Christ); bulrushes (the humble faithful who abide with Christ); church on a rock (the whole church, founded securely on the rock of faith); cross; crown (reward of the faithful Christian); emerald; hare (those who put their faith in Christ); Job (the faithful Christian); Latin cross with rays on a shield; scroll in the hands of a patriarch (the darkness faith was enveloped in before Christ); south wall of a church (associated with defenders of the faith); vine (the Christian faith); stag (the faithful Christian longing for God) • *Druidism:* three feathers (faith, hope, and the light of the world) •

faith, hope, and charity: cincture with three knots on a friar's habit (a member of the Franciscan order: the knots represent faith, hope, charity); cross with anchor and heart (faith, hope and charity, respectively); three (association); three feathers passing through a ring • *flower language:* globe amaranth; passion flower (Christian faith) • *heraldry:* hands (pledge of faith); stag (a lover of faith and trust); tree (constancy in faith); poplar (firm faith) • *see also* **confidence; devotion; piety; religion; trust**
Faith personified woman with a chalice • *attributes:* book with a cross laying on it; candle; cross with a chalice; cube; font; helmet; stag; unicorn (the steed of Faith personified)
faithfulness Antigone; blue rose (faithfulness unto death); fuchsia [flower]; mule (the faithful worker); dog; dogwood; girdle [cincture]; heliotrope [gemstone]; opal (charm to increase faithfulness in love); Penelope; spaniel; verbena; violet [flower] • *China:* dove; parrot (warning to wives to be faithful to their husbands); pigeon; pine • *flower language:* blue violet; frankincense (the faithful heart); heliotrope; key • *heraldry:* blue; dog • *see also* **constancy; loyalty; steadfastness**
faithlessness blown dandelion with no seeds remaining (a lover is unfaithful); fishhook; leather • *association:* thirteen
fall and rise *association:* H
fall of man *see* **man**
Fall [season] *see* **autumn**
falsity beans (false philosophy); black horse (false knowledge); dice; fox (false preacher); hyena; hail destroying crops (falsity destroying truth and goodness); kite [bird] (false servant); moistness; relief lacking in force; shifty eyes; sweat on the face; tapster (a falsifier of accounts); wormwood (false judgment) • *Christian Science:* Tower of Babel (false knowledge) • *false doctrine:* heron (the Christian who turns away from false doctrine); Hydra (the prolific nature of heresy, sin, false doctrine); hyena (one who thrives on false doctrine); wolf • *false prophets:* locust [insect]; tail (attribute); wolf • *flower language:* mock

orange (counterfeit) • *see also* **deceit; delusion; dissimulation; heresy and heretics; illusion; intrigue; lying; treachery**

fame gold rose; Pegasus; thorn (the road to fame); trumpet (the yearning for fame); tulip • *association:* three • *flower language:* apple blossom (fame speaks one great and good); trumpet flower; tulip • *heraldry:* serpent; torch • *portraiture:* skull with laurel (fame that will endure) • *see also* **reputation**

Fame personified Pegasus • *attributes:* chariot drawn by elephants; elephant; globe; laurel wreath; palm tree; trumpet; wings

family ace of hearts (family ties); Alastor (an evil spirit that haunts a family); berry (close kinship); bowl; dish; inverted torch on a tombstone (end of a family line); journey abroad (the cutting of family ties); pelican (parental love and sacrifice); sharing food (kinship) • *association:* six • *China:* hen crowing (the ruin of a family); unicorn (illustrious offspring of a family) • *flower language:* Virgin's bower (filial love) • *heraldry:* poplar (a flourishing family); tortoise (glorious development of family) • *see also* **children; daughters; fathers; mothers; parent and child; sons**

famine arrow; black horse; broken staff; cask; comet (omen of famine); dust; hag; lean cattle; stick (starvation); swallow [bird] or wolf (hunger)

fancy *see* **imagination**

fantasy *see* **imagination**

farewell hands clasped in a handshake on a tombstone (on a tombstone: farewell and welcome) • *flower language:* Michaelmas daisy; spruce pine

farmers *attributes:* hoe; pitchfork • *see also* **agriculture**

fascination carnation; fern; serpent • *flower language:* carnation; fern; honesty [plant]

fashion *flower language:* lady's mantle; queen's rocket (fashionable)

fastidiousness lilac [plant]; mimosa • *see also* **cleanliness**

fasting *associations:* forty; purple; violet [color]

Fasting personified crocodile with jaws bounds • *attributes:* hare

fate bouncing ball; cogwheel; dice; flax; puppet (man as the plaything of

fate); scissors; scroll (a decree of fate); spinning of thread; sword hanging overhead (vulnerability to fate; the suddenness of fate); urn; water wheel; Wheel of Fortune [tarot] (irreversible fate) • *association:* seven • *flower language:* coral honeysuckle (the color of my fate); flax; hemp • *see also* **chance; destiny; fortune; Wheel of Fortune**

Fate personified *attributes:* ball; wings

the Fates three women spinning thread • *association:* cypress (sacred to the Fates) • *attributes:* distaff (especially of Clotho); linen thread; scissors; spinning of thread

fathers bull; eagle; giant; king (a concentrated father image); old man; sky; spark (heavenly father); tetragrammatron; Yggdrasil (the all-father) • *associations:* F; iron [mineral] (the father-spirit archetype) • *China:* staff of ash wood or bamboo (mourning for a father) • *flower language:* paternal error • *God the Father:* blue (association); church spires (the largest spire represents God the Father, the smaller spires his celestial offspring); globe underfoot, glory [luminous glow around the entire body], purple, three-rayed or triangular nimbus (attributes); hand descending from heaven; one eye, especially when in a triangle or above an altar; thumb (association) • *Judaism:* swallow [bird] (paternal inheritance) • *Terrible Father:* giant; male ogre; Negro; sorcerer • *see also* **family; parent and child; trinity**

Father Time *attributes:* chariot drawn by stags; crutch; hourglass; long beard; scythe; serpent; stag; wings

fatigue afternoon; bow [archery] (exhausting strain); signs of wear (weariness of spirit)

fault *see* **defect**

favor almond (divine approval or favor); fasting (the seeking of favor or approval from a deity); thumb up • *association:* three (favorability) • *flower language:* cistus (popular favor); ivy geranium (bridal favor) • *see also* **approval**

fawning *see* **subservience**

fear aspen; chimera; female ogre (fear of maternal incest); grasshopper; jelly; loss of teeth; melting wax; paleness; Phobos; virgin; sinking in mud (fear of maternal incest) • *flower language:* peppermint (the coldness of fear with the warmth of love) • *see also* **anxiety; cowardice; horror; terror**

fearlessness *see* **bravery; courage; pugnacity**

feasts cake; sheaf with scroll (Old Testament Feast of the Pentecost); table • *associations:* tabret (goddess feasts); tent of boughs (Sukkoth, the Feast of the Tabernacles); viol (godless feasts) • *flower language:* parsley • *Judaism:* lettuce (characteristic food of feasts)

February amethyst (birthstone of February) • *emblem:* peach blossom

February personified *attribute:* heron

feces mud

fecklessness *see* **weakness**

fecundation *see* **fertilization**

fecundity acacia; agriculture; aegis (productive power); bread; bull; codfish; confetti; crocodile; dart and egg design (male generation and female productiveness, respectively); dolphin; Empress [tarot]; fire; fish; frog; hare; hollyhock; laurel; lightning; lotus; magnolia; moon (regulator of the fecundity of women and animals and the fertility of plants); mouse; orange [fruit]; parsley; plants (the healthy growth of plants indicates cosmic, spiritual, and material fecundity); pomegranate; poppy; rabbit; rice; sow [swine] (fecundity; the fecundity of evil); sparrow; spinning of thread (producing and fostering life); tortoise; tree (earth's fecundity); vegetation in abundance (fecundity and fertility); veil (with likenesses of animals on it; Wheel of Fortune [tarot]; whip • *association:* five • *China:* orchid • *Egypt:* lizard • *flower language:* hollyhock • *heraldry:* palm tree • *see also* **fertility; fruitfulness**

Feeding of the Five Thousand Christ with baskets of bread

feelings echo, forehead, mirror (all give a reflection of one's feelings); kidneys (seat of feelings in the Old Testament); liver (seat of feelings); lobster (an unfeeling, grabbing monster); raspberry (kindly feelings); swine (lack of feelings) • *associations:* F; four (the functional aspects of consciousness: thinking, feeling, sensation, and intuition) • *flower language:* garden or small double daisy (I share your sentiments--used especially in the days of chivalry) • *see also* **disposition; emotions; mood; passions; sentiments**

feet *association:* Neptune [planet]

felicity acanthus; caduceus in a woman's hand; globe; jasmine (heavenly felicity); swastika; topaz • *associations:* F (domestic felicity); right side • *China:* unicorn • *flower language:* bluebottle; centaury; sweet sultan • *Orient:* duck • *see also* **gladness; happiness**

Felicity, St. woman holding palm leaves with seven children

Felix of Cantalice, St. beggar with a wallet as a shoulder bag

fellatio blowing; kissing the head of a snake

fellowship edelweiss (sentimental, but dangerous good fellowship); garland; table • *see also* **conviviality; fraternity; friendliness**

the female hen; magnolia (feminine sweetness and beauty); mantis (female viciousness); Medusa (the dangerous female); mercury [metal]; mirror (feminine pride); night (female fertility); open mouth; orange [fruit]; peony (feminine loveliness); nymph (the fragmentary characteristics of the feminine unconscious); ring (female love); succubus (the Devil in female form); snow (female frigidity); Spring (female innocence); unicorn (feminine chastity); vineyard • *associations:* even numbers; fan; gardenia; green; lace; linden tree; M (when printed rounded); moon; pink; thimble; tree; two; violet [color]; willow tree; yin (the dark color of yin and yang) • *emblems:* crescent moon; hills; oval; spinning wheel; spot • *China:* magnolia blossom (feminine beauty); peony (feminine loveliness) • *the female principle:* alcove; amphora; anvil; arch; bag; basket; beads; bird; bower; box; chest [container]; city; conch shell; crescent; curved sword (association); darkness (association); dish; door; forest; gate; goblet; gorge; Hecate (the female principle responsible for madness and obsession); hole; house (the feminine aspect of the universe); jar; knot; lotus; mercury [metal] (the dominant female principle); moon; mother; night;

peach; pitcher [vessel]; plate; pomegranate; pumpkin; sarcophagus; saucer; scabbard; serpent; shell (association); ship; spoon swan's body; T (association); tomb; tortoise; triangle with the apex down; urn; vase; vial; wallet; waves [water] • *flower language:* justica (perfection of female loveliness); speedwell (female fidelity) • *heraldry:* green (a feminine color) • *union of the male and female principles:* caduceus; flagpole with a ball on top; guitar; hearth with a fire; horn [animal]; king and queen; maltese cross; marriage; maypole; serpent with its tail in its mouth; sexual intercourse; six-pointed star; Sphinx; swan; Temperance [tarot] • *see also* **beauty; girls; sex; vulva; women**

ferality *see* **wildness**

fermentation yeast

ferocity badger; claw; hawk; leopard; lion; lynx; ogre (primitive savage life); orange that is impure [color]; panther (martial ferocity); tiger; wolf • *China:* leopard; panther • *heraldry:* bear • *see also* **brutality; cruelty; viciousness**

fertility agriculture; amber [gemstone]; animal horn; arrow; axe; basket; bee; being bound to a stake (death of a fertility king); bell; blood; boar; bonfire; breasts, sometimes multiple breasts; breeze; bride; bridegroom; bull; caduceus; cake; Catherine wheel; cave; cedar; chest [container]; chimney sweep; clouds; clover; coat or cloak of ox skin; coconut; comb; confetti; corn [maize]; cow; cowhide; dancing; Demogorgon; dew; Diana; dog; dolphin; dove with a date tree (earthly fertility); dragon (also a guardian of fertility); eagle (especially male fertility); earthquake; eating (equivalent to the sowing of seed); effigy (has magical powers for promoting fertility); ember; Empress [tarot]; Euphrates River (the great fertilizer); field; fig; fire (sexual fertility); fireworks; flagellation; flax; flute; forest; fox; frog; full vase; gargoyle (fertility enslaved by superior spirituality); goat; goose; gourd; grapes; hammer; hare; harrow [tool]; hawthorn; hazel (love and fertility); head; hearth; heifer; hermaphrodite; hill; hoe; horse; Lady Godiva; lake (giver of fertility); lily; lion; maiden slaughtered by a tyrant (fertility conquered); manure; mare; milk; mill; mirror; mistletoe; moon (regulator of

the fertility of plants); mustard [plant]; navel; necklace; net (fertility and love); nuts; oak; obelisk; olive branch; orange [fruit]; ostrich feathers; otter (transitory fertility); oxhide; park; Phrygia; pine cone (fertility; spiritual fertility); plow; plum tree; poinsettia; pomegranate bursting open (fertility of the word); poppy; potato; quail; quince; rain; rice; ring; river; round loaf of bread; rush [plant]; Saturn [god]; satyr; scarab; scepter; scourge [whip] (promotion of fertility); seed; semen; serpent; sheepskin coat or cloak; shoes; shovel; sickle; sistrum; sleeping beauty (fertility awakened by the sun); solar wheel; spade [shovel]; spear; spice; springwort; staff; stag; stork; straw girdle [cincture]; sun; tamarisk; tear [weeping]; thaw (the return of fertility); threshing; thunder; thyrsus; Tigris River; toad; treasures hidden in a palace; tree; twelve pillars (the months of fertility); vegetation in abundance (fertility and fecundity); veil (fertility hidden underground); verbena; volcano; vulture; walnut; water; water fly (busy fertility); water lily; water mill; west wind; whip; windmill; wolf; woodpecker; wool • *associations:* black (fertilized or fertile land); dark complexion; elm; evergreens (used in fertility rites); F; five; green; hair; music; mutilation, stick dance (fertility rites); nine; nymph (fertility of nature); O [letter]; pot (usually earthen); Q; shell [biology]; sixteen • *female fertility:* garden; night; seaweed (maternal fertility) • *fertility deities:* cone (association); cypress (association); plant [botany] (association); scarecrow (goddesses); spider (attribute of goddesses) • *Great Britain:* sycamore • *heraldry:* hare • *India:* cedar • *see also* **fecundity; fruitfulness**

fertilization battering ram; cannon; hammer; harpoon; hurricane; manure; plow; scepter • *association:* Taurus

fervor *see* **passion; zeal**

festivities cider (rural festivities); candle; fireworks; flower; tabor; wreath • *association:* white garment • *flower language:* parsley • *see also* **rejoicing**

fetishes lock of hair (love fetish)

fetters *see* **bondage**

fever brass-backed bird; goat; Sirius (summer fever)

fickleness *see* **changeability; inconstancy**

fidelity buckle (fidelity in authority); carnation; doe; dog (fidelity; married fidelity, especially when shown in a woman's lap or at her feet); duck; fig; fir; Hanged Man [tarot] (power derived from fidelity, charity, wisdom, and other higher virtues); horse; ivy; lemon (especially fidelity in love); myrtle (conjugal fidelity); plum blossoms; silver; topaz; turtle dove • *association:* blue • *China:* cedar • *flower language:* ivy; lemon blossoms (fidelity in love); rosemary (fidelity between lovers); speedwell (female fidelity); veronica (especially female fidelity); wallflower (fidelity in misfortune) • *heraldry:* ring • *Orient:* mandarin ducks (conjugal fidelity); two crows together (conjugal fidelity) • *see also* **loyalty**

Fidelity personified *attributes:* bunch of keys; dog

fighting *see* **war**

filiality *see* **family; parent and child**

filth coal [carbon]; cockroach; fly [insect]; frog (uncleanliness); hoopoe; ibis; louse; maggot; mouse (untidiness); rat; russet [cloth]; sewer [drain] (vileness); swine • *see also* **impurity**

Fina, St. *attributes:* mouse; rat; white violets sprouting from deathbed

finality lighthouse (the final port); thousand petalled lotus (final revelation); tomb • *associations:* Pisces (final stage of a cycle); seventy; ten • *see also* **ending**

finance purse

fine arts acanthus • *association:* nine • *flower language:* acanthus

finesse *see* **skill**

finish *see* **ending; finality**

fire alder bark; axe and trident (fire and water, respectively); bow and arrows (fire and lightning); censer (purifying fire); eagle; ember (a concentrated expression of fire with many of its associated meanings); falcon; fir; gold robe (fire of the sun); hawk; lotus; man; oak; orange [color]; pyrus japonica (fairies' fire); red; rhododendron; salamander; scarlet; scorpion; triangle with the apex up; two pillars of Enoch (the brick pillar is proof against fire; the stone pillar is proof against water); uraeus • *associations:* F; Leo; radiance (fire in both the positive and negative sense) • *Chinese association:* odd numbers • *creative fire:* furnace; meteorite heavenly creative fire); thunderbolt (supreme creative fire); volcano • *flower language:* fraxinella; horehound • *protection against fire:* pearl, red rooster (China); swastika over a door

Fire personified *attributes:* flame on the forehead; salamander; thunderbolt

firmness alder tree; brass; bronze; copper; crozier; elephant; Justice [tarot]; legs; plane tree (firmness of character); pyramid; spine; square [shape] (firmness; the unwavering firmness of the church); stone; sumac (resoluteness) • *China:* iron • *heraldry:* poplar (firm faith) • *see also* **hardness; solidity**

fish codfish (fishery); dogfish (the lowest kind of fish); dolphin (the highest order of fish) • *associations:* Aphrodite; one hundred and fifty-three (in ancient times, held to be the number of types of fishes in existence); fishnet (fishermen; fishing); Thursday (according to the Bible, the day sea beasts were created) • *heraldry:* fish, otter (free fishing rights)

fitness *flower language:* sweet flag

five fifty (a multiplication of the values of five) • *associations:* E; N; W

flagellation *see* **whipping**

flamboyance *see* **gaudiness; ostentation**

flame miter (flame of the Holy Spirit) • *association:* orange [color] • *flower language:* fleur-di-lys; German iris; yellow iris

flashiness *see* **gaudiness; ostentation**

flattery bee; bellows; censer; claw; dog; ear (temptation through flattery); fawn; fennel; fox; honey; incense; licking; monkey; scorpion; sugar • *flower language:* Venus' looking glass

Flattery personified *attributes:* flute

fleeing *see* **escape**

Fleeting Occurrence personified *attribute:* wings

fleetness *see* **speed**

the flesh carrion: lotus (the soul transcending the flesh); spy (trust in the flesh rather than the spirit); thaw (dissolving of the flesh); thorn (temptation of the flesh); tomb (the desires of the flesh) • *associations:* base metals;

green (victory over the flesh); pink [color]

flexibility *see* **adaptability**

flies fly [insect] (in 15th and 16th century European painting, a fly painted on the work was used as a charm to keep real flies out of the fresh paint)

flight [escape] *see* **escape**

flight [flying] helmet with wings • *flower language:* Venus' car (fly with me)

flight into Egypt, the Holy Family's pyramid and star; sphinx • *association:* fallen idol

flirtation *see* **coquetry**

flogging *see* **whipping**

flood maiden killed by a natural calamity; Noah's ark (the Flood of the Bible) • *China:* black clouds (portent of a flood)

Flood personified thief

Flora [goddess] *association:* cornflower (Cyanus was turned into a cornflower by Flora) • *attributes:* crown of flowers; flower

Florence, Italy *heraldry:* red fleurdi-lys

Florian, St. soldier • *attributes:* bucket; fire (he is usually shown extinguishing the fire); millstone; pitcher [vessel]

fly with me *flower language:* Venus' car

foam white feathers (sea foam)

following *association:* T • *heraldry:* elephant (willingness to be guided)

folly alchemy (foolish occultism); ass; bear; bubble; calf; columbine; cosmetics; crab tree (an old, foolish, cowardly person); cuckoo; dog; fish; geranium; goose; hobby horse; lark (recklessness); macaroni; monkey (idle foolishness); ostrich; oyster; satyr; titmouse; turkey; young rooster • *association:* blue (Middle Ages) • *flower language:* daphne odora (painting the lily); pomegranate • *flower language:* columbine; scarlet geranium • *see also* **senselessness**

Folly personified jester • *attribute:* shell

food butter (food in general); cake (food of the rich); herb, lentils (food of the poor); leprosy (punishment for eating tabooed food); plantain (food of the pilgrim; food of the multitude seeking Christian salvation); oats (food of the lower classes) • *Greece:* red food (food reserved for the dead) • *heavenly food:* honey (food of the gods; food from heaven); manna; milk and honey • *Judaism:* lettuce (characteristic food of feasts) • *see also* **eating; sustenance**

Fool [tarot] *association:* O [letter]

foolhardiness weather cock, weather vane

foolishness *see* **folly**

fools amaranth (a cockscomb); ass ears on a human; capon (a dull fool); dove; gosling (a young fool); gudgeon (a credulous fool); gull; Hercules (in Elizabethan times: a ridiculous, boisterous, brawny tyrant); martin; snipe; woodcock • *association:* sneezing (omen that you will kiss a fool) • *attributes:* baldness; bladder; rabbit skin cap • *see also* **comedians; jesters**

foppery amaranth

force cord; diamond suit [playing cards], gold suit [tarot] (material force); flock (the collapse of a force or objective, often with a negative connotation); gun; hawk (brute force); horned serpent (opposite forces in conflict); iron; javelin (kingly force); light (creative force); locusts [insects], serpents (destructive force); oak; ocean (dynamic force); Pegasus (heightened natural forces); phallus (nature's regenerative force); serpent (force; destructive force); spine; volcano (primary forces of nature); warrior (latent force in the personality ready to aid the conscious; various forces, hostile or friendly); wild man, wild woman (primeval force); windlass (compulsion) • *associations:* K; Leo (vital forces); Pluto [planet] (explosive forces; invisible forces); Mars (driving force); R (tremendous force for good or evil); red (creative force); right side (the forces of reason) • *base force:* American Indian; leopard; monster (predominance of base forces in life being fought by spiritual forces, often by a knight); Negroes; Pan (the vitality of base forces); savages; siren [mythology] (base forces in woman); steed (control of baser forces) • *cosmic force:* flock (the disordered or semi-ordered forces of the cosmos, often with a negative connotation); gargoyle; griffin (the relationship between psychic energy and cosmic forces); harpy (evil harmonies of cosmic forces); lyre or onion (harmony of cosmic forces); ox; phallus (propagation of cosmic forces) • *flower language:* fennel • *heraldry:* wild man or wild woman as a supporter (base forces of nature subjugated and transcended) • *natural force:* cauldron (the transmutation and germination of the baser forces of nature); dwarf (hidden forces of nature); five (associated with the powers of nature); herb; maypole (the phallic reproductive power of nature, together with the vulva-circle regulation of time and motion); phallus (nature's regenerative force); sun (the active power of nature); Titan (a wild and untameable force of primeval nature); torch (the active, positive power of nature); volcano (primary forces of nature) • *see also* **energy; incentive; violence**

foresight ant; chestnut; hermit crab; honeycomb; roebuck; squirrel; tortoise; trefoil [plant] • *association:* P • *flower language:* holly • *see also* **providence**

forest Diana; foxfire (forest spirits) • *China:* wild boar (the wealth of the forest) • *heraldry:* tree (possession of forest lands)

foresters *attributes:* axe; hatchet

forethought *see* **foresight; providence**

foretokens and signs •*bloodshed:* aurora borealis • *cruelty:* second toe longer than the first (sign of a cruel husband) • *danger:* dolphin; sneezing on a Monday; sweating image • *death:* aurora borealis (death of a king or leader); bird tapping at a window or flying into a house; black hand or spot; caladrius turning away from a sick person; chirping crickets; earthquake (divine death); eclipse of the sun (death of a king); eyebrows that meet (sign of a person who will not live to marry); Gabriel hounds; golden plover song; spilling a cup of wine; vulture; washing in a stream • *defeat:* bird of prey flying from left to right before a battle • *disaster:* "blood" on the moon; earthquake (divine anger, death, intervention or sacrifice); remora; screech or squinch owl • *dishonesty:* index finger as long as the middle finger

• *divine:* shooting star • *drought:* comet • *earthquake:* comet • *end of the world:* eclipse of the sun • *evil:* being pricked on the finger by a needle; burning or tingling ears, especially the right ear (someone is speaking evil of you); comet; crow (usually); dark clouds; east wind; heart missing from a sacrificial animal; lapwing; letter [epistle]; meteor (usually); nightjar; nightmare; one eye (extra human effort devoted to one aim, usually evil); picture falling off the wall for no apparent reason; pointing; raven; red sky at morning; ruby changing color (mischief); screech or squinch owl; Sirius; sneezing (everywhere but Greece and Rome); sneezing on a Friday (you sneeze for sorrow); sneezing on a Sunday (for safety seek, the Devil will have you the whole of the week); storm clouds; sudden shiver or pain for no apparent reason); two; vulture • *famine:* comet • *flood:* black clouds (China); comet • *flower language:* small cape marigold • *good fortune:* born on a Sunday, you'll never want (or, lucky and happy, good and gay); child (beneficent change); chimney sweep; crane [bird]; finding a nail, especially a rusty nail; finding money; guelder rose (flower language); hare (China); heron; ibis; magpie (China); one hundred and forty-four; owl; ruby regaining color after it has changed; sixpence; sixty-nine; sneezing (Greece and Rome); sneezing on a Thursday (you sneeze for something better); snowball (flower language); swallow [bird] (in heraldry: messenger of good news or good fortune); unicorn (China); white horse • *kiss:* sneezing (you will kiss a fool) • *letter [epistle]:* spark in a candle flame • *love:* burning or tingling left ear, or earring falling off (your sweetheart is thinking of you); putto (profane love) • *morosity:* crooked fingers • *mourning:* glow worm • *peace:* dove with an olive branch; Phoenix [bird] • *plague:* eclipse of the sun • *rain:* chirping crickets; dolphin; east wind; rooks flying in a great flock • *reconciliation:* dove with an olive branch • *recovery:* caladrius turning toward a sick person • *riches:* crooked little finger (you will die rich) • *ruin:* hen crowing (in China, the ruin of a family); a man born during an earthquake will be the ruin of a country • *spite:* burning or tingling right ear (someone is speaking spitefully of you) • *spring [season]:* apple (generally associated with autumn, but sometimes a herald of spring); azalea; lark [bird]; lettuce (Judaism); lilac [plant]; lily of the valley; nightingale; plum blossoms; pomegranate; primrose; robin; rook [bird]; snowdrop; stork; swallow [bird]; thrush; tulip; violet [flower] • *storms:* barnacle goose; bitterns flocking together; chattering coots; eel; petrel; Phoenix [bird]; porpoise; woodpecker • *stranger:* spark in a candle flame • *sweetheart:* sneezing on a Saturday (your sweetheart will see you tomorrow) • *visitor:* magpie (China) • *war:* comet; eclipse of the sun; soldiers on horseback in the sky • *wedding:* butterfly in a house • *see also* **divination**

forge anvil with cross or sword (the forge of the universe)

forgetfulness child; dust (something forgotten or neglected); entanglement (the forgotten past); Lethe (forgetfulness of the past); lynx; ostrich; river; tobacco; yew • *flower language:* holly (Am I forgotten?); moonwort; mouse-eared scorpion grass (do not forget me)

forgiveness fasting (the seeking of favor or forgiveness from a deity); flowering staff; lamb; oak; rainbow (pardon and divine reconciliation) • *Christianity:* oak • *see also* **confession and absolution**

forlornness *see* **misery**

form Gorgon (the infinite forms in which creation is manifested); mist (the intermediate world between the formal and non-formal); yin and yang (form and life)

formality white gloves

formation Temperance [tarot] (ceaseless cycling through formation, regeneration, and purification)

fornication *see* **intercourse**

forsakenness *see* **abandonment**

fortification *see* **defense**

fortitude carp; diamond [gemstone]; ivory (moral fortitude) • *see also* **stamina; strength**

Fortitude personified female soldier; woman holding a column;

woman wrestling with a lion • *attributes:* club [bat]; circular or hexagonal nimbus; globe; helmet; lion skin; pillar; scepter; shield with an image of a lion or a ball; sword

Fortunatus *attribute:* purse

fortune dice; loom; shipwreck (tragic fortune); tide (ebb and flow of fortune); well; wheel; World [tarot] • *associations with good fortune:* Friday (Rome); nineteen; one hundred and forty-four; seventy; six; sixty-nine; three; twenty-four (generally); twenty-one; U (good, but tenuous, fortune) • *changing fortune:* rocking cradle; swinging; turning of the tide • *China:* bat [animal]; hare; magpie (emblem and foretoken); monkey (said to have the power to drive away evil and, hence, bring success, health, and protection); pheasant (occasional emblem of good fortune and beauty); red (association); swallow (emblem); tree peony; unicorn • *flower language (good fortune):* guelder rose; snowball; white heather • *foretokens and signs of good fortune:* born on a Sunday, you'll never want (or, lucky and happy, good and gay); child (beneficent change); chimney sweep; crane [bird]; finding a nail, especially a rusty nail; finding money; heron; ibis; one hundred and forty-four; owl; ruby regaining color after it has changed; sixpence; sixty-nine; sneezing (Greece and Rome); sneezing on a Thursday (you sneeze for something better); white horse • *good fortune:* albatross; bayberry candles; cinnabar orange [fruit]; clockwise swastika; clover, especially with four leaves; coral [biology]; eighteen (in the Old Testament, associated with evil, but in Christianity, with great reward); extra fingers; extra toes; flood tide; horseshoe; ladybug; meeting a fox; opal; owl (Bible); rabbit's foot; rainbow; sagebrush; six-pointed star; tortoise shell cat; verbena; white cat (except in Britain, where it is bad luck); white horse; white rooster • *heraldry:* dice (the fickleness of fortune); raven (a man who has made his own fortune); swallow [bird] (messenger of good fortune or good news) • *ill fortune:* being pricked on the finger by a needle; burning or tingling ears, especially the right ear (someone is speaking evil of you); comet; crow (usually); dark clouds; east wind; heart missing from a sacrificial animal; lapwing; letter [epistle]; meteor (usually); nightjar; nightmare; one eye (extra human effort devoted to one aim, usually evil); picture falling off the wall for no apparent reason; pointing; raven; red sky at morning; ruby changing color (mischief); screech or squinch owl; Sirius; sneezing on a Friday (you sneeze for sorrow); sneezing on a Sunday (for safety seek, the Devil will have you the whole of the week); storm clouds; sudden shiver or pain for no apparent reason); two; vulture • *Wheel of Fortune:* eight-pointed star; S (association); wheel • *see also* **chance; destiny; fate**

Fortune personified blindfold (indicates the randomness of fortune); bridle; bucket; caduceus; chariot of shell; cornucopia; dice; dolphin (usually shown riding a dolphin); globe underfoot; hand of gold or ivory; lion skin; model of a ship; rudder; sails; wheel; wings

fortune tellers gypsy • *attribute:* crystal ball

foulness *see* **offensiveness**

foundation cornerstone; legs; pavement; rock, stone (the spirit as a foundation); roots (foundation, but they do not necessarily imply stability); vine (root, basis, or foundation) • *see also* **fundamentals; support**

founders of a church *attribute:* church model being carried

fount of life Orient

four forty (a multiplication of the powers of four) • *associations:* D; M; Mercury [planet]; quadriga; quatrefoil; V

Fourth of July *association:* fireworks (United States)

fragility ant (the fragility and impotence of existence); dew • *see also* **frailty**

Fragility personified *emblem:* hemlock

fragmentation centipede, millepede (fragmentation of the psyche); multiple heads (however, it can also sometimes also positive intensification) • *involutive fragmentation of the unconscious:* Bacchante; Furies; harpy;

nymph (fragmentation of the feminine unconscious); siren [mythology]

fragrance jasmine; spikenard [perfume] • *China:* orchid

frailty anemone [flower]; spider web (human frailty); thin lips • *heraldry:* butterfly • see also **fragility; weakness**

France *association:* guillotine (the Reign of Terror) • *emblems:* Cross of Lorraine (the Free French during World War II); Eiffel Tower (especially Paris); fleur-di-lys; rooster • *heraldry:* dolphin (the provinces of France); fleur-di-lys; three toads, erect, saltant (an ancient crest) • *see also* **the French**

Francesca di Rimini two lovers sharing a book (Paolo and Francesca di Rimini)

Francis of Assisi, St. praying saint before an image or vision of the Virgin and Christ child, with the Virgin handing the Christ child to the saint; praying saint before an image of the crucified Christ, with Christ reaching down to the saint • *association:* roses springing from drops of blood • *attributes:* crucifix; deer; fish; lamb; lily; skull; stigmata; tame wolf

Francis of Rome, St. praying monk among plague victims

Francis Xavier, St. *attributes:* lily; ship

frankness diamond [gemstone]; fern; pomegranate (especially when open) • *flower language:* osier • see also **candor; honesty; truthfulness**

fraternity hands clasped in a handshake (virile fraternity); honeysuckle, lilac [color] (fraternal love); knotted ribbon; *flower language:* woodbine [monthly honeysuckle] (fraternal love) • see also **fellowship**

fraud ape; leopard; wolf • *Old Testament:* goat • see also **deceit**

Free French Cross of Lorraine (emblem of the Free French during World War II)

free will *association:* Mercury [planet]

Free Will personified *attributes:* multicolored garment

freedom bell; bird; bird freed from a cage (the soul freed from the body); bird in a cage (hope of freedom); broken handcuffs; butterfly; cat (love of freedom); cutting reins (freedom to go wild); dolphin with a trident (freedom of commerce); field (freedom from restraint); fish; goat; grazing horse (peace and freedom); hawk; inn (a place of freedom, conviviality, and protection); Jerusalem; mountain; Nike; osier; otter (free spirit); Prometheus; sandals; wind • *associations:* Aquarius (the loosening of bonds and the immanence of liberation); five; Friday's child is free and giving • *flower language:* butterfly weed (let me go); water willow • *heraldry:* eagle's claw (defense of freedom); emerald; green; lance; leopard; sword (a free man) • *Latin America:* quetzel • *see also* **autonomy; independence; liberty**

Freemasons *attribute:* apron • *emblem:* Maltese cross

the French frog; *attributes:* Phrygian cap (supporters of the French Revolution); scepter tipped with a fleur-di-lys (French kings) • *see also* **France**

frenzy *see* **agitation; excitement**

freshness bride; bridegroom; dew; hyssop; morning (bringer of freshness) • *association:* green • *flower language:* damask rose • *see also* **newness**

Freya *associations:* birch; Friday

friction rubbing [motion]

Friday Born on a Friday, worthily given (or, is loving and giving); Friday's child is free and giving • *associations:* black (the liturgical color for Good Friday); Freya; marriage on a Friday is associated with losses; Taurus; Venus [goddess]

friendliness bough; cherry blossoms; jasmine; myrtle; plane tree; robin; swallow [bird], tea (sociability); tassel • *flower language:* peppermint (cordiality); white jasmine • *see also* **conviviality; fellowship; gregariousness; hospitality; welcome**

friendship acacia; amazone; branch with berries or green leaves; brooch given as a gift (broken love or friendship); cup; hand held up, palm facing out; hands clasped in a handshake; ivy; jasper; lute; moss; mutilation (covenant of friendship); onyx (promotes happiness in friendship); salt; Saul (perfect friendship); sharing food; snowdrop (friendship in adversity); topaz; water lily (companionship) • *associations:* five (new friends); heart suit [playing cards]; lilac [color] •

China: glycine (tender and delicate friendship) • *flower language:* acacia; arbor vitae (unchanging friendship); blue or red periwinkle (early friendship); glycine (your friendship is pleasing and agreeable to me); ivy; oak geranium (true friendship); rose acacia; zinnia (thoughts of absent friends) • *heraldry:* emerald; ivy (strong and lasting friendship); palm tree • *see also* **affection; attachment; love**

Friga *see* **Freya**

frigidity fish, sometimes two fish (sexual frigidity); hydrangea; icicle; snow (especially female frigidity) • *flower language:* ficoides (your looks freeze me) • *see also* **coldness; coolness**

friskiness *see* **playfulness**

frivolity butterfly; cuckoo; weather cock, weather vane • *flower language:* bladder nut; London pride

frog toad (inverse or infernal aspect of the frog)

frolic lamb

frost maiden killed by a natural calamity; north wind

Frost personified thief

frown *flower language:* currants (thy frown will kill me)

frugality squirrel • *associations:* Scotland; Sparta • *flower language:* chicory; endive • *see also* **economy**

Frugality personified *attribute:* chicory

Fruit of Salvation *see* **salvation**

fruitfulness almond; apricot, lotus blossom, Ouroboros (self-fructification); basket with flowers or fruit; cherry; chrysanthemum; cornucopia; fig; goldfinch; grapes; hollyhock; pimpernel; snail; strawberries, sometimes with other fruit (fruits of the spirit); topaz • *associations:* gold; yellow, especially bright yellow • *China:* lotus • *flower language:* hollyhock • *see also* **abundance; fecundity; fertility; generation; prosperity**

frustration broken column (frustrated hope); forgotten or legendary fairies (frustrated acts) • *see also* **disappointment**

fulfillment hanging [suspension] (unfulfilled longing); return; ribbon knotted to form a circle (fulfillment of an undertaking) • *see also* **gratification**

fullness *heraldry:* apple (fullness of life)

fundamentals cornerstone (something fundamental, or of primary importance) • *see also* **foundation**

funerals *associations:* crown (former association); evergreens; footprints; horse, especially a riderless horse with empty boots turned backward in the stirrups; jar; muffled drum; sweet briar (funeral bouquet) • Greek *association:* flute • *see also* **burial**

the Furies *associations:* cypress; juniper; narcissus [flower] • *attributes:* red eyes; red girdle [cincture] with black clothes

furnace anvil (primal furnace)

fury badger; boiling; Cain; crocodile; dog; eagles's scream; Gordian knot; horn [animal]; labyrinth; lion; red eyes (demonic fury); Strength [tarot]; Taurus (slow to anger, but full of fury once provoked); wolverine • *Egypt:* crocodile • *see also* **anger**

Fury personified *attributes:* camel; hedgehog; leopard; shears; torch

fusion Gorgon (fusion of opposites) • *association:* fourteen • *see also* **unification; union**

futility blindman's bluff (trying to solve a problem without sufficient knowledge); bottomless cask (the apparent futility of earthly existence); relief lacking in force; rosary (the futility of aspiration); smoke (the futility of earthly glory) • *see also* **uselessness**

future boy; buds (future promise); child; curtain (veil of the future); scroll that is unrolling (the unrolling of life: the upper roll is the future, and the lower roll is the past); stranger (the future made present) • *associations:* east; fountain; right eye; right side • *Judaism:* apple eaten with honey (the hope for sweetness and joy in the future)

G

G *association:* seven

Gabriel ragged pilgrim (occasional representation) • *associations:* eighteen; seven; twelve (Gabriel and Uriel together) • *attributes:* lily; olive branch; palm tree; scepter; shield inscribed with A.M. [Maria regina], AMGPT [ave Maria gratia plena Dominus tecum—Hail Mary full of grace, the Lord is with thee], Maria, or MR [Maria regina]; wings of many colors

gaiety brussels sprouts; bubble; fiddle, fiddler; hummingbird; lark; primrose; thyrsus • *flower language:* butterfly orchis; shamrock (light-heartedness); yellow lily • *heraldry:* angel • *see also* **frivolity; merriment**

gain *flower language:* cabbage • *association:* J

Galatea *attributes:* chariot drawn by dolphins or sea horses; chariot of shell; dolphin; sea horse

Galilee, Sea of *association:* ship on a stormy sea (Jesus calming the Sea of Galilee)

gallantry coot (courtliness); goldfinch • *flower language:* bouquet (but a large group of gathered flowers means "we die together"); sweet William • *see also* **chivalry; gentility**

gallows *association:* mandrake (said to grow under the gallows of murderers)

gambling Belial (gambling as a vice); dice; playing cards; slapping hands with someone else or spitting (binding to a bet or contract)

games *see* **sports**

Ganymede youth borne aloft by an eagle

Garden of Eden *see* **Eden, Garden of**

garrulity *see* **chatter**

Gaspar, St. *attribute:* golden casket

gates *see* **entrance**

gaudiness *see* **ostentation**

Gemini twins • *associations:* chestnut; emerald; G; lavender plant; lily of the valley; mercury [metal]; Mercury [planet]; orange [color]; spring [season]; W; Wednesday; yellow • *emblem:* double-headed eagle

Gemianius, St. *attribute:* demon underfoot

generals *attribute:* scepter tipped with eagle (victorious generals)

generation dart and egg design (male generation and female productiveness); heron (generation of life); ocean (generative source of life); phallus (propagation of cosmic forces); serpent (generative energy); tragelaph (generation and preservation) • *associations:* forty-two (creative generation); T (generative power) • *see also* **fruitfulness**

generations swastika (succession of generations)

generosity Born on a Friday, worthily given (or, is loving and giving); bulldog; eagle; Friday's child is free and giving; gladiolus; hand that is open; house chimney (the joy of giving); lion; lupin; orange tree; orange [fruit]; pear; purse (philanthropy); tourmaline; white knight; woman squeezing her breasts • *association:* E • *flower language:* honeysuckle (generous and devoted affection) • *heraldry:* gold; palm tree • *see also* **benevolence; charity; magnanimity**

Genevieve, St. *attributes:* candle; the Devil with a bellows and a candle; distaff (when she is shown as a shepherdess); key; shepherd's crook

geniality *see* **conviviality; friendliness**

genitals center; eyes; foot (especially the penis); legs; thighs • *association:* Mars • *see also* **clitoris; phallus; scrotum; testicles; vulva**

genius Melusina (intuitive genius); pearl (genius in obscurity) • *China:* pearl (obscure genius) • *flower language:* acanthus (persistent genius); cereus (modest genius); plane tree • *see also* **intellect; sagacity**

gentiles ass (the gentile nations); Esther (the church of the gentiles); tamed falcon (a gentile convert to Christianity) • *attribute:* myrtle (gentiles converted by Jesus Christ)

gentility *flower language:* corn cockle;

pompon rose • *see also* **chivalry; gallantry**

gentlemen *attribute:* gold headed cane

gentleness deer; dove; Eve; fuchsia; gazelle; giraffe; linden; maiden; pigeon; roebuck; sheep; strawberry (gentle-heartedness); topaz (ardent love and gentleness); turtle dove; west wind • wisteria (the gentleness and devotion of womanhood) • *heraldry:* lamb; rose [flower] • *see also* **kindness; mildness; tenderness**

Gentleness personified *attribute:* lamb

geography five circles intertwined (the five continents: Asia, Europe, America, Africa, Australia)

geometry compasses [dividers] • *association:* D

Geometry personified *attributes:* compasses [dividers]; eagle; ferule; rule [measuring]; square [tool]; T-square

George, St. soldier with a dragon • *attributes:* armor with a red cross; broken lance; cauldron of boiling oil; dragon underfoot; helmet; horse; red Latin cross; sword and broken lance; white flag with a red cross; white shield with a red cross

Gerald of Auriliac, St. *attribute:* monastery model held in the hand

Gerald of Mayo, St. *attribute:* shamrock

Germanus of Constantinople, St. *attribute:* mirror with the image of the Virgin Mary

Germany *emblems:* beaver (formerly an emblem of Germany, now an emblem of Canada); bluebottle; cornflower; counterclockwise swastika (Nazi Germany); eagle; Maltese cross

germination black (germinal stage of a process); cauldron (the transmutation and germination of the baser forces of nature); corn [maize] (germination and growth); darkness (the germinant); night • *see also* **evolution; growth**

Gertrude, St. attributes: crown; lily; taper [wick]

Gervase and Protase, Saints two saints, one with a whip, one with a sword (St. Gervase and St. Protase, respectively)

Gervase, St. *attributes:* club [bat]; scourge [whip]

gestation, spiritual furnace; oven
Gethsemane angel holding a chalice (Christ's agony in Gethsemane); broken communion cup (Christ's agony in Gethsemane); olive tree, especially a gnarled tree; palm, cypress, and olive trees together; pointed cross emerging from a chalice
Gherardesca, Ugolina della old man dying in prison with dead children
Ghismonda *association:* cup with a heart in it
ghosts beans; dung (offensive to ghosts); firefly (a ghost of the dead, especially a dead warrior); purgative (the driving out of ghosts); shadow • *association:* sheet
ghoul hyena; rat
Gideon soldier kneeling before a fleece • *attributes:* fleece with bowl; pitcher [vessel] with light
gifts azalea (fatal gifts); manna (a free and valuable gift); bracelet (a gift to bind); gloves and ring, or gloves alone (traditional courting gifts); Magic [tarot] (gifts of the spirit); pomegranate (gifts of God) • *association:* U (receipt of a gift) • *Christianity:* hare: a Christian's haste to obtain divine gifts • *see also* **Holy Spirit; offerings**
Giles of Provence, St. man protecting a stag that has been shot by an arrow • *attributes:* crozier; hand pierced with arrows; hermitage
girls dabchick; dove (a girl 10 to 20 years of age); quail (a girl up to 10 years of age); white rose (girlhood) • *attribute:* braids (but note these are also the attribute of a courtesan) • *see also* **maidens; women; youth**
giving *see* **generosity**
gladiators *see* **warriors**
gladness Born on a Thursday, merry and glad (or, has far to go); girdle [cincture]; dove with ark (glad tidings); meadow; myrrh; Wednesday's child is merry and glad); white knight; wine • *flower language:* myrrh; spring crocus (youthful gladness) • *see also* **felicity; happiness**
gloom crooked fingers (sign of a crabbed disposition); December; ebony; ember; midnight; pine; shadow; tomb; vale • *see also* **despair; despondency; displeasure; melancholy**
glorification *see* **exaltation**

glory amaryllis; club suit [playing cards]; cicada (evanescent worldly glory); column [architectural] (especially a free standing column); hibiscus (short-lived glory); laurel; medal; pyramid (princely glory); smoke (the futility of earthly glory); sun; trumpet (glory; the yearning for glory); wings • *associations:* blue; bright yellow (divine wisdom, glory, and goodness); gold (the glory of God; the glory of faith triumphant); mandorla (spiritual glory); Rome (past glory); white • *flower language:* glory flower (glorious beauty); laurel; mountain laurel; Venice sumac (splendor) • *heraldry:* cherub; crescent (hope for greater glory); sun; tortoise (glorious development of family) • *see also* **grandeur; honor; magnificence**
Glory personified *attribute:* pyramid
gluttony Beelzebub; filled bowl; stomach; swine; vulture • *association:* the Netherlands
Gluttony personified *attributes:* bear; crown of vines; fruit in a bowl; hedgehog; swine; vine; wolf
Gnosticism eagle atop a ladder
God abandonment (loss of contact with God or nature); acacia thorn (the divine power to repel evil); almond (divine approval or favor); altar (the presence of God); amaranth (love of God excluding all other affections); amulet (the divine present in the worldly); angel, bird, cherub (messenger of God); angel with a scepter (divine authority); anointing with oil (endowing the soul with divine love); archangel (primordial divine power of the highest level); ark (the covenant God made with Noah and the church); Ark of the Covenant (the presence of God); arrow (the light of divine power); aspalathus (the wisdom of God); bite (a mark of divine love); black clerical garments (the hope of inner resurrection through service to God); bondage (man irrevocably tied to God and the universe); book (divine knowledge); breath (the divine element in man); burning bush (God appearing to Moses for the giving of the Law); butterfly (the unconscious attraction toward God); carnation, lamb (God's love); carpenter; cherry tree; crescent and many stars (God and the

heavenly host); dome (the love of God); dove with an olive branch (a soul that has made its peace with God); empty throne, flaming wheels with wings or eyes, Pole Star (the throne of God); flaming pillar or tree trunk (the God of light and wisdom); flaming sword (authority of God); Gordian knot, labyrinth (the difficulty of uniting oneself with one's spirit and with God and/or remoteness from one's spirit and from God); grail; hand emerging through a cloud (the omnipotent God); heaven (union with God); Leviathan (God's playfulness); lightning (act of God); moorings; nightmare (the longing of man for God); nuditas temporalis (worldly things abandoned in service to God); obelisk (finger of God); ostrich (one who trusts in God; man deserted by God); rainbow (God's covenant with man); rainbow and ark (God's covenant with man and Noah); Red Sea, Shiloah [pond in Jerusalem] (protection of God); returning to one's birthplace or homeland (the equivalent of dying in the positive sense of reintegration with the spirit of God); rose [flower]; seaweed; Shekinah (presence of God); spark; sphere; stole [religious garment] (submission to God's will); sun (eye of God); tabernacle on an altar (presence of God); thunder (voice of God); turtle dove (obedience to God's law); two-branched candelabrum; vine (the relationship of God and his people); vineyard (where God's children flourish) • *associations:* blue (divine contemplation); center; D; five; fifty (a special rapport with God); gold (the glory of God); hexagon (the six attributes of God, i.e., power, wisdom, majesty, love, mercy, and justice); long life (implies living in concord with God); red (the love of God); Sophia (creative spirit of God); three hundred (the breath of God); T; three; yellow (God the Son) • *attributes:* blue and red clothes (God's love and authority); gloves (used in medieval plays); white • *Christianity:* eagle (Jesus Christ as mediator between God and man); IHS on a cross (God's love for humanity revealed in Christ's death on the cross); potter's wheel (the faithful Christian's life shaped by God); stag (the faithful Christian long-

ing for God); white bird (a divine messenger); work in a vineyard (work of good Christians for God) • *emblems:* circle (monogram of God); finger pointed to the sky (one God); five-pointed star (the manifested nature of God); orb with a cross (recognition of God's ultimate dominion over the world); six-pointed star (God the creator; the omniscience of God); triangle with the apex up (the godhead); triple tiara (the three estates of God) • *flower language:* wood sorrel • *God the Father:* blue (association); church spires (the largest spire represents God the Father, the smaller spires his celestial offspring); eye, especially when in a triangle or above an altar; globe underfoot (attribute); hand descending from heaven; three-rayed nimbus (attribute); thumb (association); triangular nimbus (attribute) • *grace of God:* Born on a Tuesday, full of [God's] grace; eagle (the Christian soul strengthened by grace; divine grace descending); gazelle; hand raised with two fingers extended to give a blessing (the grace of Christ); light; manna; oil (especially olive oil); rain; salamander (the Christian who resists temptation through grace); starfish (the grace of God not quenched in a sea of sin) • *Judaism:* bramble (divine love); fever (punishment for disobedience); hawk (the providence of God); lily (trust in God); shofar (the call of God; supreme loyalty to God); tallith (when worn by the entire congregation in a synagogue: a sign that all men are equal before God); yarmulke (subservience to God) • *praise of God:* angel holding censer; angels with musical instruments; jasmine and palm; lute; organ [music] (praise of God from the church); wood sorrel (flower language) • *providence of God:* hair; hawk (Judaism); pomegranate; quail; rain; rainbow; raven, especially carrying a loaf of bread; sheaf • *punishment by God:* Assyria; fever (in Judaism, for disobedience); fire and brimstone [sulfur]; Gehenna; Hell; horde of grasshoppers or locusts; khamsin; leprosy (divine punishment, especially for pride); pine pitch; rider on a red horse (war as a punishment of God); scroll; volcano (divine punishment or destruction); vulture pecking at someone's liver in Hell • *word of God:* analogion; Bible; honey; L (association); lamp, especially an oil lamp; lighthouse; manna; pulpit; stag; tablet; unicorn; white horse, especially with a rider • *wrath of God:* angel holding a flaming sword; angel sheathing sword (God's wrath turned aside); cedar (occasionally, God's power to weaken the strong); earthquake (omen of divine anger); plague; press [tool]; scroll; smoke (anger and wrath of God); thunderbolt; wine press • *see also* **the Creator; deities; divinity; trinity; worship**

goddesses alb (an undertunic in Greece and Rome, later a woman's chemise, and then adopted for wear by priests of a goddess) • *association:* tabret (goddess feasts) • *attributes:* girdle [cincture] (fertility goddesses); grapes with wheat (earth goddesses); griffin with a ball underfoot (water goddesses); hooked nose (White Goddess); lion (earth goddesses); spindle (earth, vegetation goddesses); spider (fertility goddesses); violet hair (goddesses with a Spring festival) • *emblems:* crescent (virgin goddesses) *Great Goddess:* nine (association); white flower (attribute) • *love goddesses:* golden hair, lion (attributes) • strawberry (emblem) • *moon goddesses:* dog (emblem); dolphin, ibis (associations); spindle (attribute); wafer (sacrifice to moon goddesses) • *mother goddesses:* heifer, white cow (associations); sap (celestial milk of the mother goddess); star of the sea, usually seven-pointed (emblem)

Godiva, Lady nude woman on horseback, covered with long hair

gods ash tree (Yggdrasil, meeting place of the gods); Beelzebub (the worship of false gods); breeze (the voice of the gods); cake (offering to a god); centaurs (the teachers of the gods); giant bird (a creative deity); crow (a demiurgic power); elephant (the mount of deities); epileptic seizure (communion with a deity); fire, potter (creator deities); freckles (deities do not see or obey people with freckles); goat, raven, stag (messenger of a god); lion (avenging deity); mantle [clothing] covering a deity (the unrevealed aspects of the deity); mountain (place of communion with a deity); nymphs accompanying a deity (expression of a deity's ideas); puppet (man as the plaything of deities); reaper (death deity); veil (protection from a deity); well (access to earth gods, hence the custom of throwing money in a well to make a wish) • *associations:* beer, wine (in ancient times, beer was the drink of the gods, but it was later replaced by wine); cypress (nature deities); eagle (war deities); eight; fillet; four (occasionally); hearth (home deities such as Penates, Lares, etc.) red (dawn deities); two-wheeled plow • *attributes:* axe; conch shell, crown; dolphin, fish, hippocampus, seal [animal], trident (sea deities); crown of reeds, oar, reed, urn lying on its side (river deities); cup (Norse deities); dragon (beneficent Chinese deities); elephant (the mount of deities); hammer (thunder deities); nimbus (deities; deified Roman emperors); quiver (for arrows); seesaw (wind deities); north, trees (home of the gods); south (to face south was to speak with the authority of the gods); spectacles [eyeglasses] (twin deities); temple; three eyes; throne (seat of a deity) • *days associated with gods:* Sunday (Helios; Sol); Monday (Diana; Luna); Tuesday (Mars; Tiu); Wednesday (Mercury, Woden); Thursday (Jupiter; Thor); Friday (Freya; Venus); Saturday (Saturn) • *Egypt:* boat (the throne of a god); palm tree (residence of the gods); • *emblem:* zigzag (thunder deities) • *fertility gods:* cone (association); cow (attribute); cypress (association); plant [botany] (association); scarecrow • *sky gods:* blue eyes (attribute); column [architecture], especially a free-standing column; falcon (Egypt—attribute); hanging [execution] (sacrifice to a sky deity); light complexion (attribute); necklace (sky goddesses); short legs (attribute); whirlwind (the angry voice of a sky deity); yelow hair (attribute) • *supreme gods:* face; father; flame; glory [luminous glow around the entire body] (attribute); light complexion (attribute); net (attribute); oak (emblem); Pole Star (throne of the supreme deity); seated man or woman (supreme deity, but may also be his or her representative); six-pointed star (the androgynous nature of the supreme deity); sky (dwelling of the supreme deity); sphere; spider; thunder (the voice of the supreme deity); thunderbolt (attribute); tower • *underworld gods:* blackbird; cypress (association); dark complexion (attribute); disheveled hair (attribute); harlequin (association) • *see also* **the creator; God; goddesses** and the names of specific deities, such as **Athena, Vulcan,** etc.

gold lion • *associations:* excrement (associated with gold, and with what is highest in value); yellow

Golden Age palace of mirrors, glass or crystal that suddenly appears (primitive awareness of the Golden Age) • *association:* arbutus

Golden Age personified *attributes:* acorn; crown of flowers; olive branch

Goliath youth holding large head (David with Goliath's head) • *attribute:* sling, especially with five stones (David and his battle with Goliath)

good *see* **goodness**

good and evil balances [scales] (any binary function, such as good/evil, life/death, etc.); centaur (man torn between good and evil); feathered serpent (duality, such as good and evil, rain and drought, etc.); half man/half goat; Pegasus (innate capacity for spiritualization and changing evil into good); strawberry (good hidden under evil); war (struggle of good against evil); winnow, winnowing (the separation of good from evil) • *associations:* P, R, Z (potential for good and evil) • *emblems:* six-pointed star; yin and yang

good fortune *see* **fortune**

Good Friday *association:* black (the liturgical color for Good Friday)

Good Government personified *attribute:* scepter

good health *see* **health**

good luck *see* **fortune**

good nature *see* **benignity**

good omens *see* **foretokens and signs**

Good Samaritan *attribute:* napkin with cruse of wine

Good Shepherd sheep on a man's shoulders

good will *see* **benevolence**

good works *see* **benevolence**

goodbye *see* **farewell**

goodness beryl; Born on a Sunday, you'll never want (or, lucky and happy, good and gay); bread; caduceus (good conduct); castle of light (the abode of a heavenly power, or a good power); cherry tree (goodheartedness); crane [bird] (good life and works); divorce (the apparent or delusive separation of goodness from truth); feeding (dispensing goodness to the mind and soul); flour; flower; hail destroying crops (falsity destroying truth and goodness); Hermit [tarot]; hyssop; incense (spiritual goodness); lamp linen; manna; myrrh (natural good and wisdom); rudder (moral rectitude); rue [plant]; sun (potential good); three feathers (goodness in thought, word, and deed); topaz (divine love and goodness); wood (celestial goodness in its lowest corporeal plane) • *associations:* bright yellow (divine wisdom, goodness and glory); eight (good deeds); little finger; orange-yellow (divine goodness or wisdom); • *China:* unicorn (emblem of perfect good) • *flower language:* apple blossom (fame speaks one great and good); goose foot; sweet basil • *see also* **good and evil; morality; righteousness; virtue**

Gospel cresset; cross on an orb (the triumph of the Gospel); double-headed lectern (the Gospels and the Epistles); eagle (the inspiration of the Gospel); four rivers gushing from a rock; four scrolls; four streams running down a hill with a lamb with a nimbus (the four Gospels, with the hill as the church and the lamb as Christ); four urns with water flowing from them (the four Gospels and the four evangelists); gargoyle on the outside of a church (evil passion driven out of man by the Gospel); lizard (the Gospel's illuminating light); mill; quatrefoil (the four Gospels); torch; well; willow • *association:* four

gossip barber; bowl; burning or tingling ears, especially the right ear (someone is speaking spitefully of you); dandelion seeds floating free; ear; tongue • *flower language:* cobaea • *see also* **chatter; scandal**

government rudder; young man (the governed) • *China:* green sedan chair (attribute of a lower government official); unicorn (wise government); wild pear tree (good government) • *emblem:* rudder with a caduceus and cornucopia (the government of Caesar) • *Judaism:* bee (government in good order) • *see also* **Good Government personified**

governors of Roman provinces *attribute:* crown of laurel

grace of God *see* **God**

gracefulness birch; box tree; cat; cowslip; daffodil; elm; fuchsia; gazelle; greyhound; hart; hind [deer]; jasmine; lily; maiden; Mercury [god] (manly grace); Narcissus; rue [plant]; stag; Sunday's child is full of grace; swan; tiger; • *associations:* seven; twelve; two (tact) • *flower language:* cowslip (winning grace); multiflora rose; yellow jasmine (grace and elegance) • *heraldry:* pearl, usually on a ring (high grace); linden (often only the leaf is represented; star • *see also* **elegance; poise**

Graces, Three *see* **Three Graces**

Grail, Holy golden cup

Grammar personified woman watering plants from a pitcher • *attribute:* ferule; hen; wand; whip

grandeur ash tree; cactus; House of God [tarot] (megalomania); king (the grandeur of universal and abstract man); ocean; plane tree • *China:* unicorn • *heraldry:* castle • *see also* **glory; magnificence; majesty**

grandiloquence *see* **eloquence; talk**

Granida and Dafilo kneeling youth offering a shell as a cup to a maiden

gratification Scylla (the immediate expectation of the fruits of action as an impedance to moral progress)

gratitude dancing; flax; ibis; lion; mouse; sunflower • *flower language:* agrimony; dahlia (my gratitude exceeds your care); white bellflower • *see also* **thanksgiving**

Gratitude personified *attribute:* beans

the grave bandages (the winding sheet of the tomb); cave; closet; ditch; earth [soil] (the great sepulcher); pebble, potsherd (thrown on the grave of a suicide); whale; white pebble

(graveside gift for rebirth and resurrection); womb • *association:* elm (cemeteries) • *flower language:* basil • *see also* **burial; funerals**

gravity eyebrows set close to eyes; lead [metal] (gravity and density, especially in a spiritual sense); millstone

gray *association:* seven

Great Britain *emblems:* bulldog; lion

Great Goddess *association:* nine • *attributes:* white flower

Great Mother dove (the cosmic All Mother); earth [soil]; Eve (the mother of all things); forest; lioness • *associations:* abyss; pot (particularly earthen) • *emblem:* dog • *see also* **Mother Earth; Mother Nature**

Great Spirit holly oak

greatness acorn (latent greatness or strength); ass; reed (humiliation of greatness) • *association:* Rome • *flower language:* apple blossom (fame speaks one great and good)

greed camel; carnivorous bird; claw; dog; fish; fly [insect]; horse leech (unending greed); mantis (cruelty and greed disguised by a hypocritical attitude of prayer or religiosity); mill; palm of the hand being itchy (mercenary intent); parrot; plover; swine; wolf • *China:* wolf • *see also* **avarice; money**

Greek Orthodox Church *emblem:* Eastern cross

green *associations:* spring [season]; two

Green Knight *association:* holly

greeting *see* **salutation**

gregariousness kangaroo; pelican; rabbit; rook [bird]; sheep; tea (sociability) • *see also* **friendliness**

Gregory of Nazianus, St. *attribute:* epigonation

Gregory the Great, St. praying pope with a monk, surrounded by flames; praying saint before an image or vision of Christ bearing a cross • *attributes:* church model being carried; cross with two horizontal arms (not to be confused with either the cross of Lorraine, or the eastern cross); crozier terminating with a cross with two horizontal arms; dove; feather; scroll with Gregorian music; scroll with the words "Ora pro nobis Deum"; shroud pierced with knife and showing blood; triple tiara

grief absinthe (both the plant and the flower); black gloves; bladder; briars; dancing; dandelion; hand or hands laid on one's own head; lemon; lily; marigold; marjoram; mutilation; opal (drives out grief); pine; rending of garments; tear [weeping]; thorn • *associations:* black; brown; gray; U • *flower language:* aloe; harebell; marigold • *Judaism:* torn garment (grief and mourning) • *Orient:* marigolds and poppies (soothing of grief) • *see also* **mourning; sorrow**

Grim Reaper *attribute:* hourglass; scythe

grocers bottle with colored liquid (sign of a pharmacist, later also of grocers and confectioners)

grossness *see* **offensiveness; rudeness**

groups branding (membership in or separation from a group)

growth cedar; clockwise spiral; clockwise swastika; corn [maize] (germination and growth); cremation (destruction of what is base to make way for what is superior); Empress [tarot]; mustard plant or oak (great growth from small beginnings); oak; plantain (food of the multitude seeking Christian growth or salvation); seed; stag; tetractys (birth, growth, and death); willow (quick growth) • *associations:* five; green • *spiritual growth:* doctor, nurse, poet, priest (promoters of spiritual growth); nest (haven for spiritual growth); pilgrimage (process of spiritual growth) • *see also* **development; evolution; expansion; germination**

guardianship angel with one hand extended; cherub; dragon (guardian of fertility symbols, such as gold, jewels, etc.); eyes (guardian of the inner man); lizard; seraph; shepherd (guardian of ancient wisdom); serpent (guardian of the springs of life, immortality, the superior riches of the spirit); teeth (guardian of the inner person); wyvern • *China:* dragon • *heraldry:* key • *see also* **safety**

Guatemala *emblem:* quetzel

guidance brook (spiritual guidance); compass [direction]; dolphin; index finger (fortunate guidance); lamp; lodestone; navigator, sailor (guide of the soul); Mercury [god]; pentagon; priest (spiritual mentor); rudder; shepherd; staff; star (especially spiritual guidance); sun (guiding light); torch (spiritualization through illumination and guidance) • *China:* white rooster • *flower language:* star of Bethlehem • *heraldry:* elephant (willingness to be guided) • *see also* **leadership**

guile *see* **cunning**

guilessness *see* **ingenuousness; innocence**

guilt abandonment; albatross; black pebble; blood; harpy (guilt and punishment); loss; Furies (guilt turned to destruction; guilt turned upon itself to the destruction of the guilty); washing (purification from guilt); white pebble (not guilty) • *see also* **remorse; shame**

gullibility *see* **fools**

H

H *association:* eight

Habakkuk *attribute:* model of a temple

habits handcuffs (bad habits); mill (habitual and uncreative thinking)

Hades *associations:* antique key; asphodel • *attributes:* helmet; two pronged fork • *see also* **Hell; infernality; underworld**

Hagai *associations:* temple under construction; timbers

hair maidenhair fern (pubic hair)

Halloween goblin; ghost; witch • *emblem:* jack o'lantern; pumpkin

Hamlet *attribute:* skull

handicaps crutch (handicap, especially temporary) • *see also* **blindness; cripples**

Hanged Man [tarot] *association:* L

hanging [execution] elder tree (in legend: the tree that Judas hanged himself on); noose; rope; scaffold • *association:* mandrake (thought to grow under the gallows of murderers) • *see also* **execution**

Hannibal *association:* elephant

Hanover, House of *heraldry:* white horse

Hanukkah eight-branched menorah, especially when displayed in the home or synagogue

happiness amethyst; apple tree (man's happiness); blue flower (spiritual happiness); bluebird; bluebottle; Born on a Sunday, you'll never want (or, lucky and happy, good and gay); breasts; cicada; confetti; cotton blossoms; crane [bird]; garden; grail (source of happiness); house chimney; leaf; lily of the valley; maple (bourgeois earthly happiness); maple in the autumn (past happiness); morning (pristine happiness); myrtle; opal (increases happiness in love); peridot; rice; ruby; ship plowing waves; sugar (a plea for happiness); smoke coming from the chimney of a house; summer (extended peace or happiness); swallow [bird] (contentment in poverty); tunicle (contentment and joy of heart); two eyes: one opened and one closed (happiness and sorrow); vine; water buffalo; Wednesday's child is merry and glad; white stone • *associations:* A; bat [animal]; C; Q; red (China); six; sixteen; sixty; three; Venus [planet] • *flower language:* bridal rose; Cape jasmine (transport of joy; I am too happy); houstonia (contentment); lily of the valley (return of happiness); meadow saffron (my happiest days are past); mugwort; spiderwort, especially Virginia spiderwort (transient happiness); sweet sultan (supreme happiness); vernal grass (poor but happy); volkemania (may you be happy); woodbine [monthly honeysuckle] (domestic happiness); yellow violet (rural happiness) • *heraldry:* ass; camel; emerald; green; ship; vine • *domestic happiness:* butterfly; F (association); holly; japonica (China); martin [bird]; onyx (promotes happiness in marriage and friendship); stork (domestic happiness and peace); two fish; woodbine [monthly honeysuckle] (flower language) • *see also* **bliss; contentment; felicity; gaiety; gladness; joy; love; merriment**

harbingers *see* **foretokens** **and** **signs**

hardheartedness *see* **coldheartedness; cruelty; hardness; meanness**

hardiness crocus

hardness adamant [mythical stone]; brass; copper; diamond [gemstone]; ebony; iron; ivory; millstone; stone • *flower language:* ebony (you are hard); scratch weed • *see also* **firmness**

hardship *see* **trouble**

hare *association:* rabbit

harlots *see* **prostitutes**

harmlessness *see* **innocence**

harmony good digestion (a sign of harmony with God and nature); healing (the spiritual process by which certain qualities are harmonized and spiritualized); lyre or onion (harmonious union of cosmic forces); music (harmony; harmony arising from chaos; harmony of the universe); Lovers [tarot] (harmony of inner and outer life); musician (one in harmony with divine nature); nightingale; organ [instrument]; stone (harmonious reconciliation of self); swastika with straight ends, surrounded by a circle or triangle • *associations:* blue; Libra; six; sixty; twelve • *China:* fish • *heraldry:* stag (one who loves harmony and justice); swan (one who loves harmony) • *see also* **agreements; concord; disharmony**

harpies *attributes:* golden apple, golden balls (attributes of the harpies that accompany Avarice personified)

harshness *see* **brutality**

harvest autumn; copper; flail; holly; press [tool]; rising of the Pleiades (early or spring harvest); scythe; sheaf with a sickle; sickle; threshing; windmill • *association:* October (harvest; resowing)

haste almond; bird; Hamlet • *flower language:* woodbine (I will not answer hastily) • *see also* **speed**

hat *association:* hood (shares in the symbolism of the hat and head)

hate eel; half man/half goat (love and hate); hippopotamus; Lovers [tarot] (antagonism); rat; spade [shovel];

Strength [tarot] (triumph of love over hate); winter • *association:* yellow • *flower language:* basil; fumitory; St. John's wort (animosity) • *see also* **malice**

Hathor *association:* heifer

Hatred personified *attribute:* scorpion

haughtiness amaryllis; crane [bird]; nose in the air; raised eyebrows; swan • *flower language:* double larkspur; tall sunflower

haven nest (haven for growth of the spirit)

Hawaii *associations:* grass skirt; kukui tree (Molokai Island); lei; palm tree; pineapple; ukelele

hawks *association:* falcon (may partake of the symbolism of hawks, with which they are frequently confused)

head [anatomy] attic; belfry; copestone; doctor holding a pincers with a stone (quack operation for stones in the head); globe • *associations:* hat, hood (both share in the symbolism of the head); Mars

healing coral necklace; dog; hazel; herb. Judgment [tarot]; oil; olive tree or branch; peony; pine cone; serpent (the power to heal); serpent sloughing off its skin; wings • *China:* red (association) • *flower language:* balm of Gilead; European sweet brier (I wound to heal); hazel; marsh mallow

health agate; bell; caduceus (health of the body and spirit); corn [maize]; dahlia; lion; lizard; malachite; morning (bringer of health); pearl; signs of wear (poor health); Solomon's seal (amulet for good health); urn • *associations:* five (health and love); eight (healthiness); marriage on a Tuesday; orange [color]; pink [color] (good health); S; seven • *China:* five bats [animals] (the blessings of longevity, wealth, health, virtue, and a natural death); monkey (said to have the power to drive away evil and, hence, bring success, health, and protection) • *flower language:* Iceland moss • *heraldry:* emerald; fish; green

Health personified *emblem:* sage [herb]

hearing mole [animal] (keen hearing)

Hearing personified *attributes:* lute; organ [instrument]; stag

heart anthurium; cabinet; cave; coffer; goblet (the human heart, especially when covered); knocking (heartbeat); lotus; peach with a leaf attached (the heart and tongue); pear; raspberry (the human heart); rose [flower]; Strength personified standing on a wine press (the conquest of the spirit over the heart); tunicle (joy and contentment of heart); white gloves (pure heart) • *associations:* F; O [letter]; R; sun • *flower language:* crimson polyanthus (the heart's mystery); deep red carnation (alas, my poor heart); frankincense (faithful heart); red and white roses together (warmth of heart); spindle tree (your image is engraved in my heart; your charms are engraved in my heart); water lily (purity of heart); white rose (heart of ignorant love)

heartache opal (prevents heartache and fainting) • *flower language:* cranberry

hearth ember

heat cockroach; russet [cloth]; south wind; sulfur (vital heat); summer; vulture • *association:* orange [color] • *China:* odd numbers (association) • *Egypt:* lizard (devouring heat) • *see also* **warmth**

heathenism *see* **paganism**

heaven acanthus; arch; beanstalk; church spire with a finger pointed to the sky (reminder of heaven); circle; disease (pathway to heaven); dome (the canopy of heaven); eagle with a lion's head (conflict between heaven and hell); father; fir (the elect who are in heaven); harp (the mystic ladder to heaven; worship in heaven); hyacinth [gemstone] (the desire for heaven); jasmine (heavenly felicity); Jerusalem; leaven (kingdom of heaven); man; meteorite (heavenly creative fire); milk and honey (heavenly food); nest; palm tree (martyrdom to attain heaven); paradise; pentagon (heavenly wisdom); pillar, sometimes four pillars (support of heaven); Pole Star (eye of heaven); rain (spiritual influences from heaven); sapphire (heavenly truth, meditation, reward); ship of fools (sailing or living as an end in itself and not in the sense of seeking a safe arrival in heaven); shooting star (heavenly omen); spider; spire, thrush (aspiration to heaven);

squirrel (heavenly meditation); sun; walled city (the heavenly Jerusalem) • *associations:* blue; bull; gold; harp; lark; stag; three • *bliss of heaven:* fruit; lily; wreath of roses • *China:* orange [fruit] (an imperial sacrifice to heaven) • *entrance to heaven:* door; gate, especially of pearl or gold; gold key (key to heaven's gate); iron key (locks heaven's gate); rood screen; Solomon's seal (key to the kingdom of heaven); St. Peter (holds the keys to heaven's gate) two brass mountains • *flower language:* flowering reed (confidence in heaven) • • *heavenly beings:* light complexion, white garment, wings (associations) • *ladder to heaven:* beanstalk; harp; weaving • *messenger of heaven:* angel; Mercury [god]; seraph • *see also* **paradise; Valhalla**

heaven and earth angel (heavenly influences acting upon the earth); communion rail, ocean (separation of heaven and earth); cranberry (the divine seed present in all lower nature); drum (the mediator between heaven and earth); god naked to the waist (the top half represents the sky, the clothed bottom half represents the earth); House of God [tarot] (the power of the heavenly over the earthly); Jordan River (the flow of life essence from heaven to earth); key of gold with a key of silver; lyre (the relationship between heaven and earth); pumpkin; two linked rings, one above the other; zither (synthesis of heaven and earth) • *association:* odd numbers • *connection of heaven and earth* beanstalk (ladder to heaven); bridge; center; chains; column [architectural]; cross; eight (association); golden chain (the spirit binding earth to heaven); hanging bell; harp (the mystic ladder to heaven); king and queen together; ladder; mast; Milky Way (pathway to heaven); mountain; pillar; rainbow; scepter; sigma, sigmoid; smell; spindle; spire; snail's track; tower; tree (connection of heaven, earth, and the underworld); weaving (ladder to heaven) • *intersection of heaven and earth:* altar; church; crossroads (intersection of any binary form: space/time; body/spirit, heaven/earth, etc.); temple

heavens bell; canopy; eagle; mill,

spinning wheel (the revolving heavens); seven-branched menorah (the seven celestial spheres); single arch; starred girdle [cincture]; tent • *associations:* cornflower; Wednesday (the day on which heavenly bodies were created); zero [ether] • *see also* **sky**

heaviness elephant (ponderousness); millstone (heavy burden) • *association:* seven (heavy responsibilities)

Hebe *attributes:* eagle and jug; pitcher [vessel]

Hecate three faces in the moon: Kore, Artemis, and Hecate • *association:* purple foot • *attributes:* dagger; key; lash; lion; torch; whip

Hecla, St. *attribute:* flaming pillar

Hector chariot with a body dragging behind (the victory of Achilles over Hector)

hedonism ship of fools (sailing or living as an end in itself and not in the sense of seeking a safe arrival in heaven) • *associations:* Aeolian harp (those given to wine, women, and luxurious living); five; Greece • *see also* **pleasure; sensuality**

height *see* **elevation**

heirs *see* **inheritance**

Helen of Troy young man bearing a maiden off to a harbor (the abduction of Helen of Troy)

Helena, St. *attributes:* crown; hammer (especially a hammer and nails); Latin cross borne by angels; model of a sepulchre

Heliades a group of maidens, arms upraised and sprouting poplar branches • *association:* amber

Helios *see* **Sol; sun**

Hell cave; deepness; descending stairs (journey to Hell or the infernal world); fire (the torments of Hell); fire and brimstone (the vengeance of Hell); Gehenna; lion-headed eagle (conflict between heaven and Hell); pine pitch (punishment in Hell); pit; sulfur (the fumes of Hell); whale; worm • *associations:* adamant [mythical stone]; brimstone; fire; nine; noise; red • *entrance to Hell:* brass gate; descending stairs; open jaws of a whale • *see also* **devils; hades; infernality; Satan; underworld**

Hellespontic sibyl *attributes:* cross; nails [for wood]

help bird (supernatural assistance);

mule (mutual help among underdogs) • *association:* two (helpfulness) • *flower language:* juniper • *heraldry:* ship (succor in extremity) • *see also* **relief; support**

Help personified *attribute:* stork

helplessness broken sword; fawn; hands laid on one's own head; hands thrown up in the air; infant; kitten; scarecrow; sheep • *China:* swallow's nest (insecurity)

Hephaestus *see* **Vulcan**

Hera *see* **Juno**

heralds *attributes:* caduceus; hazel wand • *see also* **foretokens and signs**

Hercules infant holding a snake, or wrestling with two snakes; infant in the path of a plow; man attacking a horse with a club; man wrestling with a lion; soldier accompanied by Mercury [god] • *associations:* black poplar; cypress; death on a funeral pyre; thumb • *attributes:* bow with quiver (occasionally); caduceus; club [bat]; lion skin; mace [weapon]; ox and ass yoked together drawing a plow; tambourine (attribute of Hercules when dressed as a woman)

heresy and heretics centaur; dog; dragon; frog; Hydra (the prolific nature of heresy, sin, and false doctrine); idol (apostasy); locust [insect]; mule; ostrich; reptile; wolf; woodpecker • *attributes:* red-hot sepulcher; yellow garments (Middle Ages) • *Christianity:* ape (early Christianity); dragon; ship on a stormy sea (the church surviving persecution, schism, and heresy) • *see also* **doctrine**

Heresy personified *attributes:* dragon; scorpion

hermaphroditism arum; swan; Virgo

Hermaphroditus lovers in a pool

Hermes *see* **Mercury [god]**

Hermit [tarot] *association:* I [letter]

hermits cabin (hermitage); crow • *associations:* milkwort; owl • *attributes:* lantern; loincloth or other garment of palm leaves (occasionally, and especially desert hermits); long hair; skull (hermit saints)

Hero and Leander woman on a seashore with a torch (the woman is Hero)

heroes eagle (heroic nobility); king (a concentrated father and hero image); prince; Punch and Judy (the anti-hero

overcoming learning, domesticity, death, and the Devil); sun; white horse (the hero's steed); white knight; young man • *association:* light complexion • *attributes:* golden hair, lion skin, phallus (sun heroes); ribbon knotted to form a circle

heroines *association:* light complexion

heroism breastplate; Hercules (expiation of sins through heroic striving and heroism); ointment; white flower; wren • *association:* Rome (heroic death)

Hesione man chained to a rock, attacked by a monster

Hestia *attribute:* lamp

the hidden black knight; golden fleece, occasionally a white fleece (hidden treasure); nuts (the hidden; hidden riches); papyrus; tower (hidden truth) • *association:* nine (hidden factors)

hiding arch, bush, rock, roof (places for lurking, ambush, spying, illicit love); dabchick; fox; serpent; turtle dove (seclusion) • *association:* Pisces (seclusion) • *see also* **privacy; secrecy**

hierarchies *association:* seven (the transformation and unification of all hierarchical orders)

high priest *emblem:* pomegranate

High Priest [tarot] *association:* H

High Priestess [tarot] *association:* B

highness *see* **elevation**

Hilary of Poitiers, St. *attributes:* child; stick; three books with a writing pen

Hilda, St. *attribute:* three coiled serpents

hindrances *see* **obstacles**

Hippolytus, St. soldier • *attribute:* bunch of keys

history Clio; Janus (the past and the present together; history and prophecy) • *see also* **past**

History personified Clio • *attributes:* cube; tablet with a stylus; wings

Hitler, Adolf *association:* six hundred and sixty-six

hoarding squirrel

hoaxes *see* **jests**

holiness agate; angel; asperges; Bible; clouds; crossroads (intersection or conjunction or any binary form: sacred/profane, space/time, heaven/earth, etc.); desert; diamond [gemstone];

fasting; holly; lotus (the supremely sacred flower); myrrh (sacred ointment); pomegranate; round loaf of bread (sacred food); sandalwood; sky; spikenard; tamed falcon (a holy man); verbena • *associations:* blue; forty; fourteen; gold; Jerusalem; one hundred and ten [110]; Rome; seven; twelve • *attributes:* circular nimbus (sacred persons no longer living); square or rectangular nimbus (holy persons still living) • *Bible:* brass • *China:* lotus (a sacred flower); red-faced person (theater) • *Egypt:* goat (a sacred animal) • *Orient:* nimbus

hollowness bubble; mask

Holy Family *associations:* ass, date [fruit], fallen idol, pyramid and star (the flight into Egypt)

Holy Ghost *see* **Holy Spirit**

Holy Grail golden cup

Holy Innocents children holding palm leaves; soldiers killing babies (slaying of the Holy Innocents)

Holy Roman Empire *emblem:* double-headed eagle

Holy Scripture *see* **Scripture**

Holy Spirit columbine (especially prior to the 16th century); double-headed eagle; dove, usually white (especially when shown descending and/or with a three-rayed nimbus, or star around its head); dove on a font cover (regeneration through the Holy Spirit); flame; goose with flames coming from its mouth; hand raised in blessing with first two fingers extended (love of God and communion with the Holy Spirit); Mercury [god]; miter [hat] (the flame of the Holy Spirit); nine-pointed star; rushing wind (occasionally); sails; sanctuary lamp when lit (the presence of the Holy Spirit in Catholic, Anglican and some other Christian churches); seven-pointed star; squirrel (striving of the Holy Spirit); winged wheel • *associations:* blue; fifty; index finger; orange [color]; Pentecost (the descent of the Holy Spirit to the Apostles in particular and mankind in general); S • *attributes:* red; three-rayed nimbus • *nine gifts of the Holy Spirit:* [the nine gifts as listed in Galatians 5:22-23, are love, joy, peace, patience, gentleness, goodness, faith, meekness, and temperance] nine; nine flames; nine-pointed star; nine stars • *seven*

gifts of the Holy Spirit: [the seven gifts as listed in Revelation 5:12 are power, riches, wisdom, strength, honor, glory, and blessing] columbine with seven blooms; septfoil; seven; seven-branched menorah; seven doves; seven flames; seven grains; seven lamps; seven-pointed star; seven stars • *six gifts of the Holy Spirit:* [the six gifts as listed in Isaiah 11:2 are wisdom, understanding, counsel, might, knowledge, and fear of the Lord] six (but can also be used for the six sins against the Holy Spirit); six flames • *see also* **trinity**

homage incense (homage to a deity); linen

home hearth (also an attribute of home deities); nest; rubbing a stone into a round shape (perfecting a home for the self) • *association:* O [letter] • *China:* mulberry tree (the comforts of home)

home rule two keys crossed

Homer old man beside youth who has a tablet and stylus (the old man is Homer); old man playing a viol covered with laurel • *attribute:* crown of laurel

homesickness cairngorm

homicide *see* **killing; murder**

homosexuality lisping; pansy (a male homosexual); transvestitism (a sign of homosexuality); water fly (an effeminate homosexual) • *association:* lilac [color]; pink [color] • *see also* **effeminacy**

honesty ass; compasses [dividers] (right conduct); honesty [plant]; open book; square [tool] • *China:* man with a black face (on the stage: a humble but honest person) • *heraldry:* lozenge [shape] • *see also* **candor; sincerity; truthfulness**

honor beard; beech; being carried on the shoulders or in a chair; blue rose (martial honor); bouquet; bowing; burial (honoring the dead); column [architectural] (especially when free-standing); cowherd (honored in Greece; dishonored in Egypt and Great Britain); ermine; golden chain; gong; hexagonal nimbus (honor one degree below a saint); honey; medal; palace; red carpet; square or rectangular nimbus (attribute of a person honored while still living); umbrella;

wreath on the head • *heraldry:* cherub; crescent (high honors, especially in the Crusades); head (honor for special services); lance (defense of honor; palm tree (royal honor); Pegasus (energy leading to honor); seraph; spear • *see also* **distinction; exaltation; glory; integrity; merit; respect; salute**

hope almond; anchor; bird in a cage (hope of freedom; hope of salvation); bluebottle (hope in love); breasts; broken column (frustrated hope); bubble (fragile hope); candle; Christmas (renewal of love and hope); cross with anchor and heart (faith, hope and charity, respectively); crossed fingers; daisy; emerald; empty chair (undying hope); fir; flaming torch (hope of resurrection); green; green eyes; infant; iris [flower]; jasmine (divine hope); match [fire]; opal (gives hope and self-confidence); parsley (hope of redemption); pomegranate flower; rabbit; rainbow; rose [flower] (messianic hope); sapphire; scepter and censer (messianic hope); scythe (hopes for renewed rebirth); seed; ship; sieve; spider (hope and despair); stars; stole [religious garment] (hope of immortality); swallow [bird]; three feathers passing through a ring (faith, hope, and charity); tower; web (false trust or hope) • *associations:* blue; E; eighty (enduring hope); three • *Bible:* carnelian (emblem of hope and patience) • *Druidism:* three feathers (faith, hope and the Light of the World) • *flower language:* coronella (may success crown your wishes); flowering almond; hawthorn; snowdrop; spring crocus (pleasures of hope); spruce pine (hope in adversity) • *heraldry:* cinquefoil [plant]; clover; crescent (hope for greater glory); emerald; green • *Judaism:* honey and apples eaten at the New Year (the hope for sweetness and joy, respectively, in the future); five (ancient association); matzo; • *see also* **aspiration; wishing**

Hope personified *attributes:* basket with fruit or flowers; crow; flower (occasionally); ship; sickle

hopelessness partridge (hopelessness of worldly endeavor) • *flower language:* great or major convolvulus (extinguished hope); love-lies-bleeding (hopeless, not heartless); yellow tulip (hopeless love)

Horatio [Horatius Cocles] soldier fighting enemy on bridge

Horn, Cape *see* **Cape Horn**

horror aspen; Gorgon (a condition beyond the endurance of the conscious mind) • *flower language:* cereus; dragonwort; mandrake; serpentine cactus; snake's foot • *see also* **alarm; fear; terror**

horse hippogryph (combines the favorable aspects of both the horse and lion) • *association:* horseshoe (associated with a horse's vitality and sexual potency)

Horus eagle; five-pointed star

Hosea *association:* Trumpet of Zion • *attributes:* lion; mantle [clothing] that is cast off; shattered idol; skull

hospitality bough; bread; breaking of bread; closed gate (inhospitality); hearth; holly; house; linden; multiple arches; oak; oak wreath; ointment; open door or gate; pillow; roof; salt • *associations:* heart suit [playing cards]; orange [color] • *flower language:* oak • *heraldry:* cherry tree; tent; vine • *see also* **conviviality; friendliness; welcome**

Hospitality personified *attribute:* cornucopia

the Host biscuit (the Host, distributed without love); tabernacle on an altar (the reserved Host); vigil candle or sanctuary lamp (the presence of the Host at the altar in Catholic, Anglican and some other Christian churches); wafer

hotheadedness *see* **anger**

house hut (shares both house and tree symbolism) • *see also* **home**

House of God [tarot] *association:* P

housewives broom [for sweeping]; placed by the door of a cottage (the woman of the house is not at home); goose (the good housewife); sewing, sweeping (typical activities of a housewife) • *attributes:* broom [for sweeping]; kerchief on the head; ladle; needle • *see also* **wives**

Hubert, St. *attributes:* stag with a crucifix between his antlers; horse

hubris *see* **pride**

Hugh of Grenoble, St. *attribute:* three flowers held in the hand

humanity earthenware; engine, dynamo (the inhumane forces of modern society); myrtle (humaneness); Neptune [god] (the negative aspect of spirit and of humanity); ogre (prehuman savage life); reptile (lack of human warmth); rock (the spirit of human life); Sisyphus (senseless human endeavor); spider web (human frailty); tailor (imperfect humanity) • *associations:* middle finger; nine, X (humaneness) • *flower language:* French willow (humanity and bravery); oak leaf

humbleness bowing; broom [plant]; bulrushes (the humble faithful who abide with Christ); cottage (the humble life); grass (humble usefulness); hind [deer] (low birth); lentil; meadow; rabbit; strawberries and violets (the truly spiritual are always humble); striking sails; violet [flower] (humble life); weather cock on a church, especially when shown crowing (St. Peter, his denial and repentance, hence, a reminder to be humble) • *China:* man with a black face (on the stage: a humble but honest man) • *flower language:* broom [plant] • *see also* **insignificance; lower classes; modesty**

humiliation ashes and dust (deep humiliation); branding; cloak; clouds; ear being cut off; flint (indifference to insult); gallows, gibbet, hanging, tickling (disgraceful deaths); hair being cut off; pointing (an affront); reed (humiliation of greatness) • *association:* yellow • *heraldry:* chains (the refusal to be defamed or humiliated) • *see also* **mockery; satire; shame**

humility amethyst; ant; ashes; asphodel; ass; bare breasts; bare feet; basin, or basin and ewer (the humility of Christ's love); black clerical garments; carry sandals; cincture; clerical turned collar; coat or cloak of cat skin, mouse skin, or the skin of an ass; convolvulus; daisy; dove; fern (solitary humility); foot; heather; hyssop; kneeling; lark (the humility of the priesthood); lily of the valley; lying prone; manger (humility from which greatness arises); moss; mouse; ox; pansy; pavement; reed; rush [plant]; sandals; shoes; snail; sparrow; tonsure; washing someone else's feet • *asso-ciations:* black; black and white together (the humility and purity of life, respectively); blue; gray; violet [color]; white • *Christianity:* columbine • *flower language:* field lilac; small bindweed • *Greece:* ball [sphere] (in classical times) • *heraldry:* blue; cherry tree; fish

Humility personified *attribute:* lamb.

humor *see* **frivolity; wit**

hunger swallow [bird]; wolf • *see also* **appetite; famine; voracity**

hunters hound; Orion; • *attributes:* bow and arrow (weapon of the hunter and of the common soldier); lance; scarlet coat • *heraldry:* squirrel (a great hunter)

hunting bow and arrow; falcon; forest; greyhound • *association:* scourge [whip] • *heraldry:* eagle's claw (in some parts of Germany: free hunting rights); falcon, especially when bird is hooded (hunting skill); grouse (a forbearer who fought a gallant duel or was a great hunter); hare (hunting skill); hood for a falcon (hunting prowess); pheasant; stag (possessor of hunting rights)

husband and wife *see* **marriage**

husbands second toe longer than the first toe (sign of a cruel husband) • *China:* parrot (warning to wives to be faithful to their husbands)

Hyacinth, St. Dominican carrying a statue of the Virgin Mary over water • *attribute:* monstrance

Hygeia *attribute:* moon

Hylas youth being embraced by naiads with overturned pitcher

Hymen [god] *attributes:* torch; veil

Hypnos *attribute:* poppy

hypnotism basilisk

hypocrisy crocodile; fox; lead [metal]; mantis (cruelty and greed disguised by a hypocritical attitude of prayer or religiosity); mask; monkey; mule; ostrich; swan; vulture; wolf • *attribute:* whitened sepulchre • *flower language:* manchineal tree • *see also* **dissimulation; falsity**

Hypocrisy personified *attribute:* veil

hypothesis kite [toy]

hyssop thyme (the opposite of hyssop)

hysteria siren [alarm]

I

I [letter] *association:* J (symbolically the same as the letter I, this is especially true in any but modern times); nine

Icarus man and youth flying together (the youth is Icarus; the man is Dedalus) • *association:* wax

ice *association:* crystal

id bite (the dangerous action of the instincts upon the psyche, especially in the case of an animal bite); boar; giant; gold; horseman (the ego trying to control the id); skidding (loss of control of the id by the ego and superego) • *see also* **personality**

the ideal Empress [tarot]; Pole Star; sixteen (ideal age for a lover); the spirit

ideals exile (banishment of a principle or ideal); flag; murder (removal of an idea or principle from one's mind or from existence); nectar (the soul's entire service to the highest ideals); torch (high ideals) • *see also* **principles**

ideas acorn (a germinal idea); beheading (an idea, opinion, or institution at the end of its cycle); blue bird; caulking (the limitation of ideas); corpse (the end of a cycle or idea); crow (a demiurgic power); file [rasp] (refined ideas or expressions; ideas free from superstition); finger snapping (the beginning or end of a cycle, idea, or process); House of God [tarot] (the wild pursuit of fanciful ideas); Icarus (the limitation of ideas); idol (fixed ideas which bar the way to truth); king (the ideas of a nation); kite [toy] (hypothesis); leaves (true ideas); leper (the lower mind troubled with conflicting emotions, desires, and ideas); murder (removal of an idea or principle from one's mind, or from existence); nymphs as the companions of a god (expression of the god's ideas); old man (old or tired ideas); relief that is more than sufficient (the powerful surge of an idea or emotion in all its nascent strength); ruins (sentiments, ideas, or customs which are dead and irrelevant to present life, but which

nonetheless persist); signs of wear (extinct or outmoded ideas); young man (new ideas) • *see also* **beliefs; opinions**

identification flag; transvestitism (identification with a deity, parent, or ideal of the opposite sex)

identity seal [stamp]

idleness kite [toy]; monkey (idle foolishness); playing cards; smoking a pipe; spitting; whistling; whittling • *flower language:* marigold; mesembryanthemum; wild violet (love in idleness) • *see also* **laziness; sloth**

idolatry Babylon; bat [animal]; dragon; lizard; mole [animal]; prostitute (an idol worshipper) • *associations:* Egypt; gold; kiss; roof (place for idolatry) • *Bible:* bat [animal] • *Judaism:* Greece (association) • *see also* **paganism**

Idolatry personified *attributes:* blindfold; monkey; statue

Ignatius of Loyola, St. praying saint before an image or vision of Christ bearing a cross • *attributes:* crown of thorns; eucharist; heart crowned with thorns

ignominy hanging [execution], tickling (an ignominious death)

ignorance ass; bandaged eyes; blindfold; blindman's bluff (trying to solve a problem without sufficient knowledge); blindness; child; darkness; deluge (awakening of the mind from ignorance and error); Devil [tarot] (the half knowledge of the senses); devil with a black face; dragon; drugs; dwarf; House of God [tarot] (spiritual truth breaking down ignorance); jackdaw; lead [metal]; low forehead; manger (ignorance from which wisdom arises); owl eyes; peasant; poppy; sleep; squinting eyes; stable (light and revelation arising from ignorance); tapster (a very ignorant person); tusk (spiritual power overcoming ignorance and evil) • *associations:* black; dark complexion • *flower language:* white rose (heart of ignorant love)

Ildefonso, St. man being robed in a chasuble by the Virgin Mary

illegitimacy *association:* left side

illiteracy signing one's name with an X

illness *see* **disease; sickness**

illogic *see* **irrationality**

illumination alchemy; dew (spiritual illumination); east; hidden treasure (fruits of supreme illumination); Judgment [tarot]; lizard (the Gospel's illuminating influence); minaret (torch of spiritual illumination); Orient; thunderbolt; torch (spiritualization through illumination and guidance); white knight • *see also* **light**

illusion clouds; mist; smoke (illusion obscuring the truth); sweat on the face; web • *see also* **falsity**

image *flower language:* spindle tree (your image is engraved in my heart)

imagination bird; cap with colored feathers; dove on one's shoulder (creative imagination); Eurydice (undeveloped imaginative or intuitive sensibility); fan; flying; fog or mist (the unreal); House of God [tarot] (the wild pursuit of fanciful ideas); man; Merlin (enslaved imagination); mirror; moon; Moon [tarot] (imagination; arbitrary fantasy; imaginative sensitivity); Pandora, Pandora's box (the wild tendencies of imagination); Pegasus; seraph (imagination, love, and spirit); siren [mythology] (corrupt imagination); white horse; winged horse (imagination; the flight of the imagination); white horse; wings • *association:* N • *flower language:* lupin • *heraldry:* helmet with any kind of strange crest • *see also* **creativity**

imitation bullfinch; monkey

immaculate conception *see* **Virgin Mary**

immateriality voice (immaterial existence)

immaturity boy; buds; calf; lizard; rabbit (uninhibited, but often immature, sexuality)

immobility lizard

immobilization bondage (immobilization through sin or evil)

immorality light heels, round heels; macaroni • *association:* Babylon

immortality acacia; acanthus; amber [gemstone]; apple; barnacle goose; beauty; bee; berry; bird; cedar; cicada; cinnabar orange [fruit]; crystal ball; cypress; dragonfly; dryness; egg; emerald; evergreens; falcon, especially when spiraling; fir; Gemini (the dual physical/spiritual, mortal/immortal nature of all things); golden apple; golden hair; green; hammer; hart; hawk; Hercules (the quest for immortality; the individual fleeing himself in the quest for immortality); horn [animal]; horseman (bearer of immortality); ivy; jade; juniper; lamp; lily; lotus; maggot; mistletoe; myrtle; ox skull (death, but when adorned and shown with horns, immortality); peach; peacock; Phoenix [bird]; pine; pomegranate flower; pyramid; ribbon knotted to form a circle; rock; rowan; sage [herb]; salt; scarab; sea urchin; serpent (guardian of the springs of life, immortality, and the superior riches of the spirit); the soul (man's immortal part); spiral; stag; stars; stole [religious garment] (hope of immortality); tree; tusk on a grave; white stone; woodpecker; yew • *association:* eight; Wandering Jew (the imperishable part of man which cannot die) • *China:* peach, peach tree • *flower language:* amaranth • *Judaism:* duck

impartiality bandaged eyes; blindfold • *China:* pigeon (impartial filial duty) • *heraldry:* squirrel • *see also* **equality**

impatience Charybdis, Scylla (the desire for immediate fruits of an action as an impedance to moral progress); hands on hips • *flower language:* balsam; cochorus (impatient of absence); red balsam (impatient resolves); touch-me-not (impatient desire); yellow balsam

impediments *see* **obstacles**

imperfection tailor (imperfect humanity); • *flower language:* henbane • *see also* **defect**

Imperfection personified *attribute:* henbane

impetuousness *flower language:* almond (the impetuousness of youth)

impetus *see* **incentive**

impiety chaff (the ungodly); hippopotamus

importance cornerstone (something fundamental, or of primary importance) • *attribute:* white garment (important people) • *see* **persistence**

impossibility blue bird; blue dahlia; blue or golden flower; blue rose; golden or, occasionally, white fleece (conquest of the impossible)

impotence ant (the fragility and impotence of existence); devil with a yellow face; loss of teeth (fear of loss of potency); snow; tailor; wall • *see also* **weakness**

impracticality Tower of Babel (an impractical dream)

impregnability castle; cave; larch • *see also* **defense**

impregnation sowing seed; whispering in the ear

impression *flower language:* withered white rose (transient impression)

imprisonment bird cage; cage; chains; entanglement (being caught in the universe and being unable to escape by any means); handcuffs • *see also* **bondage; confinement**

improvement Hanged Man [tarot] (reversal of one's way of life by surrendering to higher wisdom); rose quartz (enhancer of inner and outer beauty); sneeze on a Thursday, you sneeze for something better • *association:* Taurus (invigoration) • *heraldry:* snail (acquired possessions to be preserved and enlarged)

improvidence cicada; grasshopper; long fingers

imprudence *see* **folly**

impulsiveness Fool [tarot] (blind impulse); myrtle (mastery of impulses) • *see also* **capriciousness**

impurity dog; dragon; dregs (the lower instincts that remain unpurified); fly [insect]; swine • *see also* **filth**

inactivity *see* **lethargy; sloth**

inanity *see* **senselessness**

incapacitation *see* **disabling**

incarnation Cancer [zodiac] (the threshold through which the soul enters upon its incarnation); Fall of Man (incarnation of the spirit) • *see also* **Jesus Christ**

incentive oil; sails; whip • *associations:* Mars (driving force); S • *see also* **anima; stimulation**

incest swan (incestuous maternal relationship) • *fear of incest:* devouring (especially maternal incest); dragon; female ogre; journey (flight from the mother for fear of incest); nightmare (sexual repression, especially of incest); sinking in mud (maternal incest); wolf devouring children

incipience aquatic plants (the nascent character of life); chaos, inability to speak, night (incipient creation); mud (a nascent state) • *see also* **latency**

incompletion broken column (unfinished work); forgotten or legendary fairies (frustrated acts); tailor (an incomplete person)

incongruence digestion (good digestion is a sign of congruity with nature, and vice versa)

inconsequence *see* **insignificance**

inconsistency *see* **changeability; inconstancy**

inconstancy April; ass; butterfly; columbine; Eve; fan; Helen of Troy; hyena; mercury [metal]; moon; ostrich; primrose; tongue; tulip; weather cock, weather vane; wind • *associations:* N; yellow • *flower language:* abatina; evening primrose; lady slippers; Near East tulip; pink larkspur; wild honeysuckle (inconstancy in love) • *see also* **changeability**

Inconstancy personified *attributes:* ass; lobster; monkey; wheel

incontinence *association:* eleven

incorruptibility box tree; cedar; house of cedar; marigold; peacock (the incorruptible soul); salt • *flower language:* cedar of Lebanon • *see also* **purity**

increase ascending (a raise in value or worth; an increase in intensity); clockwise swastika; full sails (swelling powers); phallus; rain (an increase in spiritual energy); sun • *associations:* sixteen; seventy-two (a ritual number involving solar increase and lunar wisdom) • *see also* **expansion**

indecision *association:* green; T

indefatigability *see* **energy**

independence acorn; beggar; hands on hips; larch; rattlesnake • *emblem:* cabbage (the self-willed) • *flower language:* white oak; wild plum tree • *heraldry:* millstone (going one's own way) • *see also* **autonomy; freedom**

indestructibility bone (the indestructible part of man) • *association:* I [letter]

indeterminacy mist

Indians of North America *attributes:* feathered headdress; tomahawk

indifference blown dandelion with many seeds remaining (a lover is indifferent); candytuft; fish, sometimes two fish (sexual indifference); flint (indifference to insult); globe amaranth; mustard [plant]; poppy; raven (an indifferent sinner); spitting • *association:* gray • *flower language:* agnus castus; chaste tree; dogwood blossoms along (Am I perfectly indifferent to you?); pigeon berry; senvy • *see also* **stoicism; stolidity**

indigence *see* **poverty**

indignation *see* **anger**

indigo [color] *association:* five

indiscretion heron; magpie; reed • *flower language:* almond; aloe; bulrush; feathery or split reed; snapdragon

individuality knot (an individual's existence); room [chamber]; seal [stamp]; semen (the purest part of an individual) • *heraldry:* cat

individuation hands clasped in a handshake; incest; seal [stamp]; tree (the slow process of individuation)

indolence *see* **laziness**

indomitability *see* **defense; steadfastness**

indulgence apple (indulgence in earthly desires); cat, chocolate, swine (self- indulgence); hawthorn; plucking flowers (sexual indulgence)

industry ant; beaver; bee; caduceus (commerce and industry); cogwheel; distaff; factory chimney; flax (domestic industry); hammer; lavender [plant]; loom; mole [animal]; spider; steel; water wheel • *associations:* diamond suit [playing cards]; smoke • *China:* mulberry tree; silkworm • *flower language:* bee orchis; flax; red clover • *heraldry:* beaver; bee (well-governed industry); saw [tool] • *see also* **diligence; work**

Industry personified *attributes:* ivy; tortoise

inelegance *see* **clumsiness; crudity**

inertia famine (mental and spiritual inertia); flagellation (encouragement against spiritual laxity or inertia); horizontal column; loitering (spiritual inertia); slime (inertia preceding rebirth) • *association:* gray • *see also* **languor; laziness; sloth**

inertness drought (an inert spiritual condition); ice; lead [metal]

inexorability scythe (inexorable march of time)

inexperience *see* **neophytes**

infamy *see* **humiliation**

infancy bandages (the swaddling clothes of infants); east; Gabriel hounds (the lost souls of unbaptized infants); lisping; thumb in mouth, especially sucking the thumb

infanticide elves (dark colored elves are generally unfavorable and may kill babies); lamia

infatuation *see* **love**

inferiority abyss; dwarf; goat (usually moral inferiority, but occasional moral superiority because it is associated with high peaks in its wild state); gorge (inferiority in the face of overwhelming odds); ice (resistance to all that is inferior); leather medal (farcical award for stupidity or inferiority); scales [biology] (moral or cosmic inferiority); scales [biology] on mermaids, dragons, the Devil (the inferior continuing in the superior); serpent (the inferior within the superior); trapezoid (an inferior form); X (in the United States: brand of an inferior product) • *flower language:* cornflower (devotion to an inferior)

infernality descending stairs (entry into the infernal world); rat; reptile; sulfur; south (infernal regions); yellow (infernal light) • *associations:* black magic; inverted five-pointed star; jewels; wings of skin • *see also* **devils; Hades; Hell; Satan; underworld**

infidelity *see* **unfaithfulness**

the infinite eight; Gorgon (the infinite number of forms in which creation is manifested); one; three hundred; knot; zero

infirmity *see* **affliction; disease; sickness**

inflexibility *see* **steadfastness**

influence High Priestess [tarot] (hidden influences); potter's wheel (divine influence on life); rain (spiritual influences from heaven)

informants *see* **betrayal**

information *see* **knowledge**

ingenuity *see* **cleverness**

ingenuousness dove; Eve; forget-me-not; sheep; shining face • *flower language:* blueberry, mouse-eared chickweed (ingenuous simplicity) • *see also* **innocence; unworldliness**

ingratitude child; fox; ivy; lynx; owl; swine; tooth; viper • *flower language:*

buttercup; crowfoot, especially celery leaved crowfoot; kingcup; wild ranunculus

inheritance son (heir) • *Judaism:* swallow [bird] (paternal inheritance)

inhibition acanthus (stunting); fly [insect] (the priest, or other inhibitor of the preconscious who taints innocent joys); ice (stultification of potentialities); loss of teeth; policeman (the censorious super-ego inhibiting forces of the pre-conscious); Pygmalion (inhibitions overcome) • *see also* **repression**

inhospitality closed gate

inhumanity engine (the inhumane forces of modern society)

initiation bath; burial (initiation into manhood); circumcision (initiation, especially into the Jewish faith); Emperor [tarot]; five-petalled lotus; flagellation; gypsum; honey; rain; riding a goat; serpent with a sheep's head; tarot deck (comprises an image of initiation; World [tarot] (the final crown of the initiate) • *association:* green (spiritual initiation); N

initiative High Priestess [tarot] (a balance between initiative and resistance); spark • *association:* A • *kabala:* fifty

injustice broken tablet; gall (the bitterness of injustice); hops • *flower language:* hops

Injustice personified *attribute:* toad

Inner Temple of the Inns of Court *heraldry:* Pegasus

innocence basin, especially with a ewer; blue eyes; breasts; bride; calf; child; cotta; cradle; daisy; dove; fawn; flowering staff; fly [insect] (the priest, policeman, or other inhibitor of the preconscious who taints innocent joys); garment (the lack of innocence as a result of the Fall of Man); gazelle; gold and silver plumed dove (the treasures of purity and innocence); goose; hands clasped behind the back; hind [deer]; hyssop (innocence regained); infant; jester (absolute innocence); lamb; maiden; marguerite [flower]; mother's milk or cow's milk; nuditas virtualis; opal (protection of innocence); palm of the hand held up and out; pearl; plucking flowers (innocent joys); primrose; sheep; shining face; stole [religious garment]; sum-

mer; spring (especially female innocence); surplice; virgin; washing the hands; water; whistling (pretense of innocence); white flower; white gloves; white horse; white knight; white pebble (not guilty); white robe • *association:* blue; green • *Christianity:* alb (the innocence and prophetic office of Christ) • *flower language:* daisy; white lilac (youthful innocence) • *heraldry:* hands; rose [flower]; silver • *see also* **Holy Innocents; ingenuousness; unworldliness**

Innocence personified *attributes:* lamb; serpent; washing hands

Inns of Court *heraldry:* Pegasus (Inner Temple)

inquiry *see* **investigation**

inquisition Astaroth

Inquisition, Spanish yellow garment (worn by those condemned by the Spanish Inquisition and by the executioner)

inquisitiveness *see* **curiosity; investigation; searching**

insanity *see* **madness**

insatiability bottomless pit or well (insatiable desire)

inscrutability Gordian knot, labyrinth, Solomon's knot (divine inscrutability) • *associations:* Orient; Orientals • *see also* **mystery**

insects *China:* green clouds (a plague of insects)

insecurity *see* **helplessness**

insensibility elephant; hippopotamus

insensitivity leather; lupin; rhinoceros; Strength [tarot]

insidiousness fox rat; worm (insidious destroyer) • *see also* **cunning**

insight *see* **sagacity**

insignificance farthing; gnat; minnow; molehill; mouse; sou; sparrow; spitting into the ocean; thimble; water fly; worm (an insignificant man); wren • *see also* **humbleness**

insincerity foxglove • *flower language:* foxglove; great bindweed

Insinuation personified *attribute:* convolvulus

insolence *see* **mockery**

insolubility *association:* odd numbers

inspiration angelica; black bird (ancient times); breast milk from a Muse falling on a book or musical instrument; eagle (the inspiration of the Gospels); goose; incense; kettle; laurel;

Solomon's seal; toad; trefoil [plant]; wine • *associations:* eight (occasionally spiritual inspiration, but more often material and personal); little finger; U • *flower language:* angelica • *divine inspiration:* dove on the shoulder of an Apostle; eagle (the inspiration of the Gospels); flame on the head; flaming mountain; lark (inspired visionary); lizard; white rose (inspired wisdom) • *heraldry:* angel • *poetic inspiration:* fingertips (association); forge; manna; Pegasus; wind (inducer of poetic inspiration)

instability cormorant; dahlia; dragonfly; prostitute (instability caused by object interest); sand; swallow [bird] • *association:* two • *flower language:* dahlia

Instinct personified *attribute:* elephant

instincts American Indians; bite (the dangerous action of the instincts upon the psyche, especially in the case of an animal bite); body hair; cellar; centaur; Devil [tarot]; dragon; dregs, lees (the lower instincts that remain unpurified); dwarf; Eve; fox (base instincts); goat; Helen (the instinctive and emotional aspects of woman); horse; keel (lower instincts and desires); knight (the spirit controlling the instincts and desires); moorings (the attachment of the spiritual and instinctual); monster (the instincts that hinder man in his search for truth); Negro; prison (the early state of the soul in which the spirit is in bondage to the lower instincts and desires); savage; tramp [hobo] (the primitive, instinctive, natural self); sewer [drain]; steed (the force of instincts); wild man, wild woman; wolf (the lesser instincts taking control of more human instincts, but with the possibility of improvement) • *associations:* black; left hand; square [shape] • *heraldry:* serpent

institutions beheading (an idea, opinion, or institution at the end of its cycle) • *association:* six

instruction *see* **teaching**

insufficiency wings of Icarus (functional insufficiency)

insult *see* **humiliation**

integration hermaphrodite (integration of opposites); Hermit [tarot] (the successful union of personal will with cosmic will); sheaf; rose [flower] (integration of the personality) • *see also* **reintegration**

integrity Lovers [tarot]; quartz; topaz • *associations:* green (spiritual integrity); white • *China:* iron • *see also* **honor**

intellect air (the mental plane); androsphinx [human head on a lion's body] (the union of intellect and physical power); anvil; birds that are solitary by habit (the isolation of those who live on a superior mental plane); blacksmith (mental qualities disciplined by the spirit); blindfold (mental or spiritual blindness); brain; checkers; crystal; cylinder (the mechanistic intellect); diamond [gemstone]; gold (divine intelligence); Grecian lute (triumph of the intellect); Greece (intellectual keenness); heart [organ] (the seat of true intelligence as opposed to reasoning); hermaphrodite (intellectual activity); hippopotamus (intellectual pride); horn [animal]; hound; Icarus (the intellect rebelling against the spirit; the intellect in the merely technical and non-spiritual sense; man's questing intellectual spirit; the intellect trying to escape the world); iron (mental power; the mind); jackal; lamp, especially an oil lamp; light; Mercury [god] (intellectual contemplation; intellectual energy); needle; Pegasus (intellect and morality); Prometheus (the intellect in the merely technical and non-spiritual sense, in open rebellion against the soul); reins; sphere (intellectual life); Sphinx; terror (intellectual lack of will); Strength [tarot] (the triumph of intelligence over brutality); thorn (sharp intelligence); two eyes (binary functions such as male/female, sun/moon, intelligence/love, etc.); Vulcan (intellect rebelling against the soul); white horse; wings • *associations:* C (intellectual qualities); blue stockings (attribute of a woman having intellectual or literary interests); E (intellectual character); J; forty (the highest functioning of the intellect); Mercury [planet]; O; one (intellectual power); P; seven; yellow • *flower language:* Venice sumac (intellectual excellence); walnut • *heraldry:* ash tree; gold • *lack of intellect:* dove; jay; kangaroo; low forehead; mole eyes (intellectual and spiritual blindness);

Taurus (association); woodcock • *see also* **cleverness; genius; mentality; mind; sagacity; stupidity; wit**
intelligence *see* **genius; intellect**
intemperance bottle; fox; leech; ostrich • *Christianity:* eleven (association) • *see also* **drunkenness; intoxication**
Intemperance personified *attribute:* fox
intensification ascending; multiple heads (deterioration, fragmentation, however, it can sometimes indicate a positive intensification); twenty; zero (when used after another number); wand
intercession *see* **mediation**
intercourse *see* **sex**
interdependence knot; plait
intermediacy clouds, mist (the intermediate world between the formal and non-formal)
intermingling knot; plait; Wheel of Fortune [tarot] (intermingling of the disparate)
intersection *see* **conjunction**
intervention earthquake, thunderbolt (divine intervention)
intimacy knot, plait (intimate relationship)
intoxication grapes; ivy; poppy; rhododendron (the danger of intoxication); wine; wormwood • flower language; vine • *see also* **drunkenness; intemperance**
intractibility *see* **stubbornness**
intransigence brass (obstinate resistance); chestnut (obstinate durability); donkey; folded hands with interwoven fingers; granite, marble (inflexibility); knot (an unchanging psychic situation); mule; sheep; swine • *association:* Scotland • *see also* **constancy; steadfastness; stubbornness; tenacity**
intrepidness *see* **bravery intrigue** harlequin (mischievous intrigue) • *association:* tea (amorous intrigue and scandal); three • *see also* **dissimulation; falsity; trickery**
introspection fishing; Hamlet; mirror • *associations:* B; G • *see also* **contemplation; reflection; thought**
introversion flagellation • *association:* left side
intuition chalice; crystal (intuitive knowledge); Eurydice (half formed intuitive vision; undeveloped imaginative or intuitive sensibility); intestines; jewels hidden in caves or underground

(the intuitive knowledge of the unconscious); Jupiter [god] (intuition of the supernatural); Melusina (intuitive genius); Moon [tarot]; prince; rudder; sibyl (intuition of the higher truths); stomach; sulfur (intuition and reason); tarot cards XII to XXII; woman (the intuitive and the changing); young man • *associations:* blue; four (the functional aspects of consciousness: thinking, feeling, sensation, intuition); G; L; Mercury [planet]; Neptune [planet]; two; white (spiritual intuition); yellow • *Judaism:* hare
inversion acrobat; Gemini; hourglass (perpetual inversion of the upper and lower worlds); jester (inversion of the king; inversion of normal order); riding a goat (inversion of the normal order); wolf
investigation facing north (to face north is to pose a question); fishhook (the means of investigation for esoteric knowledge or of the unconscious); journey; Magic [tarot]; smelling • *see also* **searching**
invigoration *association:* Taurus
invincibility *see* **defense**
inviolability *see* **defense**
invisibility cloak; girdle [cincture]; hood; red cap; ring; veil • *association:* Pluto [planet] (invisible forces) • *Ireland:* hazel wand
invitation angel with two hands extended; hand extended; hand with palm outward
invocation raised arms
involution black knight; counterclockwise spiral; disheveled hair; evening; hiding (the period of life before and after its involution as matter, or before and after the manifest life appears); House of God [tarot]; jester (willful involution); lion being devoured by an eagle (the victory of the evolutive over the involutive); Moon [tarot]; night; orgy; Pan (involutive or base life); threshing; turtle; two dolphins swimming in opposite directions (involution and evolution); tomb (involution and hope of regeneration); winter (involutive death with the promise of rebirth); woman (the involutive) • *associations:* the first six signs of the zodiac (Aires, Taurus, Gemini, Cancer, Leo, Virgo); left side • *involutive fragmentation of the unconscious:* Bacchante; Furies; harpy siren [mythology]

invulnerability *see* **defense**

Io *association:* heifer

Ireland *association:* green; orange [color] (Protestants in Northern Ireland); *emblems:* clover; harp; potato; shamrock

Irene, St. *attribute:* vase of ointment, usually with a lid

Iris [goddess] *emblem:* rainbow

iron *association:* Mars

Iron Age several soldiers attacking women and children

Iron Age personified *attribute:* shield with an image of a serpent with a human head

irony *flower language:* sardony

irradiation parasol

irrationality body hair (irrational power); checkers (the effort to control irrational impulses by containing them in a given order); Fool [tarot]; ocean (immense illogic); Pandora, Pandora's box; submarine boat; werewolf (the irrationality latent in man and the possibility of it reawakening) • *association:* left hand

irregularity renaming; trapezium (in comparison with a trapezoid, it shows an even greater degree of abnormality and irregularity); trapezoid; twisting • *see also* **abnormality**

irritability crab; crab tree; crooked fingers (sign of a crabbed disposition); dog; holly; wasp

irritation *see* **annoyance**

Isaac *associations:* brazier with wood and knife (Abraham and Isaac); hairy arms (Jacob's deception of Isaac) • *attributes:* cross made of faggots; knife; ram [sheep] (the sacrifice of Isaac)

Isaiah *attributes:* branch [plant]; sack; saw [tool]; scroll; tongs holding a glowing coal

Ishtar *attribute:* two looped reeds

Isidore, St. *attribute:* writing pen

Isis buckle (the goodwill and protection of Isis) • *associations:* duck (the bringing forth of the sun by Isis); goose; heifer; ibis; sulfur and eggs (worship of Isis) • *attributes:* heather; lamp; lotus; sistrum; swallow [bird] • *emblems:* frog; star-of-the- sea (usually seven- pointed)

Islam *emblems:* crescent and star; crescent moon • *see also* **Muslims**

Isle of Man. Parliament two keys crossed

isolation birds that are solitary by habit usually represent the isolation of those who live on a superior mental plane; black knight; city (lack of emotional, spiritual, or natural contact); crow (the isolation of one who lives on a superior plane); desert island; fog; hermit; island; ivory tower (retreat from the world, especially by an intellectual or an academic shutting one's eyes to reality); lighthouse; moon; tower • *see also* **loneliness**

Israel eagle (God's providential care over Israel); Gabriel (protector of Israel) • *association:* tent (Israel in the wilderness) • *attribute:* multicolored garment (Israelite) • *emblems:* grapes (Tribe of Ephraim); lily of the valley; lion (Tribe of Judah); serpent (Tribe of Dan); six-pointed star; wolf with lion (Tribe of Benjamin) • *Israel in Egypt:* pyramid and star; Sphinx; whip with a pile of bricks • *twelve tribes of Israel:* six-pointed star (the six points indicate the omniscience of God, the twelve corners signify the twelve tribes of Israel); twelve (association); twelve pillars

Issachar *association:* ass with two burdens

Italy *emblems:* gondola (Venice in particular, but often Italy as a whole); leaning tower (Pisa, in particular, but often Italy as a whole)

J

J *association:* one

Jachin and Boaz two pillars shown apart

Jacob bloodstained garment being given to an old man (Jacob being given Joseph's garment); full moon and the sun surrounded by twelve stars (respectively: Jacob's wife, Jacob, and their twelve sons); hairy arms (Jacob's deception of Isaac) • *association:* twelve (the twelve sons of Jacob) • *attributes:* ladder, especially with angels on it; mummy; stone

James the Great, St. pilgrim; soldier on a white horse killing Saracens • *attributes:* banner and white horse; gourd; scroll; shell; staff, especially crossed with sword, and/or with hat, scallop shell, wallet, letters "S.J."

James the Less, St. *attributes:* fuller's bat; halberd; knife; saw [tool], especially with the handle upright; square [tool]; three stones; windmill

Januarius, St. two vials on a book

January *association:* garnet • *China:* plum tree (emblem)

Janus head with two faces • *attributes:* key; serpent

Japan *emblems:* camellia japonica; cherry blossoms; chrysanthemum; dragonfly

Jason *associations:* fleece hanging from a tree, guarded by a dragon; two fire-breathing bulls

jealousy ass; barley; Cain; cuckoo; green eyes; handkerchief; humming-bird; jaundice; leopard, especially when crouching; orange [fruit]; serpent; sparrowhawk; stepmother; swan; tiger; trout; woman's eyebrows that meet; yellow rose • *associations:* Juno; yellow • *flower language:* French marigold • *see also* **envy**

Jepthah's daughter *attribute:* tambourine

Jeremiah *association:* cistern • *attributes:* cross with scroll; potter's wheel; scroll; smashed bottle; stone; wand and staff

Jericho, Fall of seven ram's horns; seven trumpets

Jerome, St. kneeling desert hermit with a stone in his hand; man at prayer, beating his breast with a stone; man being scourged by angles; praying desert hermit with a crucifix; saint praying in the desert or the wilderness • *attributes:* Bible or book with stone and whip; cardinal's hat; church model being carried; crucifix; fawn; hare; lion; skull; staff with white banner with red cross; stag; trumpet

Jerusalem furnace full of inferior metal; rose garden (the new Jerusalem); walled city (the heavenly Jerusalem)

jests winking eye • *flower language:* southernwood

jesters *attributes:* bladder; cap with bells; fox tail • *see also* **comedians; fools**

Jesuits *emblem:* heart crowned with thorns

Jesus Christ anchor; Ark of the Covenant; balances [scales]; basin, or basin and ewer together (the humility of Christ's love); bell (Christ's joy; the coming of Christ in the eucharist); book with seven seals and a lamb; book with the Greek letters alpha and omega; caladrius; carpenter; Christ child holding an apple (Christ as the new Adam); cornerstone; cross on an orb or globe (the triumph of Christ); dawn (the advent of Christ); day star; dew; diamond [gemstone]; dolphin (rarely); door; eagle (also Christ swooping down to save a soul); east; fern (although sometimes considered the Devil's plant); fish; fisherman; frankincense (the priesthood of Christ); grape leaves or vine; horde of locusts (a nation without Christ); giant carrying a baby on his back (St. Christopher with the Christ child); griffin (the omniscience of Christ); holly, tonsure (Christ's crown of thorns); honey (Christ and his work); horseman, especially when on a white horse (Christ; Christ's spiritual conquest); index finger upraised (Christ as the one way to salvation); kestrel (Christ in the world); lamb, especially with a cross or when it has a nimbus; lamb standing up (the triumphant, risen Christ); light; lighthouse; man rising from a coffin; manger with enthroned lamb (the humiliation and exaltation of Christ, respectively); moon (the physical nature of Christ); morning star; myrrh and aloes; oak; orpheus; otter (Christ's descent into Hell); ox; pear (Christ's love of mankind); pelican (allegory of Christ; when feeding her young, the atoning work of Christ); pilgrim (Christ at Emmaus); plowman; Pole Star; pomegranate; purple dove; quince; plane tree (the charity of Christ); Prometheus (prefiguration of Christ); rain (the impartiality of Christ); ram [sheep]; remora; rock, especially when surmounted by a cross; roebuck; rose [flower]; scroll in the hands of a patriarch (the darkness faith was enveloped in before Christ); serpent at the foot of the cross (Jesus overcoming the evil that leads man into sin); serpent on a tau cross; seven seals [stamps] (the seven main events in Christ's life: incarnation, baptism, the passion, visit to Hell, resurrection, ascension, descent of Holy Spirit); shepherd; split nut, especially a walnut (the outer casing represents his flesh, the shell the wood of the cross, and the kernel his divine nature); sunflower (the turning of the soul to Christ); sunrise; three tabernacles, usually on a mountaintop (the transfiguration of Christ); torch; turtle dove; unicorn; vine; wine press • *apostles of Christ:* book (attribute); eleven (the eleven faithful apostles—association); flame on the head (the apostles at Pentecost—attribute); scroll (the apostles, but especially the evangelists—attribute); star (the ten apostles who neither denied nor betrayed Christ—association); twelve (association); twelve clusters of grapes; twelve doves; twelve men rowing a ship (the apostles moving the church); twelve men, often each with a sheep; twelve sheep; twelve stars • *ascension of Christ:* bee (the risen Christ); Christ with a banner (refers to the period after the resurrection and before the ascension); eagle; fiery chariot; horse; ladder • *associations:* B; blue (occasionally, Christ in his earthly ministry); eight hundred and eighty-eight [888] (the sacred number of Christ in Hebrew); five (the five wounds of Christ); G; hart; middle finger (the salvation of Christ); owl; ship on a stormy sea (Christ calming the sea at Galilee); thirty-three (the number of years in Christ's life); vesica; white • *attributes:* alb; crown of thorns; cross within a circle; cruciform nimbus; daisy; globe underfoot; glory [luminous glow around the entire body]; golden girdle [cincture]; gourd; lily; lily of the valley; pearl; rod of Jesse; shepherd's crook; staff; three-rayed nimbus; two doves, usually carried by St. Joseph in a basket (the

presentation of Christ at the Temple); whip (the cleansing of the Temple); white hair (the Son of Man and the eternity of his existence) • *betrayal of Christ:* fuller's bat; hand with money in it (the betrayal of Christ by Judas); the head of Judas; St. Peter's ear being cut off; lantern (attribute); thirty pieces of silver (the betrayal of Christ by Judas) • *blood of Christ:* birds feeding on grapes (the faithful gathering sustenance from the blood of Christ); red dawn; wine of the eucharist • *body of Christ:* church; gingerbread, especially at Christmas; host [eucharist]; lamb with a white flag with a cross (the body of Christ, that is, the church) • *burial of Christ:* ciborium (the grave of Christ); ivory (the incorruptibility of Christ's body in the tomb—association); ointment (attribute); rose on a corpse; three (days that Christ was entombed—association); two (angels at the tomb of Christ—association) • *the church and Christ:* bride and groom (the church and Christ, respectively); cassock (devotion to Christ and the church); dolphin with an anchor or boat (the church being guided to salvation by Christ); moon (the church reflecting the light of Christ, however, sometimes the synagogue with the church represented by the sun); Rose of Sharon (Christ's love of the church); vine with branches (Christ and the church, especially when the apostle's emblems such as keys, ship, shell, saw, etc., are in the branches); Virgin Mary (the mother church that Christ left in the world) • *cross of Christ:* aspen, elder tree, holly, sycamore (the wood of the cross); rood beam (the necessity of the cross of Calvary in passing from the Church Militant to the Church Triumphant); six (the six hours Christ spent on the cross (association); sword held with the hilt upward; T (association); tree; trident (in ancient times, a disguised cross, or a sign of the trinity, later used as an inversion of the trinity) • *crucifixion of Christ:* brass serpent (association); Cain (the Jews killing Christ); chasuble (the seamless garment for which the soldiers cast lots—attribute); column [architecture] (attribute); cross with lamb; crossed legs, right over left (the traditional position of Christ's legs on the cross—attribute; crown of thorns (attribute); crucifixion of a lamb; dogwood blossoms (attribute); dolphin speared by a trident; Eastern cross (the mercy shown to the thief to the right of Christ); five candles, five carbuncles [gemstones] (the five wounds of Christ); golden plover (the soul of the Jew who crucified Christ and is doomed forever to lamenting the act); holly (emblem); host (breaking the host symbolizes the death of Christ's body upon the cross; when shown with a chalice it symbolizes the sacrifice of Christ upon the cross); IHS on a cross (God's love for humanity revealed in Christ's death on the cross—the letters stand for "in haec salus": in this [cross] salvation); ladder (attribute); lamb with cross; lance (attribute); lancing piercing a heart (emblem); nails for wood (early use showed four nails; later three became customary—attribute); pallium; Phoenix [bird] (Middle Ages); reed with hyssop (attribute); rooster; seamless garment (attribute); six (the number of hours Christ was on the cross—association); skull and crossbones at the foot of the cross (refers to the legend that the cross of Jesus rested on the bones of Adam—association); soldiers gambling for a tunic, straws, or three dice (the casting of lots for Christ's clothing—association); spear (attribute); sponge (attribute); staff crossed with a sword (attribute); sun and moon (alludes to the convulsion of the heavens and the sorrow of all creation—association); sword and torch crossed (attribute); thorns; vinegar, or vinegar and gall (attribute) • *death of Christ:* altar shaped as a tomb; banner with a cross (Christ's victory over death); palm tree (Christ's victory over death) *Devil and Christ:* monk offering a stone to Christ (the Devil tempting Christ in the wilderness); serpent battling with a fish (the Devil fighting with Christ); stag trampling on snake or dragon (Christ's victory over Satan) • *divinity of Christ:* ring finger (association); water mixed with wine at the eucharist (Christ's humanity and divinity, respectively) • *dual nature of Christ:* balsam with an olive branch; centaur; fleur-di-lys with the letters IHC, or IHS; griffin; lily with IHC in a triangle; mermaid, merman; two (association); two-branched candelabrum; two candles • *emblems:* alpha and omega [Greek letters]; cedar, especially a cedar of Lebanon; fleur-di-lys; fountain; IHC (from the first three letters of Christ's name in (Greek); IHS (from the Latin *Iesus hominum salvator,* Jesus, savior of men; or, when printed with a cross, *In haec salus,* in this [cross], salvation); IX (the Greek initials for Jesus Christ, usually printed with the I bisecting the X); Jesse tree (the royal human genealogy of Christ); seven candles; stone; sun (seldom used in modern times); sun with the letters IHC (the first three letters of Christ's name in the Greek); tiger; weasel; X; XP [chi rho] (usually shown with the P bisecting the X) • *entry into Jerusalem:* palm tree (association); procession in a church *flight into Egypt:* ass, date [fruit], fallen idol, pyramid and star (all are associations) • *grace of Christ:* cruse of oil (the inexhaustible grace of Christ); hand raised with first two fingers extended in blessing • *human nature of Christ:* grain; little finger (association); water mixed with wine at the eucharist (Christ's humanity and divinity, respectively) • *humiliation of Christ:* of thorns; INRI (Latin initials for "Iesus Nazarenus Rex Iudaeorum," Jesus Christ King of the Jews, a mocking title given by Pontius Pilate); manger with enthroned lamb (the humiliation and exaltation of Christ, respectively); open hand (the slapping and mocking of Christ during the Passion—association); scarlet or purple robe (given to Christ by the Roman soldiers to mock him during the Passion) • *incarnation of Christ:* gladiolus; griffin; leopard (the incarnation that was necessary for the redemption of sin); swallow [bird] • *innocence of Christ:* alb (the innocence and prophetic office of Christ); daisy (the innocence of the Christ child) • *justice of Christ:* Christ with a glory [luminous glow around the entire body] (Christ as judge); four dogs (the mercy, justice, truth, and peace of Christ); three dogs (the mercy, justice, and truth of Christ) • *kingship of Christ:* Christ dressed in vestments with crucifix;

crown (attribute); griffin; Jesse tree (the royal genealogy of Christ); lion; salamander (Christ as the king of fire, but may also be the Devil personified); scarlet or purple robe (given to Christ by the Roman soldiers to mock him during the Passion); scepter, especially tipped with a cross (attribute); stole [religious garment]; crown (attributes) • *last supper of Christ:* altar shaped like a table; chalice; ciborium; eucharist; paten (dish used at the last supper); pyx; table • *light of the world, Christ as the:* candle; torch in Nativity scenes; two burning torches • *man and Christ:* birds feeding on grapes (the faithful gathering sustenance from Christ, usually through the eucharist); birds in a vine (souls abiding with Christ); eagle (Christ as mediator between God and man); hen with chicks (the solicitude of Christ); vine with branches (Christ and his followers) • *man's sin borne by Christ:* lamb lying down; scapular; stole [religious garment]; yoke • *mercy of Christ:* four dogs (the mercy, justice, truth, and peace of Christ); three dogs (the mercy, justice, and truth of Christ) • *Middle Ages:* brass (Christ's divinity); leopard • *miracles of Christ:* Christ with baskets of bread (the Feeding of the Five Thousand); man carrying a bed (the Healing of the Paralytic); water pots (first miracle of Jesus) • *nativity of Christ:* ass; Christmas rose (flower language); Christmas starwort (flower language); cradle; frankincense (attribute); Glastonbury thorn (association); hawthorn (association); hellebore; lady's bed straw (the manger of Christ—association); manger (attribute); myrrh (attribute); ox with an ass (attribute); poinsettia; rosemary; shepherd's crook (attribute); stable; staff (attribute); torch in nativity scenes (Christ as the light of the world) • *passion of Christ:* holding a chalice (Christ in Gethsemane); broken communion cup (Christ's agony in Gethsemane); carbuncle [gemstone]; chains; cincture (the flagellation of Christ); cord (attribute); cross; cross with a winding sheet or shroud; crucifix; dalmatic (association); dandelion; goldfinch; INRI (Latin initials for "Iesus Nazarenus rex Iudaeorum,"

Jesus Christ King of the Jews, a mocking title given by Pontius Pilate—emblem); iris [flower] (attribute); Latin cross; maniple (the bands that held the wrists of Christ in the Garden of Gethsemane and when he was dragged through the streets—association); myrrh and aloes; passion flower; poppy (occasional association); rod (attribute); scarlet or purple robe (attribute); scourge [whip] (attribute); thistle (association); torch with a crossed sword (attribute); towel with a pitcher (associated with Pontius Pilate washing his hands during the passion); unbalanced balances [scales] (the trial of Christ—association); violet [color] (association); whipping post (attribute) • *peace of Christ:* four dogs (the mercy, justice, truth, and peace of Christ); olive tree or branch • *redemption by Christ:* blood; Christ child holding an apple or orange (Christ as the future redeemer of mankind); lamb with a white flag (the lamb is Christ, a cruciform flagstaff indicates the way he redeemed man) • *resurrection of Christ:* angel holding a trumpet (resurrection day); Christ with banner (refers to the period after the resurrection and before the ascension); date tree; empty tomb; frog (emblem); gourd; gourd and an apple (the resurrection of Christ as an antidote for sin); Jonah (the precursor of the resurrection of Christ); Phoenix [bird] (early use); lion (Middle Ages); trumpet (association); whale; white flag with a red cross • *sacrifice of Christ:* altar with flames; chalice with a wafer; ox (especially in the early church); Lent • *second coming of Christ:* androsphinx [human head on a lion's body] (the Beast of the Second Coming); Christ with a glory [luminous glow around the entire body] (Christ as judge of mankind); empty throne; lion with a human head and hands (the Beast of the Second Coming) • *suffering of Christ:* passion flower; pelican; Phoenix [bird] (early use) • *temptation of Christ:* monk with claw or cloven hoof showing from under the habit (the Devil in his temptation of Christ); three (association) • *truth of Christ:* four dogs (the mercy, justice, truth, and peace of Christ); three dogs (the mercy, justice, and truth of Christ)

• *wounds of Christ:* alb with the sleeves, chest, and hem embroidered; five (association); Jerusalem cross; pentagram (association) • *see also* **evangelists; eucharist; Gethsemane; trinity; Virgin Mary**

Jews ox (the Jewish nation); salt water (the tears shed by the Jewish race); synagogue • *attributes:* amber [gemstone] (Tribe of Benjamin); yellow hat (Middle Ages); yellow robe; yellow star of David (Nazi Germany) • *bondage in Egypt:* bricks and whip; charoset; maror; mint [plant] • *Christianity:* scorpion; sycamore (the unbelieving Jew) • *emblems:* ass (early Judaic Christians); grapes (Tribe of Ephraim); lion (Tribe of Judah); serpent (Tribe of Dan); wolf with lion (Tribe of Benjamin) • *see also* **Israel; Judaism; synagogue; temple**

jilting cicada (the discarded lover)

Joachim, St. *attributes:* doves in a basket; lamb; lily

Joel *association:* pointed hood

John, St. bleeding shroud pierced by a knife (St. John's shroud, usually held by St. Gregory the Great); nymph with St. John (his victory over worldly temptations); saint praying before an angel and eating a scroll or book (St. John at the Apocalypse); serpent emerging from a cup or chalice (attempted poisoning of St. John); woman rising from a coffin (Drusiana and St. John) • *attributes:* book with an eagle on it; cauldron of boiling oil; chalice or cup (the attempted poisoning of St. John); eagle (by itself, or holding a book and/or inkhorn, or rising from a cauldron; green mantle [cloak]; ox with an eagle, lion, and angel (St. Luke, St. John, St. Mark, and St. Matthew, respectively); red; ship (occasionally); white; writing pen

John Berchmans, St. *attributes:* cross; rosary

John Chrysostom, St. *attributes:* beehive; book with a chalice; dove; writing pen

John Climactus, St. *attribute:* ladder

John Gualberto, St. praying saint before an image or vision of the crucified Christ, with Christ inclining his head to the saint • *attributes:* crutch; sword

John of God, St. *attributes:* crown of thorns: heart [organ]; pomegranate surmounted by a cross

John the Baptist severed head on a horse or a platter • *attributes:* animal skin; axe; banner with cross, held by lamb; banner with cross, or with words "Ecce Agnus Dei"; book with seven seals and a lamb; camel's hair clothes; girdle [cincture] with a locust [insect]; honeycomb; lamb (attribute of John the Baptist as the forerunner of Christ); Latin cross made of reeds; locust [insect]; Maltese cross; pelt; scroll with the words "Ecce Agnus Dei"; scroll with the words "Vox clemantis in deserto"; small cross of reeds; staff with white banner with red cross; white dove • *emblem:* strawberry

John the Hospitator, St. *attribute:* boat

joining *see* **unification; union**

jokes *see* **jests**

Jonah *attributes:* dolphin; gourd; whale

Jophiel *attribute:* flaming sword (held when he drove Adam and Eve from the Garden of Eden)

Josaphat, St. deacon with wings • *attributes:* chalice; crown

Joseph fourteen sheaves (Joseph, his wife, and their twelve sons) • *associations:* eleven (the eleven brothers of Joseph); ten (the ten wicked brothers of Joseph) • *attributes:* bloodstained tunic (Joseph's garment presented to Jacob); coat of many colors; cup in a sack of corn; Egyptian column; mummy; pit; scepter and chain (Joseph's advancement); sheaf (Joseph's dream); well with a fruitful bough above

Joseph, St. carpenter, especially being visited by an angel • *association:* several people praying before an altar on which wands are piled • *attributes:* axe; bright yellow mantle; dove on a rod, staff or wand (the rod, staff, or wand may be flowering); flowering rod, staff, or wand; lily, especially with carpenter's square; plane [tool]; saw [tool]; square [tool] with lily

Joseph of Arimathea, St. *association:* Glastonbury thorn • *attributes:* crown of thorns; grail; nails [for wood]; shroud; tomb

Joshua *association:* ten (the ten servants of Joshua) • *attributes:* grapes; trumpet with sword, pitcher, or scepter

journey *see* **travel**

Jove *see* **Jupiter [god]**

joy amber [gemstone] (joy after sorrow); apple; blue aureole (celestial joy); bell; bubble; butterfly; cherry in Christ's hand (the delight of the blessed); crocus; dancing; diamond [gemstone]; elbows that are itchy; elf (the joys of natural life); flower; flute (phallic, lascivious instrument of erotic anguish or joy); fly [insect] (policeman, priest, or other inhibitor of the preconscious who taints innocent joys); harp; hops (mirth); jasper; lark; laurel; oil; palm tree; persimmon; plucking flowers (innocent joys); raspberry; scattered flowers; ship plowing through waves; tambourine; tear [weeping] (the joy of ecstasy); turtle dove; vineyard (place of joy); white rose; wreath of roses (heavenly joy) • *associations:* three (joyfulness); pink [color]; stringed musical instruments; white; yellow • *China:* chrysanthemum (joviality); red (association) • *Christianity:* alb (eternal joy); bell (Christ's joy); dalmatic; tunicle (joy and contentment of heart) • *flower language:* Cape jasmine (transport of joy); celandine (joys to come); cowslip (early joys, particularly of youth); saffron crocus (mirth); wood sorrel • *heraldry:* cinquefoil [plant]; cup; rose [flower]; silver; wings on a shield (the joy of flourishing prosperity) • *Judaism:* apple eaten with honey (the hope for sweetness and joy in the future) • *see also* **bliss; ecstasy; gaiety; happiness; merriment**

Judah lion cub • *emblems:* five hearts (the five sons of Judah); lily

Judah, Tribe of *emblem:* lion

Judaism acacia (the "burning bush" of Moses and, hence, the giving of the Law); Ark of the Covenant (Old Testament worship; Jewish worship); bull with censer (Yom Kippur, the Day of Atonement); burning bush (God appearing to Moses for the giving of the Law); circumcision (initiation into the Jewish faith); hands upraised with middle and ring fingers separated (Jewish blessing); Old Testament (Jewish worship); shank bone (a reminder of burnt offerings and of the ancient glory of the Temple); synagogue; tent of boughs (Sukkoth, the Feast of the Tabernacles) • *association:* yellow • *attributes:* hand with the middle and ring fingers separated, breastplate (Jewish priests) • *emblems:* eight-branched menorah; seven-branched menorah; six-pointed star (star of David) • *see also* **Jews; synagogue; temples**

Judaism personified crayfish (attribute of the synagogue as the Jewish faith personified)

Judas hanging man; man with a demon whispering in his ear; man with money in his hand; man with a rope around his neck; scorpion • *associations:* dirty yellow; elder tree (in legend: the tree that Judas hanged himself on) • *attributes:* lantern; money bag; money in two hands; polygonal nimbus (usually black); purse; red hair; silver coins (usually thirty); yellow shield • *emblem:* aspen

Jude, St. *attributes:* boathook with a builder's square; closed book; club [bat]; fish and loaves of bread; flail; fuller's club; halberd; inverted cross; knotted club; lance; sailboat, especially when the mast is cross shaped; saw [tool]; spear; square [tool]; sword

Judea *emblem:* elephant

judges capon (a bribe for judges) • *attributes:* black robe; ermine; gavel

judgment balances [scales]; breastplate; chair; darkness, hail (a terrible judgment); eyes; green leaf (sound judgment); Jupiter [god]; linden; man's head on a woman's body (solid and profound judgment); pendulum (balance of judgment); sitting; sword suit [tarot] or silver key (discernment); wormwood (false judgment) • *associations:* five (sympathy, good judgment, and understanding, but these can be perverted); Leo (clear judgment) • *see also* **discretion; taste**

Judgment Day wheat with tares (the believers and nonbelievers, respectively, in the church, that will be separated out at Judgment Day) • *associations:* Gabriel (messenger of Judgment Day); silver cord; trumpet

Judith head that is severed being held by a woman with a sword, being put in a sack, or laying at her feet

Julia, St. *attribute:* cross with rope on it

Julian the Hospitator, St. *attributes:* falcon; oar; ship; stag; sword (occasionally);

Julius Caesar *attribute:* severed head at the feet or in the hand

July *associations:* harvest; lion; ruby • birthstones: ruby; star ruby • *China:* lotus

June *associations:* alexandrite; chalcedony; crab; harvest • birthstones: agate; alexandrite; pearl • *China:* pomegranate blossoms • *emblem:* white flower

Juno woman with an anvil tied to her feet (Juno as Air personified) • *associations:* blue; goose; iris [flower] • *attributes:* anvil, bird (both when Juno is personifying Air); chariot drawn by peacocks; cuckoo; hind [deer]; peacock; scepter tipped with a cuckoo; spear • *emblem:* dittany (for Juno as Lucina, "the bringer of light" who took responsibility for mothers and babies during childbirth)

Jupiter [god] infant suckled by a goat; swan embracing Leda (the swan is Jupiter); white bull bearing a maiden to the sea (Jupiter raping Europa) • *associations:* beech; blue; cypress; dandelion; goat; index finger; indigo [color]; single arch; three; Thursday; tin • *attributes:* chariot drawn by eagles; cow; eagle; horse; lightning; oak wreath; scepter, especially of ivory; thunderbolt • *emblems:* oak; zigzag (Jupiter as the maker of thunderbolts)

Jupiter [planet] *associations:* blue; D; slate violet [color] • *emblem:* eagle carrying a flaming pentagram

jurisdiction cathedra; crozier

jurisprudence *see* **law**

justice angel holding a sword upright; balances [scales]; crane [bird]; dalmatic; elm; ermine; flower; gate; hand; Justice [tarot] (spiritual justice); myrtle; Nestor; old man; ostrich; plummet [tool]; pointed sword; reed; ring; rock; surplice (man renewed in truth and justice); sword (administration of justice); sword suit [tarot] (the meting out of justice); sword with balances [scales]; tablet; throne; wings • *associations:* bed (the dispensation of justice); blue (justice untempered by love); D; diamond suit [playing cards]; eight (justice with mercy); four (justice without mercy); fourteen; Libra; pebble (used to vote for guilt or innocence); purple; six • *China:* iron • *flower language:* rudbeckia; sweet scented tussilage (justice shall be done to you) • *heraldry:* bridge; gauntlet; lozenge [shape]; palm tree; purple; silver; stag (lover of justice and harmony); sword; tree

Justice personified *attributes:* balances [scales]; bandaged or blindfolded eyes (impartiality); circular nimbus; cornucopia (Middle Ages); fasces; globe; hexagonal nimbus; Phoenix [bird]; scepter; sword

Justice [tarot] *association:* H

Justin Martyr, St. *attribute:* sword

Justina, St. woman with a sword through the breast or throat • *attributes:* garment of palm leaves; pot, usually earthen; unicorn

K

Kansas *emblem:* sunflower

karma *association:* nine

key name (the key to power); Solomon's seal (key to the kingdom of heaven)

Kheperi *attribute:* male scarab

kidneys *association:* Venus [planet]

killer hunter

killing breaking of bread, fracture, fragmentation (killing in a ritual sacrifice); kite [bird] (senseless killing); stake being driven through the heart (method for killing a vampire); worm (a killing libidinal figure) • *see also* **compassion; gentleness; murder; sympathy; tenderness**

kindness bluebell; hyacinth [flower]; milk; mulberry tree (kindliness and sharpness combined); raspberry • *Egypt:* lizard • *flower language:* bluebell; flax (I am sensible of your kindness) • *heraldry:* stag

kings aurora borealis, eclipse (omen of the death of a king); balm; Gog and Magog (the king and the people); head; javelin; jester (the inversion of the king); Jupiter [god]; lion; monster ravaging the countryside (a bad king); prince (rejuvenated form of the king) • *associations:* purple; R (often stands for rex [king] or regina [queen]); ten; yellow • *attributes:* crossed legs, right over left; crown; elephant, horse, mule (mount of a king); ermine robes; scepter; throne • *Christianity:* scepter tipped with a cross (Jesus Christ as king); triple tiara (the three estates of the kingdom of God) • *Egypt:* flail (emblem of the king of Egypt) • *England:* scepter tipped with a dove, scepter tipped with an orb and cross (attribute of English kings) • *France:* scepter tipped with a fleur-di-lys (attribute of French kings) • *Greece:* sounding of a bronze gong (the death of a king) • *heraldry:* apple (earthly kingdom); pomegranate (the perfect kingdom) • *see also* **majesty; power**

kinship *see* **family; relationship**

kissing sneezing (omen that you will kiss a fool); sneezing on a Tuesday (omen that you will kiss a stranger); X

kites [birds] jackdaw (shares the unfavorable symbolism of kites and crows)

knees and calves *association:* Saturn [planet]

knights *art:* crossed legs, right over left (knights templar) • *association:* grail (knights of the round table) • *attributes:* armor; ostrich feathers (knightly dignity); spear; spurs; sword • *flower language:* helmet flower, monkshood (knight errant) • *heraldry:* red (desire to serve one's country as a knight); unicorn

knowledge arched, golden, or pearl gate (entrance to knowledge); banyan tree (expanding knowledge); berry; black horse (false knowledge); book; cathedra; comb; compasses [dividers]; crocodile; crystal (intuitive knowledge); dabchick (a seeker of the wisdom of the deeps); diamond [gemstone] (moral and intellectual knowledge); duck (love of knowledge of profound mysteries); eating (the acquisition of knowledge); eyes; fishhook (the means of investigation for esoteric knowledge or knowledge of the unconscious); flowing or full robe; hazel; high forehead; High Priest [tarot] (traditional teaching suitable for the masses; knowledge); High Priestess [tarot]; jewels hidden in caves or underground (the intuitive knowledge of the unconscious); key (especially forbidden knowledge); ladder (the gradual acquisition of knowledge); lasso; light; multicolored garment (diverse and wide knowledge); noose; open book (perfect knowledge); owl; papyrus, especially when rolled; pool [water] (cosmic knowledge); rudder, steering oar (the skill, knowledge and/or bravery of the user); rune (ancient knowledge); sieve (knowledge of self through action); silver key (psychological knowledge); Tiresias (lunar knowledge); white horse (celestial knowledge) • *associations:* brown (practical knowledge); eight (the perfect blending of knowledge and love, conscious and unconscious, action and reaction, etc.); G; heart suit [playing cards]; light complexion; lips; purple • *Christian Science:* Tower of Babel (false knowledge) • *flower language:* parsley (useful knowledge) • *kabala:* two • *spiritual knowledge:* grail; jewels (when protected by a dragon or by other obstacles: the difficulty in obtaining spiritual knowledge) • *see also* **esoterica; learning; Tree of Knowledge; wisdom**

Kore three faces in the moon (Kore, Artemis, and Hecate)

labia *see* **vulva**

labor *see* **childbirth; work**

labyrinth Gordian knot; honeycomb; web

Lachesis *attribute:* spindle

lack ghost (lack of substance); nuditas temporalis (lack of worldly things, especially in service to God); swine (lack of feeling); terror (lack of intellectual will)

ladder to heaven beanstalk; harp; weaving

Lady of the Lake *attribute:* censer

ladybug *association:* scarab

lamb, sacrificial sheep with its feet bound

lamentation aspen; poplar; roof (place for lamentation) • *flower language:* aspen; deep red carnation (alas, my poor heart) • *see also* **grief; mourning**

lamia *attribute:* comb

Lancaster, House of *emblem:* white rose

land grass (acquisition of a territory by conquest); Tuesday (according to the Bible, dry land, pastures, and trees were created on Tuesday)

language Tower of Babel (confusion of speech) • *associations:* curly hair (one who has a facility with foreign languages); lips; tongue

languor afternoon; allspice; bed; cat; couch (a place for reverie, languor, seduction); goldilocks [plant] • *see also* **inertia; laziness; sloth**

Laocoon and his sons two youths and a man wrestling a serpent

Lao Tzu *China:* pine (emblem)

Lares hearth (altar for Lares, Penates, and other home gods)

lasciviousness boar; bull tied to a fig tree (lascivious fury appeased); camel; cat; cicada (restraint of vice and lasciviousness); faun; flute (a phallic and lascivious instrument); frog; hare; lute; monkey; mullet; nymph; partridge; pheasant; quail; satyr; sparrow; swine; tongue • *see also* **debauchery; vice**

Last Supper *see* **Jesus Christ**

latency acorn (latent greatness or strength); captive (the spirit held latent); fairy, seed (latent possibilities); lion (an index of latent passions); Uranus [god] (latent thought); woman held as a captive (higher nature held by latent desire); zero (the latent and potential) • *association:* W (things held in abeyance) • *see also* **incipience; suspension**

laughter *see* **frivolity**

Laurence, St. *see* **Lawrence, St.**

law bridle; chains (legal control); chrysalis (passive and blind obedience to the laws of nature); claw; Emperor [tarot]; gavel; High Priestess [tarot]; Judgment [tarot] (active administration of the law); kneeling (submission to the laws of order); Pasiphae (the deliberate flouting of natural and divine law); plowman (obeyer of natural law); reins; river (obedience to the law); scroll (law; legal document); tablet; web, especially a spider web (the law of man, which catches small transgressors, but lets the big ones get through); yoke • *associations:* F (protection of law and trial); index finger; Libra (legality); scarlet (jurisprudence) • *Christianity:* double headed lectern (the Law and the Gospels) • *Judaism:* acacia (the "burning bush" of Moses, and hence, the giving of the Law)

lawlessness nymph

Lawrence, St. deacon carrying processional cross; man being scourged • *attributes:* censer; dalmatic; dish of money; flaming tunic; garment of palm leaves; gold and silver coins in a dish; gridiron; iron carding comb for wool; money bag

lawyers shark • *attribute:* ermine

laxity *see* **laziness**

Lazarus man rising from coffin • *attribute:* tomb

laziness cat; crayfish; flagellation (encouragement against spiritual laxity or inertia); ibis; lotus; snail; worm • *associations:* Ireland; Latin America; Taurus • *see also* **idleness; inertia; languor; sloth**

Laziness personified *attribute:* frog

leadership aurora borealis (omen of the death of a king or leader); poet (a spiritually advanced person capable of leading others to higher qualities); shepherd's crook (divine leadership); stick; sword • *associations:* A; J • *heraldry:* ram [sheep] • *see also* **guidance**

Leander of Seville, St. *attribute:* writing pen

learning bracelet; candle; conch shell; dew (spiritual illumination); dominoes; eating (the acquisition of knowledge); hare (love of learning); Hermit [tarot]; journey; lamp, especially an oil lamp; spectacles [eyeglasses]; stomach (learning and truth); rabbit (desultory learning and reading) • *heraldry:* star; swan (a learned person) • *see also* **education; knowledge; studying; wisdom**

leaving *see* **farewell**

Lebanon *emblem:* cedar of Lebanon

lechery Asmodeus; centaur; lobster; Peeping Tom spying on Lady Godiva;

ratsbane (lechery causing disease and death); sparrow • *see also* **lust**

Leda swan embracing a young girl (the girl is Leda, the swan is Zeus)

left side *association:* rear; two; woman

legality *association:* Libra

legislators Solon

legitimacy ring • *association:* right side

leisure sitting, especially on the ground • *attributes:* long nails [bodily]; soft hands (the leisure class)

Lent *associations:* forty; purple; violet [color]

Leo [zodiac] *associations:* dandelion; east; gold; Hermit [tarot]; I [letter]; K; lion; marigold; orange [color]; palm tree; peony; peridot; ruby; sun; yellow

Leonard, St. *attributes:* broken chains; dalmatic with a fleur-di-lys

leopard panther (frequently confused with the leopard, with which it shares symbolism, especially in heraldry)

lesson Hanged Man [tarot] (a public lesson); index finger upraised

lethargy *see* **inertia; languor; laziness; sloth**

Lethargy personified *attribute:* poppy

Leto *associations:* date tree (sacred to Leto); peasants by osiers, turning into frogs

letters [epistles] capon (a love letter); sneezing on a Wednesday (you sneeze for a letter); spark in a candle flame (a stranger or letter will come)

Leucothea *emblem:* gull

Levi association and *emblem:* sword and water pitcher • *attribute:* censer

levity *see* **frivolity**

liars *see* **lying [prevarication]**

Liberal Arts personified, Seven *attribute:* scroll (the Seven Liberal Arts, especially Logic, but also Music, Astronomy, Arithmetic, Geometry, Rhetoric, and Grammar)

Liberalis, St. man in armor, often shown leaning against a spear or holding a banner

liberality cornucopia; St. Julian • *China:* bamboo (open-mindedness) • *heraldry:* cup; purse (a liberal blessing); swan with a crown on its neck (liberal views); vine

liberty broken chains; butterfly; oak; ocean; Phrygia; rod; sandals; shoes; stocks [for restraint] (loss of liberty); Sun [tarot] (liberation from physical limitations); sword; torch (revolution and ultimate liberty) • *associations:* Aquarius (the loosening of bonds; the immanence of liberation); green • *flower language:* live oak • *heraldry:* cat • *see also* **freedom**

Liberty personified *attribute:* two crowns

libido drunkenness (closely related to fornication as a libido symbol); elephant (the power of the libido); fire; heat; intoxicant; locomotive; metal; monster; phallus; Sphinx; worm (a killing libidinal figure) • *see also* **sex; vitality**

Liborius, St. *attributes:* peacock; pebble

Libra *associations:* ash tree; blue; copper; green; H; jasper; lilac [plant]; rose [color]; sapphire; smoky quartz; tourmaline; Venus [planet] • *emblem:* balances [scales]

Libyan sibyl [Libyana] *attribute:* torch

licentiousness *see* **debauchery; lasciviousness; sex; vice; wantonness**

lies *see* **lying [prevarication]**

life acorn; apron (purity of life and conduct); aquatic plant (the nascent character of life); asp; bacon; Balder (the life principle); banana (continuing life); beetle (life reduced to smallness); broken cup (broken life); butterfly; candelabrum (life; spiritual life); candle (especially the life of an individual); Capricorn (the dual tendencies of life toward the high and the low, the physical and the spiritual); carrion (low life); Catherine wheel; chess; clay cup (man's life); crane [bird] (good life and works); diamond [gemstone]; disguise (entrance into a new life); Egyptian cross [ankh]; elf, fairyland (the real joys of the natural life) firebrand; flour (abundant life); flowering tree; fly [insect] (diminutive life); fountain (life; future life); grasshopper (the carefree life); green; gypsy (the footloose life); hare; heron (the generation of life); hiding (the period of life before and after its involution as matter, or before and after manifest life appears); house chimney; loom (the mysterious strands of life woven into one span); lotus; Lovers [tarot] (harmony of inner and outer life); manna (bread of life); marigolds mixed with red flowers (the varying course of life); milk (elixir of life); mistletoe; mother (the life principle, indifferent to individual human suffering); mummy; myrtle; naked child (new life); ocean (generative life); ogre (prehuman savage life); orange [fruit]; Ouroboros (continuity of life); oyster (lowest form of animal life); Pan (base of involutive life); phallus (perpetuation of life); plant [biology]; pulse; rabbit, especially a young rabbit; Rachel (the contemplative life); rain; red flower (animal life); river (obedience to life, time, and the law); road; rock (the spirit of human life); rocking cradle (the ups and downs of life); sandals (lowest form of material life); scarab (creation and revival of life); scarlet; scroll; serpent (subterranean life); sewing; shuttle [weaving] (man's life); singing (fostering and bringing forth life); solar wheel; spark; sphere (intellectual life, wheel of life); Sphinx (watchdog over the ultimate meaning of life, which remains forever beyond man's reach); spindle; spine; spinning of thread (the bringing forth and fostering of life); stag (purity and solitude of life); swinging (life's changing fortunes); tarot deck (the flow of life; portrays the complementary struggles in man's life: self vs. others, physical vs. spiritual, etc.); tea (the brew of life); thirst (blind appetite for life); thread; thyrsus; tortoise (Chaos, with the hope of renewal of life); train [transportation]; Tree of Life (the life of the cosmos); unrolling carpet (the unfolding of life); upright torch; vale (protected life); violet [flower] (humble life); waves [water] (the flux and reflux of life); weaving, especially as a feminine activity; well; wool (homely and simple life) • *associations:* black (mineral life); black and white together (the humility and purity of life, respectively); blood; bone; bread (life; the means of sustaining life); eighteen; five (organic fullness of life); green (victory over the vicissitudes of life); right side; six (life; family life); Spring • *brevity of life:* ashes; bubble; eyebrows that meet (sign of a person who will not live to marry); flower (especially with dewdrops); grass; hourglass; insect; lantern (transitory life in the face

of the eternal); skull; skull and crossbones; smoke; spindle; wildflower (a short, perhaps unhappy life); World [tarot] *China:* red (association); sheep (the retiring life) • *Christianity:* hare (the rapid course of life); hart (the faithful partaking of the waters of life) • *cycle of life:* agriculture (cyclic existence); earth [soil] (the cycle of existence as a symbol of man's life); flower; Temperance [tarot] (ceaseless cycling through formation, regeneration, and purification) • *divine life:* food (the visible form of divine life); potter's wheel (the Christian's life shaped by divine influence) • *Egypt:* palm tree (life in the abstract) • *emblem:* skull and crossbones (danger to life) • *eternal life:* butterfly; chancel arch (passage from this world into eternal life); crown; dove with olive branch; egg surrounded by serpent (the eternal germ of life encircled by creative wisdom); flowing fountain; harbor; holly; monolith; obelisk; peacock; seaweed; skull and crossbones (meditation on the eternal life that comes after death); tree; wine (youth and eternal life) • *flower language:* lucerne • *heraldry:* apple (fullness of life); butterfly (transitory life); palm tree • *life force:* balances [scales] (any binary function, such as life and death, good and evil, etc.); fossil; lake (transition between life and death, often in a destructive sense); ocean (mediator between life and death); painted veil; sarcophagus (the earth as the beginning and end of material life); skull with a cross (meditation on the eternal life that comes after death); spiral (mystery of life and death); starling (life in death); uraeus (power over life and death); wood • *material life:* bubble (the emptiness of material existence); Death [tarot] (dematerialization); dove embedded in lead (the spirit embedded in matter); earth [soil] (the moral opposite of what is heavenly and spiritual; the end of material life; the sustainer of material life); eating (material existence); Eve (the material and formal aspect of life); four (the material aspect of life—association); goat; green (material decay—association); hare (material existence); mother; plant [biology] (the healthy growth of plants indicates cosmic, spiritual, and material fecundity); sarcophagus (the earth as beginning and end of material life); sandals (the lowest form of material life); Scorpio (association); turtle (material existence) *Norse:* cup (life token) • *primitive life:* monolith; monster; reindeer; reptile • *renewal of life:* Sun [tarot]; thirty-six (Judaism); water cress • *River of Life* Jordan River; meadow (association); • *seat of life:* king; nostrils (seat of the breath of life) • *source of life:* chalice; east; heat; ocean; Orient; serpent (guardian of the source of life); slug [animal]; water • *Tree of Life:* ankh [Egyptian cross]; cross, especially when flowering; date tree (Near East); mast; maypole; poplar; seven branched menorah; squirrel (messenger of the Tree of Life); trident • *unfolding of life:* mat being unrolled; unrolling papyrus or scroll (the top roll is the future; the bottom roll is the past) • *universal life:* ocean; Temperance [tarot] • *see also* **living**

light axe (the power of light); butterfly (the unconscious attraction toward light, truth, or God); candelabrum (the spiritual light of salvation); diamond [gemstone]; gold (pure light); iris [flower]; lamp; lotus; necklace; oil; onion; pyramid (eternal light); rod; ruby; slug [animal] (the tendency of darkness to move toward light); south (light; spiritual light); stable (light and revelation arising from ignorance; the realm of ignorance from which light emerges); sun (creative light; guiding light; the source of light); toe (ray of light) • *associations:* one; stag; Sunday (according to the Bible, the day God created light); white; yellow (infernal light); white • *Christianity:* candle, torch in Nativity scenes, two burning torches (Jesus Christ as the light of the world) • *divine light:* arrow (the light of divine power); bo tree; crystal ball; flaming pillar or tree trunk (the God of light and wisdom) • *Druidism:* three feathers (faith, hope, and the Light of the World) • *see also* **illumination**

light-heartedness *see* **gaiety; happiness**

lightness butterfly; linden leaf; shuttle [weaving] • *flower language:* larkspur

lighting arrow; axe; bow with arrows

(fire and lightning); drum (thunder and lightning); eagle; spear • *association:* Z • *emblems:* peridot; zigzag • *see also* **thunder**

limitation bowl; caulking (the limitation of ideas); circumference (objects contained within are limited, defined, and of the manifest world); dish; meadow; spy; Sun [tarot] (liberation from physical limitations); wall • *associations:* D; square [shape] • *Christianity:* purple mantelleta (worn by bishops as a sign of limited authority or jurisdiction); red mantelleta (worn by a cardinal as a sign of limited authority or jurisdiction) • *see also* **restraint**

limitlessness circle; field (limitless possibility); freedom from restraint)

link *see* **connection**

Lioba, St. *attribute:* washing of feet in a basin

lion *association:* hippogryph (combines the favorable aspects of both the horse and lion)

literature feather as a quill pen; laurel wreath (distinction in literature or music); scroll with pencil or quill • *association:* blue stockings (attribute of a woman having intellectual or literary interests) • *China:* sturgeon (literary eminence) • *portraiture:* laurel (implies the subject was a literary or artistic figure) • *see also* **poetry; writers**

liveliness *see* **vivacity**

liver hepatica • *associations:* E, I [letter]; N; O [letter]; W

lividness *association:* white

living sailing (living to transcend existence); ship of fools (sailing or living as an end in itself and not in the sense of seeking a safe arrival in heaven) • *association:* spring [season] (the living) • *attributes:* beard (in early art, living persons were shown with a beard, the dead were shown clean shaven); rectangular nimbus (indicates the holiness of a person still living); square or rectangular nimbus (attribute of a person honored while still living) • *see also* **life**

loathing *see* **disgust**

loftiness *see* **elevation**

logic mill (logic as a protection against passion); myrrh; ocean (immense illogic) • *associations:* E; right hand; thumb • *see also* **rationality; reason**

Logic personified Aristotle • *attri-*

butes: lizard; scorpion; scroll; serpent; tamed falcon

Loki milkmaid (disguise of Loki)

Lombardy *heraldry:* poplar

loneliness bluebottle (single wretchedness); city; cottage in a vineyard; ocean; owl; pelican; room [chamber] • *see also* **isolation; solitude**

longevity agate; algae; bamboo; bat [animal]; carp; cat; cedar; Chinese evergreen; crane [bird]; crow; deer; dove; eagle; elephant; elm; fig; heron; ivy; juniper; malachite; oak; peach; pine; sage [herb]; sea coral; stag; stork; sturgeon; tortoise; tree; turtle; walnut • *China:* bat [animal]; crane [bird]; deer; dove; five bats [animals] (the blessings of longevity, wealth, health, virtue, and a natural death); fox; hare; knot; peach tree; pigeon; sea coral; stork; tortoise; unicorn • classical times: holly oak • *Orient:* lobster • *see also* **aged**

longing ascending stairs (longing for a higher world); aspiration (the yearning of lower nature for the higher); breeze (amorous yearning); cairngorm (homesickness); cold [temperature] (longing, especially for solitude); cross (man's longing for the higher world); dangling, hanging (unfulfilled longing); harp (longing for love or death); hyacinth [gemstone] (the desire for heaven); journey (unsatisfied longing); nightmare (the longing of man for God); poison ivy; sitting at a window; talking and singing birds (amorous yearning); trumpet (yearning for fame, glory, and power) • *association:* ocean (longing for adventure) • *see also* **aspiration; desire; wishing**

Longinus, St. soldier with lance, on horseback • *attributes:* lance; pyx

loose women *see* **courtesans; mistresses; promiscuity; prostitutes; wantonness**

loquacity *see* **chatter**

loss abandonment (loss of contact with God or nature); Gordian knot, labyrinth (the loss of the spirit in the process of creation and the need to find it again); Mars (associated with the idea that there is no creation without sacrifice); river (the sense of loss); russet mantle [clothing] (loss of good reputation) skidding (loss of control of the id by the ego and superego)

• *associations:* blue (loss of love); fourteen; marriage on a Friday; V • *flower language:* dried white rose (death is preferable to loss); mourning bride (I have lost all)

lotus *associations:* honeysuckle (shares in the symbolism of the lotus); wheel

Louis IX, St. man with a crown and scepter at his feet • *attributes:* cross; crown; crown of thorns; fleur- di-lys; lily; nails [for wood]

Louis XII of France, King *heraldry:* hedgehog surmounted by a crown

Louis XIV of France, King *emblem:* sun

love amaranth, globe amaranth (steadfast love); amethyst (usually deep love, sometimes dalliance); animal fat; apricot flower (timid love); Balder; barley, especially red barley; beryl; bird; blown dandelion with many seeds remaining (a lover is indifferent); blown dandelion with some seeds remaining (a lover is unfaithful); bluebottle (hope in love); breasts; brooch given as a gift (broken love or friendship); broom [plant] (rejected love); Buddha; burr sticking to one's clothing (being in love); butterfly; cactus (ardent love); camomile (love in adversity); capon (love letter); carbuncle [gemstone]; carnation (love; first love); cat's eye [gemstone] (platonic love); chameleon; chaos (absence of love); charity (universal love); chrysolite (unrequited love); clover (ardent but humble love); cocoa tree; coconut; crocus (illicit love); daffodil, nightingale (unrequited love); dimple; divorce (the apparent or delusive separation of love from wisdom); dolphin; doves, especially when billing (love; amorous delight); ear burning or tingling, or an earring falling off (your sweetheart is thinking of you); fever; flame; flower (love, especially female love); fuchsia (confiding love); gazelle, rose [flower] (the beloved); golden arrow (kindles love); goose; hand flat on the heart; hands clasped in a handshake; harp (longing for love or death); hazel (love and fertility); heart [organ] (love; romantic love; love as the center of illumination and happiness); half man/half goat (love and hate); hearth; honeysuckle; hyacinth [flower] (love and its woes); ivy; jasmine; knot; lamp; lead arrow (drives love away); lilac [flower] (first love); linen; lock of hair (love fetish); louse [insect]; magnolia (love; love of nature); malachite (success in love); morning (renewal of love); mirror; mulberry tree (tragic love); muteness (inability to express love from within); myrtle (love; everlasting love); net (love and fertility); nightingale (night love); ointment; olive (courageous love and faith); opal (increases faithfulness, tenderness, and happiness in love); orange [fruit]; orchid; papyrus; pea; periwinkle; pillow; pin; pomegranate; Pyramus and Thisbe (perfect love); red flower; red rose; robin; rochet (loving administration); roebuck; ruby; scarf; seal [stamp]; seraph (the spirit of love and imagination); sheep; shoes; smoke; soldier on a couch with a woman, his weapon put aside (love conquering war); sparrow; spice; starfish (inextinguishable power of love); Strength [tarot] (triumph of love over hate); sulfur and eggs (cure for unrequited love); summer; sunflower (infatuation); sycamore; talking and singing birds (amorous yearning); thrush; tomato; topaz (ardent love and gentleness); turtle doves; two eyes (binary functions such as intelligence and love, male and female, sun and moon, etc.); Venus [goddess] (love in the physical or sexual sense, occasionally love in the spiritual sense); virgin (love of self); warmth; wasp (generally an unfavorable symbol, but also can mean love); white rose (chaste love); willow (forsaken love); wolfsbane (illicit love); yeast • associations: balcony; birch; blue (love; heavenly love; loss of love; nonerotic, tender love); blue eyes (sign of being in love); crimson; eight (the perfect blending of knowledge and love, the conscious and unconscious, action and reaction, etc.); five (love and health); Friday (works of love); hair; hook; lark; mugwort (love potions); Phrygia; purple; red; rye; scarlet (mutual love); six; sixteen; three; Venus [planet] (love in all its forms); violet [color] (love of truth) • carnal love: arrow piercing a heart (emblem); arum (flower language); balcony; balsam (flower language); billy goat (Christianity); blue (in the Middle Ages, worldly love—association); blue eyes

(association); braided hair (association); burr sticking to one's clothing (association); bush, hedge (places for illicit love); cactus; candle; canoe; carnation (first love); cicada (the jilted lover); clover (ardent but humble love; cuckoo plant (flower language); Cupid (association); flute; heart; heliotrope (intoxicated with love); Lovers [tarot]; melting wax (hot love); milkmaid (robust, but not too discriminate love); nightingale (worldly love); perfume; putto (harbinger of profane love); red double pink (pure and ardent love—flower language); ruby; salamander (the ardent lover); scarf; spearmint (burning love); tea (amorous intrigue and scandal—association); topaz (ardent love and gentleness); Venus [goddess] (love in the physical or sexual sense, although occasionally in the spiritual sense); wagtail; wake robin (flower language); wind and rain (physical love) • China: orchid; peony • conjugal love: duck; geranium; ivy; linden (flower language); lyre (emblem); maple; myrtle; pair of geese (China) • declaration of love: bouquet; moss rose (confession of love), red tulip (flower language); tulip • divine love: amaranth (love of God excluding all other affections); anointing with oil (endowing the soul with divine love); basin and/or ewer (the humility of Christ's love); bite (mark of divine love); blue and red (love and authority, often used for the color of God's clothes—association); bramble (Judaism); burning bush; butter (divine love and wisdom); carnation; Christmas; columbine; cross with anchor and heart (faith, hope, and charity, respectively); diamond [gemstone]; dianthus; dome; flaming heart (Christian love); frankincense; grapes (the spiritual nature of love and wisdom); hand raised with first two fingers extended (love of God and communion with the Holy Spirit); heart; lamb; light; narcissus (divine love triumphing over worldliness); oil; ointment, unguent (divine love and truth); olive (courageous love and faith); pear (Christ's love of mankind) red (association); red rose; topaz (divine love and goodness); vase with flame coming from its mouth (attribute of Sacred Love personified); X (association) • *emblem:* arrow piercing a heart (love, especially romantic love) • *female love:* carnation; carnation pink (flower language); flower (love, especially female); marigold (endurance in love, especially of women); ring; twisted belt (a woman in love) • *fidelity in love:* lemon; lemon blossoms (flower language) • *flower language:* ambrosia (love returned); American cowslip (you are my angel, my divinity); arkansa coreopsis (love at first sight); balsam (ardent love); blue violet; cabbage rose (ambassador of love); campion rose (only deserve my love); carnation (woman's love); Carolina rose (love is dangerous); catchfly (pretended love); creeping willow (love forsaken); dandelion (love's oracle); four leaf clover (be mine); garden or small double daisy (I share your affection—used especially in the days of chivalry); flower; honey (sweet and secret love); lotus flower (estranged love); magnolia (love of nature); maiden blush rose (if you love me, you will reveal it; if you love me, you will find it out); marigolds mixed with roses (sweet sorrows of love); moss rose; Near East tulip (violent love); paleness (lovesickness); peach blossom (I am your captive); peppermint (the combination of the coldness of fear with the warmth of love); purple lilac (first emotions of love); red bay; red catchfly (youthful love); red chrysanthemum (I love); red double pink (pure and ardent love); red single pink (pure love); rose, especially a red rose; scabious (unfortunate love); strawberry tree (love and esteem); Syrian mallow (consumed by love); violet; white rose (heart of ignorant love); wild violet (love in idleness); woodbine (bond of love; inconstancy in love); yellow chrysanthemum (slighted love); yellow tulip (hopeless love); yellow sweet brier (decrease of love) • *fraternal love:* Castor and Pollux; Gemini; lilac [color] (association); mock orange, woodbine [monthly honeysuckle] (flower language) • *heraldry:* apple; dove (loving constancy); ivy (constant love) • *maternal love:* cinquefoil [flower]; coltsfoot (maternal care); hind [deer]; linnet; mare (mother as protector);

Melusina (heraldry); moss (flower language); panther (a beautiful woman, normally tender, but fierce in defense of her children—heraldry); pheasant; warmth (maternal comfort); woman nursing a child; wood sorrel (maternal tenderness—flower language) • *Rome:* lapis lazuli (association) • *secret love (flower language):* honey flower (sweet and secret love); motherwort; toothwort; yellow acacia • *self-love:* Narcissus; narcissus [flower]; poet's narcissus (flower language); virgin • *true love:* emerald; forget-me-not (flower language) • *see also* **affection; attachment; courtship; desire; family; friendship; happiness; marriage; parent and child; passion; selfishness; self-love; vanity**

love goddesses *attributes:* golden hair; lion • *emblem:* strawberry

Love personified chariot drawn by four white horses (attribute of Cupid personifying love) • *association:* goat • *attributes:* jewels (attribute of Profane Love personified); vase with flames coming from its mouth (attribute of Sacred Love personified)

lovelessness cold [temperature]

loveliness gentian; moon (serene loveliness) • *China:* peony • *feminine loveliness:* justica (in flower language: perfection of female loveliness); peony • *flower language:* Australian rose (thou art all that is lovely); hyacinth (unobtrusive loveliness); Indian double pink (lovely always); orange blossoms (your purity equals your loveliness); red rosebud (you are pure and lovely); white camellia japonica (perfected loveliness) • *see also* **beauty; comeliness**

the Lover personified *attribute:* lute

lovers bush, hedge (refuge of the lover); cicada (the discarded lover); pilgrim; pipe [music] (phallus, especially when played by a male lover); salamander; bush, hedge (refuge of the lover); pilgrim; shepherd (the rustic lover); sneeze on a Saturday, your lover will see you tomorrow • *associations:* hawthorn trained over a bench to make a bower; sixteen (the ideal age for a lover) • *attributes:* lute; paleness (lovesickness); staff, especially with purse • *flower language:* rosemary (fidelity between lovers) • *see also* **courtship; suitors**

Lovers [tarot] *associations:* F; V

lower classes archer (a soldier of the lower classes); crow (a plebeian); dahlia (the dignity of the lower or middle class); beans, lentils, oats (humble foods); beer (the drink of the common man, but in ancient times, the drink of the gods); gallows (typical execution of lower class criminals, especially thieves); grass; hind [deer] (low birth) • *associations:* garlic; musical instruments of wood • *England:* bricks (associated with lower class upstarts) • *see also* **humbleness; peasantry**

Lowliness bramble; sandal (the lowest form of material life); swineherd • *association:* yellow • *see also* **baseness**

loyalty changing clothes (changing loyalties, personalities, roles, opinions, beliefs, etc.); crane [bird]; dog (from the Middle Ages to present); hearth (filial loyalty); shamrock; shofar (supreme loyalty to God); sunflower; violet [flower] • *association:* red • *heraldry:* blue; greyhound • *see also* **allegiance; constancy; faithfulness; fidelity**

lubricity *see* **lechery; lust**

Lucia, St. sword piercing a woman's neck

lucidity *see* **clarity**

Lucifer *see* **Satan**

Lucina dittany (emblem of Juno as Lucina, "the bringer of light" who took responsibility for mothers and babies during childbirth)

luck *see* **fortune; misfortune**

Lucretia soldier in a bedchamber, holding a naked woman at swordpoint (rape of Lucretia) • *attribute:* dagger

Lucy, St. *attributes:* cord; knife; lamp; ox; two eyes carried on a platter; wound on the neck

Luke, St. bull with wings and nimbus; ox with an eagle, lion, and angel (St. Luke, St. John, St. Mark, and St. Matthew, respectively) • *attributes:* painting of the Virgin Mary; palette; writing pen

Lumiel *associations:* nine (all angels, but especially Lumiel); ten; twenty; zero

Luna *association:* Monday • *attributes:* bow and arrows; chariot drawn by one white horse and one black horse; crescent moon

lunacy *see* **madness**

the lunar *see* **moon**

lungs *associations:* J; S

lurking *see* **hiding**

lust ape; ass; baboon; burning; cat; cobbler (from the vagina symbolism of shoes); cosmetics; crane [bird]; crocodile; dark complexion (lustiness); flute; fly [insect]; fox (bucolic lust); full, thick head of hair; gadfly [insect] (noisome lust); goat; hare; hare of white at the Virgin Mary's feet (her triumph over lust); heated plow; honey; horse; leopard; liver; marrow; meadow; nanny goat; neighing; night (the lustful female); nuditas criminalis; oven; oyster; pipe [music]; porpoise; satyr; scorpion; swine; syrinx; turtle; whale; wine; woodpecker; wren; wryneck (feminine lust) • *associations:* orange [color]; sphinx (occasionally) • *see also* **desire; lechery**

Lust personified *attributes:* boar; goat; greyhound; hare; mirror; two doves; plow; rooster; satyr; sparrow; swine; toad hanging from the breasts of a woman, or eating female genitalia; torch; veil

luster *see* **brilliance**

Luther, Martin *association:* six hundred and sixty-six [666] (number of the Beast of the Apocalypse, also applied to other Protestants and Adolf Hitler) • *emblem:* anthurium

luxury angora cat (expensive luxury a pampered and spoiled person, especially a woman); Babylon; bath; butter; carpet; fig; ointment; orchid; panther; peach; pheasant; silk • *association:* sixteen

Lydia, St. *attribute:* snail with scallop shell

lying [prevarication] blister on the tongue (sign of a lie); crossed fingers, especially when hidden; duck; Liguria; macaroni; mole [animal]; Pytho; russet [cloth] (love of lies and darkness); two faces; whetstone • *flower language:* bugloss; dogsbane; jasmine; manchineal tree; yellow lily • *United States:* index and little finger raised (bull horns, and by extension, bull excrement, meaning a lie, or nonsense) • *see also* **dissimulation; falsity; intrigue; treachery**

Lying personified *attribute:* bugloss

M

machinery iron

madness bat [animal]; bee; buttercup; cuckoo; disheveled hair; hare (madness, especially youthful madness); Hecate (the feminine principle responsible for madness, obsession); horn [animal]; mare (erotic madness); moon; mouse; narcissus fumes; rosemary; rue (antidote for madness); turkey; wind • *association:* nudity • *see also* **psyche**

maenads *attribute:* tambourine

magi *associations:* casket of frankincense; casket of myrrh; gold

magic angelica; black robe; book; brooch in the shape of an animal (endows the wearer with characteristics of that animal); cat (magical forces); clockwise swastika (white magic); drum (a vehicle for magic); echo (magical in that it may remember what it hears); effigy (has magical properties for warding off evil spirits, for fertility, and for placating the gods); engine; harlequin (magic transformations); herb; moon; Moon [tarot]; pentagram; rune; painting, picture (magic access to the soul); mummy (magic beyond the grave); foot; tattoo (counter-magic); tattoo (counter-magic); whistling (magical act) • *associations:* clock, engine (related to the creation of beings that pursue their own autonomous existence); excrement; hair; left side; mandrake; mask; menstrual blood; nail clippings; one hundred twenty (a magical number); wand • *black magic:* bat [animal]; counterclockwise swastika; dancing; Devil [tarot] • *magic power:* abnormality (an indication of magical powers); blue flower (magic or special powers); cat, crow (possessors of magic powers); crossroads (a place of magic power); foot; footprint (thought to have the magic powers of the maker); gloves (thought to have the magic power of their owner); hair; mandrake (association); mermaid, merman (the power of song-magic); rubbing [motion] (the transfer of magical powers) • *magic spells:* circle or wheel of fire; kiss (breaking a spell);

frog or seal [animal] (may be a human under a magic spell); oats (the bewitching soul of music—flower language); yarrow (flower language—association) • *see also* **enchantment**

magicians *attributes:* cape; magic wand; top hat

magnanimity lion at the feet of saints and martyrs • *association:* yellow • *heraldry:* bull; ox; red • *see also* **generosity**

magnetism, personal *see* **charisma**

magnificence Emperor [tarot]; magnolia; plane tree; sun; tulip • *flower language:* Asiatic ranunculus (your charms are resplendent); calla aethiopica (magnificent beauty) • *heraldry:* sun (magnificent example) • *see also* **glory; grandeur; majesty**

magnitude point (that which has no magnitude)

maidens dimple (attribute of attractive children and maidens); paleness (maidenhood) • *see also* **girls; virginity; women**

majesty cedar; Chariot [tarot]; lily; mountain; oak; throne • *association:* six • *flower language:* crown imperial; lily, especially the imperial lily • *see also* **grandeur; kings; magnificence**

male and female anvil with cross or sword (male and female: the anvil is female); chess (the sexes meeting on equal terms); dart and egg design (male generation and female productiveness); Endymion (man trespassing into woman's realm); rising mist (the female principle in nature desiring the male); triangle within a circle; wheels within wheels

male principle air; cydippe; father; fire; gun; hammer; head; heaven; light; lily; lion; oboe; menhir; phallus; Pierrot (the male principle still in a state of innocence); pillar; plow; rod; rooster; sky; spade [shovel]; staff; sword; torch; triangle with the apex up; vowel; wand; yang (the light color of yin and yang) • *associations:* monolith; odd numbers; one; straight sword • *union of the male and female principles:* caduceus; flagpole with a ball on top; guitar; hearth with a fire; horn [animal]; king and queen; maltese cross; marriage; maypole; serpent with its tail in its mouth; sexual intercourse; six-pointed star; Sphinx; swan; Temperance [tarot]

males bull, hound, lion (male sexual desire); cherry tree (masculine virtue); closed mouth, or mouth with tongue sticking out; dragonfly (male dominance); hare (generally a male figure, but sometimes a woman of loose morals); slug [animal] (the male seed); spaniel (emasculation); sun; thunderbolt (male orgasm); whistling (a typical male activity, sometimes considered taboo for women) • *associations:* carp (a masculine fish); hook; lilac (male homosexuality)

malice adder (hidden evil; deadly malice); ape; elf (dark colored elves are generally unfavorable and may kill babies); goblin; leaven; lizard; monkey; rattlesnake; tongue (malicious talk); troll [folklore] • *association:* orange is impure [color] • *flower language:* lobelia • *see also* **hate**

malignancy octopus

Malignity personified *attribute:* quail

Mami *emblem:* bricks

Mammon idol (Mammon worship)

man *see* **mankind; men; women**

manger *see* **Jesus Christ**

manhood *see* **male principle; men**

manias *see* **obsessions**

manifestation circumference (objects contained within are limited, defined, and of the manifest world); Wheel of Fortune [tarot]

mankind Adam (the weak, sinful side of man); belly (the physical side of man); bird cage (man's contrariness); bone (the indestructible part of man); breath (the divine element in man); bucentaur (the dual nature of man); caterpillar (man in his world); Caucasian (the spiritual side of man); devil (the unrealized dark side of man); earth [soil] (the cycle of man's existence); Egypt (the animal in man); giant (universal man); gypsy (primitive man); king (the grandeur and universal aspect of man; archetypal man); king that is sick (the negative aspect of man); ladder (the ceaseless striving of man); lighthouse (the remoteness and solitude of man); Magic [tarot] (man in his struggle with occult powers); monster (the instincts that hinder man in his search for truth); Moon [tarot] (upward progress of man); Mount Ararat (the second cradle of mankind); ostrich (sinful man); pansy; plow (man's earthly consciousness); pottery vase; puppet (man as the plaything of deities or fate); Sagittarius (the complete man in both animal and spiritual nature); Saturn [god] (man as an existential being); savage (natural man); shuttle [weaving] (man's life); sorcerer (the dark unconscious of man); the soul (man's creative or eternal part); steed (the animal in man); tower; Wandering Jew (alludes to the imperishable part of man which cannot die); werewolf (the irrationality latent in man and the possibility of it reawakening); white surplice (man renewed in justice and in truth); worm (insignificant man) • *associations:* blue (the spirit of man); four (usually a human number, but may also be associated with divinity); Friday (according to the Bible, land beasts and man were created on Friday); Leo (spiritual beginnings of man); red (body of man); square [shape] (man not yet at one with himself); yellow • *China:* orchid (the perfect or superior man) • *Fall of Man:* angel holding a flaming sword (expulsion from the Garden of Eden); ape with an apple in its mouth; apple; clothing (lack of innocence as the result of The Fall of Man); elephant; five (associated with mankind after The Fall); giant (man before The Fall); orange [fruit] shown in Paradise (The Fall of Man and his redemption); precipice; serpent encircling a tree; skull; spade [shovel]; thistle • *mankind and God:* blood (Christ's redemption of man); nightmare (man longing for God); olive tree or branch (reconciliation of God and man); ostrich (man deserted by God); pear (Christ's love of mankind); pilgrim (man in his search for salvation); rainbow and/or ark (God's covenant with Noah and man); stole [religious garment] (man's sin borne by Christ) • *natural mankind:* American Indian, gypsy, Negro, nuditas naturalis (the natural state of man); savage, tramp [hobo] (the primitive, instinctive self); shadow (the primitive side of a person); wild man, wild woman (the primitive, instinctive, natural, and emotional self); young man (the primitive mind) • *see also* **men; people; women**

Manlius Torquatus head with the body it was severed from

marble mud (the opposite of marble)

March [month] *associations:* heliotrope [gemstone]; ram [sheep] • birthstones: aquamarine; bloodstone • *China:* tree peony (emblem)

Marcus Curtius soldier on horseback, leaping into a pit

Margaret of Antioch, St. woman emerging from the stomach of a dragon • *attributes:* cross with martyr's palm; crown; dragon led by a cord or underfoot; garment of palm leaves; pearl

Margaret of Cortona, St. praying saint before an image or vision of the crucified Christ, with Christ inclining his head to the saint • *attributes:* bulldog (occasionally); spaniel

Mark, St. ox with an eagle, lion, and angel (St. Luke, St. John, St. Mark, and St. Matthew, respectively) • *attributes:* fuller's club; lion; rope around the neck; writing pen • *emblems:* lion, especially with wings; ox with wings

marriage bed; blue ribbon; bracelet; bull tied to a tree (a man subdued in marriage); butterfly (conjugal bliss); butterfly in the house (omen of a forthcoming marriage); cage; cat (guardian of marriage); chains; dog (marital fidelity, especially when shown on a woman's lap or at her feet); elm tree with vine (marriage; the ideal husband and wife relationship); eyebrows that meet (sign of a person who will not live to marry); fasces (unity, especially in marriage); five-petalled lotus; hands clasped beneath the hand of God (the blessing of marriage by the church); hands clasped in a handshake (mystic marriage); ivy (wedded love); knot, especially interlaced with initials; lotus (the sexual prison of marriage); lute (marital bliss); marjoram; myrtle (conjugal fidelity); needle; onyx (promotes happiness in marriage); pansy; peach; pin; plague; quince; ring; sea coral; sistrum; stocks [for restraint]; torch; two fish (the joy of union; marriage; domestic felicity); verbena;

Wednesday (the best day for a marriage); well with trees (divine marriage); white dress • *associations:* bright yellow; five; gold; orange [color]; ring finger; six; ten; three • *China:* fish (connubial bliss); japonica (happiness in marriage); pair of geese (conjugal affection); Mandarin ducks or two crows (conjugal fidelity); peach tree • *days associated with marriage:* Monday for health/ Tuesday for wealth/ Wednesday the best of all/Thursday for crosses/Friday for losses/Saturday, no luck at all. • *Egypt:* rook [bird] • *emblem:* two circles or rings, intertwined, side by side (marriage; permanent marriage union) • *flower language:* American linden; ivy; ivy geranium (bridal favor); pink pink (newlyweds) • *Germany:* wimple (attribute of a married woman) • *Orient:* two crows (conjugal fidelity) • *see also* **betrothal; brides; husbands; love, conjugal; wives**

Marriage personified *attribute:* quince

Mars [god] *associations:* goose; miner; ram [sheep]; red, especially brilliant red; Tuesday • *attributes:* chariot drawn by wolves; drum; goblet; horse; iron; spear; thorn

Mars [planet] *association:* chive; eight; K; magenta; P • *emblem:* dragon biting the hilt of a sword

Mars and Venus [deities] lovers under a net; soldier on a couch with a woman, his weapon put aside

Marsyas *attributes:* flute; pipe [music]

Martha, St. *attributes:* asperges with water pot; aspergillum; bunch of keys, usually attached to her girdle; dragon underfoot; ladle

Martin of Tours, St. soldier holding cloak and sword • *attributes:* chasuble; cloak split in two with a sword; crozier; goose; horse

martyrdom bear; being bound to a stake; blood; branch [plant], especially a branch with thorns; burning faggots; carbuncle [gemstone]; cauldron; club [bat]; cross; dish; ember; fire; flame; gridiron; guillotine; harrow [tool]; heated plow; large fork; millstone; myrrh and aloes; palm branch; red rose, especially in art; spear; stone; swan song; sword and palm branch; tiger; wound • *associations:* eleven; red

* *attributes:* crown (victory over sin and death; a martyr of royal blood); crown of stars, usually held in the hand (virgin martyrs); crown of thorns; palm branch; red; sword; thorns; white (saints who were not martyrs) * *flower language:* deep red rose

Mary Magdalene woman casting off her jewels * *attributes:* box, vase, or dish of alabaster; crucifix; box, jar or vase of ointment, usually with a lid; crown of thorns; long flowing hair; skull; stool [for sitting]; whip

Mary Magdalene of Pazzi, St. praying woman before an image or vision of the crucified Christ, with Christ presenting instruments of the Passion to her; praying woman before an image or vision of the Virgin and Child, with the Virgin handing the Christ Child to the woman or placing a veil on her head

Mary of Cleophus, St. *attribute:* windmill with ship and fish

Mary of Egypt, St. *attributes:* lion scratching out graves in the desert; long flowing hair; ointment; three loaves of bread

masculine principle *see* **male principle**

masculinity beer; bull; carp; cherry tree (masculine virtue); cydippe * *associations:* M (when printed angularly); sun * *see also* **men; virility**

masher wolf

mass *see* **eucharist**

Massachusetts *emblem:* codfish

master old man * *heraldry:* horse (master of the horse); key (master of the cellar)

mastery digestion; whip

masturbation Aladdin's lamp, genie issuing from a lamp (male masturbation and its objectified emotional consequences); Pandora, Pandora's Box (female masturbation and its objectified emotional consequences)

materialism Devil [tarot] (domination of the soul by matter); frog (worldly things and those who indulge in them); Hanged Man [tarot] (detachment from materialism); hippopotamus (gross materialism); House of God [tarot] (materialism struck down by spiritual light to render regeneration possible); nuditas temporalis (contempt for worldly things;

lack of worldly things, especially when abandoned in service to God); pitcher overturned (the emptiness of worldly things, especially in a still life painting); plum (object or situation of value); prostitute (instability caused by object interest); raven; reptile; rhinoceros; serpent; skull (useless nature of earthly things); thorn (materialism killing spirituality); turtle (highly concentrated materialism); Vulcan (a weak materialistic, and corrupt soul) * *association:* index finger * *see also* **matter**

maternity *see* **motherhood**

Mathematics *see* **Arithmetic personified**

Matilda, St. *attribute:* purse

matrimony *see* **marriage**

matter anvil; belly (destruction of matter); black globe (prime matter); hiding (the period of life before and after its involution as matter, or before and after the manifest life appears); lake (prime matter); lead [metal]; mud (emergence of matter); serpent (matter seducing strength); weaving as a feminine activity (the world of matter); yin and yang * *associations:* square (material things); the first six signs of the zodiac (Aries, Taurus, Gemini, Cancer, Leo, Virgo) relate to involution or matter * *material life:* bubble (the emptiness of material existence); dove embedded in lead (the spirit embedded in matter); Death [tarot] (dematerialization); earth [soil] (the moral opposite of what is heavenly and spiritual; the end of material life; the sustainer of material life); eating (material existence); Eve (the material and formal aspect of life); four (the material aspect of life—association); goat; green (material decay—association); hare (material existence); mother; plant [biology] (the healthy growth of plants indicates cosmic, spiritual, and material fecundity); sarcophagus (the earth as beginning and end of material life); sandals (the lowest form of material life); Scorpio (association); turtle (material existence) * *material world:* crow (a demiurgic power); cylinder (material thoughts; the mechanistic intellect); Death [tarot] (dematerialization); gold suit [tarot] (material forces); hood (detachment from the material world); key of silver (material power); ladder (surmounting the difficulties of the material world); last six signs of the zodiac [Leo, Scorpio, Sagittarius, Capricorn, Aquarius, Pisces] (materialization or evolution—association); O [letter] (association); six (material comforts—association); spiral (escape from the material to the spiritual world—association); square [shape] (association); three (material success—association); two (the material—association); water mill (the material world of phenomena); yin (the dark of yin and yang); zigzag (association) • *matter and spirit:* Cancer [zodiac] (the mediator between the formal and non-formal worlds); dove embedded in lead (the spirit embedded in matter); mist (the intermediate world between the formal and non-formal); Sphinx (spirit triumphant over matter); Strength [tarot] (spirit ruling over matter); swine (desire that seeks sustenance in matter rather than in spirit); Temperance [tarot] (the interaction of matter and spirit); yin and yang • *see also* **materialism; the physical**

Matthew, St. man with wings usually with book and/or pen and/or with an angel dictating and pointing toward heaven; ox with an eagle, lion, and angel (St. Luke, St. John, and St. Matthew, respectively) • *attributes:* axe; cherub; dolphin; halberd; inkhorn (St. Matthew and other evangelists, but often the inkhorn is held by an angel in the latter cases); lance; money chest; money bag or purse, especially three money bags or purses; wings (occasionally); writing pen

Matthias, St. *attributes:* book with a halberd or sword; double-headed axe with a stone or open Bible; hatchet; lance with three stones; saw [tool]; scimitar with book, the book usually is closed; square [tool]; sword held by the point; tall cross alone

maturity candlestick (the beauty of ripe age); fruit; summer • *association:* forty • *flower language:* pomegranate flower alone (mature elegance) • *see also* **middle age; aged**

Maturity personified *attribute:* compasses [dividers]

Maundy Thursday *association:* black (the liturgical color for the day)

Maurice, St. soldier with palm, banner with eagle, and red cross on breastplate • *attributes:* banner with eagle; breast plate with red cross; palm tree

Maurus, St. *attribute:* crutch; spade [shovel]; wolf

May *association:* robin • *birthstone:* emerald • *China:* magnolia blossom • *flower language:* hawthorn

May Day *association:* red flag • *flower language:* hawthorn

meanness covering one's face, heart, or flanks with fat; diamond [gemstone]; eyebrows that meet; flint; granite; House of God [tarot] (smallmindedness); kite [bird]; rat; squinting eyes • *flower language:* cuscuta; dodder; ebony (you are hard) • *see also* **cruelty; selfishness**

measuring compasses [dividers]; rule [measuring]; wand

meat carver *heraldry:* cup (holder of the honorary title of royal cup-bearer or meat carver)

mechanics cogwheel; cylinder (the mechanistic intellect); dynamo; wrench

meddling nose

Medea witch with a cauldron

mediation angel kneeling (intercession); Cancer [zodiac] (the mediator between the formal and non-formal worlds) • *associations:* blue; G

medicine barber (primitive medicine) • *emblem:* caduceus (the medical profession) • *see also* **physicians**

mediocrity island (refuge from mediocrity or the passions)

meditation hill, mountain peak (place of worship and meditation); pansy; rosary; wings • *heavenly meditation:* sapphire; skull with a cross (meditation on the eternal life that comes after death); squirrel • *see also* **contemplation; thought; worship**

Medusa woman with serpents for hair; youth holding severed head with snakes for hair (Perseus with Medusa's head)

meekness birch; clerical turned collar; elephant; lamb; yoke • *China:* willow (emblem) • *see also* **timidity**

Meekness personified *attribute:* elephant

meeting ash tree (Yggdrasil, the meeting place of the gods); crossroads (meeting place of demons, witches, etc.) • *flower language:* chickweed (rendezvous); everlasting pea (an appointed meeting); nutmeg geranium, lemon geranium (unexpected meeting); pimpernel (assignation)

megalomania House of God [tarot]

Meinrad, St. *attribute:* two ravens

melancholy bagpipe; balm tea (cure for melancholy); bear; cat; cypress and marigolds; Death [tarot]; dove; ebony; geranium; hare; heron; lion; lodge; monkey; pale cheeks; pelican; raven; sparrow; swan song; wolf • *associations:* brown; Friday; yellow • *flower language:* night smelling geranium; dark geranium; sorrowful geranium (melancholy mind) • *see also* **despair; despondency; displeasure; gloom; sadness; sorrow**

Melancholy personified *attributes:* compasses [dividers]; plane [tool]; purse; rule [measuring]; saw [tool]; skull; sitting position; square [tool]; wings

Melchior *association:* casket of frankincense

Melchizidek *attributes:* bread with chalice; censer and/or crown and/or scepter

Melager *associations:* boar surrounded by hunters; firebrand

melody cicada; thrush (melodiousness) • *see also* **music**

Melpomene *attributes:* crown of flowers held in the hand; dagger (17th century on); mask with a frown (17th century on); scepter underfoot; sword

membership branding (membership in or separation from a group); tattoo

memories cellar (childhood recollections); edelweiss (noble memories); firefly; heron (silent memories); hollow [topography]; mirror (unconscious memories); palace of mirrors, glass, or crystal, that suddenly appears by magic (ancestral memories of mankind; unconscious memories); perfume; sleeping beauty (memories dormant in the unconscious); Uranus [god] (man's ancestral memories) • *association:* violet [color] • *flower language:* adonis (sorrowful or painful memories); white periwinkle (pleasant recollections) • *see also* **memory; remembrance**

memory beads; brain; elephant; ivy (tenacity of memory); jasmine; king that is old (world memory); mirror (magic in that it may remember what it sees); table; Uranus [god] (man's memory); wallet; wreath • *flower language:* blue periwinkle, white periwinkle (pleasures of memory); red bay; rosemary; silver-leaved geranium (recall); syringa • *see also* **memories; remembrance**

men ass (a man 80 to 90 years of age); bull (a man 20 to 30 years of age); bull tied to a tree (a man subdued in marriage); burial (initiation into manhood); cat (a man between 70 and 80 years of age); cuckoo (the eternal bachelor); dog (a man 60 to 70 years of age); fallen pine (a man fallen in misfortune); fox (a man 40 to 50 years of age); lion (a man 30 to 40 years of age); marrow (manly prowess); Mercury [god] (manly grace); sorcerer (a wise old man); toe (a man's way of life); trident (the male as creator); vein (vital male energy); weaving as a masculine occupation (an incomplete man); white horse (manhood); white rooster (a man of holy ways); wolf (a man 50 to 60 years of age) • *association:* hawthorn trained over a bench (old men) • *heraldry:* raven (a man who has made his own fortune) • *see also* **boys; effeminacy; homosexuality; male principle; males; masculinity; virility**

menstruation acacia gum (menstrual blood)

mentality blindness (mentality immersed in the concerns of the lower life); brass; bronze; cold [disease] (inhibition of psychic powers); muscular and/or hairy man (energetic and strong mentality); iron (mental power); pain (mental or physical disharmony or disorder); smoke (mental darkness) • *associations:* cone (psychic wholeness); prune (mental and physical constipation) • *flower language:* clematis, kennedia (mental beauty) • *mental plane:* air; birds that are solitary by nature (usually, the isolation of those who live on a superior mental plane); navel (the point on the mental plane midway between higher and lower nature); breeze (the spirit energizing the mental plane) • *mental qualities:* bishop (spiritualized mental qualities); cattle (baser mental qualities); soldier (striving mental qualities) • see also **intellect; mind**

mentor priest (spiritual mentor)

merchants *attribute:* purse • *folklore:* eight hours of sleep (the amount needed by merchants) • *heraldry:* diamond [shape]; ship (merchant riches); trident (upper class merchant) • *see also* **commerce**

Mercury [god] *associations:* crane [bird]; goose; little finger; rooster; three maidens with baskets on their heads • *attributes:* balances; caduceus; club [bat]; cow; cydippe; flute; golden chain; hazel wand; helmet with wings; lyre; moon; pipe [music]; purse; sandals with wings; severed head; staff; stork; wings; winnow (occasionally) • *emblems:* olive tree or branch; spade [shovel]

Mercury [planet] *associations:* blue; E; five; H; mercury [metal]; plaid; Q; slate violet [color]

mercy angel holding a branch with white flowers; blunted sword; cedar; crozier; cruse of oil (the inexhaustible grace and mercy of Christ); Eastern cross (the mercy shown the thief to the right of Christ); gate; marigold; pillow; rain; rainbow (God's mercy); rue [plant]; thumb up; willow branch • *associations:* eight (justice with mercy); seventy-two; six • *see also* **compassion; kindness; pity; ruthlessness; sympathy**

Mercy personified woman expressing milk from her breasts

merit coriander (concealed merit); garland; laurel • *association:* scarlet (general virtue and merit) • *flower language:* coriander (concealed merit); full moss rose (superior merit); laurel (reward of merit); red primrose (unpatronized merit) • *heraldry:* gannet (one who subsists on virtue and merit without material help); martlet (subsisting on virtue and merit) • *see also* **distinction; honor; value; worth**

mermaids *attributes:* comb; green hair

merriment Born on a Thursday, merry and glad (or, has far to go); cherry; Wednesday's child is merry and glad; • *flower language:* mundi rose (you are merry) • *see also* **frivolity; gaiety; happiness; joy**

mesmerism basilisk

message lightning, meteorite, thun-

der (divine message) • *flower language:* iris (I have a message for you)

messengers banshee (messenger of death); clouds; crow; fish with a bird's head, usually a swallow's (messenger of cyclic regeneration); squirrel (messenger of the Tree of Life or Yggdrasil); starling • *attribute:* caduceus • *heraldry:* squirrel (important service as a messenger); swallow [bird] (messenger of good news or good fortune) • *divine messengers:* angel; cherub; dove; eagle; Elijah (messenger of the Messianic Age); Gabriel (messenger of the Day of Judgment); goat; Mercury [god]; raven; seraph; stag; tide; white bird • *attribute:* wings

Messiah myrtle (messianic promises); rose [flower]; scepter and censer (messianic hope) • *Judaism:* open door (opened on Seder nights to allow entrance for Elijah announcing the Messianic Age; wine (set out on Seder nights, for Elijah, messenger of the Messianic Age)

metamorphosis *see* **change**

metaphysics *association:* V (metaphysical gifts)

meticulousness Hermit [tarot]

Micah *association:* temple on a hill or mountain • *attributes:* broken sword with a lance; lance broken with a sword

Michael angel with a dragon underfoot; soldier with wings • *associations:* eleven; nineteen • *attributes:* balances [scales]; flaming sword and a shield; shell

mid- Winter *association:* starling

midday *associations:* eagle; south

middle navel • *association:* three (beginning, middle, and end) • *see also* **center**

middle age autumn; evening; fox (a man between 40 and 50 years of age); hen (a woman 40 to 60 years of age); goose (a woman 40 to 60 years of age); lion (a man between 30 and 40 years of age); noon; scarf; west • *see also* **maturity**

Middle Ages *emblems:* dominoes; monks

middle classes dahlia (the dignity of the lower or middle classes) • *see also* **bourgeoisie**

Middle East *emblems:* camel; scimitar

Middle Easterners *attribute:* turban (Muslims and Sikhs in particular)

Midwest [United States] *emblem:* corn [maize]

might *see* **power**

mildness heifer; rabbit; spring [season]; stag; west wind • *association:* twelve • *flower language:* mallow • *heraldry:* emerald; stag • *see also* **gentleness**

the military banners in superfluous numbers (aggressive militarism); Castor and Pollux (power in battle); crossed swords (military strategy or power); lizard (military strategy); scepter (military command) • *heraldry:* oak leaves, serpent (military distinction) • *United States:* Pentagon [building] (the U.S. military establishment; the U.S. military-industrial complex) • *see also* **warriors**

milk foam; goat's milk (milk of the poor); sap (milk; celestial milk of the mother goddess)

Milky Way snail's track

Milo of Croton man with hands caught in a tree, attacked by a lion

mimicry mockingbird

mind ache (mental or spiritual disorder); air (the mental plane); attic; boil [disease] (a psychological affliction or spiritual shortcoming); bubble (mindlessness); cave; chains (the attachment of the mind to the lower world); deluge (awakening of the mind from ignorance and error); effigy (the psychic aspect of a person); eyes (abode of the mind); feeding (dispensing goodness to the mind and soul); frankincense (purification of the mind); Gordian knot, labyrinth (mental torture); Gorgon (a condition beyond the endurance of the conscious mind); griffin (the relation between psychic energy and cosmic force); head; husband and wife (mind and emotion, respectively); iron; musician (the mind which fosters higher emotions); Psyche; sun; raven; Vulcan (the creative mind which has been captured by the lower qualities); white horse (the pure and perfect higher mind); young man • *associations:* blue (purification of the mind); four; yellow • *flower language:* African marigold (the vulgar mind); hundred-leaved rose (dignity of the mind); plane tree (cultivation of the mind); sorrowful geranium (melancholy mind) • *heraldry:* gold (elevation of the mind) *lower mind:* ashes; dust (the unstable lower mind); leopard (the opinionated lower mind full of errors that are mingled with the truth); leper (the lower mind troubled with conflicting emotions, desires, and confused ideas); raven; Trojan • *mind and body:* banyan tree (the close union of the spiritual and physical in man); hawk eating a hare (the triumph of the mind over the flesh); lion with a human head (in Egypt, the union of the intellect with physical power); room [chamber] (privacy of mind and body) • *mind and spirit:* blindness (the mind not awakened by the spirit); feeding (dispensing goodness to the mind and soul); fairy (the lesser spiritual moods of the universal mind); Mephistopheles (the negative aspect of the psychic function which has broken away from the spirit to acquire independence); nine (associated with the three worlds: corporal, intellectual, and spiritual); red horse (the mind energized by the spirit) • *see also* **brain; conscious; intellect; mentality; super-ego; superconsicious; unconscious**

minerals *association:* black (mineral life)

miners gnomes

Minerva *see* **Athena**

mining gnomes

Minstrel [tarot] *association:* A

Miriam *attribute:* tambourine

mirth *see* **joy**

Mirtillo and Amarillis coronation of a youth by a maiden, or vice versa, in a pastoral setting

misanthropy thistle • *flower language:* fuller's teasel; wolfsbane

mischief ferret; fox; goblin; harlequin (mischievous intrigue; tricks played on others); magpie; ruby (changes color to presage mischief, regains color when the danger is over); scorpion (mischief and discord)

misconception breeze (the clearing away of misconception)

miserliness *see* **avarice**

misery closed gate; eating ashes (utter misery); gall; marigold; willow; winter • *association:* U • *flower language:* bluebottle (single wretchedness); wood anemone (forlorn) • *see also* **dreariness**

misfortune bat [animal]; bitter herbs; black rooster; blackbird; blackthorn; chains (more than one chain usually indicates punishment, suffering, slavery, hopeless misfortune); counterclockwise swastika; crutch; darkness; darnel; dimple in the cheek or chin; ebb tide; fallen pine (a man fallen in misfortune); flat feet; hag; marriage on a Saturday, no luck at all; meadow; meeting several foxes; screech or squinch owl; wings • *associations:* eighteen (in the Old Testament, an evil number, but in Christianity, a number of great reward); fifteen (generally an unlucky number); marriage on a Saturday; thirteen • *Christianity:* Friday • *flower language:* wallflower (fidelity in misfortune) • *foretokens and signs of misfortune:* being pricked on the finger by a needle; burning or tingling ears, especially the right ear (someone is speaking evil of you); comet; crow (usually); dark clouds; east wind; heart missing from a sacrificial animal; lapwing; letter [epistle]; meteor (usually); nightjar; nightmare; one eye (extra human effort devoted to one aim, usually evil); picture falling off the wall for no apparent reason; pointing; raven; red sky at morning; ruby changing color (mischief); screech or squinch owl; Sirius; sneezing (everywhere but Greece and Rome); sneezing on a Friday (you sneeze for sorrow); sneezing on a Sunday (for safety seek, the Devil will have you the whole of the week); storm clouds; sudden shiver or pain for no apparent reason); two; vulture

mission wings (divine mission)

missionaries *attribute:* hat • *emblem:* crutch (those who care for the aged or crippled)

mistakes forest

mistresses bird in a cage (a kept woman); Lillith (a discarded mistress taking revenge) • *see also* **courtesans; promiscuity; prostitutes**

Mithra *attributes:* grapes; key; nimbus; scepter; sunflower

mixing *see* **intermingling**

mockery ape; hyena; lemon; lizard (disrespect for elders); macaroni (insolence); music; owl (object of ridicule); poison ivy (ridicule); scarlet robe (the mocking of Christ); southernwood

[plant]; winking eye • *see also* **humiliation; satire**

moderation *see* **restraint; temperance**

modesty alyssum (exemplary modesty); ash tree; bluebottle (the modesty of the Virgin Mary); briars; falcon; flowers of the field; lily of the valley; linden; reseda; scepter with an eye on it; veil; turned clerical collar; violet [flower]; wren • *associations:* blue; brown • *China:* bamboo • *flower language:* sweet violet; trillium (modest beauty); white lilac; woodruff (modest worth) • *heraldry:* beetle • *Rome:* slender fillet • *see also* **humbleness**

Modesty personified *attribute:* scepter tipped with an eye

Molokai Island [Hawaii] *emblem:* kukui tree

monarchs *see* **kings**

Monastic Life personified *attribute:* crane [bird]

monasticism Cockaigne (ridicule of monasticism); crane [bird] (good order in monastic life); unicorn • *association:* brown • see also **monks**

Monday marriage on a Monday was said to ensure good health; Monday's child is fair in the face (or, full in the face); Born on a Monday, fair of face • *associations:* Cancer [zodiac]; Diana; Luna; moon; works of divination

money bacon; coins (the unfavorable aspects of money); copper; rubbing the fingertips • *associations:* diamond suit [playing cards]; F (to the Anglo-Saxons) • *see also* **avarice; greed**

Monica, St. *attributes:* sash [clothing]; tear [weeping]

monkeys *association:* banana

monks *attributes:* sandals; three knots in a monk's cincture (the vows of poverty, chastity, and obedience; in the Franciscan order they represent faith, hope, and charity); open book (often the rule of the order to which the monk belongs); tonsure (although in the early church, these were also worn by members of the secular clergy) • *see also* **monasticism**

monomania one eye (extra human effort devoted to one aim, usually unfavorable)

monotony smoking a pipe; wood pigeon (monotonous chanting) • *see also* **boredom**

monsignori *attribute:* black cassock with red piping

monsters aquatic monster (a cosmic or psychological situation at a deeper level than symbolized by land monsters); insect (a reduced primeval monster); lobster (an unfeeling, grabbing monster); monsters carried in a procession (indicates they are dominated); ostrich (a monster of chaos); sword (antithesis of the monster) • *see also* **demons**

months twelve pillars • *see also* the names of individual months, such as **January, February,** etc.

mood clothes; eyes (expressive of mood or character); fairy (the lesser spiritual moods of the universal mind); tail (indicates the mood of an animal) • *see also* **disposition; emotions; feelings; temper**

moon cup; fan; index and little finger raised (the horns of the moon); ox; shepherd • *associations:* B; C (the crescent moon); cow (the earth and the moon); curved sword; dew; Diana; fan (phases of the moon); frog; left side; Luna; Monday; nine; north (new moon); pearl; pumpkin; scythe; seven; shell; silver; silver earring (moon worship); silver gray; south (full moon); tarot cards XII to XXII; Tiresias (full moon); two; water lily; Wednesday (according to the Bible, the day heavenly bodies were created); white • *China:* hare (association) • *emblem:* triangle with the apex down • *Greece:* sounding of a bronze gong (done at the eclipse of the moon) • *Orient:* rabbit on a disk of gold or white (emblem) • *see also* **sun and moon**

moon goddess wafer (sacrifice to moon goddesses) • *associations:* dolphin; ibis • *attribute:* spindle • *emblem:* dog

Moon [tarot] *association:* R

morality caduceus (moral equilibrium); Cato (moral virtue); chaos (death of religion and morality); Hermit [tarot]; ivory (moral fortitude); kneeling (moral strength); light (moral value); Lovers [tarot] (moral beauty); Pegasus (morality and intellect); rudder (moral rectitude); rule [measuring] (standard of morality); spider (morally and physically repulsive sex); swine (moral plunge into corruption) • *associations:* Libra (moral and psychic

equilibrium); one (moral purpose); Libra; three (moral and spiritual dynamism) • *moral inferiority:* goat (usually, moral inferiority, but occasionally moral superiority because it is associated with high peaks in its wild state); scales [biology] • *moral progress:* leprosy (rotting of the spirit from lack of moral progress); petrification (detention of moral progress); Scylla (the immediate expectation of the fruits of action as an impedance to moral progress) • *moral superiority:* goat (usually, moral inferiority, but occasionally moral superiority because it is associated with high peaks in its wild state); plane tree • *see also* **goodness; righteousness; virtue**

morning brook; east wind; heron; ibis; incense; plantain; womb • *association:* spring [season] (early morning)

morning star hart

morosity *see* **gloom**

Morpheus *attributes:* ebony couch (the bed of Morpheus); poppy

mortality earthenware; Gemini (the dual mortal/immortal, physical/spiritual, etc., nature of all things); gravestone; handful of earth; skeleton at a feast (reminder of mortality); skull; swan • *associations:* black; square [shape] • *heraldry:* hourglass • *see also* **death**

mortification *see* **humiliation; self- denial**

Moses basket in bulrushes, or an infant in a basket (the birth of Moses); infant placed before a king and offered two dishes (the infant is Moses); *associations:* acacia or shittim (reputed to be the burning bush in which God appeared to Moses); miter (the two rays of light that came from the head of Moses when he received the Ten Commandments); staff striking rock and producing water; two tablets of stone • *attributes:* bulrush; burning bush (God's appearance before Moses); grapes; shepherd's crook; staff; staff with serpent (Moses and Aaron before Pharaoh); two tablets of stone (Moses and the Ten Commandments, if oak leaves are included they indicate sturdiness and regeneration)

mother basket; box; breasts; cask; cauldron; cave; city; cow (especially a heifer or white cow); cradle; cross-roads; dolphin; egg; furnace; germinating seed; goose; harbor; hen; High Priestess [tarot]; hippopotamus (mother principle); hollow [topography]; journey (search for the lost mother); lioness; mare; matron (domineering mother); mold [tool]; moon; ocean; oven; panther; red rose; seaweed (maternal fertility); spoon; tomb; vein (maternal links); Virgin Mary (the mother church that Christ left in this world); vulture; water; waves [water] (maternity and death); woman nursing a child; wood • *associations:* darkness; lozenge [shape]; nine • *China:* mulberry staff (mourning for a mother) • *Great Mother:* abyss (association); pot, particularly earthen (association); dog (emblem); dove (the cosmic All Mother); earth [soil]; Eve (the mother of all things); forest; lioness • *incest with mother:* journey (flight from the mother for fear of incest); sinking in mud (fear of maternal incest); swan (incestuous maternal relationships) • *maternal love:* cinquefoil [flower]; coltsfoot (maternal care); hind [deer]; linnet; mare (mother as protector); Melusina (heraldry); moss (association); panther (a beautiful woman, normally tender, but fierce in defense of her children—heraldry); pheasant; warmth (maternal comfort); woman nursing a child; wood sorrel (maternal tenderness—association) • *mother goddesses:* heifer (association); sap (celestial milk of the mother goddess); star of the sea (usually sevenpointed—association); white cow (association) • *Terrible Mother:* Diana; dragon; female ogre; hag; Hecate; Hercules (the fight against the Terrible Mother); Juno; key (attribute); lamia; Lillith; mare; matron; Medusa; Sphinx; stepmother; whip (attribute)

Mother Earth   bare feet (direct contact with Mother Earth); goose • *see also* **mother**

Mother Nature   Sun [tarot] • *see also* **mother**

Mother's Day   *United States:* white carnation

motherhood *see* **mother**

motion   jar (still motion); legs; palace; Pole Star (unmoved mover); sphere (creative motion); triskele; uraeus

motivation   heat

mountains   edelweiss (ostentatious or feigned mountaineering skill or courage); hollow [topography] (an inverse form of a mountain)

mourning   ashes; bare feet; bay wreath; black clothes, feathers, gloves, robe, or veil; bloodstone; cutting off a finger; cypress; cypress wreath; daffodil; disheveled hair; dust; extinguished hearth; fasting; flag at half-mast; glow worm (harbinger of mourning); hair (either cutting the hair, or letting normally short hair grow long); heliotrope [gemstone]; jet [mineral]; kingfisher; laurel; laying the hands on one's own head); lilac [plant]; lying prone; mourning dove; mutilation; owl; ring; roof (place for mourning); sackcloth, especially with ashes; scabious; sitting at a window, or on the ground; smiting one's thigh; umbrella; urn; violet [plant]; white wimple with a black robe; willow; willow wreath; wreath; yew • *associations:* black; blue (half-mourning); purple; Saturday (works of mourning); violet [color] • *China:* ash tree staff, bamboo staff (mourning for a father); mulberry staff (mourning for a mother) • *flower language:* myrobalan; weeping willow • *Judaism:* bare feet; long flowing hair; torn garment • *Middle Ages:* hyacinth [flower] • *Orient:* white • **grief; lamentation**

Mucius Scaevola   Roman soldier with his hand held in a brazier

multiplicity   monolith (unity counterbalancing multiplicity); nymph (multiplicity and dissolution)

munificence *see* **generosity**

murder   black hand or spot (impending death or murder); breaking of bread in a ritual sacrifice); dark colored elves may kill babies; lamia (infanticide); reaping or wine press (slaughter); red hand; wolf • *see also* **death**

murderers   hazel wand (said to find murderers, water, buried treasure, thieves); mandrake (said to grow under the gallows of murderers)

the Muses   *associations:* heron (sacred to the Muses); laurel • *attributes:* horse; violet hair

music   cicada; harp (music; religious music in general, specifically the Book of Psalms); laurel wreath (distinction in music or literature); long fingers;

oats (the bewitching soul of music); Orpheus; seven- stringed lyre (the seven note scale in music); swan; twelve- stringed lyre (the twelve note scale in music) • *associations:* linen; seven; timbrel (a musical instrument usually associated with women) • *flower language:* oats; reed • *heraldry:* dolphin (love of music); stag (skill in music) • *see also* **harmony; melody**

Music personified *attributes:* bell; lute; organ [instrument]; viol • *emblem:* harpy

Muslims *attribute:* turban (Middle Eastern peoples generally, Muslims in particular) • *see also* **Islam**

mutability *see also* **changeability**

mutation *see* **change; transformation**

mutilation beaver, scythe (self-mutilation); scar (a remnant of mutilation, usually with a sinister connotation)

mutuality mule (mutual help among underdogs); onyx (reciprocity); spindle (mutual sacrifice); two millstones (mutual converse of human society)

mystery cedar; cloak; closed door; clouds; darkness; devouring; flower; grail; key; lake; nut, especially a hazel nut; serpent (great mysteries); Sphinx; veil, especially a painted veil; water; Wheel of Fortune [tarot] • *associations:* spiral (mystery; the mystery of life and death); thirty-three • *attributes of mysterious persons:* dark complexion; gloves; mask • *flower language:* crimson polyanthus • *see also* **inscrutability**

mystic center globe; hole; lotus; Mount Ararat; navel; palace; paradise; pearl; pyramid; seed; spark (souls scattering from the Mystic Center into the world of phenomena); swan; swastika; temple; threshing floor; throne; Thule [classical land]; treasure in a cave; web; whale • *association:* one

mysticism book (spiritual or mystic power); Hanged Man [tarot]; hood • *associations:* nine (a mystic number); Y (search for the esoteric or mystic) • *see also* **occultism**

mythology lightning flash through a cloud

N

Nahum angel's feet emerging from a cloud above a mountain (Nahum's vision) • *association:* broken yoke

name *heraldry:* blackbird (a clear sounding family name)

Naphtali association running hind [deer]

narcissism *see* **self-love**

Narcissus [mythology] narcissus [flower]; youth gazing into a pool

narcotics hemp; henbane

narrowmindedness lobster (bigotry); wax seal [stamp]

nascence *see* **incipience**

nations horde of locusts (a nation without Christ); king (a nation; the ideas of a nation) • *folklore:* a man born during an earthquake will be the ruin of his country • *heraldry:* peacock (the pride of a nation)

National Socialism *emblem:* counter-

clockwise swastika

nationalism flag

nativity *see* **birth; Jesus Christ**

Natural Disasters personified thief

nature abandonment (loss of contact with God or nature); albatross (beneficent nature); buffalo (untamed nature); censer (spiritual nature); child (unity with nature); city (lack of emotional, spiritual, or natural contact); conch shell (the spiritual and natural means of development rendered active); Diana; digestion (good digestion is a sign of congruity with nature, and vice versa); disease (natural or spiritual disorder or disharmony); dragon (nature; evil nature); Euphrates River (the irreversible process of nature); fairyland (the real joys of the natural life); fishing (communion with nature); garden (nature subdued);

grafting (artificial interference with the natural order of things); hunchback (nature perverted); judge (restorer of natural balance); leaven (spiritual nature permeating lower nature); magnolia (love of nature); mold [tool]; musician (harmony with nature); myrtle; Ouroboros (the self-sufficiency of nature); Pan; pot, usually earthenware (nature's inexhaustible womb); rising mist (the female principle in nature desiring the male); river (the creative power of nature and time); serpent (evil nature); Sun [tarot] (Mother Nature); tide (the balance of nature); titan (a wild and untameable force of primeval nature); weaving as a feminine activity (order and balance in nature); whale (grandeur or nobility of nature); wolf (untamed nature); woman (the passive principle in nature) • *associations:* cypress (nature deities); nymph (fertility of nature); oval (natural biological objects); two • *creative nature:* Gemini (creative and created nature); gourd; river (the creative power of nature and time) • *emblem:* six-pointed star (the natural and the supernatural) • *flower language:* magnolia (love of nature) • *higher nature:* cow's milk; mother's milk; navel (the point on the mental plane midway between higher and lower nature); woman as a captive (higher nature held by latent desire) • *lower nature:* Eve; flesh; heel (the lower nature of the soul); Helen; horse (the baser forces in man); leaven (spiritual nature permeating lower nature); navel (the point on the mental plane midway between higher and lower nature); prostitute; slavery (subjection to lower nature); sores (the suffering of lower nature); thief (lesser nature that robs the self of primordial wealth); victory (subdual of lower nature—that which is conquered often represents the very inferiority of the conqueror himself) • *natural forces:* cauldron (the transmutation and germination of the baser forces of nature); dwarf (hidden forces of nature); five (associated with the higher power of nature); herb; maypole (the phallic reproductive power of nature, together with the vulva-circle regulation of time and motion); Pegasus (heightened natural forces); phallus (nature's regenerative force); sun (the active power of nature); Titan (a wild and untameable force of primeval nature); torch (the active, positive power of nature); volcano (primary forces of nature) • wild man or wild woman as a heraldic supporter (base forces of nature subjugated and transcended) • *natural mankind:* American Indian, gypsy, Negro, nuditas temporalis (the natural state of man); savage, tramp [hobo] (the primitive, instinctive self); wild man, wild woman (the primitive, instinctive, natural, and emotional self); shadow (the primitive side of a person); young man (the primitive mind) • *see also* **baseness** (for lower nature); **elevation** (for higher nature)

Nature personified   *attributes:* green; vulture

nausea   stomach (seat of nausea)

navel of the world   *see* **mystic center**

navigation   compass [direction]; compasses [dividers]; oar; rising of the Pleiades (start of the navigation season); rudder; sextant

navy   *see* **the military; sailors**

Nazi Germany   *emblem:* counterclockwise swastika

neatness   *see* **cleanliness**

negativity   flock of birds (usually have a negative connotation); jay (generally has a negative connotation); Neptune [god] (the negative aspect of the spirit and of humanity); Pluto [god] (the negative aspect of the spirit); thumb down; X (negation) • *associations:* even numbers; two (negative and positive)

neglect   dust (something forgotten or neglected) • *flower language:* laurestina (I die if neglected); thrift, throatwort (neglected beauty)

negligence   cicada

Negroes   ace of spades; crow • *United States:* watermelon (pejorative association)

Nemesis   *attributes:* blindfold; bridle; globe underfoot; griffin; rope and vase; rudder; wings

neophytes   boy; bride • *association:* green • *Judaism:* frog • *see also* **apprentices**

Neptune [god]   *associations:* gall [biology] (consecrated to Neptune); Hermit [tarot]; I [letter]; Neptune [planet]; nine • *attributes:* aquamarine [gemstone]; chariot of cockle shells, drawn by sea horses; dolphin; horse; trident

Neptune **[planet]** *associations:* brown; lavender [color]

Nero house of gold (Nero's Palace of the Sun) • *associations:* fiddle; silver doors (Nero's Palace of the Sun)

nerve gall [biology]

nerves harp (soothing of strained nerves) • *associations:* K; Mercury [planet]; N

Netherlands *emblems:* tulip; windmill; wooden shoes

neutrality valley • *association:* green

neutralization *association:* gray

New England *association:* maple leaf

New Testament *see* **Bible. New Testament**

New Year April; bayberry candles; birch; olive branch • *association:* A • *Judaism:* honey and apples (the hope for sweetness and joy, respectively, in the new year)

newness infant (new beginning; new era); prophet (beginning of a new era); naked child (new life); young man (new ideas) • *associations:* S (new cycles); thirteen (new beginning) • *flower language:* China rose, damask rose (beauty ever new) • *see also* **freshness**

newlyweds *see* **marriage**

news mushroom (bad news) • *flower language:* guelder rose; snowball (both good news)

Nicholas of Myra, St. bishop bearing a youth aloft (the bishop is St. Nicholas of Myra); child kissing the hand of a saint (the saint is St. Nicholas of Myra); three children in a tub with a bishop (the bishop is St. Nicholas of Myra) • *attributes:* anchor; money bag; ship; three balls

Nicholas of Tolentino, St. *attributes:* crucifix entwined with lilies; star on the breast; two doves in a dish

Nicodemus *attribute:* myrrh

night bat [animal]; black robe; black rooster; blanket (the night sky); cat; hourglass; mouse; owl; panther; serpent; wolf; womb • *associations:* black; dark blue; dew (nightfall); indigo [color]; north; pinching; west; west wind • *China:* even numbers (association) • *flower language:* blue, minor, or night convolvulus • *see also* **day and**

night

Night personified *attributes:* black mantle [clothing]; chariot drawn by black horses (usually two horses); ebony throne; lamp; mask; one black rat and one white; owl; poppy; scepter of lead; wings, usually with two infants

Nightingale, Florence *attribute:* lamp

nightmares onyx (protects against nightmares)

Nike *attribute:* palm tree

Nilus, St. abbot anointing a boy's lips with lamp oil (the abbot is St. Nilus)

nimbleness eel; goat; hart; hind [deer]; roebuck; mountain goat; squirrel; stag

nine ninety (multiplies the meanings of nine) • *associations:* I [letter]; Neptune [planet]; R

nirvana lotus

no *see* **negativity**

Noah ark and/or rainbow (the covenant God made with Noah and the church); carpenter building an ark; dove with a twig (signal of land to Noah on the ark) • *association:* three (Noah's three sons) • *attributes:* oar; olive branch; raven; vine

nobility Antigone; ash tree; bear; beauty; buckle; buskin; eagle (heroic nobility); ermine; falcon; gloves, especially the left glove; green leaf; hawk (nobility; fierce nobility); herb; Hercules; lapis lazuli; legs; orchid; owl (lack of nobility); snow covered mountain; strawberry leaves; swan • *associations:* lisping (Spain); M; musical instruments of metal; purple; white • *attributes:* crossed legs, right over left; horse; long fingernails; soft hands • *Greece:* grasshopper • *heraldry:* castle; gold; lozenge [shape]

nomads *association:* tent

nonchalance *see* **poise**

nonsense *United States:* index and little finger raised, (bull's horns, and by extension, bull excrement, meaning a lie, or nonsense)

noon *associations:* eagle; south

Norbert, St. chalice or monstrance with a spider; demon underfoot

normality two eyes (physical and spiritual normality) • *association:* right side

north eagle (Norse symbol for the

north wind); pine tree (associated with northern areas); reindeer (emblem of the north polar region)

Northern Ireland *association:* orange [color] (Protestants in Northern Ireland)

nostalgia *see* **memories**

nothingness snow; wind • *associations:* black; zero

Notoriety personified *attribute:* cornet

noumena Cancer [zodiac] (the mediator between the formal and non-formal worlds)

nourishment *see* **eating; sustenance**

November *birthstone:* topaz • *China:* gardenia (emblem)

November personified man or woman sower

nudity swan (chaste female nudity)

nuisance *see* **annoyance**

numbers three hundred (a large or infinite number); zero (an intensifier after another number) • *lucky numbers:* twenty-one; twenty-four (generally) *mystic numbers:* nine; one hundred and twenty [120] • *unlucky numbers:* twenty-eight; twenty-two (generally) • *sacred numbers:* fourteen; forty; one hundred and ten [110]

nuns *attribute:* veil

nurses crutch (emblem of those who care for the aged or cripple); three feathers (the end of nurse's training)

nurture *see* **care; sustenance**

nymphs *association:* grotto (Diana and her nymphs)

O

O [letter] *association:* six

oath *association:* phallus

Obadiah *attribute:* pitcher [vessel] with loaves of bread • *association:* two caves

obedience bee; camel; chrysalis (passive and blind obedience to the laws of nature); dog; folded hands; plowman (obeyer of natural law); river (obedience to time, life, the law); Sparta (obedience through custom); stole [religious garment]; shofar, turtle dove (obedience to divine will); stork; swallow [bird]; three knots in a monk's girdle [cincture] (the vows of poverty, chastity, and obedience); yoke • *association:* green • *see also* **submission; subservience**

Obedience personified *attributes:* ass with a millstone; camel; yoke

objectivity Moon [tarot]

objects *see* **materialism; matter**

obligation *see* **duty**

obliteration *see* **destruction**

oblivion *see* **forgetfulness**

obscenity skunk

obscurance clouds, smoke (obscuring of the truth, especially by illusion);

forest (obscuring of reason)

obscurity pearl (obscure genius); shadow; turtle; wool • *association:* gray • *China:* pearl (obscure genius)

observation *see* **sight**

obsessions dismemberment, dispersal (being possessed by the unconscious, unconscious manias, or unconscious obsessions); Hecate (the feminine principle responsible for madness, obsession)

obstacles bear; Charybdis, Scylla (the immediate expectation of the fruits of action as an impediment to moral progress); idol (fixed ideas that bar the way to truth); Punch and Judy (contagious humor and common sense overcoming all obstacles); quicksand or reef (obstruction of destiny); rubbing [motion]; thorn; trout (stubbornness overcoming obstacles) • *association:* C (success despite obstacles) • *flower language:* harrow; mistletoe (I surmount all obstacles) • *heraldry:* remora

obstinacy *see* **intransigence**

obstructions *see* **obstacles**

occultism alchemy (foolish occultism); lake; Magic [tarot] (man in

his struggle with occult powers; occult wisdom); papyrus • *associations:* nine; R • *see also* **mysticism; supernatural**
occupation *see* **work**
ocean *see* **sea**
October *birthstones:* aquamarine (occasionally); opal; tourmaline • *association:* scorpion • *China:* chrysanthemum
October personified man or woman sower
Oda, St. *attribute:* magpie
oddity giraffe (in Renaissance art, often depicted because of its unusual appearance rather than for any symbolic value)
Odin *attributes:* eagle; goat; horse; wolf • *association:* eight hundred (the number of Odin's warriors at Valhalla) • *emblem:* ash tree
Odysseus *attributes:* red beard; ship
offense Ajax; rags thrown in the water (an offense cast off)
offensiveness bittern; crab; dung (offensiveness, especially to ghosts); mallow (rankness); skunk; tusk (an offensive weapon) • *see also* **rudeness; repulsiveness**
offerings cake (offering to a god); fist placed over the heart (tearing out one's heart as an offering); gingerbread (offering to a god; burial offering) • *Judaism:* shank bone (a reminder of burnt offerings and of the ancient glory of the Temple)
office collar; golden chain, scepter (high office); mace [weapon] (divine office); necklace; sash [clothing]
officials rod (official power) • *China:* blue sedan chair (high government official); canopy; green sedan chair (lower government official); peacock tail feathers
offspring *see* **children**
Ohio *emblem:* buckeye (horse chestnut)
ointment myrrh (sacred ointment)
Olaf, St. *attribute:* double axe with crown
old age *see* **aged**
Old Age personified *attribute:* skull
Old Testament *see* **Bible. Old Testament**
Old Testament personified synagogue
Olympic Games *emblems:* five linked rings; torch
omens *see* **foretokens and signs**

omnipotence hand emerging through a cloud (the omnipotent God)
omnipresence *see* **ubiquity**
omniscience one eye; papyrus, especially when rolled; scepter tipped with an eye; six- pointed star
Omobuono, St. *attribute:* flash
one church spire with a finger pointed to the sky (one god); index finger upraised (the number one, signifying the best) • *associations:* A; J (one, especially in a magnified sense, multiplied ten times); K (the number one in a magnified sense); Q (primarily associated with the number eight, but sometimes with the numbers one and seven); S; sun
oneness *see* **unity**
Onuphrius, St. man covered by long hair • *association:* lion scratching out graves in the desert • *attributes:* coins underfoot; girdle, lion, especially two lions; loincloth, or other garment of palm leaves; raven with a loaf of bread of leaves
open-heartedness *see* **generosity; truthfulness**
openmindedness *see* **liberality**
openness *see* **candor**
opiates hemp; henbane
opinions bed (a phase of thought or opinion); beheading (an opinion, thought, or institution at the end of its cycle); changing clothes (changing opinions, personalities, roles, loyalties, beliefs, etc.); cloak (mental covering, often revealing the wearer's opinions, prejudices, mental state, beliefs, etc.); leopard (the opinionated lower mind full of errors that are mingled with the truth); oppressors (opinions that oppose truth); lowered mast (change in opinions or beliefs) • *association:* two • *see also* **beliefs; ideas; thoughts**
opportunity basket with flowers or fruit; door or gate, especially when open
Opportunity personified *attributes:* balances [scales] on a razor's edge; globe underfoot; loose hair over the brow; wings
opposites amulets (the divine present in the worldly); beheading (the separation of the body and the spirit); bucentaur (the dual nature of man); Capricorn; Castor and Pollux; checkers; cross; double spiral; feathered serpent;

feathered serpent with horns (opposite forces in conflict); Gemini; half man/half goat; hart and panther; heron; High Priestess [tarot]; hippopotamus; horn [animal]; horned serpent (opposite forces in conflict; duality intensified); Janus; Justice [tarot] (balance of opposites); maypole; moon (opposing values such as male/female, constancy/inconstancy, etc.); poplar; spectacles [eyeglasses]; Sphinx; swan; tarot deck; transvestitism (identification with a deity, parent, or ideal of the opposite sex); twilight (the dividing line which both joins and separates pairs of opposites); twin mountain peaks; twin serpents; twins; two eyes; two pillars close together; Virgo; yin and yang • *associations:* eight; H; Mercury [planet]; six; W (twin formations) • *conjunction of opposites:* alcohol; banyan tree (the close union of the spiritual and physical in man); cross; crossroads; Gorgon (fusion of opposites); hermaphrodite (integration of opposites); intersection; maypole; molten metals; rose with thorns; scissors; Sphinx; staff surmounted by a crescent; swan; two (association) • *reconciliation of opposites:* mistletoe; plumed serpent; split scepter

opposition *association:* eight • *flower language:* belvedere, licorice, tansy (I declare against you); tremella nestoe

oppression griffin (those who oppress Christians); Prometheus (the will to resist oppression); russet [cloth]

Ops *attribute:* lion

optimism bull (optimism or rising prices on the stock market); light; monkey; rose colored glass (optimistic or unrealistic view) • *association:* C • *Judaism:* five (in ancient times)

oracles judge; naiad; rowan • *flower language:* dandelion (love's oracle) • *see also* **prophets; revelation**

oral-genital sex *United States:* sixty-nine (simultaneous oral-genital sex)

orange [color] *association:* one

Orange, House of *association:* orange [color]

order bee (good order); clock; gavel; incest (corruption or perversion of the natural order); jester (inversion of the normal order); kneeling (submission to the laws of order); music; navel; necklace (order from chaos); Pandora,

Pandora's box (rebellion against divine order); Pleiades; riding a goat (inversion of the normal order); stars in a constellation; tablet (divine order); tamed tiger (the defense of order against chaos); weaving as a feminine activity • *associations:* four (order; terrestrial order); index finger; M; seven (perfect order; planetary order); square [shape]; ten; twelve (universal order) • *Judaism:* bee (government in good order) • *see also* **discipline; organization**

Order of the Bath *association:* red ribbon

Order of the Garter *association:* blue ribbon

ordinariness potato

ordination chalice on a closed book, with a stole [religious garment]; chrism; hands laid on the head • *attribute:* stole [religious garment]

organization chrysalis • *associations:* four (rational organization); fourteen; square [shape] • *see also* **order**

orgasm flock of birds taking flight; "little" death; vampire (aftermath of orgasm) • *female:* blowing; earthquake; waves [water] • *male:* erupting volcano; lightning; thunderbolt • *see also* **sexual intercourse; sex**

orgies *associations:* dancing; holly

Orient abacus (the mysterious ways of the Orient); golden eagle; tea • *associations:* curved sword; gong • *emblems:* abacus (occasionally); bamboo: willow

orientation compass; east (the mystic point of reference)

origin navel; point; slug [animal] (origin of life); triangle with the apex up (the urge to escape from this world to the Origin) • *origin of life:* chalice; east; heat; Orient; ocean; serpent (guardian of the source of life); slug [animal]; water

original sin centaur on a font (the overcoming of original sin by baptism); Christ child holding an apple or an orange (Christ as the redeemer of man from original sin)

originality *associations:* ten; Uranus [planet]

Orion giant carrying a youth on his back • *attribute:* bow with quiver

Orlando and Rodomont soldier fighting with naked man on a bridge

(the soldier is Rodomont, the naked man is Orlando)

ornament scroll (sometimes merely ornament); sword (spiritual ornament) • *flower language:* hornbeam

Orpheus *attributes:* lute (occasional attribute); lyre; viol

orthodoxy dog

Osiris *associations:* goose; monolith; plant [biology]; sparrowhawk • *attributes:* balances; grain; hare; lotus; ostrich feathers; scepter; shepherd's crook

ostentation crane [bird]; dahlia (vulgar ostentation); feather; hoopoe; lily; macaroni; peacock; plume; rich clothing (worldly pomp and vanity); turkey; weather cock; weather vane • *China:* kingfisher (gaudy raiment) • *see also* ostentation; pomp • *see also* **pretension**

ostracism being sent to one's room; dunce cap; exile; solitary confinement in prison; standing in the corner

Oswald, St. *attribute:* ciborium

otherness ox (those who labor for the good of others); three (associated with other people) • *other worlds:* alcove, mirror (doorway to another world); eating the food of another world binds one to that world; fossil (a link between two worlds)

Otto III severed head held by a woman before a king (the king is Otto III)

outdoor life *association:* cabin; tent

outhouses crescent moon on an outhouse door (use reserved for females, although in more common present-day usage, any outhouse); sun on an outhouse door (use reserved for males)

outlaws forest (home of outlaws, fairies, supernatural beings)

over-confidence *see* **presumption**

ownership seal [stamp]

oxen *Christianity:* five (associated with the Five Yoke of Oxen)

P

P *association:* seven

pacification *see* **placation**

paganism ape (early Christianity); Beelzebub (the worship of false gods); dog; dragon; idol; locust [insect] (a heathen); mistletoe; swine • *Judaism:* Greece • *see also* **idolatry**

Paganism personified *attribute:* dragon

pageantry *association:* musical instruments of metal • *see also* **pomp**

pain Gordian knot; labyrinth • *association:* seven • *flower language:* dog rose (pain and pleasure); marigold; milkvetch (your presence softens my pain) • *see also* **suffering**

painter *attributes:* beret; palette

painting ape (Middle Ages); fly [insect] (in 15th and 16th century Europe, painting a fly on a painting was a charm to keep real flies out of the fresh paint) • *flower language:* auricula

Palace of the Sun house of gold (Nero's Palace of the Sun) • *associa-*

tion: silver doors

Pallas Athena *see* **Athena**

palliative sugar

Palm Sunday *England:* pussy willow (association)

pampering angora cat (a pampered and spoiled person, especially a woman)

Pan half man/half goat • *association:* crimson • *attributes:* goat; horn [animal]; pine wreath; pointed ears; reed; shepherd's crook; syrinx

Pandora *attribute:* vase

panic *see* **terror**

panther *association:* Mars

Paolo and Francesca lovers sharing a book (Paolo and Francesca di Rimini)

papacy beehive; gold rose (papal benediction); pallium (papal authority) • *attributes:* cross with three horizontal arms (attribute of the papacy, St. Peter, and of all popes except St. Sylvester and St. Gregory the Great); crozier terminating in a cross with three horizontal pieces; emerald; gloves; key; miter, especially a triple miter; three crowns; triple tiara; white cassock • *emblem:* female wolf

paradise canopy; crescent and star; date tree with doves (earthly paradise); garden; honey; morning; park; rose [flower]; sun • *art:* daisy (a flower of paradise) • *associations:* four (the four rivers of paradise); one • *see also* **Eden, Garden of; heaven; Valhalla**

paralytics *see* **cripples**

parasite briars; caterpillar; dabchick; flea; ivy; moss; moth; sponge

parchment *association:* sheepskin

pardon *see* **forgiveness**

parent and child burial (return to the primal parent); hearth (filial loyalty); heron (parental providence); hoopoe (parental care); partridge, sorrel, stork (parental affection); pelican (parental love and sacrifice); stork, swallow [bird] (filial piety) • *China:* dove, pigeon (impartial filial duty); lamb (filial piety) • *flower language:* sorrel (parental affection); virgin's bower (filial love) • *heraldry:* pelican, usually with wings spread (filial devotion) • *see also* **family**

Paris [mythology] infant fed by shepherds

Paris, France Eiffel Tower

Parliament two keys crossed (Isle of Man)

Parnassus laurel grove

parthenogenesis pearl

participation *flower language:* double daisy

parting of the ways fork in a road or path

Pasiphae hollow wooden cow (the cow Dedalus built for Pasiphae)

passage center (going through death to eternity; the connection between heaven and earth); chancel arch (passage from this world into eternal life, or from the Church Militant to the Church Triumphant); closet (passage into another existence or world); disease, Milky Way (pathway to heaven); hole (the passage between worlds or existences); hurricane, tornado (hole through which one may pass out of space and time); Nazareth (a point of progress on the path to perfection); tunnel (dangerous passage) • *Gnosticism:* eagle atop a ladder (the Way) •

passage of time: mouse; rat; raven; river (the irreversible passage of time); stain • *see also* **connection**

passion blood; blowing; breathing, especially heavy; burning; ember (dying passion); fever; fir; girding the loins (restraint of passion and turning toward the spirit); goldilocks [flower] (languishing passion); heat; helmet (protection of the soul from the assaults of the passions and desires); hops; mill (logic as a feeble protection against passion); nightingale; Pasiphae (the overthrow of reason by animal passion); press [tool]; pulse; red flower; red knight; rhinoceros (shortsighted passion); ruby; violin • *association:* orange [color] (passion tempered by earthly wisdom); scarlet • *flower language:* fleur-di-lys (flame; I burn); white dittany; yellow iris • *see also* **desire; Jesus Christ; love; zeal**

Passion personified *attribute:* pillar

passions fire (forbidden passions); gargoyle (evil passions; when on the outside of a church: evil passions driven out of man by the Gospel); goat; Gommorrah, Sodom (carnal passions); island (refuge from the passions); lion (an index of latent passions); liver, nostrils (seat of passions); Negro (the baser passions); onyx (curb for the passions); storm (passions of the soul); sulfur; volcano (tremendous passions) • *association:* eight • *see also* **emotions; feelings**

passivity earth [soil]; floating; moon; night; owl; princess, either in a secluded place or sleeping (passive potential); scythe; sleeping beauty (passive potential) • *associations:* blue; even numbers; green; tarot cards XII to XXII; triangle with the apex down; woman (the passive principle in nature) • *see also* **patience; resignation**

Passover blood on a doorpost; dandelion (a bitter herb of Passover); slain lamb; tau cross

past attic; entanglement (the forgotten past); hollow [topography]; Janus (the past and the present together); Lethe (forgetfulness of the past); light; maple in the autumn (past happiness); scales on mermaids, dragons, the Devil (the past continuing in the present); scroll that is unrolling (the upper roll is the future, the lower roll is the past);

shadow • *associations:* left eye; left side; mist (distant past); Rome (past glory) • *flower language:* meadow saffron (my happiest days are past) • *see also* **history**

pastimes *see* **amusement; sports**

the pastoral myrtle (pastoral poetry); shepherd's crook

pastures *association:* Tuesday (according to the Bible, dry land, pastures, and trees were created on Tuesday)

path disease, Milky Way (pathway to heaven); Nazareth (a point of progress to the path to perfection) • *Gnosticism:* eagle atop a ladder (the Way)

patience ass; bull; camel; chrysoberyl (patience in sorrow); cincture (patient suffering); dock [plant]; fir (patience; those who excel in patience); Hermit [tarot] (patient and profound work); iron; Job; mustard [plant]; ox; spider; stole [religious garment]; wine press (patient or solitary labor or suffering); yoke (patience; patient service) • *flower language:* dock [plant]; ox-eyed [plant] • *heraldry:* ass; bridge; lamb; ram [sheep] • *emblem:* carnelian (hope and patience) • *see also* **passivity; resignation**

Patience personified *attributes:* lamb; ox; yoke

patriarchs seven-branched menorah (the seven patriarchs of mankind) • *attribute:* cross with two horizontal arms (not to be confused with either the Cross of Lorraine, or the Eastern cross) • *China:* cedrela tree (the patriarch of a town)

Patrick, St. *attribute:* font; harp; serpent; shamrock; St. Andrew's cross

patriotism cairngorm; elm • *association:* red • *flower language:* American elm tree; nasturtium • *heraldry:* peacock

Paul, St. man suspended in a basket by a rope; saint in prison, released by an earthquake • *associations:* three (his three days of blindness); three fountains; twelve; twelve scrolls (epistles of St. Paul) • *attributes:* blindfolded severed head, on a horse; book with a sword, especially with the legend "Spiritus Gladius"; crown of laurel; fire and a serpent; Latin cross with rays on a shield; skull; sword and scabbard; sword with a serpent twined around it • *emblem:* crossed swords (one sword refers to his martyrdom, the other to his good fight for the faith)

Paul the Hermit, St. *association:* lion scratching out graves in the desert • *attributes:* loaf of bread carried by a raven; loincloth or other garment of palm leaves; palm tree; two lions; white bears

pause chair

pawnbrokers *emblem:* three balls

peace ass; beaver; bridge; broken sword; bull; caduceus; cattle in a pasture; corn [maize]; dove, dove with ark, dove with olive branch (peace; peacemaker); evening; fig; flowing or full robe; glass; grazing horse (peace and freedom); hand raised with palm outward; hands clasped in a handshake; house chimney; hyacinth [gemstone] (peace of mind); index and middle finger forming a vee; kangaroo (peacefulness); kiss; laurel; leopard or lion lying with a lamb, calf, or kid; lion eating straw; meadow; mountain; myrrh; myrtle; navel; oil; olive branch, wreath, or tree; open gate; Phoenix [bird] (harbinger of peace); pillow; pipe [music]; plow; poppy; pruning hook; ram [sheep] as a sacrifice; river; scepter tipped with a dove (peace and reconciliation); sitting; split scepter; stork (domestic peace and happiness); stream; summer (extended peace or happiness); unicorn; valley; verbena; weaving (peace and concord); white flag; wolf with lamb • *American Indians:* burying a hatchet; smoking a pipe with enemies • *associations:* blue; December (peace and quiet); green; light; two (inner peace); light complexion; silver; six; white • *China:* crab apple (perpetual peace) • *Christianity:* olive tree or branch (peace of Jesus Christ); dove with an olive branch in its mouth (a soul that has made its peace with God) • *flower language:* hazel; heart's ease (peace of mind); olive tree or branch • *funeral art:* dove with an olive branch or palm branch (eternal peace) • *heraldry:* beaver (peacefulness); dove with olive branch; hare (one who enjoys a peaceful, retired life); rhinoceros (one who does not seek combat, but will defend to the death when attacked); silver • *see also* **concord; harmony; soothing; tranquillity; truce**

Peace personified woman destroying weapons • *attributes:* caduceus; cornucopia; crown of olive branches; dove; olive branches; torch; wings, usually with dove

pearls *association:* daisy

peasantry grass; rabbit; worm • *associations:* bagpipe; beans, cabbage, turnips (humble food); beer (drink of the common man); blue clothes; pitchfork, scythe (weapons of peasants) • *attribute:* blue clothes • *see also* **lower classes**

peeping roof (a place for peeping)

peerlessness *flower language:* peach blossoms (your qualities, like your charms, are unequalled)

peevishness *see* **irritability**

Pegasus winged horse

Peitho *association:* goose

penance cutting a beard; Lent; scourge; sitting on the ground

Penates hearth (altar for home gods, Penates, Lares, etc.)

penetration middle finger upraised; phallus; thumb in the mouth or between closed fingers; window (the idea of penetration)

penis *see* **phallus**

penitence ashes; ashes and dust; black clerical garments; black knight; camel's hair clothes; fish on a confessional; hyssop; long flowing hair; maniple; nuditas temporalis; purple amethyst; rending garments; sackcloth, especially with ashes; washing of someone else's feet; whip • *associations:* black; brown; gray; purple; violet [color] • *heraldry:* holly • *see also* **remorse; repentance; remorse**

Penitence personified *attributes:* jug of water; pelican; skull

penitents *attributes:* rope around the neck; skull (penitent saints)

pensiveness cowslip; moonstone; tourmaline • *flower language:* cowslip; laburnum (pensive beauty) • *see also* **contemplation; thought**

Pentateuch scroll

Pentecost fire; miter; scroll with a sheaf of wheat (Old Testament Pentecost; Old Testament Feast of the Pentecost) • *association:* red • *attribute:* flame on the head (the apostles at Pentecost)

penury *see* **poverty**

people Gog and Magog (the king and the people); grass (common people); leaves (people coming and going); vine (relationship of God and his people) • *attributes:* dark complexion, gloves, mask (mysterious people); white garment (important people) • *see also* **mankind**

perception blindness (lack of spiritual perception); eyesight (mental perception); twilight (perception of a new state of being) • *associations:* Leo; Neptune (extra-sensory perception) • *see also* **thought**

perfection ball; circle; diamond [gemstone]; globe; heart of gold (a perfect person); grail (attainment of perfection); key of gold; key of gold with a key of silver; Nazareth (a point of progress on the path to perfection); orb; peach; Pyramus and Thisbe (perfect love); rosary (circle of perfection); rose [flower]; seven candles (a perfect number, hence, Christ); sieve; Solomon's seal; sphere; the spirit; summer; white horse (the perfect and pure higher mind); World [tarot] (perfection as the end of creation out of chaos); work (the endeavor of the soul to attain perfection) • *associations:* eleven (surfeit of completion and protection); forty-two (being cut off halfway to perfection); mandorla (perfect blessedness); nine; ninety (striving toward perfection); O [letter]; one hundred; one hundred and ten [110] (a perfect age to die); one thousand (absolute perfection—multiplications of and additions to one thousand are usually intensifiers); seven (perfection; a perfect number; perfect order); six; six hundred; T; ten; thirty-three; three; twelve; white; Z (the thing that completes perfection) • *China:* jade; orchid (the perfect or superior man); unicorn (emblem) • *flower language:* justica (the perfection of female loveliness); pineapple (perfection; you are perfect); strawberry (perfect excellence) • *heraldry:* angel (striving for perfection); pomegranate (the perfect kingdom) • *kabala:* one hundred • *see also* **excellence**

perfidy *see* **treachery**

perfume *see* **fragrance**

peril *see* **danger**

permanence *see* **endurance**

Pero woman nursing an old man (Cimon and Pero)

perpetuity *see* **eternity**

perplexity *see* **confusion**

persecution arrow; fritillary; scourge; two scourges and a pillar; north wind (religious persecution) • *persecution of Christians:* hare; hart or stag being hunted; griffin (those who oppress Christians) • *persecution of the church:* burning bush (the church being persecuted but not perishing); hare; ship on a stormy sea (the church surviving persecution, schism, and heresy)

Persephone *see* **Proserpine**

Perseus horseman on winged horse; soldier with a dragon; youth holding the severed head of Medusa • *attributes:* helmet with wings; highly polished shield; sickle; wallet; winged sandals

perseverance bulldog; carp; chimere (dutiful perseverance); hen on its nest; ibis; magnolia; Ulysses; woodpecker (perserverant action) • *association:* Scotland • *China:* carp • *flower language:* canary grass; ground laurel; swamp magnolia • *heraldry:* snail • *see also* **endurance; persistence**

Perseverance personified Phoenix [bird] (occasionally)

Persia bear (the Kingdom of Persia) • *emblem:* ram [sheep]

Persian sibyl [Persica] woman treading on a serpent • *attributes:* lamp; lantern

persistence burr (importunity); hammer (persistent thought); mantis; ruins (sentiments, ideas, or customs which are dead and irrelevant to present life, but which nonetheless persist) • *flower language:* acanthus; burdock; fuller's teasel (importunity) • *see also* **endurance; persistence**

personality American Indian, liver, Negro, savage, wild man, wild woman (all, the darker side of the personality); bubble (emptiness of personality); changing clothes (changing personalities); cloak, clothes, robe (mental covering, often revealing the wearer's personality; the outer bounds of the wearer's personality); corpse (the personality in its lower aspect); disguise (assumption of a different personality); effigy (the psychic aspect of a person); hat, helmet (the color often represents the wearer's personality); hermaphrodite (loss of the sense of separation of the personality); rose [flower] (integration of the personality); snail (the self: the shell represents the conscious, the soft inner part the unconscious or personality); tailor (an incomplete person); teeth (guardian of the inner person); warrior (forces of consciousness warring within the personality; latent force in the personality ready to aid the conscious); wild man, wild woman (the instinctive part of the personality) • *see also* **disposition; ego; id; superego**

personifications *association:* woman • *attribute:* polygonal nimbus (occasionally)

persuasion Empress [tarot] (dominance by persuasion); tongue • *flower language:* althaea frutex; Syrian mallow

pertinacity *see* **stubbornness**

perversion incest (corruption or perversion of the natural order)

perversity mule

pessimism bear (pessimism or declining prices on the stock market); blue colored glass

pest flea; fly [insect]; gadfly [insect]; louse [insect]; mosquito; starling

pestilence dragon; fly [insect]; Merehim; Sphinx • *association:* horse with three legs (attribute of Death personified in time of pestilence) • *see also* **disease; plague**

Peter, St. fisherman; man having his ear cut off (St. Peter at the betrayal of Christ); man preaching from the stern of a ship (St. Peter leading the church); saint in prison, aroused from sleep by an angel • *attributes:* bright yellow mantle; bunch of keys; chains; cross with three horizontal arms (attribute of the papacy, St. Peter, and of all popes except St. Sylvester and St. Gregory the Great); crozier terminating in a cross with three horizontal pieces; fish, especially in a net or on a hook; inverted cross; key of gold with a key of iron (the gold key opens heaven's gate, the iron key locks it); palm tree; rock; rooster, especially when crowing (St. Peter, his denial and repentance, hence, also a reminder to be humble); scourge [whip]; scroll with two keys; ship

Peter Martyr, St. axe embedded in a monk's head; crucifix held by a martyr with a hatchet in his head • *attributes:* axe, knife, sword, or hatchet in the head, occasionally in the hand; head wound

petitioning *see* **supplication**

Petroclus *association:* death on a funeral pyre

Petronius, St. model of the city of Bologna, Italy; two towers, one leaning

pettiness flea; Justice [tarot]; monkey • *flower language:* pompon rose

petulance *see* **irritability**

Petulance personified *attribute:* cymbal

Phaeton horse, chariot and man falling from the sky (the man is Phaeton) • *attribute:* fiery chariot

phallus awl; axe; battering ram; birch; bottle; branch [botany]; caduceus; column [architecture]; cone; cupola; cydippe; dagger; dart; eel; fingers, especially a single finger; fish; flute; foot (the genitals, but especially the phallus); gun; hammer; knife; lamprey; lance; lightning; lily; nails [for wood]; necktie; needle; nose; obelisk; oboe; pestle; Phrygian cap; pillar; pine cone; pipe [music], especially when played by a male lover; purple orchid; quiver [for arrows] (vulva, but also may stand for the phallus as it contains arrows, which may stand for semen); rabbit's foot; rod; scepter; scythe; serpent; spear; spindle; staff; swan's neck; thumb up; thyrsus; tongue; torch; tower; tusk; wand; whip • *associations:* little finger; neck; one; rat; thumb • *phallus and vulva:* bell; flagpole with a ball on the end; maypole (the phallic reproductive powers of nature together with the vulva-circle regulation of time and motion); Q; well with trees • *Rome:* nerve (euphemism) • *see also* **genitals; scrotum; testicles**

pharmacy bottle with colored liquid; mortar and pestle

phenomena Aquarius (the dissolution or decomposition of the world of phenomena); Cancer [zodiac] (the mediator between the formal and nonformal worlds); theater; water mill; web • *see also* **noumena**

philanthropy *see* **generosity**

Philemon old man pursuing a goose around a table

Philip, St. *attributes:* basket; book with a scroll or a tall cross; cross with a carpenter's square; inverted cross; long staff and a spear; reed surmounted by a Latin or tau cross; shattered idol; small cross, especially a Latin cross, carried in the hand; spear with a patriarchal or tau cross and long staff; tall column [architecture]; two loaves of bread

Philip Benizzi, St. monk near a tree being struck by lightning

Philip Neri, St. saint praying before an image of the Virgin Mary and the Christ child • *attributes:* chasuble; lily; vial

philosophy beans (false philosophy); gold key (philosophical wisdom); High Priest [tarot]; pine; tower (philosophical retirement) • *associations:* blue (philosophical serenity); nine; seven • *flower language:* pitch pine; plane tree (associated with Greek philosophers)

Philosophy personified *attributes:* globe underfoot; scepter

Phlegmatic Man personified *attribute:* lamb

Phoenix [bird] metal bird • *association:* incense

Phrygian sibyl [Phrygiana] *attributes:* banner with a red cross, held by a lamb; processional cross

the physical belly (the physical side of man; antithesis of the spirit or brain); sword (destruction of the physical); wind and rain (physical love) • *association:* N (physical existence) • *physical and the spiritual:* banyan tree (the close union of the physical and spiritual in man); Castor and Pollux; duality, Gemini (the physical and spiritual nature of all things); moorings (the attachment of the physical and spiritual); Sun [tarot] (balance between the physical and spiritual); sword (conjunction of the physical and spiritual); two linked rings, one above the other • *see also* **matter**

physicians doctor holding a pincers with a stone (quack operation for stones in the head) • *attributes:* black bag; caduceus; forceps; gold headed cane; lancet • *emblems:* caduceus; crutch (emblem of those who care for the aged or crippled); leech

piety elephant; elm; forehead; hart;

hippopotamus; kneeling; lamp; lizard; skullcap; stag (the strength derived from the devout by their faith in scripture) • *association:* blue • *filial piety:* lamb (China); stork; swallow [bird] • *flower language:* wild geranium (steadfast piety) • *heraldry:* marigold; sapphire (piety and sincerity) • portrait painting: skull • *see also* **faith; religion**
Piety personified *attributes:* elephant; flame on the head
Pilate, Pontius *association:* basin, or basin and ewer together (Pilate washing his hands after confronting Christ)
pilgrimage ascending stairs; journey
pilgrims *attributes:* cloak; girdle [cincture]; gourd; hat; plantain (food of the pilgrim); purse; sandals; scrip; shell; staff; wallet • *association:* road • *heraldry:* shell (especially a pilgrim to Santiago, Spain)
pioneers *associations:* cabin; covered wagons
piquancy salt
pirates black flag, especially with a skull and crossbones; buried money chest (pirate booty); crow
Pisa, Italy *emblem:* leaning tower (sometimes of the whole of Italy)
Pisces *associations:* amethyst; hematite; Jupiter [planet]; moon; Neptune [planet]; peridot; red-violet; S; tin; tourmaline; tulip; U; water lily; willow • *emblem:* two fish
pitfalls *see* **snares**
pity elephant; myrrh and aloes; pine; rue [plant] • *flower language:* black pine • *see also* **compassion; mercy; sympathy**
Pity personified *attribute:* elephant
placation bull tied to a tree (lascivious fury appeased); effigy (has magical properties for warding off evil spirits, for fertility, and for placating the gods); wound (sacrifice to placate) • *association:* two (pacification)
plague acorn, garlic (protection against the plague); arrow; comet, eclipse of the sun (omen of the plague); dragon; hornet; insects in swarms; rat; Sirius; yellow cross • *association:* ten (the ten plagues of Egypt) • *China:* green clouds (a plague of insects) • *emblem:* sword (the tenth plague of Egypt) • *see also* **pestilence**
plaintiveness gull; oboe; turtle dove
planets seven- stringed lyre (the

seven planets known to the ancients); stars on the forehead of a deity (a planet personified); twelve pillars • *associations:* seven; Wednesday (according to the Bible, heavenly bodies were created on Wednesday)
plans *association:* middle finger (system) • *flower language:* foxfire (a wild scheme pursued); nettle tree • *see also* **strategy**
Plantagenet family *heraldry:* broom plant
planting *see* **sowing**
plants *see* **vegetation**
platonic lover *flower language:* acacia; rose acacia; white acacia
play ball (childhood play); hyacinth [flower]; kite [toy] (idle recreation) • *flower language:* hyacinth • *see also* **amusement; sports**
playfulness cat; colt (friskiness); kangaroo; kitten; lamb (frolic); Leviathan (the playfulness of God); otter; puppy; squirrel; tickling
pleasure bacon (female sexual pleasure); hill (place of innocent pleasure and freedom from care); lemon (pleasant thought); mermaid, merman, siren [mythology] (sensual pleasure); nymph (worldly pleasure); poppy (evanescent pleasure); ribbon; Salome; scattered flowers; shoes; southernwood [plant] (pleasantry); Sphinx (pleasures of the body); thumb up; tobacco (ephemeral pleasure) • *China:* a perfect ring (the emperor is pleased) • *flower language:* blue periwinkle, white periwinkle (pleasures of memory); currants, especially a branch (you please all); dog rose (pleasure and pain); everlasting pea (lasting pleasure); gentle balm (pleasantry); glycine (your friendship is pleasing and agreeable to me); ivy sprig with tendrils (eagerness to please); merzion (desire to please); poppy (evanescent pleasure); spurge laurel (desire to please); sweet pea (delicate pleasures); tuberose (dangerous pleasures) • *see also* **hedonism**
plebeians *see* **lower classes**
pledges *see* **promises**
Pleiades *attribute:* crown of violets
plenty animal fat; basket with flowers or fruit; corn [maize]; filled bowl; jar, urn (source of plenty); sheaf • *associations:* one hundred; one hundred and eleven [111]; U (cauldron of plenty) •

heraldry: purple (temperance in plenty) • *see also* **abundance; prosperity**

ploy sting (swindler's ploy)

plunder buried money chest (pirate booty); harpy; wolf • *see also* **treasure**

Pluto [god] black bearded king carrying off a maid in his chariot (the rape of Proserpine by Pluto) • *attributes:* black castle (the abode of Pluto); chariot drawn by black horses, usually three; cypress wreath; ebony throne; horse, especially black

Pluto [planet] *association:* zero

poets Eurydice (the poet's anima escaping); Pegasus; wound in the neck (poet's stigma) • *attributes:* cicada (bad poets); crown of laurel • *poet's inspiration:* fingertips (association); forge; manna; wind (inducer of poetic inspiration)

poetry Calliope (heroic poetry); harp; hazel (poetic art); (lyric poetry); lyre; myrtle (pastoral poetry); Pegasus; quill feather pen; swan; weaving as a feminine activity; winged horse • *association:* crane [bird] • *flower language:* European sweet brier • *heraldry:* lyre • *see also* **literature**

Poetry personified *attribute:* lyre

poise crayfish (nonchalance); folded hands (composure) • *association:* blue; two (tact) • *heraldry:* bat [animal] (coolness in the time of danger) • *see also* **gracefulness**

poison gall [biology] (poison words); radish (charm against poisoning); rattlesnake (virulence); rue (antidote for poison); skull and crossbones • *association:* serpent emerging from a cup or chalice (attempted poisoning of St. John)

Poland *emblem:* white eagle

polar regions *north polar region:* eskimo; igloo; polar bear; reindeer • *south polar region:* penguin

polarity Wheel of Fortune [tarot] (the principle of polarity) • *association:* two

police drag net • *attributes:* blue uniform; handcuffs; nightstick [billy club]

politics *association:* Thursday (works of religion and politics) • *heraldry:* stag (political providence)

Pollux *attribute:* horse • *see also* **Castor and Pollux**

Polyhymnia *attributes:* lute (occa-

sionally); organ [music]

Polyphemus one-eyed giant • *attributes:* shepherd's crook; syrinx

Polyena woman before a tomb, held at swordpoint by a soldier

Pomona old woman and naked goddess with cornucopia (Vertumnus and Pomona, respectively) • *attributes:* fruit in a basket; pruning hook or knife

pomp *see* **ostentation**

pomposity *see* **pride**

ponderousness *see* **heaviness**

Pontius Pilate *association:* ewer or pitcher with basin and sometimes towel (Pontius Pilate washing his hands during the passion of Christ)

the poor *see* **poverty**

popes *see* **papacy**

popularity hemlock (punishment for unpopular beliefs); *association:* L • *flower language:* cistus (popular favor)

Porcia woman snatching coals from a brazier

pornography *association:* X (United States)

port lighthouse

portents *see* **foretokens and signs**

Poseidon *association:* eight (sacred to Poseidon) • *attributes:* counterclockwise spiral; whip

positive principle *association:* odd numbers

positive and negative *association:* two

possession dismemberment, dispersal (being possessed by the unconscious, unconscious manias, or unconscious obsessions); palm of the hand held out (demand for possession); spreading a skirt over someone (taking possession) • *demonic possession:* demon emerging from a victim's mouth (exorcism); epileptic seizure • *flower language:* four leaf clover (be mine); hedgehog (association)

possessions *art:* coins, jewels, purse (the power and possessions that death takes away) • *heraldry:* snail (acquired possessions to be preserved and enlarged)

possibility carnival, saturnalia (the desire to concentrate all the possibilities of existence in a given period of time); closed room with windows (the possibility of communication or understanding); field (limitless possibilities); multicolored garment (diverse possibilities); fairy, seed (latent possibilities); goblet filled with liquid (the non-formal world of possibilities); window; wings (possibility of spiritual evolution) • *see also* **potential**

pot *association:* U (world pot)

potency loss of teeth (fear of loss of potency); teeth • *association:* wart (sexual potency) • *see also* **power**

potential corn [maize] (development of a potentiality); darkness (germinant undeveloped potentialities); egg; High Priestess [tarot] (unrealized potential); ice (stultified potential); Mercury [god]; moon (potential evil); night; road; sun (potential good); sleeping beauty, sleeping princess, princess in a secluded place (passive potential); seed • *associations:* P, Z (potential for good and/or evil); zero (the latent and potential) • *see also* **possibility**

poverty bare feet; barley; basil; basilisk; beans; beggar; bowl; brown bread; carp eaten as a food; crust of bread; evergreens; goat (the poor man's cow); goat's milk; herb; hoopoe; lentil; loss of hair; mouse, especially a church mouse; potato; quail; rags; swallow [bird] (contentment in poverty); three knots in a monk's girdle [cincture] (the vows of poverty, chastity, and obedience); vinegar (poor man's wine); wheelbarrow; wolf • *associations:* ass; brown • *charity to the poor:* basket; coins at the feet of an old man; loaf of bread; open purse or money bag • *China:* quail • *flower language:* basil; evergreen clematis; Indian plum tree; myrobalan; vernal grass (poor, but happy)

power aegis (productive power); androsphinx [human head on a lion's body] (the union of intellect and physical power); asp; axe (the power of light); belt; body hair (irrational power); book (spiritual and mystical power); bow [archery] (power, especially worldly power); breathing (assimilation of spiritual power); buds (latent or undeveloped power); bull; cedar; column [architectural]; crocodile; devouring (assimilation of the powers of that which is eaten); dynamo, engine (power; technological power); diamond key (the power to act); eagle on a globe or orb (consecration of power); eagle shown as a bird of prey (the sins of worldly power and pride); Emperor [tarot] (power; sterile regulation and power); face; factory chimney; fan; fasces (controlled power resulting in authority); fir; fire; fist; foot (seat of power); gate; gauntlet; globe; gloves; granite; gun; hammer (especially physical power and strength); hand; Hanged Man [tarot] (power derived from charity, wisdom, fidelity, and other higher virtues); horn [animal]; inn (power without pomp); intersection (a point of special power); iris [flower]; jade; king (power and energy); lion-headed ox (earthly abundance and power); liver; lizard (the power of evil); magnolia; Maltese cross with triangles on the end of each arm; mermaid, merman (the power of seduction; the power of song); name (key to power); nimbus; phallus (active power); Phoenix [bird] (power to overcome change, death, tragedy); pillar; ram [sheep] with its pugnacity emphasized; reins; ring; rod (official power); rope, especially a short piece); rudder; sails when full (swelling power); scepter (power; the power of chastity); seal [stamp]; secret (the power of the supernatural); seraph; serpent (power to heal); shepherd's crook; shoes; silver key (power of the subconscious; material power); snails when eaten (sexual power); Solomon's ring (power and wisdom); Sphinx; starfish (the inextinguishable power of love); stranger (replacement of reigning power); Strength [tarot] (power through conscious awareness of eternity); tail (animal power); thunderbolt, especially when shown with wings; tooth; tornado, whirlwind (invincible power); tower; trumpet (power; yearning for power, glory, fame); tusk; two-handed sword (civil power); uraeus (power over life and death); wheel; wings • *associations:* club suit [tarot] (power of command); diamond suit [playing cards]; eight; Leo (solar power); one (willpower; intellectual power); Pluto [planet] (the will to exercise power); purple; red (victorious power); T (generative power); ten (infinite power) • *China:* willow (power over demons) • *creative power:* anvil; double-headed eagle; gourd (creative power of nature); lake (source of creative power); light; lotus; red (association); river (creative power of time and nature); scepter (crfeative power of the word); the soul (man's creative part); spire • *divine power:* archangel (primordial divine power on the highest level); arrow (the light of divine power); aureole (supreme power—normally only used for members of the Trinity and occasionally for the Virgin Mary); cedar (occasionally, God's power to weaken the strong); crozier; earth [soil]; gold rope; House of God [tarot] (the power of the heavenly over the earthly); lightning; ruby; sigma, sigmoid; six (association); thunder; thunderbolt; umbrella (divine power and protection) • *Egypt:* bee (royal power); lion's body with human head (union of the intellect with physical power); Sphinx • *flower language:* cress; crown imperial; imperial montague • *heraldry:* apple (earthly kingdom); ash tree; bear; bull; elephant; fess; hands; head; leopard (power and pride); oak; ox head (power guided by reason); peacock (power and distinction); ship; unicorn (knightly power) • *Ireland:* dwarf elder • *Judaism:* coins (in still life painting, the power and possessions that death takes away); crown, sceptor (in still life painting, the power that death takes away); gold (mystic power); key; one (associated with the power and the will of the universe) • *magic power:* abnormality (an indication of magical powers); blue flower (magic or special powers); cat, crow (possessors of magic powers); crossroads (a place of magic power); foot; footprint (thought to have the magic powers of the maker); gloves (thought to have the magic power of their owner); hair; mandrake (association); mermaid; merman (the power of song-magic); rubbing [motion] (the transfer of magical powers) • *military power:* Castor and Pollux (power in battle); crossed swords (military strategy or power) • *natural power:* river (the creative power of time and nature); sun; torch (the active power of nature) • *royal power:* Adam; bee (Egypt); peony; purple, red (associations); yellow (Chinese association) • *sexual power:* body hair (association); snail (emergence of sexual power);

snails when eatern; warts (association) • *spiritual power:* book; breathing (assimilation of spiritual power); crozier (the hooked end to draw souls to God and the pointed end to prod the slothful); hair on the head; key; stole [religious garment] (priestly power and dignity); Strength [tarot]; tusk (spiritual power overcoming ignorance and evil) • *temporal power:* Emperor [tarot]; scepter tipped with a cross; tiara • *see also* **energy; potency; strength**

Power personified   *attributes:* eagle; fritillary

powerlessness *see* **helplessness**

powers [angels]   angel with armor (a power or other lower order of angel)

praise   calf (endearment); flute; gate; harp; jasper; trumpet • *flower language:* fennel (worthy of all praise); iris • *praise of God:* angel holding censer; angels with musical instruments; jasmine and palm; lute; organ [music] (praise of God from the church); wood sorrel (flower language) • *see also* **exaltation; worship**

prattle *see* **chatter**

prayer   belfry (call to prayer or worship); censer (prayer ascending to heaven; in the Old Testament: the plea that prayers would be acceptable to God); chalcedony (secret prayer); crossed legs, right over left); eagle; hands raised and open; incense; mantis (cruelty and greed disguised by a hypocritical attitude of prayer or religiosity); orant; rosary; rose quartz (remembrance in prayer); swallow [bird] • *association:* forty • *see also* **supplication; worship**

pre-eminence *see* **supremacy**

preaching   fox (false preacher); roof (platform for preaching)

precaution   goldenrod; lavender [plant] • *association:* P • *see also* **caution**

precociousness   *flower language:* May rose

precognition *see* **prophecy**

preconscious   child; fly [insect] (the priest, or other inhibitor of the preconscious who taints innocent joys); policeman (the censorious super-ego inhibiting forces of the preconscious)

precursors   abandonment (prelude to resurrection); night (precursor of creation) • *see also* **foretokens and signs**

predation hawk • *heraldry:* eagle claw or foot (one who preys)

preference *flower language:* apple blossom; pink or rose geranium

pregnancy baking; full sails • *association:* blue eyes (Elizabethan times)

prejudice dirtiness (the accumulation of error, prejudice, sin); oppressors • *see also* **bigotry; underdogs**

preludes *see* **precursors**

preparation *see* **readiness**

presages *see* **foretokens and signs**

presence bloodstone (charm for presence of mind); tabernacle on an altar (the real presence of God) • *flower language:* milkvetch (your presence softens my pain); rosemary (your presence revives me) • *Judaism:* scroll on a gravestone (the presence of God)

present and past *see* **past and present**

presents *see* **gifts**

preservation cypress chest; oil; salt; seal [stamp]; sturgeon; tragelaph (preservation and generation) • *association:* P • *heraldry:* snail (acquired possessions to be preserved and enlarged)

Preservation personified *attribute:* sheaf of millet

presidents *attribute:* gavel

presumption antelope; covering one's face, heart, or flanks with fat; House of God [tarot] (the dangerous consequences of over-confidence); spider; Tower of Babel (sinful presumption) • *flower language:* snapdragon

pretense whistling (pretense of innocence) • *flower language:* catchfly (pretended love)

pretension stork • *flower language:* Flora's bell (you make no pretension); glasswort; pasque flower anemone (you have no claims, you are without pretension); spiked willow-herb • *see also* **ostentation**

Priapus gardener • *attribute:* purse; sickle

prickliness *see* **irritability**

pride Aeolian harp (pomposity); amaryllis; aspen; ass; camel; covering one's face, heart, or flanks with fat (hubris); crow; diamond [gemstone]; dove; eagle; eagle shown as a bird of prey (the sin of pride); elephant; Eve; eyebrows (the abode of pride); falcon; feather; fir; foxglove and nightshade together (pride and punishment); gadfly [insect] (punishment for pride); gourd; hippopotamus (intellectual pride); hops (overwhelming pride); House of God [tarot] (the sin of pride); kite [bird]; leprosy (divine punishment, especially for pride); lion; Lucifer; magnolia; mast; mirror (feminine pride); monkey; mule; neighing; peacock; riding, especially on an animal; scorpion (unbending pride); Tower of Babel; turkey • *flower language:* hundred-leaved rose; polyanthus (pride of riches); tiger flower (for once may pride befriend me) • *heraldry:* chains (the refusal to be defamed or humiliated); leopard (pride and power); oak; peacock (pride of nation) • *Judaism:* bramble (dangerous pride)

Pride personified peacock • *attributes:* bat [animal]; bloated toad; eagle; lion; mirror; peacock

priests belfry (religiosity undone by clerical weakness); bell; censer; dog; elephant (priestly chastity); fly [insect] (the priest, or other inhibitor of the preconscious who taints innocent joys); frankincense (priesthood of Jesus Christ); heron (the unfavorable aspects of the priesthood); Janus (priest and monarch); lark (humility of the priesthood); Levi (priesthood without land); linen (priestly dress); rook [bird]; shepherd; stole [religious garment] • *attributes:* alb (the innocence and prophetic office of Christ; an undertunic in Greece and Rome, later a woman's chemise, and then adopted for wear by priests of a goddess); black biretta; black cassock; thirty-three buttons on a priest's cassock (the number of years in Christ's life) • *Egypt:* leopard (the dignity of the high priest) • *Judaism:* breastplate (attribute of Old Testament priesthood); hands upraised with middle and ring fingers separated: on a tombstone, an attribute of a Jewish priest; miter (Old Testament priesthood) • *see also* **archbishops; bishops; cardinals [clergy]; deacons; deans [religious]; monks**

primal furnace anvil

prime matter black globe; lake

primitiveness Africa; cave (primitive shelter) • *association:* red (primitive wildness) • *primitive man:* gypsy, savage, tramp [hobo] (the primitive, instinctive self); wild man, wild woman (the primitive, instinctive, natural, and emotional self); shadow (the primitive side of a person); young man (the primitive mind)

the primordial monster; mud (primordial slime); ocean (primordial creation); reptile; saturnalia (invocation of primordial chaos); sea urchin (primordial seed); thief (lesser nature that robs the self of primordial wealth) • *association:* Taurus (primordial sacrifice)

Prince of Wales *emblem:* three ostrich feathers

princesses peacock (apotheosis of princesses)

principalities [angels] *attribute:* scepter tipped with a cross and lily

principles *see* **ideals**

printing black and white together (the printed word)

Printing personified *attribute:* houseleek

prisoners bread and water (prisoner's food); noose • *attributes:* ball and chain; black and white striped clothing; manacles • *flower language:* peach blossom (I am your captive)

privacy hedge; room [chamber] (privacy of mind and body) • *see also* **hiding; secrecy**

privation *see* **poverty**

prizes blue ribbon (first prize); cup; golden cup; leather medal (farcical award for stupidity); medal; plum; silver cup; red ribbon (second prize)

probation *association:* forty

probity *see* **honesty**

problems bear (a difficult problem); blindman's bluff (trying to solve a problem without sufficient knowledge); bundle; forest • *see also* **trials; problems**

processes dancing; earthquake (a sudden change in a process); finger snapping (the beginning or end of a cycle, idea, or process); tree (the slow process of individuation) • *association:* black (germinal stage of a process) • *see also* **cycles**

procrastination *see* **delay**

procreation *see* **generation; reproduction**

Procris hunter grieving over a woman shot by an arrow (Cephalus and Procris)

Prodigal Son youth praying among swine or in barnyard • *association:* calf (the Prodigal Son's return)

productiveness *see* **fecundity**

profanation threshold monsters [lions, dragons, etc.] at entrance to a holy place (warning against profanation)

Profane Love personified *attribute:* jewels

professions *see* **work**

profit *flower language:* cabbage

profligacy Aeolian harp (associated with those given to wine, women, and luxurious living); U • *flower language:* fig

profundity duck (love of knowledge of profound mysteries); Hermit [tarot] (patient and profound work); journey (desire to undergo profound spiritual experience); man's head on a woman's body (solid and profound judgment)

profusion *flower language:* fig

progress Chariot [tarot] (progress and victory); Death [tarot] (the progress of evolution); kneeling (progress by restraining the lower qualities); leprosy (rotting of the soul due to a lack of moral progress); Moon [tarot] (upward progress of man); Nazareth (a point of progress on the path to perfection); Nike; oar; petrification (detention of moral progress); road; rolled papyrus; Scylla, Charybdis (the expectation of immediate fruits of action as an impedance to moral progress); seven-pointed star (cyclic progression); torch; train [transportation]; wheel; Wheel of Fortune [tarot] • *association:* fifteen

prohibition closed door; father; hedge (a privet hedge may indicate a lack of the means of enforcement, while a thorn hedge does have the means); leprosy (punishment for eating tabooed food); wall

projects *see* **tasks**

Prometheus life sized male statue with a god (the god is Prometheus); man chained to a rock, attacked by eagles • *attributes:* torch; willow

promiscuity *see* **wantonness**

Promised Land grapes borne on a staff by two men (entry into Canaan, the Promised Land) • *association:* milk and honey

promises buds (future promises); hand flat on the heart; myrtle (messianic promises); sun (promise of salvation) • *flower language:* plum blossoms (keep your promises) • *heraldry:* hands (pledge of faith)

promotion *China:* sea coral (official promotion)

promptness *flower language:* ten week stock

proof High Priest [tarot]

propagation *see* **generation; reproduction**

prophecy alb (the innocence and prophetic office of Christ); almond; barley; bee; bird; blindness, deafness, dumbness [muteness] (indications that the person may have a sixth sense or some other compensatory power); dragon; eagle (the spirit of prophecy); gypsy; horn gate (entrance to prophetic dreams); horseman (bearer of immortality or prophecy); Janus (history and prophecy); jasper (precognition); myrtle; naiad; opal (gives prophetic powers); owl; parrot; Prometheus; scroll; sleep (giver of prophetic dreams) • *associations:* jester; swan • *flower language:* prophetic marigold; verbena • *see also* **foretokens and signs**

prophets crow; python; sibyl • *associations:* four (the four major prophets of the church) • *attributes:* book; scroll • *flower language:* St. John's wort (you are a prophet) • *false prophets:* locust [insect]; tail (attribute); wolf • *see also* **fortune tellers; oracles**

propitiousness morning (a propitious time)

Proserpine black bearded king carrying off a maid in his chariot (the rape of Proserpine by Pluto); Ceres with a chariot drawn by dragons and or with a torch (the search for Proserpine) • *association:* asphodel

prosperity acacia; bayberry candles; beehive; box tree; Capricorn; cedar; cotton blossoms; fat cattle; fig; herd, when orderly; malachite; olive branch; palm tree; peony; swastika; triskele (the revival of prosperity or life); unicorn; wall; wheat • *China:* swallow nesting on a home; yellow clouds • *flower language:* beech; red- leaved rose (prosperity and beauty); stalk of wheat • *heraldry:* tree; wings on a shield (the joy of flourishing prosperity) • *Orient:*

charcoal • *see also* **abundance; fruitfulness; plenty; wealth**

prostitutes Bacchante; prunes, especially stewed prunes; sistrum; vampire • *associations:* Aphrodite (ritual prostitution); Babylon; road • *attributes:* cosmetics; harp; red light • *Elizabethan times:* Bermuda (the brothel district); red petticoat (attribute); scourging (punishment for prostitutes) • *see also* **concubines; courtesans; mistresses; wantonness**

Protase and Gervase, Saints *see* **Gervase and Protase, Saints**

Protase, St. *attributes:* club [bat]; scourge [whip]

protection aegis; arm; armor; banner; bough; branch with green leaves; breasts; buckle (protection; the protection and goodwill of Isis); cactus; canopy; chasuble; circle; cloak; coral necklace; corset; cradle; curtain; dagger (protection against a foe); dancing; dog; door; double horse head; eagle (protection of the young); flaming sword; gauntlet; giant (protector of the common people); girdle [cincture]; gloves; hand, especially when extended; helmet (protection of the soul from the assaults of passions and desires); hen with chicks; horn [animal]; horseshoe; ibis; inn (place of conviviality and protection); king; knot; lap [anatomy]; laurel; linden; lioness; mare (maternal protection); mask; menhir; mistletoe; necklace; nest; parasol; plane tree; roof; scales [zoology]; seal [animal]; shepherd; shield; smoke; spreading a skirt over someone; tattoo; tent; umbrella (protection; divine or royal protection); uraeus; vale; veil (protection from a deity); vulture; wall, especially when viewed from the inside; warmth; wings; womb (protection from reality) • *associations:* F; scarlet • *divine protection:* Red Sea (deliverance by God's protection); reed; Shiloah (pond in Jerusalem); umbrella • *flower language:* bearded crepis; crocus (abuse not); juniper • *Greece:* asp • *heraldry:* hands; wings • *see also* **charms [amulets]; defense**

protest *see* **complaint**

Protestantism Bible (Protestantism in particular, Christianity in general); fox; tree with many branches (the divisions of Protestantism) • *associations:* orange [color] (Protestants in Northern Ireland); six hundred and sixty-six (originally applied to the Beast of the Apocalypse, but later applied by Catholics to Martin Luther and other Protestants)

providence clouds; goose; hen, especially with chicks; heron (parental providence); squirrel • *association:* Pluto [planet] • *divine providence:* Elijah's raven; hair; pomegranate; quail; rain; rainbow; raven, especially carrying a loaf of bread; sheaf • *flower language:* purple clover • *heraldry:* hedgehog (provident provider); stag (political providence) • *Judaism:* hawk • *see also* **foresight; improvidence**

providers plowman (provider of society) • *heraldry:* hedgehog (provident provider)

provocation goad; needle; red flag; Taurus (slow to anger, but furious once provoked)

prowess claw; marrow (manly prowess) • *heraldry:* helmet (martial prowess) • *see also* **skill; strength**

prudence ash tree; breasts; camel; chalice; dolphin with an anchor or boat; hawthorn; Hermit [tarot]; hyacinth [flower]; hyacinth [gemstone] (Christian prudence); padlock; rudder; sorb • *associations:* little finger; P • *China:* elephant • *flower language:* service free • *heraldry:* ermine; otter; spider; wolf • *see also* **caution**

Prudence personified head with three faces; head with two faces (occasionally a woman, but usually Janus); woman with bare breasts and a veiled face • *attributes:* circular nimbus; compasses [dividers]; dragon; hawthorn; hexagonal mirror, especially with serpent; nimbus; remora pierced by an arrow; stag; three eyes; veil

Psalms harp • *association:* fifteen (the gradual psalms)

Psyche [goddess] naked maiden with a lamp, standing over a sleeping god (Psyche standing over Cupid) • *attributes:* lamp; vase

psyche bite (the dangerous action of the instincts upon the psyche, especially in the case of an animal bite); butterfly; corset (society hampering the development of the psyche); disease (malady of the soul or psyche); griffin (the rela-

tionship between psychic energy and cosmic force); knot (an unchanging psychic situation); moon • *association:* Libra (psychic and moral equilibrium) • *psychic disturbance:* broken stone, broken necklace with scattered beads, centipede, millipede (psychic disintegration); ghost (psychic dissociation); monster (unbalance psychic function); siren [alarm]; storm • *see also* **madness**

psychology key of silver (psychological knowledge)

puberty mutilation (proof of courage at puberty)

pubic hair maidenhair fern

pugnacity bulldog; quail; sparrow • *China:* quail • *heraldry:* dolphin; unicorn • *see also* **bravery; courage**

punishment axe; bee; beheading (typical punishment of the upper classes); birch rod or switch (corporal punishment; school punishment); branding; cauldron of boiling oil; chains (usually more than one chain); club [bat]; flogging (typical punishment for sailors); flood; foxglove and nightshade (pride and punishment, respectively); gall; gauntlet; Gehenna; hanging (typical punishment for common criminals); harpy (guilt and punishment); hemlock (punishment for unpopular beliefs); hornet; iron; lash; leprosy (punishment for eating tabooed food); making bricks without straw; millstone; noise; oar; pine; plummet [tool]; prison; rod; scourging (punishment, especially for Elizabethan prostitutes and Roman debtors); sick king (punishment for the sins of a nation); smoke; spanking, standing in the corner (punishment of children); staff; stick; stones; to be thrown from a rock (punishment for a traitor); torrential rain; vulture; whip; willow switch; wormwood; wound • *associations:* black; eight; fire and brimstone [sulfur], pine pitch (punishment in Hell); forty (castigation); forty-two • *divine punishment:* Assyria; Gehenna; Hell; horseman on a red horse (war as a punishment); khamsin; leprosy (divine punishment, especially for pride); lion (avenging deity); rider on a red horse (war as a punishment of God); scroll; volcano (divine punishment or destruction); vulture pecking at someone's liver • *Judaism:* fever

(punishment for disobedience to God) • *see also* **execution; torment; torture; wrath**
purgation *see* **purification**
purification ablution (purification, especially of subjective and inner evils); aloe (purification of the dead); baptism; bath; bitterness (suffering undergone in purification of the soul); breath; bronze; cedar; censer (purifying fire); circumcision (spiritual purification); clipping the nails; cremation; cutting the hair; deluge; dew; dill; embalming (purification of the soul through faith and trust in the ideal); ember; exile; fan; feather (purification of evil); fig (purgation); fireworks; flagellation; fleur-di-lys (purification through baptism); frankincense (purification of the mind); hawthorn; holy water; hyssop (purgation); incense (purification by fire); jug of water (cleansing of the soul); lavabo; maniple; myrrh; ocean; opal (said to purify thoughts); rain; Red Sea; rue [plant]; sieve; sorrel; sparrow; spice (purification; spiritual qualities that purify the mind); spikenard; sulfur and eggs; swinging (purification by air); sword; Temperance [tarot] (purification; ceaseless cycling through formation, regeneration, and purification); urn; vulture; washing; wine; wormwood; zigzag (spiritual purification and rebirth) • *associations:* blue (purification of the mind); forty; violet [color] • *China:* willow • *Judaism:* acacia (the month of purification)
Puritanism *associations:* blue; New England; Scotland
purity alabaster; angel holding a lily; apron (purity of life and conduct); asperges; basin, or basin and ewer together; child; cotta; crane [bird]; crescent (the pure soul); crystal; desert (the realm of abstraction, truth, purity, spirituality, and holiness); dew; dove; edelweiss; elephant; ermine; fir; fish; fleur-di-lys; garden; glass; gold and silver plumed dove (the treasures of purity and innocence); golden fleece, occasionally white fleece (purity of soul); hind [deer]; iris [flower]; ivory; jade; lamb (purity; pure thought); lamp; lavabo; light; lily (purity; the purified soul); linen; lotus; mountain air; myrtle; nightingale; nuditas virtualis; ointment; orange [fruit]; pearl; pigeon; sapphire; semen (the purest part of an individual); silk; silver; sky; snow; snowdrop; spire (the pure and solitary life); stars; surplice; swan; tower; turtle dove; unicorn; virgin (purity; purified emotions); waves [water]; white bird; white gloves (pure heart); white horse (the pure and perfect higher mind); white knight; white rose, especially in painting • *associations:* black and white together (humility and purity of life, respectively); golden hair; light complexion; white • *China:* pearl; silver; white rooster • *Christianity:* alb; emerald; seamless garment • *flower language:* orange blossoms (your purity equals your loveliness); red double pink (pure and ardent love); red rosebud (you are pure and lovely); red single pink (pure love); Star of Bethlehem; water lily (purity of heart); white lilac; white lily • *heraldry:* angel (a purified existence); cup • *purity of the soul:* embalming (purification of the soul through faith and trust in the ideal); girdle [cincture] (spiritual purity invigorating the soul); golden fleece (occasionally, white); lily (the purified soul) • *spiritual purity:* girdle [cincture] (spiritual purity invigorating the soul); spice (spiritual qualities which purify the mind); zigzag (spiritual purification and rebirth) • *see also* **incorruptibility; virginity**
purpose dabchick (a sensitive purpose) • *association:* one (moral purpose)
pursuit *see* **searching**
putti *attribute:* bow and arrows
puzzles *see* **enigmas**
Pygmalion sculptor with life sized female statue (the sculptor is Pygmalion)

Q

Q *association:* eight

quacks and quackery doctor holding with a pincers with a stone, or cutting open a patient's forehead (quack operation for stones in the head)

quaking aspen; poplar

qualification *attribute:* spurs (one who is qualified)

qualities *flower language:* mignonette (your qualities surpass your charms); peach blossom (your qualities, like your charms, are unequalled) • *mental qualities:* bishop (spiritualized mental qualities); cattle (baser mental qualities); soldier (striving mental qualities) • *see also* **baseness; elevation; virtues**

quantities X (a variable or unknown quantity); Y, Z (unknown quantities)

quarreling *see* **discord; dissension**

queens lily (queenly beauty) • *association:* R (often stands for rex [king] or regina [queen]) • *Egypt:* bearded queen (the beard indicates sovereignty) • *flower language:* dame violet, queen's rocket (you are the queen of coquettes)

querulousness *see* **complaining**

questing *see* **searching**

questioning *see* **curiosity; investigation; searching**

quickness *see* **speed**

quiet *see* **silence; tranquillity**

Quixote, Don knight charging a windmill

R

Ra *association:* ass • *attribute:* uraeus

Rachel *attribute:* moon

radiance *flower language:* ranunculus (you are radiant with charms) • *see also* **brilliance**

rage *see* **fury**

raiment *China:* kingfisher (gaudy raiment)

rain arrow; bottle; chirping cricket, rooks flying in a great flock (omens of rain); comb; dolphin (harbinger of rain); east wind (bringer of rain); feathered serpent (duality, such as rain and drought, good and evil, etc.); jar (rain charm); moon (regulator of rain); white cow • *association:* eight (rain and thunder); hair; pot, usually earthenware

rainmaking gourd used as a rattle; hands clapping; rattle

raising *see* **elevation**

rallying cry bugle; trumpet

randomness blindfold (usually used as an attribute of Fortune personified, and Nemesis)

rank cloak lined with fur; collar

[clothing]; crown; fan; golden chain; necklace; oak (tree of the highest rank); umbrella; velvet and ermine robe; white garment • *associations:* J; yellow (lowest rank) • *China:* canopy, peacock tail feathers (official rank) • *heraldry:* cherub; eagle (high position); red hand; ring; seraph; swan with a crown on its neck (high rank)

rankness *see* **offensiveness**

rapacity beehive (society thriving on rapacity); eagle shown as a bird of prey; harpy; shark; vulture; wolf • *Judaism:* fox • *see also* **greed; voracity**

Rapacity personified *attribute:* raven, especially with a ring in its back

rape nightingale; maiden abducted by a black bearded king in a chariot (the rape of Proserpine by Pluto); white bull bearing a maiden to the sea (the rape of Europa by Zeus)

Raphael [archangel] angel dressed as a pilgrim • *associations:* one; six; thirteen • *attributes:* caduceus; fish;

gourd; pyx (when with Tobias); staff; sword; wallet

rapidity see **speed**

rapine see **plunder**

rarity green eyes (in Elizabethan times, valued for their rarity) • *flower language:* mandrake

rascality see **evil; wickedness**

rashness butterfly; Hamlet; ruby • *associations:* Germans, Germany • *flower language:* balsam

rationality manticore (beastly rationality); rectangle (the most rational, secure, and regular of geometric forms); square [shape] (rationality; the merely rational) • *association:* four (rational organization); right hand • *see also* **logic; reason**

ray obelisk (sun ray); toe (ray of light)

reaction see **action and reaction**

readiness *association:* violet [color] (preparation) • *flower language:* red valerian • *heraldry:* buckle; horse (readiness for action); gauntlet, javelin, lance, spear, tent (readiness for combat); key (readiness to serve)

reading rabbit (desultory reading and learning) • *associations:* book; candle; lamp

realism Grecian lute

reality clothes (concealment of reality, truth, nakedness, vice, etc.); drugs, drunkenness (escape from reality); food (the real as opposed to the illusory); ivory tower (escape from reality, especially by an intellectual or academic); linen (ultimate reality); pinching (return to reality); plain [topography] (land of reality and truth); scarecrow (disguise to avoid facing reality); Wheel of Fortune [tarot] (unchanging reality despite changing events); womb (protection from reality) • *association:* four

reaping see **harvest**

reason brain; caduceus; checkers; compasses [dividers]; divorce (the apparent or delusive separation of emotion from reason); Emperor [tarot]; forest (obscurance of reason); Moon [tarot] (rejection of reason); Pasiphae (the overthrow of reason by animal passion); rule [measuring]; snow covered mountain (cold reasoning); the soul; sulfur (reason and intuition); white horse • *associations:* club suit [playing cards]; four; Jupiter [planet];

one; right side; white • *Egypt:* crocodile (divine reason) • *flower language:* goat's rue • *heraldry:* heart; ox head (power guided by reason) • *see also* **logic; rationality; thought**

Reason personified Mercury [god]

Rebecca woman at a well being offered jewels

rebellion flood; giant (everlasting rebellion); Leviathan (rebellion against the Creator); mosquito; Pandora, Pandora's box (rebellion against divine order); pitchfork (attribute of rebellious peasants)

Rebellion personified Jew striking a bishop

rebirth ashes (an ending that is also a beginning); baptism; butterfly; chick; cradle; Death [tarot]; emerald; font; kettle (realm of rebirth); lotus (human rebirth); Mount Ararat; Red Sea; river; scythe (renewed hopes for rebirth); slime (inertia preceding rebirth); snake sloughing off its skin; son; spring [season]; treasure in a cave (rebirth of the self); well; white pebble (graveside gift for rebirth); winter (involutive death with the promise of rebirth) • *associations:* animal skin (death and rebirth); green • *heraldry:* ash tree • *spiritual rebirth:* daffodil; fishing (seeking regeneration or spiritual rebirth); zigzag (spiritual purification and rebirth) • *see also* **regeneration; renewal; revival**

recall see **memory**

recantation *flower language:* lotus leaf alone

receptiveness woman

reciprocity see **mutuality**

recklessness see **careless; folly**

reclusiveness see **isolation**

recognition pitcher [vessel]

Recognition personified *attribute:* hemp

recollections see **memories**

recompense crown • *kabala:* three hundred (compensation)

reconciliation hazel; scepter tipped with a dove (reconciliation and peace); stone (harmonious reconciliation of self); threshold (the reconciliation and separation of two worlds: sacred and profane, life and death, etc.) • *flower language:* hazel; verbena • *heraldry:* ram [sheep] • *reconciliation of God and man:* olive tree or branch; rainbow •

reconciliation of opposites: mistletoe; plumed serpent; split scepter • *see also* **forgiveness**

recovery caladrius turning toward a sick person

recreation *see* **play; sports**

rectitude *see* **goodness**

red *associations:* ladybug (connected with red in the beneficent sense); three

redemption blood (Christ's redemption of man); chalice; Christ child holding an apple or orange (Christ as the redeemer of man from Original Sin); cross (finished redemption; if the cross is on three steps, they represent faith, hope, and love); cruet; fly [insect] (sin leading to redemption); lamb with a white flag with a cross on a cruciform flagstaff (Jesus Christ and the way in which he redeemed mankind); leopard with Christ and the Magi (the incarnation that was necessary for the redemption of sin); orange [fruit] shown in paradise (the fall of man and his redemption); parsley (hope of redemption); radish; water cress • *Judaism:* lettuce • *see also* **restoration**

refinement gardenia; high forehead • *China:* bamboo; orchid

reflection bed; echo (reflection of one's inner self, feelings, or emotions); mirror (reflection of one's inner self, emotions, or feelings); Moon [tarot]; pond • *associations:* ninety; tarot cards I to XI (the reflective); two • *see also* **contemplation; introspection; reverie; thought**

reform *see* **improvement**

refreshment bottle; ewer; fountain, well (especially spiritual refreshment); pitcher [vessel]; river; Tigris River; water; well

refuge *see* **safety**

refusal *flower language:* striped carnation; variegated pink • *see also* **denial**

regard *see* **respect**

regeneration baptism; bath; chrysalis; crab; deluge (destruction and regeneration); dove on a font cover (regeneration through the Holy Spirit); dragonfly; eagle; eight-petalled rose; eight-pointed staff; farmer (the catalyst of regeneration and salvation in harmony with nature); fir; fire; fish with a bird's head—usually a swallow's (bringer of cyclic regeneration); fish-

ing (seeking regeneration or spiritual rebirth); heron; House of God (materialism struck down by spiritual light to render regeneration possible); hurricane; ibis; Judgment [tarot]; lizard; milk; mistletoe; moon (a regenerating receptacle for the soul); oak leaf; obelisk; ox head with crown; phallus (nature's regenerative force); plane tree; rose garden; serpent; spring [season]; stag; thyrsus; tomb (involution and regeneration); torch; water; waves [water]; wind; zigzag • *associations:* eight; green (regeneration of the spirit); Neptune [planet]; mandorla (perpetual sacrifice and regeneration); octagon; Pluto [planet]; R • *China:* fish • *see also* **death and regeneration; destruction and regeneration; rebirth; renewal; reproduction; revival**

regression acanthus; arson (regression, especially male); bath, especially a warm bath (return to the womb); being struck dumb; centipede; crab; darkness appearing after light; Devil [tarot] (regression or stagnation of all that is inferior, fragmentary, or discontinuous); drawbridge; eyes with no lids; fairyland (escape or regression to childhood); floating; hat that confers invisibility; herd (when disorderly: loss of unity, disintegration, degeneration, regression); hood; hunchback; invisibility; millipede; Moon [tarot]; multiplicity; Neptune [god] (the regressive and evil side of the unconscious); orgy; thumb stuck in the mouth, especially sucking the thumb; wild man or wild woman (the unconscious in its perilous and regressive aspect)

regret asphodel; bluebell (sorrowful regret); gooseberry • *flower language:* asphodel (my regrets follow you to the grave) • *see also* **remorse; sorrow**

regularity rectangle (the most rational, secure, and regular of geometric forms)

regulation Emperor [tarot] (sterile regulation and power); maypole (the phallic reproductive powers of nature together with the vulva-circle regulation of time and motion); moon (regulator of water, rain, the fecundity of women and animals and the fertility of plants) • *see also* **control**

Reign of Terror [France] guillotine

reincarnation beans; nuts; scarab • *kabala:* two hundred (association)

reintegration returning home to one's birthplace or homeland (the equivalent of dying in the positive sense of reintegration with the spirit of God)

rejection briars; broom [plant] (rejected love); Moon [tarot] (rejection of reason); thistle; thumb down; tonsure (rejection of the temporal) • *flower language:* ice plant (rejected addresses); Indian single pink (don't touch me) • *see also* **disdain**

rejoicing tambourine (rejoicing in the Lord); timbrel; wine • *see also* **festivities**

rejuvenation apple; berry; fig; fountain; kettle (magic vessel or rejuvenation); panther; pomegranate (rejuvenation of the earth); prince (rejuvenated form of the king); spice; stag; water cress • *association:* pot, usually earthenware • *heraldry:* apple

relationship berry (close kinship); knot, plait (intimate relationship); sharing food (kinship); vine (relationship of God and his people)

relativism gray hair

release broken handcuffs; dancing (release from disagreeable circumstances); key • *flower language:* butterfly weed (let me go)

reliability *see* **dependability**

relief balm; harp music, warm bath (soothing of stress) • *flower language:* balm of Gilead • *see also* **help**

religion belfry (religiosity undone by clerical weakness); bishop (religious authority); chaos (death of religion and morality); cherub; crayfish (loss of faith); cymbal (religious ardor); drunkenness (religious frenzy); elephant; flame, torch (religious zeal or fervor); High Priest [tarot] (religion; external religion); honey (religious eloquence); Hydra (the prolific nature of heresy, sin, and false doctrine); idol (outward observances regarded as true spiritual experiences); Jesus Christ; lighthouse; lizard; mantis (cruelty and greed disguised by a hypocritical attitude of prayer or religiosity); north wind (religious persecution); pulpit (religious instruction); stag (religious aspiration); stigmata (high religious character); sword with an obtuse point;

tabret, timbrel (religious ecstasy); traveller (someone engaged in personal development, especially spiritual or religious) • *associations:* blue; five (religious interest); pipe [music]; purple; Thursday (works of religion and politics) • *flower language:* aloe (religious superstition); passion flower (religious superstition); schinus (religious enthusiasm) • *religious power:* book; crozier (the hooked end is to draw souls to God and the pointed end to prod the slothful); hair on the head; key; stole [religious garment] (priestly power and dignity) • *see also* **faith; piety**

Religion personified *attributes:* crane [bird]; elephant

remembrance dew; echo (magical in that it may remember what it hears); gray hair; hydrangea; juniper; mirror; pansy; rising serpent; rosemary; sage [herb]; stone; rose quartz (remembrance in prayer); sunflower (affectionate remembrance; religious remembrance) • *flower language:* cudweed, everlasting (never ceasing remembrance); forget-me-not; holly (Am I forgotten?); mouse-eared scorpion grass; rosemary (remembrance; remembrance of the dead); white clover (think of me) • *see also* **memories; memory**

Remigius, St. *attribute:* dove with a vial in its beak

reminder church spire with a finger pointed to the sky (reminder of God); skeleton at a feast (reminder of mortality)

reminiscences *see* **memories**

remission of sins *Christianity:* fifty (association)

remorse arrow; bramble; Furies; heart pierced with an arrow; scorpion; thorn; vulture; whip; wolfsbane • *association:* scourge [whip] • *flower language:* raspberry • *see also* **guilt; penitence; regret; shame; sorrow**

remoteness albatross (distant seas; long sea voyages); Ethiopia, Thule ("far away" lands); lighthouse (remoteness and solitude of man) • *flower language:* ficoides (your looks freeze me) • *remoteness from God:* abandonment (loss of contact with God or nature); labyrinth (the difficulty of uniting oneself with one's spirit and with God and/or remoteness from one's spirit and from God)

Remus see **Romulus and Remus**

Renaissance *associations:* Netherlands; Italy

rendezvous see **meetings**

renewal asceticism (voluntary abandonment of worldly activities in preparation for renewed life on a higher spiritual plane); Christmas (renewal of love and hope); cup (renewed spiritual vigor); Judgment [tarot]; morning (renewal of life; renewal of love); new clothes, especially at Easter (renewal of the owner); surplice (man's renewal in justice and truth); tortoise (Chaos, with the hope of renewal of life); waves [water] (renewed spiritual vigor) • *association:* Pluto [planet] • *renewal of life:* Sun [tarot]; thirty-six (Judaism); water cress • see also **rebirth; regeneration; revival**

renown see **fame**

renunciation broken straw (renunciation of allegiance or an agreement); coins at the feet of an old man (renunciation of worldly goods); pilgrim; veil (renunciation of the world) • *associations:* brown (renunciation of the world); gray • *flower language:* broken straw (renunciation of an agreement)

Reparata, St. woman bearing a Latin cross • *attributes:* white banner with a red cross, held by lamb; dove issuing from a saint's mouth

repentance blackberry; heart pierced by an arrow; lily; nettle; putting a rope on one's head; raven (an unrepentant sinner); rue [plant] • *association:* violet [color] • see also **penitence**

repetition circle, ring (an eternally repeated cycle); hunter; rosary (inane repetition); wood pigeon (monotonous chanting)

replacement stranger (replacement of the reigning power)

repose bed; lotus • *flower language:* blue, minor, or night convolvulus; buckbean • see also **rest**

representative seated man or woman (the supreme deity or the earthly representative of the supreme deity)

repression attic (that which is repressed); drawbridge; entanglement; goat (repression of one's conscience);

hat that confers invisibility; hood; ice (stultification of potentialities); invisibility; jester (repressed unconscious urges); needle; net; sealed lips; wax seal [stamp] • *association:* left side • *sexual repression:* apron; nightmare (sexual repression, especially of incest); tiger (repressed sexuality)

reproduction acacia; apple; bed; cow; hare; lap [body]; loins; maypole (the phallic reproductive powers of nature together with the vulva-circle regulation of time and motion); phallus (propagation of cosmic forces) • *associations:* Leo; monolith (procreative principle); two • see also **generation; regeneration; reproduction**

Republican Party [United States] *emblem:* elephant

repulsiveness black widow spider; crab, spider (repulsive sex); frog (the repulsiveness of sin); tarantula • *association:* dirty yellow • see also **offensiveness; rudeness**

reputation russet mantle (loss of good reputation) • *flower language:* apple blossom (fame speaks one great and good) • *heraldry:* angel, martlet (good reputation); blue (spotless reputation) • see also **fame; Notoriety personified**

request see **prayer; supplication**

rescue see **help**

resemblance see **sameness**

resentment burning or tingling right ear (someone is speaking spitefully of you); cat; fork [implement]; stomach (seat of resentment) • see also **anger; bitterness**

reserve Hermit [tarot]; maple; Saturn [god] • *flower language:* maple; sycamore

resignation blackbird; hands loose at sides; hyacinth [flower]; sorrel (resignation to sorrow) • see also **passivity; patience**

resilience juniper; reed

resistance amulet (resistance to evil); brass (obstinate resistance); camel; fist; High Priestess [tarot] (a balance between initiative and resistance); ice (the coldness of the ice implies a resistance to all that is inferior); ivory; latch, especially on a door (resistance to change); leather; mule; Prometheus (the will to resist oppression); wall • *association:* two • *flower language:* tremella nestoe • *heraldry:* hedgehog

resoluteness *see* **firmness**

resolution *association:* three (resolution of conflict) • *flower language:* purple columbine; red balsam (impatient resolves)

resourcefulness hare; rabbit • *heraldry:* duck; goose

resowing *association:* October

respect bowing; carnation (admiration); golden chain; kneeling; pea; standing; veiled hands • *China:* parasol • *flower language:* daffodil (regard); sage, especially garden sage; spiderwort (esteem, but not love); strawberry tree (esteem and love) • *heraldry:* gold • *Judaism:* bare feet • *see also* **honor**

resplendence *see* **magnificence**

responsibility shoulders • *associations:* F; O [letter] (material responsibility); seven (heavy responsibilities); six; X

rest bed; chair; four o'clock [flower]; poppy • *associations:* Saturday (according to the Bible, God rested on Saturday after creating the world); seven • *flower language:* harrow • *see also* **repose**

restlessness ferret; fever • *heraldry:* helmet with any kind of strange crest • *see also* **unrest**

restoration judge (restorer of natural balance); music (a general restorative); two keys crossed (excommunication and restoration) • *flower language:* persicaria • *see also* **redemption**

restraint bear, cincture (self-restraint); black stone; bridle; cicada (restraint of vice and lasciviousness); closed gate; collar; elephant (moderation; self-restraint); ermine (moderation); fibula [clasp or buckle] (restricted virility); field (freedom from restraint); girding the loins (restraint of passion and turning toward the spirit); Justice [tarot]; pin • *associations:* O [letter]; Saturn [planet] • *see also* **limitation; temperance**

restriction *see* **restraint**

resurrection abandonment (prelude to resurrection); angel holding a trumpet (resurrection day); baptism (death and interment of the old, birth and resurrection of the new); barley; beans; black clerical garments (the hope of inner resurrection through service to God); boat; bone; bonfire; bursting pomegranate; butterfly; cauldron; cave; chrysalis; cicada; cremation; cypress coffin; daisy; date palm tree; dolphin; eagle; flaming torch (hope of resurrection); fountain; frog; glow worm; gourd, especially when used as a rattle; gypsum; hare; hart; Jonah; lotus; monolith; moon; mountain; Noah's ark; peacock; pelican; pheasant; Phoenix [bird]; quail; ram [sheep]; resin; rooster; scarab; sea urchin; snail; staff; sunrise; swallow [bird]; swan; tamarisk; trumpet; vegetation growing in cycles (death and resurrection); vine; white stone or pebble (graveside gift for resurrection); wine; wings; wreath • *associations:* myrtle; seventy; spiral • *Gnosticism:* pink [color] • *Judaism:* eight (association); lettuce • *still life painting:* egg, especially when the shell is broken • *resurrection of Christ:* angel holding a trumpet (resurrection day); Christ with banner (refers to the period after the resurrection and before the ascension); date tree; empty tomb; frog (emblem); gourd; gourd and an apple (the resurrection of Christ as an antidote for sin); Jonah (precursor of the resurrection of Christ; the resurrection of Christ); lion (Middle Ages); Phoenix [bird] (early Christianity); trumpet (association); whale; white flag with a red cross

retaliation *see* **revenge**

retirement five-petalled lotus; maple; sleep (withdrawal); squirrel (sylvan retirement); swan (Christian retirement); tower (philosophical retirement) • *China:* sheep (the retiring life) • *heraldry:* hare (one who enjoys a peaceful, retired life); owl; squirrel (sylvan retirement)

retreat ivory tower (retreat from the world, especially by an intellectual or an academic); lodge; Shangri-La; sleep; valley (secret retreat of the soul)

retribution *see* **punishment**

retrospection *see* **remembrance**

return burial (return to the primal parent); pomegranate (return of spring); thaw (return of fertility) • *association:* calf (return of the Prodigal Son) • *flower language:* jonquil (from the 19th century on: I desire a return of affection)

Reuben *attribute:* water

revelation drunkenness (revelation of inner thoughts and feelings); glass; light, scroll (divine revelation); meteorite; reflection of a lake; soldiers on horseback in the sky; stable (light and revelation arising from ignorance); thousand petalled lotus (final revelation) • *associations:* blue (the unveiling of truth); gold (revealed truth); one (spiritual truth) • *flower language:* maiden blush rose (if you love me, you will reveal it) • *see also* **oracles**

revelry faun; saturnalia; satyr; singing; wine

revenge Asmodeus; bat [animal]; Cain; cedar; centaur; Electra; ember; hawk; knife; Lillith (a discarded mistress taking revenge); thistle; vulture • *flower language:* Scotch thistle (retaliation); trefoil • *see also* **punishment; vendetta**

Revenge personified *attribute:* narcissus [flower]

reverence *see* **piety**

reverie couch (a place for reverie, languor, seduction); pansy • *flower language:* flowering fern • *see also* **reflection; thought**

reversal acrobat

reversion *see* **regression**

revival almond; scarab (creation and revival of life); spring [season]; swastika; triskele (revival of life or prosperity); violet [flower] (spring revival) • *flower language:* rosemary (your presence revives me) • *see also* **rebirth; regeneration**

revolution red banner; torch (revolution and ultimate liberty) • *association:* red

reward basket with flowers or fruit; garland of roses (reward of virtue); laurel; reaping • *flower language:* laurel • *heraldry:* gauntlet • *kabala:* four hundred • *spiritual reward:* crown; eighteen (Christian association); heaven; sapphire

Rhea *association:* staff striking rock and the rock producing water • *attribute:* lion

Rhetoric personified *attributes:* shield; sword

riches *see* **wealth**

richness *China:* mani

ridicule *see* **humiliation; mockery; satire**

ridiculousness *see* **fools; stupidity**

right side *association:* east; front; three

rightness Lovers [tarot] (the right choice)

righteousness breastplate (righteousness as a defense); chalcedony (open righteousness); cloak; cypress (occasionally the righteous man who preserves his faith); daisy (the sun of righteousness); drugs (warring against right and truth); eagle or lamb (the just); endurance (long endurance implies righteousness); flowing or full robe; girdle [cincture]; king (divine right); match [fire] (uprightness); olive branch; plummet [tool]; seven branched menorah (the Seven Righteous Men); square [tool] (right conduct); strawberry; strawberry with other fruit (good works of the righteous); stream; vulture; waves [water] • *see also* **goodness; morality; virtue**

rigidity *see* **steadfastness**

Rinaldo and Armida nymphs bathing observed by soldiers; soldier holding a mirror for his mistress; soldier sleeping beside a pillar, woman kneeling beside him; two lovers in mirror

ripeness *see* **maturity**

rise and fall *association:* H

Rita, St. *attribute:* rose [flower]

rivalry *see* **conflict**

river deities *attributes:* crown of reeds; oar; urn lying on its side

River of Life Jordan River • *association:* meadow

Rivers of Paradise, Four *association:* four

robbery *see* **theft**

Roch, St. pilgrim; saint in prison with a dog • *attributes:* dog; plague spot on the thigh; shell

Rodomont and Orlando soldier fighting with naked man on a bridge (the soldier is Rodomont, the naked man is Orlando)

Roman Catholicism *see* **Catholicism**

romance *see* **love**

Rome double-headed eagle (the union of the Roman and Byzantine empires); nimbus (attribute of deified Roman emperors); scepter tipped with eagle (attribute of Roman consuls)

Romuald, St. *association:* ladder to

heaven, or monks in white habits on a ladder • *attributes:* crutch; the Devil underfoot; skull

Romulus and Remus infants suckled by a wolf • *association:* woodpecker • *attribute:* female wolf

root *see* **foundation**

Rornvald, St. *attribute:* white beard

rosary beads; bladder nut; garland of roses (rosary of the Virgin Mary) • *association:* fifteen (the fifteen mysteries of the rosary)

rose [color] *association:* eight

Rose of Lima, St. *attribute:* crown of thorns

rotation swastika

roughness *see* **rudeness**

Round Table, Knights of the *associations:* grail; round table

royalty asp; cedar; chrysanthemum (regal beauty); dwarf elder (in ancient times, in the eastern Mediterranean area); iris [flower]; lapwing; peacock; Phoenix (royal succession); pomegranate; ruby; umbrella (royal protection) • *associations:* blue (occasionally); crimson; purple • *attributes:* bracelet; camel's hair clothes; crown; ermine; golden (occasionally white) fleece; hoopoe; sandals; scepter; shoes, especially golden; velvet and ermine robe; • *Egypt:* lotus • *emblem:* parasol • *flower language:* angrecum • *heraldry:* fleur-de-lys (especially French royalty); unicorn • *Middle East:* camel • *Spain:* lisping • *royal dignity:* canopy; diamond [shape] (royal dignity and wealth); globe (imperial dignity); lion; two-wheeled plow (emblem) • *royal power:* Adam; peony • *associations:* purple; red; yellow (Chinese association) • *Egypt:* bee • *royal weapons:* club [bat]; double-headed axe; lance; mace;

spear (in ancient times); staff; whip • *see also* **kings; queens; princes; princesses**

rudeness bittern; goat; swine; weeds • *associations:* body hair; Germany; Netherlands; Scotland; thick lips; wart • *flower language:* borage; burdock; xanthium • *see also* **offensiveness; repulsiveness**

Ruffina, St. *attribute:* pot, usually earthen

ruination *association:* P (success followed by ruin) • *China:* hen crowing (the ruin of a family) • *folklore:* earthquake (a man born during an earthquake will be the ruin of a country) • *see also* **defeat**

rule *see* **command; power**

rumor house without doors

rupture ship on a stormy sea (the church surviving persecution, schism, heresy) • *flower language:* blue-flowered or Greek valerian; broken straw (breaking of a contract) • *see also* **separation**

rural life *see* **rusticity**

ruse *see* **deceit; trickery**

Russia *emblems:* alexandrite; bear; double-headed eagle (czarist Russia); hammer and sickle (Union of Soviet Socialist Republics)

rusticity apple cider (rural festivities); cabin, cottage (the simple, carefree country life); cowslip; hemp; jay (bumpkin); shepherd's crook; squirrel (sylvan retirement) • *flower language:* French honeysuckle (rustic beauty); yellow violet (rural happiness)

Ruth *attributes:* grain; harvesting; stalk of wheat

ruthlessness *see* **cruelty; ferocity; viciousness**

S

S *association:* one

Sachiel *associations:* eighteen; fourteen

sacraments dove on a pyx (reservation of the sacrament); pyx (blessed sacrament) • *associations:* five (the five lesser sacraments); septfoil (the seven sacraments of pre-Reformation times) • *see also* **baptism; confession and**

absolution; confirmation [religious]; consecration; eucharist; marriage; ordination; unction
Sacred Love personified *attribute:* vase with flame coming from its mouth
sacredness *see* **holiness**
sacrifice Alcestes; blood, especially when spilled; breaking of bread in a ritual sacrifice (killing); Christ; comb (sacrificial remains); cornerstone (remnant of the foundation sacrifice: originally a child was used, later, small animals); cutting of the hair; earthquake (omen of divine sacrifice); eating a goose (sun sacrifice); fillet; fish; fist placed over the heart (tearing out one's heart as an offering); gallows; hanging [execution] (sacrifice to a sky god); incense (sacrifice for thanksgiving or plea for a favor); jester (sacrificial victim); offering (sacrificing lower values for higher values); pelican (parental love and sacrifice); Phrygian cap; pierced ears (blood sacrifice for the protection of a child); plate; pouring out wine (bloodletting in ritual sacrifice); rags hung on a tree (substitute for human sacrifice); spider (continuous sacrifice); spindle (mutual sacrifice); thighs (a sacrificial, holy place); Tristram (sacrifice in an unendurable situation); wallowing (sacrificial act to encourage change); wound (sacrifice to placate); yoke • *associations:* bull; calf; chalice; dove; fat; fourteen; goblet suit [tarot]; grapes; heifer; knife; lamb (sometimes, unwarranted sacrifice); mandorla (perpetual sacrifice and regeneration); Mars (the idea that their is no creation without sacrifice); ox; ram [sheep] (sacrifice; the sacrifice of Isaac); red; sheep, especially with bound feet; tattoo; Taurus (primordial sacrifice); thirty; trapezoid; white cow; wine • *China:* orange [fruit] (an imperial sacrifice to heaven) • *Christianity:* altar with flames (the sacrifice of Christ); beaver (the Christian who makes sacrifices for the sake of his spiritual life); Lent (suffering and sacrifice, especially of Christ); narcissus [flower] (the triumph of sacrifice over selfishness); pelican, usually with wings spread (Christian readiness to sacrifice) • *heraldry:* beaver; goose (self-sacrifice) • *Judaism:* altar with

flames (the Jewish altar of sacrifice); kidney • *kabala:* thirty • *self sacrifice:* beaver; Hanged Man [tarot] (spiritual self- sacrifice); lamp; pearl; swan
sadness Born on a Wednesday, sour and sad (or, full of woe); dead leaves; harp; meadow; Tuesday's child is solemn and sad; vinegar; willow; yew • *association:* blue; violet [color] • *flower language:* yew • *see also* **melancholy**
safety arch; armor; blanket; boat; caduceus in a woman's hand; castle; Castor and Pollux (safety at sea); cave; chains; church; city; cord; crossed fingers; egg; harbor; hearth; High Priestess [tarot]; house; island; lighthouse; lizard; lying down; padlock; pillow; rectangle (the most rational, secure, and regular of geometric forms); roof; rudder; screw; seal [stamp]; sedge (refuge of the lover); ship; stable; sturgeon; throne; tower; turtle; vine; wall • *association:* seven • *flower language:* rock rose; traveller's joy • *see also* **guardianship**
sagacity broom [for sweeping] (insight); tunny • *China:* elephant • *heraldry:* elephant; fox (sagacity or wit used in one's own defense) • *see also* **cleverness; genius; intellect; wit**
sages *see* **scholars; wisdom**
Sagittarius archer • *associations:* blue; dandelion; east; falcon; G; Jupiter [planet]; linden; oak; pink [flower]; Thursday; tin; topaz; turquoise [gemstone]; mimosa; purple • *emblem:* bow and arrows
sailing *association:* Netherlands
sailors anchor (as a 19th century sailor's tattoo: service in the Atlantic); dragon (as a 19th century sailor's tattoo: a sailor who had been to China); gold earring (protection from drowning) • *association:* tar • *heraldry:* dolphin • *see also* **the military**
saintliness *see* **holiness**
saints knight riding a goat • *attributes:* amaranth (crown of saints); armor, banner (warrior saints); aspergillum (saints famed for their contests with the Devil); ermine, lily (virgin saints); hexagonal nimbus (a person one degree below being a saint); scroll; white (saints who were not martyred) • *see also* **martyrdom,** and the names of particular saints, such as **Matthew, Peter,** etc.

salaciousness *see* **lasciviousness**
saliva foam; pot, usually earthen; sap
salutation hand flat on the heart; removing a glove, especially the right
salute dipping a flag; firing guns • *see also* **honor**
salvation alchemy; anchor; ark; ass; bird in a cage (hope of freedom); bottle; bulrush; candelabrum; castle of light; Christ child holding an apple (the fruit of salvation); church as an ark (the salvation of its members); cross on an orb or globe; dalmatic; dawn (the beginning of salvation); dolphin; dolphin with an anchor or boat (the church being guided to salvation by Christ); door; eagle (Christ swooping down to save a soul); farmer (the catalyst of the forces of regeneration and salvation in harmony with nature); garden; gate; grail; hart (Christian thirst for salvation); helmet, especially surmounted by a fleur-di-lys; horn [animal]; index finger upraised (Jesus Christ as the one way to salvation); Jesus Christ; lighthouse; olive branch, Red Sea (deliverance); peach (the fruit of salvation); pearl; pilgrim (man in his journey to salvation); plantain (food of the multitude seeking Christian growth or salvation); rood beam (the necessity of the cross of Calvary in passing from the Church Militant to the Church Triumphant); shield; sun (promise of salvation); thorn (the road to salvation); tower; wall • *associations:* middle finger (the salvation of Christ); twelve • *Gnosticism:* eagle atop a ladder (the way to salvation) • *heraldry:* fleur-di-lys
Samiel *associations:* four; sixteen
Samaritan, Good *attribute:* napkin and cruse of wine
sameness meadow; Temperance [tarot] (that which is always different yet always the same) • *flower language:* spiked speedwell
Samian sibyl [Samiana] *attribute:* rose [flower]
Samson man wrestling with a lion; sleeping man having his hair cut off • *attributes:* broken pillar; jawbone of an ass; lion; seven cords; two pillars
sanctity *see* **holiness**
sanctuary *see* **safety**
sanguinity *see* **optimism**
Santa Claus *association:* Christmas •

attributes: gifts; red clothing; reindeer; sleigh
Santiago, Spain *heraldry:* shell (pilgrimage to Santiago)
Saracens *attribute:* turban
Sarepta, Widow of *association:* faggots formed in a cross • *attribute:* cruse of oil
Satan ape (early Christianity); basilisk; bear; billy goat; blackbird; chains (the power of the Devil); crocodile; crow; cuckoo; demon (an agent of the Devil); the Devil with a candle and bellows (his attempt to extinguish spiritual life); dog; dragon; fish swimming into a whale's mouth (unsuspecting souls trapped by the Devil); fly [insect]; fox; frog; gray horse; headless horseman; hunter; hyena; leopard; lion (rare), sometimes shown roaring; monk offering a stone to Christ (the Devil tempting Christ in the wilderness); nightingale (the Devil's deceit); partridge (sometimes, however, the church); rat; raven; satyr (child of the Devil); scorpion; serpent; serpent battling with a fish (Satan tempting Christ); sparrow; spider; stag trampling on a snake or a dragon (Christ's power over Satan); succubus (female form of the Devil); swine; toad; vampire; viper; vulture; whale; wolf; woodpecker; wyvern • *associations:* black; blackberry; brass (occasionally); darkness; fern (used occasionally, although more often associated with Christ); fifteen; impure orange [color]; mouse (especially in the Middle Ages); red; red and black; sneeze on a Sunday, for safety seek, the Devil will have you the whole of the week); wart • *attributes:* aspergillum (attribute of saints famed for their contests with the Devil); barbed or pointed tail; bat [animal]; burning throne; cloven feet; horns; horse with three legs; owl; pitchfork; red beard; red clothing; red garters; scaly skin; trident; wings of skin • *emblem:* bear and lion together • *see also* **demons; devils**
satire barb; pepper • *flower language:* prickly pear • *see also* **humiliation; mockery**
satisfaction *see* **fulfillment; gratification**
Saturday marriage on a Saturday was once associated with misfortune •

associations: Capricorn; Saturn [god]; works of mourning

Saturn [god] infant being eaten by an old man (the old man is Saturn) • *associations:* crow; middle finger; Saturday; Saturn [planet] • *attributes:* crutch; grapes with wheat; hourglass; oar; scythe; serpent; sickle

Saturn [planet] *associations:* ass; dark green; December; four; indigo [color]; lead [metal]; M; middle finger; N; pine; sapphire; Saturday

saturnalia *associations:* dancing; holly

satyrs *attributes:* horn [animal]; ivy; pipe [music]; thyrsus; wineskin

Saul of Tarsus *see* St. Paul

savagery *see* **ferocity; wildness**

Scaevola, Gaius Mucius soldier with his hand in a brazier

scandal tongue • *association:* tea (amorous intrigue and scandal) • *flower language:* hellebore • *see also* **gossip**

Scandinavia *emblem:* five swans (the five Scandinavian countries)

scarabs *association:* ladybug

scarecrows gargoyle (scarecrow for evil spirits)

scavengers dog; crow; kite [bird]; vulture

schemes *see* **plans; strategy**

schism *see* **rupture; separation**

scholars bullfinch • *attributes:* ivory tower; writing pen • *China:* purple • *Orient:* chrysanthemum

scholarship dominoes; duck (love of knowledge of profound mysteries); hare (love of learning); key; lute • *China:* sturgeon (scholarly excellence, particularly in examinations)

Scholastica, St. *attributes:* crucifix, especially with a dove; lily

schools birch rod or switch (school authority)

science compasses [dividers]; dog • *associations:* B; Wednesday (works of science) • *heraldry:* blue; crescent; torch

Scipio book and sword offered to a warrior sleeping under a tree

scoffing *see* **mockery**

scorn *see* **disdain**

Scorpio *associations:* blackthorn; bluish green; carnation; chrysanthemum; dark red; eagle; eight; iron; Mars; moon; N; Pluto [planet]; scorpion; Tuesday

Scotland *associations:* bagpipe; frugality; tartan • *emblems:* grouse [bird]; thistle

scourge branch [plant]; locust [insect]

scourging cincture (the scourging of Christ) • *see also* **whipping**

scouts *emblems:* fleur-di-lys (Boy Scouts); squirrel tail (American scouts in the Revolutionary War); trefoil (Girl Scouts)

scribes *emblem:* feather quill pen

scripture *see* **Bible**

scrotum bag; basket; purse • *see also* **genitals; testicles**

sculpture *associations:* hammer and chisel; spindle tree (sculptors) • *flower language:* hoya • *Middle Ages:* ape

sea albatross (distant seas; long sea voyages); Castor and Pollux (safety at sea); dolphin; salt water; sea serpent (unexplored waters); white feathers (sea foam); zigzag (waves of the sea) • *associations:* dark blue (a stormy sea); eight (the eternal movement of the sea); Monday (according to the Bible, the day the waters were divided) • *attributes of sea deities:* conch shell; dolphin; fish hippocampus; seal [animal] (the steed of sea deities); trident • *emblems:* crab; dolphin with a trident (supremacy of the seas); Neptune [god]; oak wreath (victory at sea); orb with an orrery on it (sovereignty at sea); trident • *heraldry:* dolphin (seafarer); Melusina, mermaid, merman (seafaring ancestors); ship (veteran of sea expeditions)

Sea personified *attribute:* jug with water flowing from it

searching carnival, saturnalia (the desperate search for a way out of time); dabchick (a seeker of the wisdom of the deeps); deer (a Christian seeking after truth); fishnet (searching the water of the unconscious); grail (elusive quest); hound; hunter, traveller (searcher for the truth); journey (searching; searching for the lost mother); monster (the instincts that hinder man in his search for truth); plantain (food of the multitude seeking Christian growth or salvation) • *association:* Y (search for the mystic or esoteric) • *heraldry:* falcon (someone on an eager quest) • *see also* **curiosity; investigation**

seasickness beryl (charm against death, seasickness, eye and throat ailments)

seasons Temperance [tarot] • *association:* four • *see also* **autumn; spring; summer; winter**
Sebastian, St. arrow piercing a nude man; man being bound to a stake • *attributes:* crown; pillar
seclusion *see* **hiding**
Second Coming of Jesus Christ *see* **Jesus Christ**
second prizes red ribbon
second sons *heraldry:* crescent (second sons and their families)
secrecy arch; bag; bed; book (secret knowledge); box, especially a closed box; cave; closed book, chest, or door; closet; coffer; hand placed over the mouth (secrecy; member of a secret cult); hedge; key; maidenhead; padlock; seal [stamp]; serpent; Sphinx; wax; whisper; winking eye; worm • *associations:* Taurus; two; violet [color] • *flower language:* full grown rose placed over two buds; honey flower (sweet and secret love); motherwort, toothwort, yellow acacia (secret love) • *heraldry:* fish • *see also* **hiding; privacy**
security *see* **safety**
Seder *associations:* open door, wine (both provided on Seder nights for Elijah messenger of the Messianic Age)
sedition *see* **treason**
seduction cosmetics; couch (a place for reverie, languor, seduction); Empress [tarot]; handkerchief; locust [insect]; long fingernails (attribute of a seductress); mermaid, merman; mirror; serpent (seduction by strength of matter); winking eye • *see also* **allurement; temptation; wantonness**
seed meteorite; sea urchin (primordial seed); slug [animal] (the male seed)
seeking *see* **searching**
seers *see* **fortune tellers; prophets; wisdom**
selection *see* **choice**
self American Indian; tramp [hobo]; Negro; savage; wild man, wild woman (the primitive, instinctive, emotional, natural self); beetle; caduceus (self-control); chariot; clothing (reflection of one's inner self); Death [tarot] (death of the old self, not necessarily physical death); echo (reflection of one's inner self, feelings, or emotions); effigy (the psychic aspect of a person; an image of the soul); elephant; enemy

(the forces threatening a person from within); eyes (guardian of the inner person); fasting (self-mortification); fish, remora (the self hidden in the unconscious); horse; house; incest (longing for union with one's own self); mirror, reflection in water (self-contemplation; reflection of one's inner self; self-realization); moorings (the higher self); Ouroboros (the self-sufficiency of nature); phallus; rags (self-deprecation); sieve (self-knowledge through action); snail (the self: the shell represents the conscious, the soft inner part, the unconscious or personality); stone (harmonious reconciliation of self); thief (lesser nature that robs the self of primordial wealth); treasure in a cave (the self being reborn); tunic (inner self) • *emblem:* cabbage (the self-willed) • *heraldry:* raven (a self-made man)
self-assertion flag • *association:* eight (self-assertion and material success)
self-confidence Aeolian harp; carbuncle [gemstone]; opal (charm for self-confidence and hope); rooster
self-consciousness mirror; Narcissus [mythology]; reflection in water
self-control *see* **control**
self-creation birch; hermaphrodite (androgynous self-creation); scarab
self-defense armor; buckle; hedgehog; raised arms • *heraldry:* fox (sagacity or wit used in one's own defense)
self-denial amethyst; bull; Hanged Man [tarot]; midnight • *see also* **denial**
self-destruction enemies (the forces threatening a person from within); Furies (guilt turned upon itself to the destruction of the guilty); Phrygian cap; siren [mythology] or swan song (desire leading to self-destruction) • *association:* eight
self-fructification apricot; lotus blossom; Ouroboros
self-indulgence cat; chocolate; swine
self-love narcissus [flower]; virgin • *flower language:* poet's narcissus • *see also* **selfishness; vanity**
self-mutilation beaver; scythe
self-respect *see* **dignity**
self-restraint bear; cincture; elephant
self-sacrifice beaver; Hanged Man [tarot] (spiritual self-sacrifice); lamp; pearl; swan song • *heraldry:* goose
selfishness cuckoo; horse; swine;

walnut • *association:* one • *Christianity:* narcissus [flower] (the triumph of sacrifice over selfishness) • *flower language:* poet's narcissus • *see also* **egoism; meanness; self-love**
selflessness *see* **compassion; generosity**
selk *attribute:* scorpion
semblance *see* **resemblance**
semen foam; insect; marrow; milk; mixed wine; plant gum; sap; thread • *association:* pot, usually earthen • *see also* **sperm**
Semiramis woman whose hair is being tended to by a maid amid war preparations
sensationalism *association:* yellow
senselessness *see* **folly**
senility grasshopper
senses Devil [tarot] (the half knowledge of the senses); drunkenness (elevation of normal powers); harpy (unregulated appetites of sensation and desire using knowledge to promote their own ends); herb (primitive desires and ambitions aroused by the senses); metal; World [tarot] • *association:* four (the functional aspects of consciousness: thinking, feeling, intuition, and sensation)
sensitivity aspen (excessive sensitivity); dabchick (a sensitive purpose); mimosa; Moon [tarot] (imaginative sensitivity); rhinoceros (lack of sensitivity); snail • *associations:* I [letter]; K
sensuality bear; cat; chestnut; chocolate; duck; fox; gull; lisping; magnolia; mermaid; merman; silk; siren [mythology]; stomach; trombone; wine • *associations:* pink [color]; sixteen • *flower language:* cyclamen; moss rose; Spanish jasmine; tuberose • *see also* **hedonism; wantonness**
sentiments ass (sentimentality); ruins (sentiments, ideas, or customs which are dead and irrelevant to present life, but which nonetheless persist) • *association:* red • *flower language:* double aster (I share your sentiments); spearmint (warmth of sentiment) • *see also* **feelings**
separation beheading (separation of the body and spirit); branding (membership in or separation from a group); cloven hoof; communion rail (separation of heaven and earth); divorce (the apparent or delusive separation of

emotion from reason, wisdom from love, or goodness from truth); fan; jasmine; ocean; threshold, wall (the separation and reconciliation of two worlds: sacred/profane; life/death, etc.); tulip • *flower language:* ash-leaved trumpet flower; Carolina jasmine • *see also* **rupture**
September *associations:* balances; harvesting of grapes; sapphire; turquoise [gemstone] • *China:* chrysanthemum; mallow
sepulcher *see* **the grave**
seraphs angel with a candle; blue angel
Serapis *attribute:* caduceus
serenade *see* **song**
serenity *see* **peace; tranquillity**
Sergius, St. soldier • *attribute:* palm tree
serpent *see* **snake**
servants Hagar (a bondswoman unjustly oppressed); kite [bird] (false servant) • *association:* ten (the ten servants of Joshua) • *attribute:* blue clothes
service apron; bitter herbs [forced service]; black clerical garments (the hope of inner resurrection through service to God); cincture (preparation for service); broom [both the plant and the tool]; falcon [noble service]; flint (zeal to serve); hare (diligent service); jackal (cowardly service); moss; nectar (the soul's entire service to the highest ideals); nuditas temporalis (lack of worldly things, especially when abandoned in service to God); soldier; tonsure (dedication to divine service); tunicle; yoke (patient service) • *heraldry:* head (honor for special services); key (readiness to serve) • *willing service:* bare feet (Judaism); foot; stole [religious garment]; washing of someone else's feet
servility broom [for sweeping]; cutting a beard • *heraldry:* bull
Seth *associations:* thread wrapped three times around the thumb; three seeds of the Tree of Life
seven seventy (the values of seven multiplied) • *associations:* G; Q (primarily associated with the number eight, but sometimes with seven); Saturn [planet]; Y
the Seven Archangels seven trumpets

the **Seven Celestial Spheres** seven-branched menorah

Seven Gifts of the Holy Spirit *see* **Holy Spirit**

the **Seven Patriarchs of Mankind** seven-branched menorah

the **Seven Pre-Reformation Sacraments** septfoil

the **Seven Righteous Men** seven-branched menorah

the **Seven Virtues** seven women (faith, hope, charity, temperance, prudence, fortitude, justice)

Seven Liberal Arts personified *attribute:* scroll (especially Logic, but also Music, Astronomy, Arithmetic, Geometry, Rhetoric, and Grammar)

Seventh Commandment heart pierced with an arrow with a woman's head shown on the heart (sin against the 7th Commandment: Thou shalt not commit adultery)

severity Emperor [tarot]; spearmint • *association:* purple-red • *flower language:* branch of thorns

sex apple (sexual enjoyment); apron (repression or cover of sexuality); asparagus; baking; claw (degenerate sexuality); crab (repulsive sex); dancing; fig (sex in general; the breasts; an opened fig suggests the vagina; eating a fig represents erotic ecstasy); fish, sometimes two fish (sexuality; sexual coldness, frigidity, indifference); flagellation (sexual stimulation); floating (sexual ecstasy, especially female); fox; handiwork (euphemism); hawthorn; kidney; locomotive; lotus (the sexual prison of marriage); Medusa (primal sexuality); rabbit (uninhibited, but often immature, sexuality); reptile; screw; sixty-nine (simultaneous oral-genital sex); thighs (sexual vigor); transvestitism (identification with a deity, parent, or ideal of the opposite sex); trout; Venus [goddess] (love in the physical or sexual sense); water • *associations:* beech; garters; grafting; hair (especially, thick, long, full, or flowing hair); horseshoe (related to a horse's vitality and sexual potency); lips; loaf of bread (depending on the shape of the loaf); neck; Scorpio (sexual function); tailors; teeth; tinkers; Venus [planet] (sexual emotions) • *female sexuality:* bacon (female sexual pleasure); cow; floating; goose;

lioness; lying down spread-eagle (female surrender); musk; night; sleeping beauty or princess (dormant female sexuality) • *Judaism:* acacia (sexual abstinence) • *male sexuality:* bull, hound, lion (male sexual desire); phallus • *sexual desire:* bull (male); cow (female); hound (male); ibis; itching (association); lion (male); lioness (female); monkey; ocean (association); pin; quivering (association); sting • *sexual intercourse:* boring [drilling]; cracking a nut (sexual intercourse, especially between a small man and a large overbearing woman); entering a tunnel; flower, especially a white flower; intoxicant (fornication); Liguria, Pasiphae (abnormal sexual intercourse); middle finger upraised; ointment; plucking flowers; riding, especially an animal; stringing beads; thumb in the mouth or between closed fingers; trombone being played • *sexual power:* body hair (association); snail (emergence of sexual power); snails when eaten; warts • *sexual repression:* apron; nightmare (sexual repression, especially of incest); tiger (repressed sexuality) • *see also* **aphrodisiac; eroticism; libido; orgasm; wantonness**

shadow *association:* two

shaking aspen; poplar

shallowness *see* **superficiality**

Shamash *association:* measuring with a rod and a line • *emblem:* four-pointed star

shame burning; cutting one's beard; nudity; ostrich; peony • *flower language:* deep red rose (bashful shame); peony • *see also* **guilt; humiliation; remorse**

shamelessness *see* **boldness**

sharing *flower language:* double aster (I share your sentiments); garden or small double daisy (I share your affection--used especially in the days of chivalry)

shark *association:* Mars

sharpness mulberry tree (sharpness and kindness combined); scourge [whip] (sharp tongue) • *flower language:* barberry; lantana

sharpsightedness *see* **sight**

sheep golden plover (warns sheep of approaching danger) • *attributes:* branded hand (sheep thieves); scissors (sheep shearers) • *heraldry:* ram [sheep] (the right to keep sheep) • *see also* **shepherds**

shelter cave (primitive shelter); cradle; house; hut

shepherds sheep on a man's shoulders (the good shepherd) • *associations:* bagpipe; P (the shepherd's crook) • *attribute:* crozier; pipe [music] (attribute); staff; syrinx; tent

ships renaming (bad luck for a ship) • *association:* tar

shooting tailor (a bad shot with a weapon)

showiness *see* **ostentation**

shrewdness *see* **cleverness**

Shriners *emblem:* scimitar

shroud *see* **burial**

Shrove Tuesday *emblem:* pancake

shyness lizard; shrimp; thrush • *flower language:* cyclamen (diffidence); deep red rose (bashful shame); peony; vetch; wallflower; sowbread (diffidence) • *see also* **timidity**

sibyls *associations:* ten; twelve • *attributes:* book; turban *Agrippine sibyl:* whip (attribute) • *Cimerian sibyl:* horn of milk (attribute) • *Cumean sibyl:* woman with cupped hands before Apollo; bowl, cradle, manger (attributes) • *Delphic sibyl:* crown of thorns (attribute) • *Erythraean sibyl:* animal horn, lily (attributes) • *European sibyl:* sword (attribute) • *Hellespontic sibyl:* cross, nails [for wood] (attributes) • *Libyan sibyl:* torch (attribute) • *Persian sibyl:* woman treading on a serpent or dragon; lamp, lantern (attributes) • *Phrygian sibyl:* lamb carrying a banner with a red cross; processional cross (attribute) • *Samean sibyl:* rose [flower] (attribute) • *Tiburtine sibyl:* dove, rod (attribute)

sickness bed; caladrius turning away from a sick person: death; caladrius turning toward a sick person: recovery; dragon; kerchief on the head; paleness • *association:* violet [color] • *flower language:* anemone; meadow anemone • *see also* **affliction; disease; plague**

Sickness personified *attribute:* greyhound

sight eagle, greyhound, hawk, sparrowhawk (good eyesight); eyelids (observation); fog, squinting (poor eyesight); window • *association:* crystal; four (double vision) • *flower lan-*guage: hawkweed (quick-sightedness)

Sight personified *attributes:* eagle; mirror; torch

signal whistling

significance *see* **importance**

signs *see* **foretokens and signs; tokens**

silence cold [temperature]; daisy (the silence of death); hand on the mouth, index finger to the lips (silence); vow of silence); moon; oyster; padlock; peach (the virtue of silence); Sphinx; stone; tortoise; turtle • *association:* diamond suit [playing cards] • *flower language:* deadly nightshade [belladonna]; white rose • *heraldry:* rose • *see also* **peace; tranquillity**

Silence personified *attribute:* peach

Silenus *association:* ass • *attributes:* chariot drawn by an ass; vine garland; wineskin

silk *association:* mulberry tree

silliness *see* **folly**

Silver Age personified woman sower • *association:* harvest, harvesting • *attributes:* plow, especially with a sheaf of grain

silvery blue *kabala:* eight (association)

Simeon *attribute:* sword

Simeon Stylites, St. *attribute:* pillar

Simon, St. *attributes:* boathook with a fish attached; book with a fish on it; fuller's bat; oar with saw or battle axe, or two oars crossed; saw [tool], especially a large saw with one or two oars or a cross; two fish crossed

Simon Stock, St. praying saint before an image or vision of the Virgin and Child, with the Virgin presenting a scapular • *attribute:* scapular

simpletons *see* **intellect**

simplicity cottage (the simple country life); crystal; dove; flax; forget-me-not (ingenuous simplicity); sheep • *associations:* Sparta; white • *flower language:* American sweet brier; blueberry, mouse-eared chickweed (ingenuous simplicity); dog rose; single rose • *heraldry:* dove

Simplicity personified *attribute:* pheasant

simplification giant (quantitative simplification)

sin acanthus (awareness and pain of sin); Adam (man's weak, sinful side); Adam with an apple; Adam's skull with the Cross; ailanthus (virtue growing out of, but untainted by, sin); Alastor (man's inner evil driving him to sin); ape; Bacchante (a debauched and sinful woman); Bacchus; black knight; black stone; blackbird; blindfold; blot; bondage (immobilization through sin or evil); brambles, briars (sins: when growing, they may be major sins); broken handcuffs or bonds (sin overcome); bruised serpent (victory over sin); chains; cord; crown (attribute of martyrs, indicating victory over sin and death); devils; dirtiness (the accumulation of error, prejudice, sin); dragon; dragon underfoot, slain, bound, or chained (paganism or sin overcome); fire and brimstone, sick king (punishment for sins); fly [insect] (sin; sin leading to redemption); frog (sin; the repulsiveness of sin); gourd and apple (the resurrection of Christ as an antidote for sin); hunchback (sins of the past); Hydra (the prolific nature of heresy, sin, false doctrine); lamprey (debilitating sin); leopard; leopard with the Christ child and the Magi (the incarnation needed for the redemption of sin); Medusa; orb or globe with a snake around it (sin encircling the world; the spread of sin); ostrich (sinful man); person in handcuffs, or other bonds (man enslaved by sin or his earthly desires); raven; Satan; scorpion; serpent; serpent at the foot of the Cross (Jesus overcoming the evil that leads man into sin); skull; slime; snare; stole [religious garment], yoke (man's sin borne by Jesus Christ); sweat; thistle; thorn (sin; minor sin); Tower of Babel (sinful presumption); trident; troll [mythic being]; vampire; viper; web; weeds; wineskin; worm • *associations:* black; cloven feet; crimson; darkness; eleven; evil smell; red; scarlet • *Christianity:* eleven (transgression); fifty (remission of sins); six (the Six Sins Against the Holy Spirit: despair of salvation, presumption of God's mercy, impugning the known truths of faith, envy of another's spiritual good, obstinacy in sin, final impenitence) • *original sin:* centaur on a font (the overcoming of original sin by baptism); Christ child holding an apple or an orange (Christ as the redeemer of man from original sin) • *see also* **evil**

Sin personified Satan
sincerity amethyst; fern; honesty [plant]; osier (sincerity without finery or dissimulation); sapphire • *association:* blue • *flower language:* fern; garden chervil; satinflower • *heraldry:* clover; heart; silver; sapphire (sincerity and piety) • *see also* **honesty**
single men cuckoo (the eternal bachelor)
single women *attributes:* fillet (Germany); green stockings (in the Middle Ages, worn at weddings the bride's older unmarried sisters); long flowing hair (Judaism) • *heraldry:* lozenge [shape]
sinlessness *see* **innocence**
sinners billy goat; elephant; hawk (the sinner's evil mind); lion; raven (an unrepentant sinner); snail; straw; tares • *Judaism:* long flowing hair (attribute) • *see also* **evil**
sirens [mythology] *attribute:* comb
Sirocco personified manticore
Sisera woman hammering a tent peg into a soldier's head (death of Sisera)
sisters *Middle Ages:* green stockings (worn at weddings by older unmarried sister of the bride)
six sixty (a multiplication of the powers of six) • *associations:* daffodil; F; hexagon; O [letter]; Venus [planet]; X
size point (that which has no magnitude)
skepticism ebony; rabbit; Saint Thomas • *flower language:* enchanter's nightshade • *see also* **uncertainty**
skill rudder, steering oar; seven-pointed star (human skill) • *flower language:* germander speedwell; spider ophrys; Sweet William (finesse) • *heraldry:* beaver (skill, especially in castle building) • *see also* **prowess**
sky blanket (the night sky); canopy, especially a round canopy (the celestial realm); obelisk (support of the sky); parasol, umbrella (dome of the sky); single arch; sky god naked to the waist (the top half represents the sky, the clothed bottom half represents the earth) • *associations:* blue, especially light blue • *see also* **heavens**
sky deities hanging [execution] (sacrifice to a sky deity); whirlwind (the angry voice of a sky deity) • *attributes:* blue eyes; light complexion;

necklace (sky goddesses); short legs; yellow hair • *Egypt:* falcon

slander nettle; rat • *association:* gnat • *flower language:* snake's lounge; stinging or burning nettle • *see also* **calumny**

Slander personified *attribute:* hedgehog; torch

slaughter *see* **murder**

slavery apron (slave nature); bandaged eyes; bitter herbs; cage; chains; collar for restraint; gypsum; Hagar (an unjustly oppressed bondswoman); lash; oar; ring; rope; serpent; sitting in darkness; whip • *Judaism:* charoset, chicory (a reminder of their slavery under the Egyptians; the bitterness of bondage); pierced ears (in ancient Israel: the mark of a freed slave who preferred to stay with his owner)

sleep black feathers; cloak; clouds; crescent; fording (the dividing line between two states, such as sleeping/waking, consciousness/unconsciousness, etc.); honey; Morpheus • *associations:* black; dark complexion; dew; sand • *folklore:* eight hours (the hours of sleep needed by merchants); eleven hours (the hours of sleep needed by the wicked)

Sleep personified *attributes:* owl; poppy

slenderness pencil; radish; weasel; willow

slim mud (primordial slime)

slipperiness eel; Proteus

sloth ape (the slothful soul of man); Belphegor; lizard; swine; tortoise • *see also* **idleness; inertia; languor; laziness**

Sloth personified peasant • *attributes:* ass; ox; slug [animal]; snail; swine

slowness mulberry tree; snail; turtle

slumber *see* **sleep**

slyness *see* **cunning**

small- mindedness *see* **meanness**

smallness beetle (life reduced to smallness); cress (something small or worthless); mustard seed, acorn (great growth from small beginnings); shrimp; water fly; wren

smell jackal (keenness of smell)

Smell personified *attributes:* dog; flower; vase

smile *flower language:* daily rose (I aspire to your smile); oak geranium (lady, deign to smile); Sweet William

smoothness ice

snakes *association:* S

snakebite agate (protection against snakebite and contagious diseases); garlic (protection against the evil eye, vampires, colds, plague, and snakes) • *association:* fern

snares ditch (trap); net; weaving • *flower language:* dragon plant

sneakiness *see* **cunning; insidiousness**

sneezing Sneeze on a Monday, you sneeze for danger; Sneeze on a Tuesday, you will kiss a stranger; Sneeze on a Wednesday, you sneeze for a letter; Sneeze on a Thursday, you sneeze for something better; Sneeze on a Friday, you sneeze for sorrow; Sneeze on a Saturday, your sweetheart will see you tomorrow; Sneeze on Sunday, for safety seek, the Devil will have you the whole of the week.

snobbery *see* **haughtiness**

snow goose

sobriety balances [scales]

sociability *see* **friendliness; gregariousness**

socialism red flag • *association:* May 1 [Mayday]

society beehive (society thriving on rapacity); city (the society, or the beliefs of the society of which it is a part); corset (society hampering the development of the psyche); dolphin; dynamo, engine (the inhumane forces of modern society); necktie, silk (bonds of society); plowman (provider of society); theater (social life) • *association:* four hundred (American upper class society, especially in the east)

Society of Jesus *emblem:* heart crowned with thorns

Socrates old man and child with mirror; old man in prison, surrounded by youths • *attribute:* hemlock

sodomy *associations:* Greece; sailors; Sodom

soil *association:* black

Sol *association:* Sunday • *attributes:* amber [gemstone]; horse; nimbus • *see also* **sun**

solace *see* **consolation**

solar principle *see* **sun**

soldiers *see* **warriors**

solemnity Tuesday's child is solemn and sad

solicitude *see* **care**

solidarity hands clasped in a handshake

solidity alder tree; iron; rock, stone (solidity; the first solid form of creation); man's head on a woman's body (solid and profound judgment) • *association:* eight • *heraldry:* castle; fess; tower • *see also* **firmness**

solitude briars; cold temperature (longing, especially for solitude); crow; fox; heather; hermit; island; lighthouse; lodge; midnight; mountain; monk; owl; raven (solitude; the desire for solitude); rock; sparrow; stag (the life of solitude and purity); swan; unicorn; wine press (patient or solitary labor or suffering) • *flower language:* lichen • *see also* **isolation; loneliness**

Solomon idol (apostasy Solomon's apostasy); infant held by a king or a judge (the king or judge is Solomon) • *association:* temple under construction • *attributes:* model of a temple; scepter tipped with a scroll; scroll with scepter

solstices *associations:* little finger (winter solstice); middle finger (summer solstice)

the soluble *association:* even numbers

Son of Man *see* **Jesus Christ**

song hands raised and open (voice and song); lyre; mermaid; merman (the power of song- magic); Orpheus; tripod (achievement in song or dance) • *flower language:* dew plant (serenade)

sons *association:* three (three sons of Noah) • *heraldry:* crescent (second sons); martlet (fourth sons); ring (fifth sons); star (third sons)

soothing *see* **relief**

soothsayers *see* **fortune tellers; prophets**

Sophonsiba woman drinking from a cup

soporifics juniper

sorcery pentagram (protection against sorcery); siren [mythology] • *associations:* Lapland; magic wand • *flower language:* enchanter's nightshade • *see also* **enchantment; magic; magic spells; witchcraft**

sorrow aloe; amber [gemstone] (joy after sorrow); anemone [flower]; black gloves; black knight; bluebell (sorrowful regret); burial; chrysoberyl (patience in sorrow); cosmetics; cypress; elephant with drooping trunk; hya-cinth [flower]; lily; marigolds mixed with roses (sweet sorrows of love); myrrh and aloes; osprey (cause of sorrow); oven (unrevealed sorrow); purple rose; rue [plant]; sneezing on a Friday (you sneeze for sorrow); sorrel (resignation to sorrow); tear [weeping]; thistle; two eyes, one open, one closed (sorrow and happiness); web; yew • *associations:* blue; brown; purple; red eyes • *flower language:* adonis (sorrowful or painful memories); cranberry (cure for heartache); marigolds; yew • *heraldry:* beetle (a reminder of worldly sorrows) • *see also* **grief; melancholy; penitence; regret; remorse**

the soul abstinence (the soul refraining from temptation); acacia; adamant [mythical stone] (tranquility of the soul); agriculture (cultivation of, and concern with, the soul); amulet (the higher nature of the soul); anointing with oil (endowing the soul with divine love); ape (the slothful soul of man); arum; bee; barnacle goose (the unhallowed soul of a dead person); bird; bird in a cage (the soul longing for freedom); bitterness (suffering undergone in purification of the soul); blood; breath; bride; butterfly; Cancer [zodiac] (the threshold through which the soul enters upon its incarnation); candle (the external soul); cocoon; crane [bird] (the good and diligent soul); crozier (the hooked end is to draw souls to God, and the pointed end is to prod the slothful); deer (the soul; aspiration of the soul, especially a jumping deer); Devil [tarot] (domination of the soul by matter); doll; dove, usually white (the departed soul); dove with an olive branch in its mouth (a soul that has made its peace with God); dragonfly (the soul of a dead person); drinking (the soul acquiring truth); dummy, effigy, mannequin (an image of the soul); eagle shown as a bird of prey (the demon that ravages souls); equinox (the point of balance and change reached within the soul's development when a new process is started); fairy (the supranormal powers of the human soul); feeding (dispensing goodness to the mind and soul); fire; fish; fish swimming into a whale's mouth (unsuspecting souls trapped by the Devil); flame;

flower; foot; fountain; garden; gardener (cultivator of the soul); gazelle; globe; glow worm (a departed soul); goose; grain (cultivated higher emotions in the soul); hair (the external soul); hart (piety and aspiration of the soul); head that is severed (life of the soul after death); hearing (intuitive perception of truth in the soul); heel (the lower nature of the soul); herd in orderly condition (coordinated desires and emotions working for the evolution of the soul); infant with wings; jug of water (cleansing of the soul); legs (support of the soul); liver (seat of the soul); lotus (the soul transcending the flesh); magic, especially white magic (inner and unobserved processes within the soul which raise the lower qualities to a higher level); magnolia (the lofty soul); mandrake (the soul in its negative and minimal aspects); mirror; moon (the soul; a regenerating receptacle for the soul); nail clippings (part of the soul); name; nectar (the soul's entire service to the highest ideals); Negro (the soul before entering on the path of spiritual evolution); nut; peacock (the incorruptible human soul); pearl; pilgrim; photograph, picture (magical access to the soul of the subject); prison (the early state of the soul in which it is in bondage to the lower instincts and desires); Prometheus (the intellect, in the merely technical and non-spiritual sense, in open rebellion against the soul); prostitute (the soul seeking satisfaction instead of wisdom); Psyche; Queen [tarot]; nine (associated with the three worlds: corporal, intellectual, spiritual); reins (the relationship of the soul and body); scarecrow; shadow (the soul; a departed soul; existence between the soul and body); sheep (the soul's higher qualities and virtues); sleep, sneezing (opportunity for the soul to leave the body); spark (souls scattering from the Mystic Center into the world of phenomena); stake driven through heart (nailing the soul in a particular place); stars; storm (passions of the soul); swan; temple; tragelaph (the body, soul, and spiritual life); tunic; valley (secret retreat of the soul); Vulcan (intellect rebelling against the soul; a weak, materialistic, and corrupt soul); walled city (the tran-

scendent soul); wings; work (the endeavor of the soul to attain perfection) • *associations:* eight (entering into a new state or condition of the soul); M (enlightenment of the soul and spirit); Neptune [planet] (the deepest layers of the soul); six • *body and soul:* bite (the seal of the spirit upon the flesh); crossroads (intersection of body and soul); duality (the physical and spiritual nature of all things); empty vase (the body separated from the soul); green (victory of the spirit over the flesh); helmet (protection of the soul from the assaults of passions and desires); nine (associated with the three worlds: corporal, intellectual, spiritual); reins (relationship of the body and soul); shadow (the evil or base side of the body; existence between body and soul) • *China:* fox (the transmigrated soul of a deceased person); red (association) • *Christianity:* Antichrist (adversary of the soul); birds in a vine (souls abiding with Christ); dove drinking from a cup or eating bread (the soul being fed by the eucharist); eagle (Christ swooping down to save a soul; the Christian soul strengthened by grace); sunflower (the soul turning to Christ) • *conductors of the souls of the dead:* dolphin; Mercury [god]; navigator; sailor; shepherd • *defect in the soul:* abortion (a defect in the soul or spirit); amputation; disease (malady of the soul or psyche); insanity (a disordered condition in the soul); lameness; maiming (weakness or defect in the soul; revenge for the maiming shows that some vestige of moral strength remains); rags (a wound to the soul: the particular garment that is in rags gives a more precise meaning to the wound) • *Egypt:* eagle • *emblem:* six-pointed star • *flower language:* oats (the bewitching soul of music) • *Norse:* cup (container of the soul) • *purity of the soul:* embalming (purification of the soul through faith and trust in the ideal); girdle [cincture] (spiritual purity invigorating the soul); golden fleece (occasionally, a white fleece); lily (the purified soul) • *Rome:* larvae (evil souls) • *the soul escaping the body:* bird freed from a cage; chrysalis; dove or naked child issuing from a person's mouth; empty vase (the soul separated from the body); sleeping, sneezing (opportunity for the soul to leave the body) • *unbaptized souls:* Gabriel hound, nightjar (the lost soul of an unbaptized infant) • *see also* **body; spirit**

sound drum (primordial sound)

sourness Born on a Wednesday, sour and sad (or, full of woe); lemon • *flower language:* barberry (sourness; tartness) • *see also* **bitterness**

south *associations:* eagle; heat • *emblems:* cotton, honeysuckle, magnolia (southern United States); lion with four wings (in Egypt: the south wind)

South Africa *emblem:* mimosa

South Seas *associations:* coconut; grass skirt; palm tree

sovereignty beard; carpet; castle; chair; crown; father; orb; orb with a cross (recognition of God's ultimate dominion over the world); orb an with orrery on it (sovereignty at sea); osprey; rudder in a globe; shepherd's crook; sitting; sun; thunderbolt; tuna; uraeus; whip (sovereignty by force) • *Egypt:* bearded queen • *heraldry:* bee; ermine; key; trident (maritime dominion)

sowing eating (equivalent to the sowing of seed); setting of the Pleiades (new sowing) • *association:* October (resowing)

space whirlwind • *associations:* fifty; seven • *time and space:* blue (association); crossroads (intersection or conjunction of any binary form: space and time, heaven and earth, etc.); hurricane, tornado (hole through which one may pass out of time and space); Pole Star (a hole in time and space); twelve (association)

Spanish Inquisition yellow (worn by both the executioner and those condemned by the Spanish Inquisition)

sparrowhawk hawk (frequently shares the symbolism of falcon and sparrowhawk, with which it is frequently confused)

sparrows *association:* five (the Five Sparrows Sold for a Farthing)

speech *see* **chatter; eloquence; talk**

speed deer; dolphin; eagle; flying; gazelle (graceful speed); giraffe; greyhound; hare; helmet with wings; Mercury [god]; mercury [metal]; mullet; ostrich; rabbit; roebuck; seraph; swastika; thunderbolt, especially when shown

with wings); wind; winds; wolf • *association:* R • *flower language:* hawkweed (quick-sightedness); larkspur • *heraldry:* hare; lance • *see also* **haste**

Speed personified *attribute:* tamed falcon

spells *see* **magic**

sperm barley grains; cereal grains; confetti; corn [maize]; rice; wheat grains • *see also* **semen**

spheres *see* **celestial spheres**

spinning distaff • *association:* Athena

spinsters *see* **single women**

spirit asceticism (voluntary abandonment of worldly activities in preparation for renewed life on a higher spiritual plane); amazement (part of the process of spiritual awakening); amphibian (the parting of spirit and matter); angel (spiritual influences acting upon the earth); arrow (a spiritual weapon); ascending (the human condition being transcended and a higher spiritual level being attained); Athena (man's higher nature); beheading (separation of the body and spirit); belly (antithesis of the spirit or brain); bird; bite (the seal of the spirit upon the flesh); bishop (spiritualized mental qualities); blacksmith (mental qualities disciplined by the spirit); blue flower (spiritual happiness); book (spiritual or mystical power); breath; breeze (the spirit energizing the mental plane); brook, stars (spiritual guidance); caduceus (health of the body and spirit); candelabrum (spiritual salvation; the spiritual light of salvation); castle (an embattled spiritual power ever on watch); castle of light (spiritual attainment); Caucasian (the spiritual side of man); censer (spiritual nature); centaur (the unconscious uncontrolled by the spirit); cherry blossoms (spiritual beauty); city (lack of emotional, spiritual, or natural contact); cold temperature (a spiritualized atmosphere); conch shell (the spiritual and natural means of development rendered active); crystal; cup (renewed spiritual vigor); cydippe (spiritual value); daffodil (spiritual rebirth); the Devil with a bellows (his attempt to extinguish spiritual life); dew, minaret (spiritual illumination); Eve, Helen (that which diverts man from spiritual progress); fairy (personification of the stages in the development of the spirit; the lesser spiritual moods of the universal mind); Fall of Man (incarnation of the spirit); fishing (seeking regeneration or spiritual rebirth); flagellation (encouragement against spiritual laxity or inertia); furnace, oven (spiritual gestation); girding the loins (restraint of passion and turning toward the spirit); golden carriage (spiritual qualities allied with wisdom); golden chain (the spirit binding earth to heaven); Gordian knot, labyrinth (remoteness from one's spirit and from God; the difficulty of uniting oneself with one's spirit and with God; the loss of spirit in the process of creation, and the subsequent need to find it again); grapes (the spiritual nature of love and wisdom); Hanged Man [tarot] (spiritual self-sacrifice); hawk; healing (the spiritual process by which certain qualities are harmonized and spiritualized); heaven, paradise (union with the spirit; spiritual reward); hippogryph (a spiritual mount); holly oak (the Great Spirit); honey (spiritual wisdom); House of God [tarot] (materialism struck down by spiritual light to render regeneration possible); ibis (spiritual awakening); idol (outward observances regarded as true spiritual exercises); incense (spiritual goodness); journey (desire to undergo profound spiritual experience; spiritual pilgrimage); Justice [tarot] (spiritual justice); knight (the spirit controlling the instincts and desires); leaven (spiritual nature permeating lower nature); light; lion; loitering (spiritual inertia); Magic [tarot] (gifts of the spirit); man; manna (spiritual sustenance); meteorite (spiritual life descending to earth; spiritual messenger); miner (extraction of spiritual values); monster (predominance of the baser forces in life being fought by the spiritual forces, often in the form of a knight); mountain (communion with the spirit; loftiness of spirit); nest (haven from growth of the spirit); onyx (strengthens spiritual thought); pine cone (spiritual fertility); plant [biology] (the healthy growth of plants indicates cosmic, material, and spiritual fecundity); rain (spiritual influences from heaven); red horse (the mind energized by the spirit); rock,

stone (the spirit; the spirit as a foundation; the spirit of human life); scissors (spiritual decision); seraph (the spirit of love and imagination); serpent (guardian of the springs of life, immortality, and the superior riches of the spirit); shield (defense of the spirit); signs of wear (weariness of spirit); Sophia (the creative spirit of God); south (spiritual light); spiral (escape from the material to the spiritual); spy (trust in the flesh rather than the spirit); stairs (spiritual ascension; the forces of the spirit struggling against the forces of evil); steel (the all-conquering spirit); strawberries and violets (the truly spiritual are always humble); strawberry, sometimes with other fruit (fruit of the spirit); Strength personified standing over a wine press (the conquest of the spirit over the heart); sun; sword (a spiritual weapon); temple on a hill (the spiritual Zion); tonsure (spiritual thoughts); tragelaph (body, soul, and spiritual life); traveller (someone engaged in personal development, especially moral or spiritual); treasure (spiritual truth; something of spiritual value); trumpet (call of the spirit); Victory personified (spiritual worth); waves [water] (renewed spiritual vigor); white dove with blue wings (spiritual or celestial thoughts); wind; wine (a spiritual drink) • *associations:* B; blue (the spirit of man); gold (spiritual worth or superiority); green (spiritual initiation; spiritual integrity; victory over the flesh; regeneration of the spirit); Leo (spiritual beginnings of man); M (enlightenment of the soul and spirit); mandorla (spiritual glory); Neptune [planet] (spiritual aspirations); nine (the three worlds: corporal, intellectual, spiritual); one (spiritual revelation); three (spiritual and moral dynamism); V (success on earth with spiritual gifts); white (spiritual intuition); X (spiritual love); yang [the dark color of yin and yang] • *Christianity:* beaver (the Christian who makes sacrifices for the sake of his spiritual life); hare (a Christian's haste to obtain divine gifts) • *desire and spirit:* helmet (protection of the soul from the assaults of passions and desires); knight (the spirit controlling the instincts and desires); prison (the early state of the soul in which the spirit is in bondage to the lower instincts and desires); swine (desire that seeks sustenance in matter rather than spirit); woman as captive (higher nature held by latent desire) • *heraldry:* eagle (lofty spirit); goat (striving after higher things); ocean (spiritual exploration); unicorn • *matter and spirit:* Cancer [zodiac] (the mediator between the formal and non-formal worlds); dove embedded in lead (the spirit embedded in matter); mist (the intermediate world between the formal and non-formal); Sphinx (spirit triumphant over matter); Strength [tarot] (spirit ruling over matter); swine (desire that seeks sustenance in matter rather than in spirit); Temperance [tarot] (the interaction of matter and spirit); yin and yang • *negative aspect of the spirit:* Neptune [god] (the negative aspect of the spirit and of humanity); Pluto [planet] (association) • *physical and the spiritual:* banyan tree (the close union of the physical and spiritual in man); Castor and Pollux; duality, Gemini (the physical and spiritual nature of all things); moorings (the attachment of the physical and spiritual); Sun [tarot] (balance between the physical and spiritual); sword (conjunction of the physical and spiritual); two linked rings, one above the other • *spiritual abundance:* fruit; nine (association); ten (association) • *spiritual disorder:* abortion (defect in the soul or spirit); ache; blindfold (mental or spiritual blindness); blindness (the mind not awakened by the spirit; lack of spiritual perception); boil [disease] (a psychological affliction or spiritual shortcoming); brown (associated with spiritual death and degradation); Caliban; cancer [disease]; captive (the spirit held latent); darkness (spiritual darkness); deafness (inability to hear the voice of the conscience or the spirit); devastation (barrenness and unproductiveness of the spirit); disease (natural or spiritual disorder or disharmony); drought (an inert spiritual condition); entombment (detention of the spirit in the world); fracture, fragmentation (destruction or disintegration of the spirit); gangrene; Gordian knot, labyrinth (remoteness from one's spirit and from God); hood

(spiritual blindness); Icarus (intellect rebelling against the spirit); lameness; leprosy; (rotting of the spirit due to a lack of moral progress); loss (spiritual bankruptcy); Mephistopheles (the negative aspect of the psychic function which has broken away from the spirit to acquire independence); mole eyes (intellectual and spiritual blindness); pain; rotting; sick king (sterility of the spirit); thorn (materialism killing spirituality) • *spiritual elevation:* flying; magic, especially white magic (inner and unobserved processes within the soul which raise the lower qualities to a higher level); mountain; wings on an orb • *spiritual energy:* fountain; rain (an increase in spiritual energy) • *spiritual enlightenment:* crown, especially a jewelled crown; fire (spiritual enlightenment and zeal); M (associated with enlightenment of the spirit and the soul) • *spiritual evolution:* lotus; Negro (the soul before entering on the path of spiritual evolution); orb with wings; pilgrimage (the process of spiritual evolution); search for treasure (the search for spiritual evolution); sword; wings (the possibility of spiritual evolution); World [tarot] (truth and spiritual evolution attained on earth) • *spiritual growth:* doctor, nurse, poet, priest (promoters of spiritual growth); nest (haven for the growth of the spirit); pilgrimage (process of spiritual growth) • *spiritual knowledge:* grail; jewels (when protected by a dragon or by other obstacles: the difficulty in obtaining spiritual knowledge) • *spiritual power:* book; breathing (assimilation of spiritual power); crozier (the hooked end is to draw souls to God and the pointed end to prod the slothful); hair on the head; key; stole [religious garment] (priestly power and dignity); Strength [tarot]; tusk (spiritual power overcoming ignorance and evil) • *the spiritual principle:* bishop; eagle; feather; head (as opposed to the body, which represents the physical); spark (the spiritual principle giving birth to each individual) • *spiritual purity:* girdle [cincture] (spiritual purity invigorating the soul); spice (spiritual qualities which purify the mind); zigzag (spiritual purification and rebirth) • *see also* **elevation; the soul**

spirits blue flame on a candle (a passing spirit); fireflies (dead spirits, especially dead warriors); foxfire (forest spirits); ghosts (disembodied spirits); obelisks (penetrating spirits); otters (free spirits); purgative (driving out spirits); putti (angelic spirits); sons (earthly spirits); swallows [birds] (wandering spirits); tree (home of gods and spirits) • *China:* white rooster (guide of transient spirits) *evil spirits:* Alastor (an evil spirit that haunts a family); Demogorgon; demon; epileptic seizure (possession by evil spirits); gargoyle; larvae (in Rome: evil souls); toad • *protection against evil spirits:* obelisk; onion; onyx; purgative (drives out evil spirits)

spirituality desert (the realm of abstraction, truth, purity, ascetic spirituality, spirituality in general, and holiness); gargoyle (fertility enslaved by superior spirituality); gothic arch; heaven; maniple; tulip; wings • *associations:* blue; brown (Victorian lack of emotion or spirituality); purple; six

spiritualization bird; Pegasus (innate capacity for changing evil into good, and for spiritualization); serpent with a sheep's head; torch (spiritualization through illumination and sublimation); wings

spit *see* **saliva**

spite *see* **resentment**

spleen *see* **anger**

splendor *see* **glory**

spoiling angora cat (a pampered and spoiled person, especially a woman)

sports blue ribbon, loving cup, purple fillet (victory in sports); *flower language:* hyacinth • *Rome:* parsley (victory in sports) • *see also* **amusement; play**

spring [season] almond; butterfly; cherry blossoms; child; clockwise swastika; cuckoo [bird]; cuckoo plant; fig; flower; furze (spring equinox); lizard; maiden (any new start, such as spring, dawn, etc.); parsley; peony; prince awakening a sleeping princess (spring reawakened by the sun); Proserpine; radish; rising of the Pleiades; serpent with a sheep's head; white hand • *associations:* A; Aphrodite; Aries; east; emerald; five; furze (spring equinox); green; index finger (spring; spring equinox) • *China:* ox; peach tree; tree

peony; willow • *emblem:* hare (Middle' Ages) • *herald of spring:* apple (generally associated with autumn, but sometimes a herald of spring); azalea; lark [bird]; lilac [plant]; lily of the valley; nightingale; plum blossoms; pomegranate; primrose; robin; rook [bird]; snowdrop; stork; swallow [bird]; thrush; tulip; violet [flower] • *Judaism:* lettuce

Spring personified *attributes:* flower; garden; hoe; spade [shovel]; violet hair (attribute of goddesses with a spring festival)

spying balcony; bush (a spot for lurking, ambush, spying, illicit love); ear (eavesdropping) • *see also* **betrayal; treachery**

squalor *see* **filth**

square *associations:* D; four

squire green knight

stability donkey; globe amaranth; hill; island; keel; king; larch; peony; pyramid; seat (place to sit); throne • *associations:* cube; four; six (stabilizing influences); seven; square [shape] • *flower language:* cress • *heraldry:* blue; bridge • *see also* **constancy; dependability**

stages feast (a completed period of stage of development) •*association:* violet [color] (a transitional stage, such as between sleeping and waking, worldliness and spirituality, etc.)

stagnation Devil [tarot] (regression or stagnation of all that is inferior, fragmentary, or discontinuous); leprosy (rotting of the spirit from lack of moral progress); pond; slime; turtle • *see also* **decay**

stamina bulrush (lack of stamina); ostrich; spine • *heraldry:* ass; camel • *see also* **fortitude; strength**

standard rule [measuring] (standard of morality)

Star [tarot] *association:* Q

stars *associations:* glow worm; tremella nestoe; Wednesday (the day the stars were created according to the Bible)

starting *see* **beginning**

starvation *see* **famine**

the state mace [weapon] (authority, especially of the state); two-handed sword

stateliness *see* **elegance**

steadfastness amaranth, globe amaranth (steadfast love); anchor; cedar (steadfast faith); cold temperature (resistance to all that is inferior); column [architecture]; oak; rock (steadfastness; Christian steadfastness) • *association:* M (indomitability) • *flower language:* arbor vitae (unchanging friendship); globe amaranth; laurel (I change but in death); wild geranium (steadfast piety) • *heraldry:* buckle; tortoise • *Orient:* charcoal • *see also* **constancy; intransigence; stubbornness; tenacity**

steadiness *see* **stability**

stealing *see* **theft**

stealth *see* **cunning**

Stephen, St. deacon with processional cross; deacon with stones • *attributes:* Old Testament; blood-stained stones; censer; dalmatic, especially with three stones; garment of palm leaves; shell-shaped stones

sterility mule; salt; salt water; sick king; willow • *see also* **barrenness**

stewardship scorpion (defensive stewardship) • *see also* **care**

stickiness tar

stigma wound in the neck (poet's stigma)

stillness *see* **tranquillity**

stimulation fennel (stimulant); flagellation (sexual stimulation); spurs (stimulus to action) • *see also* **incentive**

stinginess *association:* Netherlands

stock exchange bear (pessimism or declining prices on the stock market); bull (optimism or rising prices on the stock market)

stoicism box tree • *flower language:* box tree • *see also* **indifference**

stolidity bulldog; ox • *association:* Taurus • *see also* **indifference**

stomach *associations:* earth [soil]; Mercury [planet]; Z

stones in the head doctor cutting open a patient's forehead, doctor holding a stone with a pincers (quack operation for stones in the head)

storms Bacchante (storm spirit); clouds; falcon; giant bird; manticore (storm demon) • *association:* dark blue (stormy sea) • *foretokens of storms:* barnacle goose; bitterns flocking together; chattering coots; eel; petrel; Phoenix [bird]; porpoise; woodpecker

strain *see* **stress; tension**

strangeness *see* **oddity**

strangers snare (a strange woman);

sneezing on a Tuesday (you will kiss a stranger); spark in a candle flame (a letter or a stranger will come) • *flower language:* American starwort (welcome to a stranger)

strategy crossed swords (military strategy or power); lizard (military strategy) • *flower language:* nettle tree (concert; plan); walnut • *heraldry:* castle; cat; fox (strategic cunning); serpent • *see also* **plans**

straying *see* **wandering**

strength acorn (latent greatness or strength); Ajax; arm; Atlas; bear; beauty; belt; brass; bull (brute strength); cable; carbuncle [gemstone]; chains; club [bat]; condor; copper; Death [tarot]; girdle [cincture]; hammer (physical power and strength); hand of iron; Hercules; hippopotamus (strength and vigor); horn [animal]; iron; kneeling (moral strength); lion; liver; long hair worn by a man; maniple; mother; muscular and/or hairy man (energetic and strong mentality); neck; Nike; oak; oak wreath; ox; pillar; pyramid; ram [sheep]; salt; serpent (strength seduced by matter); sheaf; shoulders; steel; stone; sword; tamed tiger (strength and valor in the fight against evil); thighs; tower; tusk • *associations:* K; M (strength of character); Taurus • *China:* bear; elephant; iron; jade; tortoise • *flower language:* cedar; cedar of Lebanon; fennel • *heraldry:* orange [color]; tower • *see also* **fortitude; power; prowess; stamina**

Strength personified *attributes:* broken pillar; dragon; eagle

stress bow [archery] (exhausting strain); harp; harp music (soothing of stress) • *see also* **tension**

strictness Justice [tarot] (strict and correct behavior)

strife *see* **discord**

striving ladder (ceaseless striving of man); one eye (extra human effort devoted to one aim, usually unfavorable); soldier; squirrel (striving of the Holy Spirit) • *associations:* ninety (striving toward perfection); six (effort and trial) • *heraldry:* angel (striving for perfection); goat (striving after higher things)

struggle antelope; cross; gazelle; fighting a monster (struggle to free the conscious from the unconscious);

gazelle; lion; Magic [tarot] (man in his struggle with occult powers); tarot deck (portrays the complementary struggles in man's life: self vs. others, physical vs. spiritual, etc.) • *see also* **striving; trials; trouble**
stubbornness ass; bear; donkey; hawk (a wild and intractable woman); horse; lead [metal]; mule; neck; raven; trout (stubbornness overcoming obstacles) • *association:* seven • *flower language:* burdock; xanthium (pertinacity) • *see also* **steadfastness; tenacity**
students *see* **apprentices; catechumens; neophytes; scholars**
studying *see* **learning**
stultification *see* **inhibition; repression**
stupidity ass ears on a human; baboon; beetle (a stupid person); calf; coot (a common or stupid fellow); geranium; goat; goose; Hercules (in Elizabethan times: a ridiculous, boisterous, brawny tyrant); horse; jackdaw; kangaroo; lapwing (a stupid conceited fellow who things he knows better than his elders); leather; leather medal (farcical award for stupidity or inferiority); mullet; oyster; sheep • *flower language:* almond; scarlet geranium • *see also* **intellect**
Stupidity personified *attribute:* ass
Styx blue boat (Charon's boat on the Styx)
subconscious cellar (the morbid terror lurking in the subconscious); Empress [tarot]; floating (refusal to explore the subconscious); night; potato; silver key (power of the subconscious); World [tarot] (merging of the subconscious and the super-conscious with the conscious) • *associations:* blue; left hand; Neptune [planet] • *see also* **unconscious**
subdeacon *attributes:* maniple; tunicle (used at high mass)
subdual *see* **subjugation**
subhumanity one eye
subjectivity mace [weapon] (the subjective assertive tendency in man); Saturn [god] (subjective evil)
subjects Gog and Magog (the king and his subjects)
subjugation branding; bull tied to a fig tree (a man subdued in marriage); Emperor [tarot]; garden (nature sub-

dued); slavery (subjection to lower nature); tamed lion (subjugation of virility); victory (subdual of lower nature—that which is conquered often represents the inferiority of the conqueror) • *see also* **defeat; conquest; submission; victory**
sublimation cremation; decoration; Prometheus; red knight; thread; winged animals (the sublimation of that animal's specific virtues); weapons (the powers of sublimation and spiritualization); winnowing • *association:* purple
submission broken mast; camel; grass, especially a lawn; kneeling (submission to the laws of order); ox; sitting down; stole [religious garment] (submission to God's will); yarmulke (submission to God); woman • *flower language:* grass; harebell • *see also* **defeat; obedience; subjugation; surrender**
subservience dog; fawn; footstool (the lowest subservience); greyhound; licking; livery [clothing]; spaniel • *associations:* Germans; Germany • *see also* **obedience**
substance bricks; ghost (lack of substance); plant gum (the seminal substance)
substitute rags thrown in the water (substitute for drowning); rags hung on a tree (substitute sacrifice)
subterranean life serpent
subtlety spider
suburbia *emblems:* charcoal grill; lawn [grass]
subversion House of God [tarot] (sudden subversion); young man
success basket with flowers or fruit; black flag (success in battle); crown; elephant with trunk held up; flood tide; malachite (success in love); Temperance [tarot] (successful combination); Wheel of Fortune [tarot] • *associations:* C (success despite obstacles); eight (self-assertion and material success); L; P (success followed by ruin); V (success on earth with spiritual gifts); three (material success) • *China:* monkey (drives away evil, and, hence, brings success, health, and protection); swallow nesting on a house • *flower language:* coronella (may success crown your wishes)
succession Phoenix [bird] (royal

succession); swastika (succession of generations)

suffering amphisbaena (anguish caused by an ambivalent situation); bed; bitterness (suffering undergone in purification of the soul); carbuncle [gemstone]; chains; chalice; corrosion; cross (the suffering of existence); flute (erotic anguish, but also erotic joy); harp; Lent (suffering and sacrifice, especially of Christ); ox; Prometheus (magnanimous endurance of unwarranted suffering); rust; scorpion; sores (suffering of lower nature); tears [weeping] (suffering endured pursuing truth); thorn; wheelbarrow; wine press (patient or solitary labor or suffering) • *association:* violet [color] • *heraldry:* nails [for wood] • *Judaism:* matzo • *see also* **pain**

sufficiency *association:* three

Sufficiency personified *attribute:* pomegranate

suicide asp (Cleopatra's suicide, and by extension, any suicide); boar (irrational urge toward suicide); elder tree (in legend, the tree that Judas hanged himself on); flint, pebble, potsherd (thrown on the graves of suicides); scorpion • *associations:* Japan; Rome; Sweden

suitors *flower language:* field or double daisy (considering a suitor, especially in chivalry when turned in a wreath and worn by a woman) • *see also* **courtship; lovers**

Sukkoth *association:* tent of boughs

sulfur *association:* Mars

summer coconut (endless summer); cricket [insect]; dragonfly; firefly; red heather (mid-summer); Sirius (summer fever); vulture • *associations:* harvest; middle finger (summer solstice); noon; south; south wind • *China:* lotus

Summer personified *attributes:* fruit in a cornucopia; scythe; sickle

summons bugle, trumpet (call to action); conch shell (primitive summons); shofar, trumpet (call of the spirit)

sun amber [gemstone]; asp; axe, especially double-headed; axle tree; circular temple; eating a goose (solar sacrifice); fir; fire, torch (solar principle); flower (the work of the sun); fox (a solar animal); gold (solar light);

gold earring (sun worship); golden egg (laid on the waters or chaos by the primeval goose); golden robe (the fire of the sun); goose; Helios (the sun in its astronomic and spiritual aspect); horse chestnut [buckeye]; obelisk (solar ascension); pyramid; prince awakening a sleeping princess or sleeping beauty (the spring awakening ·the spring); staff • *associations:* A; ass; eight (in Egypt, Babylonia, and Arabia); F; golden beard; gnat (sunshine); gooseberry; Leo (solar power); monolith (solar principle); one; orange [color]; pheasant; right side; round tower (solar worship); silver doors (palace of the sun); south; sparrowhawk; straight sword; Sunday; tarot cards I to XI; vulture • *China:* red; red crow • *Egypt:* duck (associated with Isis bringing forth the sun); eight • *emblems:* cabbage; Catherine wheel; chariot drawn by four horses; chrysanthemum; chariot drawn by four horses; clockwise swastika; cone; counterclockwise swastika (the autumnal sun); dandelion; eagle; ember; eyes; face; fiery chariot; falcon; golden ball; hand with fingers extended; hawk; head; hedgehog; horse, especially a white horse; horse with a flaming mane; lion; lodestone; lotus; marguerite [flower]; marigold; orange or yellow flower; pansy; parasol; red hand; rooster; round canopy; round table; scarab; sea urchin; solar wheel; sunflower; torch; triangle with the apex up; triskele; two lions back to back (sunrise and sunset); umbrella; wafer; wheel • *flower language:* scarlet lychnis (sunbeaming eyes) • *Orient:* rooster on a red or gold disk (emblem) • *sun and moon (associations):* seventy-two (a ritual number involving solar increase and lunar wisdom); two; two eyes (binary functions such as sun and moon, male and female, intelligence and love, etc.) • *sun heroes:* golden beard (attribute); golden hair (attribute); lion skin (attribute); phallus (attribute); son • *sun rays:* arrow; comb; crown; dart; flaming sword; golden bough (the rays of the setting sun); golden hair; obelisk; ribbon; rope; shower of gold; spear; tassel; web • *sunrise:* east; eight-pointed star; elephant; fanlight (rising or setting sun); scarab; Sisyphus (rise and fall of

the sun); young lion; young man •
sunset: beetle; fanlight (rising or setting
sun); golden bough; dead rook [bird]
(Egypt); lion; old man; red swan; Sisyphus (rise and fall of the sun); willow; west • *Syria:* eagle with human
arms (sun worship) • *see also* **Apollo;**
dawn; Sol
Sun [tarot] *association:* S
Sunday Born on a Sunday, you'll
never want (or, lucky and happy, good
and gay); Sunday's child is full of grace
• *associations:* God; Helios; Sol; the
sun; works of light
superego policeman (the censorious
super-ego inhibiting forces of the preconscious) • *see also* **personality**
superconscious ellipse; gold key (key
to the superconscious); Jupiter [god]
(superconsciousness); World [tarot]
(merging of the subconscious and the
super-conscious with the conscious)
superficiality duck; idol (outward
observances regarded as true spiritual
exercises)
superfluity *association:* Z
superhumanity fairy (the supranormal powers of the human soul);
three eyes
superiority ace [playing cards], especially the ace of spades; chair (implies the occupant's superior position
to those who are standing); cloak (superior dignity); cold temperature (resistance to all that inferior); crow (the
isolation of one who lives on a superior
plane); eagle carrying a victim (victory
of the superior over the inferior); goat
(usually moral inferiority, but occasionally moral superiority because it is
associated with high peaks in its wild
state); gold (superiority, especially on
a spiritual plane); island; knight riding
a goat; plane tree (moral superiority);
salt; scales on mermaids, dragons, the
Devil (the inferior continuing in the
superior); serpent (the inferior within
the superior); trousers; whip • *China:*
orchid (the superior or perfect man) •
flower language: full moss rose
(superior merit) • *see also* **excellence;**
perfection; supremacy
supernatural blindness (may be an
indication that a person has heightened
or supernatural powers); blue flower,
dwarf (has supernatural powers);
forest (home of outlaws, fairies, super-

natural beings); Jupiter [god]; king;
king that is crowned (the consummation or victory of the supernatural); red
bird (in ancient times); secret (the
power of the supernatural); smoke •
association: radiance • *China:* fox (possessor of supernatural powers, such as
transformation); hare (a supernatural
creature) • *emblem:* six-pointed star
(the natural and supernatural) • *see*
also **occultism**
superstition file [rasp] (ideas free
from superstition); nightingale •
associations: black; bushy eyebrows;
Ireland • *flower language:* aloe, passion
flower (religious superstition); St.
John's wort
supplication kneeling; myrtle • *see*
also **prayer**
support corset; crutch (hidden or
shameful support); nails [for wood];
obelisk; pillar: especially four pillars
(support of the heaven or the sky); rod;
staff; throne; thighs (dynamic support
of the body) • *association:* V • *flower*
language: black bryony (be my sup-
port) • *heraldry:* fess • *see also* **founda-**
tion; help
supremacy aureole (supreme power:
normally only used for members of the
Trinity, but occasionally for the Virgin
Mary); crown, dolphin with a trident
(supremacy of the seas); legs, especially
when bestriding something; riding,
especially riding an animal; stars
(supremacy in a particular area) • *see*
also **superiority**
supreme deities face; father; flame;
seated man or woman (may also be his
or her representative); sky (dwelling of
the supreme deity); six-pointed star
(the androgynous nature of the
supreme deity); sphere; spider; tower •
attributes: glory [luminous glow
around the entire body]; net; Pole Star
(throne of the supreme deity); thunder
(the voice of the supreme deity);
thunderbolt • *emblem:* oak • *see also*
divinity; God
sure-footedness *see* **nimbleness**
surfeit *see* **excess**
surprise dwarf (the unexpected); •
association: seven (unexpected and
willful action); W • *flower language:*
betony; truffle
surrender hands raised and open; lying down (female surrender); striking

sails; white flag • *see also* **defeat; submission**
survivor salamander (a soldier who has survived a battle)
susceptibility *see* **vulnerability**
suspension Hanged Man [tarot] (a suspended decision); hanging *see also* **incipience; latency**
suspicion *see* **uncertainty**
sustenance birds feeding on grapes (the faithful gathering sustenance from the blood of Christ); bread (the means of sustaining life); breasts; earth [soil] (the sustainer of material life); manna (spiritual sustenance); milk • *see also* **care; food**
swaddling bandages (swaddling clothes)
swearing *see* **allegiance; promise; truth**
sweat foam • *association:* pot, usually earthen
sweethearts *see* **lovers**
sweetness almond; angel; bee; cherry (sweetness of character derived from good works); Empress [tarot]; gillyflower; honey; lamb; lily of the valley; linden; magnolia (feminine sweetness and beauty); marigolds mixed with roses; spring [season]; sugar; violet [flower] • *China:* jasmine blossom • *flower language:* honey flower (sweet and sacred love); white lily • *Judaism:* honey and apples (when eaten on the New Year: the hope for sweetness and joy, respectively)
swelling bottle; full sails (swelling powers)
swiftness *see* **speed**
swindling hawk (swindler); sting
Switzerland *emblem:* edelweiss
sword knife (a base, secret weapon, the inversion of the sword, which is an heroic weapon)
Sylvanus, St. *attribute:* cliff
Sylvester, St. *attributes:* bull; cross with two horizontal arms (not to be confused with either the cross of Lorraine, or the Eastern cross); crozier; dragon underfoot; miter; ox; picture of Saints Peter and Paul; triple tiara
sympathy amethyst; elm tree with vine (natural sympathy); leather (lack of sympathy); poplar • *associations:* fifty (sympathy and understanding); five; green; I [letter]; violet [color] • *flower language:* balm; sea lavender • *see also* **compassion; consolation; kindness; pity**
synagogue billy goat; Hagar; moon (generally the church reflecting the light of Christ, however, sometimes the synagogue with the church represented by the sun); two eyes, one opened and one closed (the church and synagogue, respectively) • *emblem:* owl (pejorative) • *see also* **Judaism; temple**
syphilitics *attribute:* baldness
Syrinx nymph hiding in the woods
system *see* **plans; strategy**

T

tabernacle tent • *association:* tent of boughs (Feast of the Tabernacles)
taboo *see* **prohibition**
taciturnity Sparta • *heraldry:* fish
tact *see* **poise**
tailors *attributes:* needle; scissors; sitting cross-legged • *heraldry:* scissors
talent borage (the flower only); sweet brier • *flower language:* white pink
Talents, the Five *association:* five
talk burning or tingling ears (someone is speaking of you; evil gossip); carp; goose; Hermit [tarot]; leech (grandiloquence); madder [plant] (talkativeness); sieve (small talk); Sparta (brevity of speech); tongue (malicious talk); Tower of Babel (confusion of speech) • *flower language:* southernwood (bantering) • *heraldry:* fish (taciturnity) • *see also* **chatter; eloquence; gossip**
tameness *see* **docility**
Tancred and Clorinda female soldier dying, comforted by male

soldier; soldier pouring water on a dying woman from his helmet

Tannhauser *attribute:* flowering staff

Tantalus man in a pool reaching up for dangling fruit

tardiness *see* **delay**

tartness *see* **sourness**

tasks key (a task to be performed and the means for carrying it out); ribbon knotted to form a circle (fulfillment of an undertaking) • *association:* four (taskmasters) • *see also* **work**

taste egg whites (tastelessness); fuchsia; tongue (sense of taste); white gloves (good taste) • *flower language:* fuchsia • *see also* **bitterness; judgment; sourness**

Taste personified ape • *attributes:* fruit in a basket; tamed falcon

Taurus bull • *associations:* apple tree; copper; diamond [gemstone]; F; foxglove; Friday; indigo [color]; orangered; poppy; rose quartz; rose [flower]; ruby (occasionally); spring [season]; V; Venus [planet]

taverns branch with green leaves; alcoholic beverage bottle (sign of a tavern); red lattice window

teachers centaurs (the teachers of the gods) • *association:* four

teaching book; cathedra; Hanged Man [tarot] (a public lesson); High Priest [tarot] (traditional teaching suitable for the masses); pulpit (religious instruction); seed (divine instruction) • *see also* **education**

tears [weeping] *associations:* crystal; plant gum • *flower language:* helenium

technology dynamo, engine (technology; technological power)

tedium *see* **boredom**

teenage boys billy goat (a male child 10 to 20 years of age); calf (a boy up to 20 years of age) • *see also* **boys; men; youth**

teenage girls dabchick (a girl 10 to 20 years of age) • *see also* **girls; maidens; women; youth**

temper ferret (fiery temper); pepper; monkey (sanguine temper); stomach (seat of temper) • *see also* **anger; disposition; mood**

temperance azalea; camel; cincture; compasses [dividers]; cup; hearth; lamb; lettuce; level [tool]; Phoenix [bird]; scepter with an eye on it (can also be an attribute of Modesty personified) • *associations:* fourteen; twelve • *Egypt:* bull • *flower language:* acalia; azalea • *heraldry:* fish; purple (temperance in plenty); ram [sheep] • *see also* **restraint**

Temperance personified woman holding two vases • *attributes:* ass; bridle; clock; circular nimbus; hexagonal nimbus; hourglass; pitcher [vessel]; spectacles [eyeglasses]; sword in sheath, or with hilt bound; torch; windmill

Temperance [tarot] *association:* N

tempests *see* **storms**

temples tent • *associations:* eleven (the eleven curtains of the Temple); fifteen (the fifteen steps of the Temple) • *Judaism:* burned eggs, shank bone (a reminder of burnt offerings and of the ancient glory of the Temple) • *see also* **Jews; Judaism; synagogue**

the temporal *see* **matter; power; worldliness; worldly things**

temptation abstinence (the soul refraining from temptation); Adam; apple; bee; bellows; blackbird; ear (temptation through flattery); emerald (victory over the flesh; the overcoming of temptation); flower; fruit in a basket; Lillith (temptress); Lovers [tarot]; Mammon; nymph; Pandora, Pandora's box (wicked temptations of mankind); serpent; siren [mythology]; snare; spider; thorn (temptation of the flesh); toy • *Christianity:* chestnut (triumph over the temptations of the flesh); monk with claw or cloven hoof showing from under his habit, serpent battling with a fish (the Devil's temptation of Christ); salamander (the Christian who resists temptation through grace) • *flower language:* apple; quince • *see also* **allurement; seduction**

ten *association:* twenty

Ten Commandments clerical collar with two tabs (the two tablets of the Ten Commandments) • *associations:* miter (the two rays of light that came from the head of Moses when he received the Ten Commandments); ten; two tables or tablets of stone

tenacity box tree; bulldog; claw; ivy (tenacity; tenacity of memory); nails [for wood] • *heraldry:* bear; buckle; eagle's claw • *see also* **stubbornness; steadfastness**

tenderness gray hair; opal (increases tenderness in love); reseda; snail •

China: glycine (tender and delicate friendship) • *flower language:* wood sorrel (maternal tenderness) • *heraldry:* linden (often the leaf only is represented) • *see also* **gentleness; kindness**

tension bow [archery] (the tension between physical and spiritual forces); death (escape from unendurable tension); square [shape] (tense domination) • *see also* **stress**

tenuousness *association:* U (tenuous good fortune)

Teresa of Avila, St. praying saint before an image or vision of the crucified Christ, with Christ presenting the crucifixion nails or showing his wounds; praying saint before an image or vision of the Virgin and Child, with the Virgin and St. Joseph handing a cloak to the saint; woman with a dart with a flaming tip piercing her breast • *attributes:* dove; heart

Terpsichore *attributes:* crown of flowers; harp; lyre (occasionally); viol

Terrible Father giant; male ogre; Negro; sorcerer

Terrible Mother Diana; dragon; female ogre; hag; Hecate; Hercules (the fight against the Terrible Mother); Juno; lamia; Lillith; mare; matron; Medusa; Sphinx; stepmother • *attributes:* key; whip

territory *see* **land**

terror bat [animal]; cellar (the morbid terror lurking in the subconscious); Deimos (panic); goblin; guillotine • *see also* **fear; horror**

Terror personified *attribute:* trumpet

testicles eyes (can also be female genitals); gemstones; nuts; stones • *see also* **genitals**

Texas *emblem:* yellow rose

Thalia *attributes:* mask with a smile (17th century on); scroll; viol

thanksgiving cornucopia; incense (sacrifice for thanksgiving or for a favor); sheaf • *associations:* American pilgrim; orange [color]; pumpkin; red; turkey • *see also* **gratitude**

theater black blanket hung on an Elizabethan theater (a tragedy being performed); buskin, mask with a frown (tragedy); mask with a smile, sock [stocking] (comedy); white stone (theater admission) • *associations:* K; scaffold

Thebes city with seven gates

Thecla, St. woman tied between two bulls • *attribute:* lion

theft heart pierced with an arrow with a coin on the heart (sin against the 8th Commandment: Thou shalt not steal); partridge; Thursday's child is inclined to thieving • *see also* **thieves**

Themis *attribute:* balances

Theodore, St. soldier with a crocodile or dragon • *attributes:* crocodile; dragon

theology two dogs fighting (quarreling theologians) • *association:* three (the Three Theological Virtues: faith, hope, and charity)

theory kite [toy]

Therese of Lisieux, St. *attribute:* crucifix with roses

Theseus *associations:* crane [bird]; sword and sandals under a rock

thesis and antithesis echo; Gemini; mirror; rose with thorns; weapons (thesis and antithesis as the counterpart of monsters or enemies)

thieves dog (an object of contempt, a thief and a scavenger, but since the Middle Ages can also mean loyalty); fox; hazel wand (said to find water, buried treasure, murderers, thieves); jackdaw; magpie • *associations:* eastern cross (the mercy shown the thief to the right of Christ); gallows (typical execution of thieves); two (the two thieves on crosses with Christ) • *attributes:* branded hand (sheep thief); gloves; long fingers (occasionally) • *Rome:* Spain (association) • *see also* **theft**

thighs *association:* Jupiter [planet]

things *see* **matter; objects**

thinking *see* **thought**

thinness pencil; radish; weasel; willow

third son *heraldry:* star

thirst wine press

Thomas, St. *attributes:* book with a spear; girdle [cincture] with arrows and stones; dagger; lance with spear and arrows; man pierced with spears, especially when on a cross; rule [measuring]; spear with builder's square, arrows, or book

Thomas a Becket, St. bishop with a sword piercing his head • *attribute:* chasuble

Thomas Aquinas, St. monk driving off a young woman with a torch; praying bishop attacked by soldiers •

attributes: book; chalice; dove; lily; monstrance; ox; sun on the breast
Thomas of Canterbury, St. *attribute:* axe
Thomas of Villanueva, St. *attribute:* purse
Thor *associations:* acorn; goat; Thursday • *attributes:* gauntlet; girdle [cincture]; hazel; iron glove; red beard
thorns tonsure (Jesus Christ's crown of thorns)
Thoth *associations:* crane [bird]; goose • *attributes:* balances; caduceus
thought bed (a phase of thought or opinion); bird; burning or tingling left ear (your sweetheart is thinking of you); crest; drunkenness (revelation of inner thoughts and feelings); Emperor [tarot]; falcon (evil thought or action); feather; flag; flying; forge; hammer (persistent thought); hat; helmet (the color often represents the wearer's thoughts or personality); helmet with the visor down (hidden or suspect thoughts); helmet with wings (poetic thought); jerkin (ambiguity of thought); lamb (pure thought); lemon (pleasant thought); mill (habitual or uncreative thinking); mirror; moonstone; mountain air (heroic and solitary thought); oar (creative thought); opal (purifies thoughts); pansy; snow covered mountain (abstract thought); sphere; three feathers (good thought, word, and deed); Uranus [god] (latent thought); white dove with blue wings (celestial thoughts); wings • *associations:* blacksmith; cylinder (material thoughts); four (the functional aspects of consciousness: thinking, feeling, sensation, and intuition) • *flower language:* enchanter's nightshade (dark thoughts); purple violet (you occupy my thoughts); pansy; single aster (I will think of it); zinnia (thoughts of absent friends) • *heraldry:* snail (deliberation) • *lofty thoughts:* helmet; giraffe; snail (heraldry); winged sandals • *spiritual thoughts:* onyx (strengthens spiritual thoughts); tonsure • *see also* **beliefs; contemplation; ideas; introspection; meditation; opinions; pensiveness; perception; reason; reflection; reverie**
thoughtfulness *see* **pensiveness**
thoughtlessness *see* **carelessness**
threat black hand; fist; gun; red hand (threat of death); skunk; sword hanging overhead (constant threat) • *see also* **danger; warning**
three *associations:* C; L; Mars; triangle; U
Three Graces *attributes:* myrtle; rose [flower] • *flower language:* hundred-leaved rose (emblem)
threshold Cancer [zodiac] (the threshold through which the soul enters upon its incarnation); fossil; guard (force gathered on the threshold of transition); key (threshold of the unconscious) • *see also* **entrance**
thrift *see* **frugality**
throat beryl (charm against death, seasickness, eye and throat ailments) • *associations:* L; Venus [planet]
throne of a deity empty throne; flaming wheels with wings or eyes; Pole Star; temple • *Egypt:* boat
thrones [angels] angel with a throne; winged wheel
thunder axe; drum (thunder and lightning); hammer (attribute of thunder gods); oak; zigzag (emblem of thunder gods) • *association:* eight (rain and thunder) • *see also* **lightning**
thunderbolt *see* **lightning**
Thursday Born on a Thursday, merry and glad (or, has far to go); marriage on a Thursday was thought be good for crosses (i.e., religion); Thursday's child is inclined to thieving • *associations:* Jupiter [god]; Sagittarius; Thor; works of politics and religion.
Tiburtine sibyl [Tiburtina] *attribute:* rod
ties *see* **bonds**
tigers *association:* Mars
tightness screw
time bird; carnival, orgy, saturnalia (the desperate quest for a way out of time); distaff (time; cosmic time); dragon biting its own tail; fossil; hourglass (the fleeting quality of time); lion; maypole (the phallic reproductive powers of nature, together with the vulva-circle regulation of time and motion); mill; pendulum; pulse; pyramid; river (the creative power of time and nature); obedience to time, life, and the law; sand; Saturn [god] (destructive and devouring time); scroll; scythe; sheen; sickle; spring [season]; sundial (natural time in the general rather than the personal sense); swan;

thief; water mill; water wheel; well; whistling, whittling (frittering away time); wind; wings (time; attribute of Father Time); zenith (the point at which one passes out of time into timelessness) • *associations:* black; ocean; sixty; white (timelessness) • *Egypt:* baboon • *flower language:* pitch pine; white polar • *passage of time:* blot; dancing; dust; mouse; procession; rat; scythe; stain; swallow; raven; river (the irreversible passage of time); wheel • *time and eternity:* ford, fording (the dividing line between two states such time and eternity, consciousness and unconsciousness, etc.); Ouroboros • *time and space:* blue (association); crossroads (intersection or conjunction of any binary form: space and time, heaven and earth, etc.); hurricane, tornado (hole through which one may pass out of time and space); Pole Star (a hole in time and space); twelve (association)

Time personified *attribute:* serpent

timelessness zenith (the point at which one passes out of time into timelessness) • *association:* white

timidity amaryllis; apricot flower (timid love); deer; doe; dove; four o'clock [flower]; giraffe; grasshopper; hare; hind [deer]; knight pursued by a hare; mole [animal]; mouse; quivering; rabbit; turtle dove • *association:* two • *flower language:* cyclamen (diffidence); marvel of Peru; sowbread (diffidence) • *see also* **meekness; shyness**

tinkers *attribute:* pigskin bag

tiredness *see* **fatigue**

Titus, St. *attribute:* columns in ruins

Tityus vulture tearing at the liver of a naked man

Tiu *association:* Tuesday • *see also* Mars [god]

Tobias *attribute:* dog

toil *see* **work**

Toil personified *attribute:* yoke

tokens *flower language:* laurestina; ox-eyed daisy

tolerance *associations:* D; I [letter] • *heraldry:* beaver

tomb *see* **the grave**

tomorrow sneezing on a Saturday (your sweetheart will see you tomorrow)

Tomyris severed head placed in an urn (Tomyris with the head of Cyrus)

tongue peach with a leaf attached (the heart and the tongue); scourge

[whip] (sharp tongue)

torment fire; Gehenna (eternal torment); gnat; harpy; mosquito • *see also* **punishment; torture**

torture fork [implement]; Gordian knot, labyrinth (mental torture); lead [metal]; scorpion; scourge [whip]; spread-eagle body position; thumbscrews; wheel • *see also* **punishment; torment**

totality *see* **wholeness**

touch *see* **contact**

Touch personified *attributes:* ermine; hedgehog; tamed falcon

toughness *see* **durability**

towns *heraldry:* dolphin (coastal towns)

Towns personified *attribute:* turreted mural crown

tracking *heraldry:* foot (the discovery of an important track or fact which gains lasting merit)

trade *see* **commerce**

tradesmen brooch (may indicate the wearer's trade)

traditions drum (communication, especially of word or tradition); father; Hermit [tarot]; house; old man; ruins (customs, traditions, ideas, or sentiments which are dead and irrelevant to present life, but which nonetheless persist); torch (life or tradition passed on from one generation to the next)

tragedy black blanket hung on an Elizabethan theater (a tragedy being performed); buskin (tragedy, especially in drama); Dido; mask with a frown; mulberry tree (tragic love); nightingale (tragic victim); Phoenix [bird] (power to overcome tragedy); shipwreck (tragic fortune); swan song (tragic art)

traitors *see* **betrayal**

tranquillity adamant [mythical stone] (tranquillity of the soul); agate; broccoli; December (peace and quiet); evening; fishing; herd (when orderly); kingfisher (rural tranquillity); jar (still movement); oil; potato; water buffalo (serenity) • *associations:* blue (tranquillity; philosophical serenity); bluish purple; brown; rush plant • *flower language:* buckbean; Christmas rose (tranquillize my anxiety); madwort; mugwort; stonecrop • *see also* **peace**

Tranquillity personified *attribute:* alyssum

transcendence ascending (the human

condition being transcended and a higher spiritual level being attained); Ascension Day; flame; lotus (the soul transcending the flesh); ship (transcendence; living to transcend existence); stairs; threshold; walled city (the transcendent soul); wheel; whirlwind

transference rubbing [motion] (transference of magical power)

transformation catastrophe (the beginning of a transformation); chrysalis; cicada (metamorphosis); Death [tarot]; fog; harlequin (magic transformations); stranger (mutation); tomb • *associations:* M; seven (the transformation and unification of all hierarchical orders) • *China:* fox (possessor of supernatural powers, such as transformation) • *kabala:* forty • *see also* **change; transition; transmutation**

transgression *see* **sin**

transience *see* **transitoriness**

transition bridge; clouds (the intermediate world between the formal and non-formal); guard (force gathered on the threshold of transition); lake (the transition between life and death, often in a destructive sense); threshold (transition between two worlds) • *associations:* eleven; violet [color] (a transitional stage) • *see also* **change; transformation**

transitoriness anemone [flower] (brief blossoming); ashes (brevity of life); blot; bubble; butterfly; candle, lantern (transitory life in the face of the eternal); cherry blossoms (short-lived beauty); cicada (evanescent worldly glory); clouds; comet (a brilliant, but short-lived career); dew; fabric (the transitoriness of this world); flower (evanescence of life, especially when it has dewdrops on it); garment; grass; hailstones; Helen; hibiscus (short-lived glory); hourglass (the transiency of life); insect; jewels (the transience of earthly possessions, especially in a still life); lantern (transitory life in the face of the eternal); leaves; lightning; maple tree in autumn; moon; nymph; otter (transitory fertility); paper; poppy (evanescent pleasure); rush [plant]; shuttle [weaving]; sewing; skull, skull and crossbones (transitory nature of earthly life); smoke; spider web; spindle; stain; stubble in a field; swan; tent; tooth; violet [flower]; wildflower (a

short, perhaps unhappy life); wings (attribute of Fleeting Occurrence personified); World [tarot] (transitory life) • *association:* eyebrows that meet (sign of a person that will not live to marry) • *flower language:* night blooming cereus (transient beauty); spiderwort, Virginia spiderwort (transient happiness); withered white rose (transient impression) • *heraldry:* butterfly; candle; hourglass

Transitoriness personified *attribute:* peacock

transmigration *China:* fox (the transmigrated soul of a deceased person)

transmutation cauldron (the transmutation and germination of the baser forces of nature); incense (transmutation of the physical into the spiritual); swine (transmutation of the higher into the lower) • *see also* **transformation**

transparency crystal

trap *see* **snare**

trauma tunnel (birth trauma)

travel globe; gull • *associations:* five; I [letter]; one; W • *see also* **voyages; wandering**

travelers pilgrim (the human being on earth, traveling toward the Mystic Center); sparrow • *attribute:* staff • *emblem:* stork • *heraldry:* fusil; elephant, parrot (one who has made distant journeys); shell (successful distant journey) • *see* **wandering**

treachery cat; cloven hoof; dagger; fish hook; hatchet; lapwing; laurel; scorpion; siren [mythology] (a treacherous woman); tiger; tongue, especially a forked tongue; viper • *association:* Neptune [planet] • *China:* white face in the theater (a treacherous, but dignified man) • *flower language:* bilberry; common laurel • *see* **betrayal; deceit; disloyalty; spying; treason**

treason lark • *association:* yellow • *flower language:* whortleberry • *see also* **betrayal; disloyalty; treachery**

treasure box; castle of light; finding a key (the stage prior to finding treasure); golden fleece, occasionally a white fleece (hidden treasure); Hesperides (treasure hunt); morning (release of treasures locked in darkness or myth) • *see also* **plunder**

treasurer *heraldry:* cup; purse

treaty hands clasped in a handshake

tree beanstalk (Tree of the Universe); hut (shares both house and tree symbolism); oak (a tree of the first rank) • *association:* Tuesday (according to the Bible, the day dry land, pastures, and trees were created)

Tree of Knowledge *fruit:* apple (the usual fruit); lemon, orange [fruit], pear, pomegranate, quince, especially in hotter countries (occasional substitutes for the fruit of the Tree of Knowledge)

Tree of Life ankh [Egyptian cross]; cross, especially when flowering; mast; maypole; poplar; seven-branched menorah; squirrel (messenger of the Tree of Life); trident • *Near East:* date tree

tremulousness aspen; poplar

triad three pillars (any triad, such as goodness, power, and wisdom; faith, hope and charity, etc.)

trials harrow [tool]; red knight (the ability to overcome baseness and all trials through sacrifice); thorn; yoke • *associations:* F (protection of law and trial); forty; forty-two; six (trial and effort); V • *see also* **problems; striving; struggle; trouble**

tribulations *see* **trials**

tribute *see* **honor**

trickery *see* **deceit; dissimulation; falsity; lying**

trinity anemone [flower] (in early Christianity); empty throne with a dove and a crucifix; pansy, triangle within a circle (trinity and unity); three-lobed or trefoil arch; three fish (Trinity Sunday); empty throne with a dove and crucifix; triangular temple • *associations:* A; blue; three • *attributes:* aureole, especially gold or white (occasionally also used for the Virgin Mary); three-rayed nimbus • *emblems:* clover; fleur-di-lys; shamrock; three candles; three circles intertwined; three fish; three hares turned so they appear to have only one pair of ears; three linked rings; three pillars; three-branched candelabrum; trefoil [design]; tri-colored rainbow; triangle within three circles; triangle, especially when formed with fishes; trident (in ancient times, a sign of the Trinity, later used as an inversion of the Trinity); triquetra • *see also* **God; Holy Spirit; Jesus Christ**

Triton *attribute:* conch shell

triumph arch; banner; chariot; Chariot [tarot]; Grecian lute (triumph of the intellect); myrtle; Nike; riding, especially on an animal; salamander (enduring and triumphant faith); single arch; symmetry • *flower language:* mistletoe (I surmount all obstacles) • *heraldry:* red • *see also* **victory**

triviality bear; gnat • *see also* **insignificance**

Trojan War horse of wood

trollops *see* **prostitutes; wantonness**

trophies *flower language:* Indian cress, nasturtium (war trophies)

tropics banana; coconut; monkey; palm tree

troubadours lute (instrument of troubadours) • *heraldry:* peacock

trouble bear; billows (overwhelming trials); blackthorn; broom [for sweeping] (the power to do away with worry and trouble); dark clouds, storm clouds, barnacle goose (foretokens of trouble); dragon's teeth (seeds of dissension); flak; fly [insect] (minor troubles); knot; lichen (hardship); rat (major troubles); siren [both mythological and mechanical] (psychic disturbance); road; rubbing [motion]; sloe; thunder; vulture (foretoken of major troubles) • *association:* green (victory over the vicissitudes of life) • *flower language:* blackthorn; branch of thorns, lantana (rigor); hyacinth (love and its woes) • *see also* **problems; struggle; trials**

Troy *emblem:* eagle; young man bearing a woman off to a ship (abduction of Helen of Troy)

truce caduceus; laurel; white flag • *see also* **peace**

truculence *see* **ferocity; threat**

trust ivy; ostrich (one who trusts in God); pillow; raven (trust in divine providence); spy (trust in the flesh rather than the spirit); web (false hope or trust) • *heraldry:* key; stag (lover of trust and faith) • *Judaism:* key; lily • *see also* **confidence; faith**

Trust personified woman with a boat in her hand (Claudia personifying Confidence or Trust)

trustworthiness steel; brown face (applies only to Caucasians) • *association:* brown • *flower language:* plum blossoms (keep your promises) • *see also* **dependability**

truth aqueduct, artery (channels of truth from a higher to a lower nature); Bible; bittersweet [plant]; butterfly (the unconscious attraction toward light, truth, or God); cincture; clothes (concealment of reality, truth, nakedness, vice, etc.); clouds (obscuring of the truth); deer (a Christian searching after truth); desert (the realm of truth, abstraction, purity, ascetic spirituality, spirituality in general, and holiness); divorce (the apparent or delusive separation of goodness from truth); dove; dragon (the enemy of truth); drawing water from a well (acquiring truth); drinking (the soul acquiring truth); drugs (warring against right and truth); dryness; fig; flour; fountain; gold (revealed truth); goose; hail destroying crops (falsity destroying truth and goodness); hand or hands raised and open (swearing the truth); hearing (intuitive perception of truth in the soul); hound (seeker of truth); House of God [tarot] (spiritual truth breaking down ignorance); hunter (searcher for truth); ice (latent truth); idol (fixed ideas which bar the way to truth); irrigation (the bestowing of truth upon the lower qualities); lace; lantern (transitory truth); leopard (the opinionated lower mind full of error that are mingled with the truth); manna; milk; mirror; monster (the instincts that hinder man in his search for truth); moonlight (distorted truth); myrrh; open book (dissemination of the truth); oppressors (opinions that oppose the truth); partridge; plain [topography] (land of truth and reality); pomegranate; rock; salt; salt water; sibyl (the intuiting of higher truth); smoke (illusion obscuring truth); spitting (a sign of truth); square [tool]; stomach (truth and learning); surplice (man renewed in truth and justice); tears [weeping] (the suffering endured pursuing truth); thorn (the road to truth); torch; tower (hidden truth);

traveling (seeking after truth); treasures hidden in a palace (spiritual truths); trumpeting elephant; veil; wine; World [tarot] (truth and spiritual evolution attained on earth) • *associations:* blue (truth; the unveiling of truth); cube; eighty-one (the number nine, that is, truth, multiplied by itself); nine; ring finger; square [shape]; twenty-one (absolute truth); violet [color] (love of truth); yellow • *flower language:* white chrysanthemum; woody or bittersweet nightshade • *heraldry:* holly; vine • *divine truth:* linen; sapphire; unguent (divine love and truth)

Truth personified *attributes:* crown of laurel; globe; mirror, especially a hand mirror; peach; sun

truthfulness crystal; mantis; white knight • *heraldry:* cube • United States: cherry tree (associated with the Parson Weems story of George Washington and the cherry tree that he wrongfully chopped down, but had the truthfulness to admit to) • *see also* **candor; frankness; honesty**

Tuccia *attribute:* sieve

Tuesday Born on a Tuesday, full of [God's] grace; marriage on a Tuesday was associated with good health; Tuesday's child is solemn and sad • *associations:* Mars; Scorpio; Tiu; works of wrath • *emblem:* pancake (Shrove Tuesday)

Tullia *association:* chariot drawn over a corpse

turning swastika • *turning point:* ford, fording (marks a decisive stage in action, development, etc.); oak

twin formations *see* **opposites**

twins spectacles [eyeglasses] (twin deities)

two twenty (multiplies the powers of two) • *associations:* B; K; moon; T

tyranny emperor; giant; hand of iron; iron glove; iron hand; yoke • *Egypt:* crocodile • *Elizabethan times:* Hercules

U

U.S.S.R. *see* **Russia**

ubiquity serpent encircling a globe (the omnipresence of sin); wings, especially four wings

ugliness bear; toad • *China:* monkey

Ugolina della Gherardesca old man dying in prison with dead children

Ulysses *attribute:* red beard

unanimity *see* **concord; harmony**

unbelief *flower language:* Judas tree

unbeliever owl; stumbling ass; swine • *Christianity:* sycamore (the unbelieving Jew)

uncertainty convolvulus; Lovers [tarot]; mercury; mushroom; rabbit; wool • *association:* gray • *flower language:* convolvulus • *see also* **skepticism**

unchasteness *see* **wantonness**

uncleanliness *see* **filth**

uncleanness swine (a ritually unclean animal); washing (purification of ritual uncleanness) • *attribute:* cloven feet (unclean animals)

the unconscious Bacchante (involutive fragmentation of the unconscious); box; cave; cellar; centaur (the unconscious uncontrolled by the spirit); chaos; dismemberment, dispersal (being possessed by the unconscious, unconscious manias, or unconscious obsessions); dragon; drowning (being overwhelmed by conscience or the unconscious); dwarf; earthquake (upheaval in the unconscious); entanglement; fish (the self hidden in the unconscious); fishing (inquisitiveness about the unconscious); Fool [tarot]; forest; fountain; giant; Gordian knot; gorge; harpy (involutive fragmentation of the unconscious); Hercules (the fight against the unconscious); hold of a ship; hollow [topography]; horse; island (consciousness and will as refuge from the unconscious; the synthesis of consciousness and will); jester (repressed unconscious urges); jewels hidden in caves or underground (the intuitive knowledge of the unconscious); journey into caverns or into Hell (exploration of the unconscious); key (threshold of the unconscious); labyrinth; lake; lion (the danger of being devoured by the unconscious); mercury; mermaid, merman; monkey (unconscious activity); monster; moon; Neptune [god] (the regressive and evil side of the unconscious); night; nymph (unconscious; the fragmentary characteristics of the feminine unconscious); ocean swells or a stormy sea (activity or disturbance in the unconscious); rear; reef (danger lurking in the unconscious); remorse (the self in the unconscious); sailor (dealing with the unconscious); secret chambers; serpent (the unconscious expressing itself suddenly and unexpectedly with terrible or frightening results); sewer [drain]; siren [mythology], Furies (involutive fragmentation of the unconscious); sorcerer (the dark unconscious of man); submarine boat, fishnet, fish hook (means of exploring the unconscious); tomb; treasure in a cave (value found in the unconscious); trident; Uranus [god]; water (the personal unconscious); wild man, wild woman (the unconscious in its perilous and regressive aspects); woman • *associations:* left side; tarot cards XII to XXII • *collective unconscious:* mother; Negro; ocean; water • *conscious and unconscious:* child (conjunction of the conscious and unconscious); circumference (viewed from without: the circumference is the defense of the conscious against the unconscious, or chaos); dawn (the unconscious broadening into consciousness); eight (associated with the perfect blending of the conscious and unconscious, knowledge and love, action and reaction, etc.); ford, ice (the dividing line between two levels such as the conscious and unconscious, sleeping and waking, time and eternity, etc.); gorge [topography] (that part of the conscious through which parts of the unconscious may be glimpsed); H (associated with the union of the conscious and unconscious); king and queen, marriage (the union of the conscious and unconscious); snail (the self: the shell represents the conscious, the soft inner part the unconscious or personality); Sun [tarot] (balance between the conscious and unconscious); World [tarot] (the merging of the subconscious and the super-conscious with the conscious) • *conscious threatened by the unconscious:* erupting volcano (the sudden attack of the unconscious on the conscious); fighting a monster (fighting to free the conscious from the unconscious); fingers; locomotive; man-eating monster; nightmare; quicksand • *flower language:* Burgundy rose (unconscious beauty) • *heraldry:* serpent • *unconscious memories:* mirror; palace of mirrors, glass, or crystal that suddenly appears by magic • *see also* **subconscious**

unconsciousness ford, ice (the dividing line between two states such as consciousness and unconsciousness, sleeping and waking, etc.)

unconventiality actor, artist, tinker, writer (people living outside the conventions of society)

unction chrism; oil

underdogs mule (mutual help among underdogs) • *see also* **victims**

understanding coot; eyes; light; ostrich (lack of understanding); silver key; window (possibility of understanding) • *associations:* fifty (understanding and sympathy); five (sympathy, good judgment, and understanding, but these can be perverted); Jupiter [planet]

undertakings *see* **tasks**

underworld abyss; Gordian knot; kettle; labyrinth; lion; tree (link of heaven, earth, and the underworld) • *associations:* adamant [mythical stone] (occasionally); brass (occasionally); lupin; myrtle; nine; pot, usually earthen; Spain (Celts and Greece) • *emblem:* triangle with the apex down • *underworld beings:* blacksmith; chimera; Demogorgon; eleven (association); red hair (attribute); scales [biology] (attribute) • *underworld deities:* blackbird; cypress (association); dark complexion (attribute); disheveled hair (attribute); harlequin (association) • *underworld entrance:* brass gate; descending stairs; key; river • *see also* **Hades; Hell; infernality**

the undifferentiated universal solvent; viper • *association:* gray

uneasiness *see* **anxiety**

unendurability Gorgon (a condition beyond the endurance of the conscious mind); Tristram (sacrifice in an unendurable situation)

unfaithfulness blown dandelion with some seeds remaining (a lover is unfaithful); columbine; cuckoo; Helen of Troy; yellow rose • *flower language:* dried white rose • *see also* **disloyalty**

unfavorability *see* **adversity; negativity**

unfolding of creation octopus; unrolling papyrus; web

unfolding of life mat being unrolled; unrolling papyrus or scroll (the top roll is the future; the bottom roll is the past)

the unformed *association:* jester

ungodliness chaff (the ungodly)

unguent myrrh (sacred ointment)

unhappiness *see* **despair; despondency; displeasure; gloom**

unicorns hart (a substitute)

unification necklace; sheaf • *association:* seven (the transformation and unification of all hierarchical orders) • *see also* **fusion; union; unity**

uniformity *see* **sameness**

unimportance *see* **insignificance**

union cord; crossroads; Gordian knot, labyrinth (the difficulty of uniting oneself with one's spirit and with God); hands clasped and raised overhead; heaven (union with God); Hermit [tarot] (the successful union of personal will with cosmic will); incest (longing for union with one's own self); knot; Lovers [tarot]; lyre (harmonious union of cosmic forces); Magic [tarot] (union of personal and divine will); marriage (urge to unite the discrete); rainbow; ring; two fish (the joy of union); yoke • *association:* V (joining) • *flower language:* Lancaster rose; whole straw • *union of the male and female principles:* caduceus; flagpole with a ball on top; guitar; hearth with a fire; horn [animal]; king and queen; maltese cross; marriage; maypole; serpent with its tail in its mouth; sexual intercourse; six-pointed star; Sphinx; swan; Temperance [tarot] • *see also* **conjunction; connection; fusion; unification; unity**

Union of Soviet Socialist Republics *see* **Russia**

United States Pentagon [building]

(the U.S. military establishment; the U.S. military-industrial complex) • *emblems:* American Indians, bison (the west); corn [maize] (the midwest); cotton, honeysuckle (the south); eagle

unity center; child (unity with nature); circle (the ultimate state of oneness); elm tree with vine; fasces (unity, especially in marriage); globe; head; hermaphrodite; monolith (unity counterbalancing multiplicity); mountain peak; onion; Ouroboros (cosmic unity); pansy (trinity and unity); point; pomegranate; seamless garment (Christ's garment at the Crucifixion, hence: purity, divinity, unity); sphere; the spirit; throne; triangle with the apex up (aspiration of all things to unity); triangle within a circle • *associations;* one • *flower language:* red and white roses together • *see also* **completion; unification; union; wholeness**

universality giant (universal man); ocean, Temperance [tarot] (universal life); pool [water] (universal consciousness) • *association:* L

universe anvil (the force that created the universe); anvil with cross or sword (the forge of the universe); armillary; beanstalk (the Tree of the Universe); bondage (man irrevocably tied to the Creator and to the universe); clock; egg; head; head of an eagle (the center point of the universe); house (the feminine aspect of the universe); music (harmony of the universe); north (furthest bounds of the universe); organ [instrument]; round table; Sophia (wisdom of the universe); spider web (the negative side of the universe); spiral (evolution of the universe); threshing floor; tree; zither (the strings correspond to the levels of the universe) • *association:* ten (the totality of the universe • *Egypt:* ellipse • *Judaism:* one (power and will of the universe) • *see also* **world**

the unknown sea serpent (formerly used on maps to denote unexplored waters); X, Y, Z (unknown quantities)

unlucky numbers thirteen; twenty-eight; twenty-two

unmarried men *see* **single men**

unmarried women *see* **single women**

unnaturalness *see* **abnormality; irregularity**

unpleasantness *see* **offensiveness; repulsiveness**

unpopularity hemlock (punishment for unpopular beliefs)

unpredictability dwarf • *association:* Pluto [planet] • *see also* **caprice**

unproductiveness *see* **barrenness; sterility**

unreality fog; mist; rose colored glasses [spectacles] (optimistic or unrealistic view)

unrepentance raven (an unrepentant sinner)

unrest comet; itch; mosquito; raven • *see also* **restlessness**

untidiness *see* **filth**

untrustworthiness crow; green eyes; pale face

unworldliness ivory tower (retreat from the world, especially by an intellectual or an academic) • *see also* **ingenuousness; innocence**

upheaval thunder (cosmic upheaval)

upper classes beheading (typical punishment of the upper classes—the poor were hanged); carriage (vehicle of the upper classes); silk • *heraldry:* trident (upper class merchant) • *Spain:* lisping (association) • *United States:* four hundred (upper class society, especially in the eastern U.S.)

Upper Kingdom of Egypt *emblems:* lily; white crown and flowering rush

uprightness *see* **righteousness**

upstarts *England:* bricks (associated with lower class upstarts)

upward *see* **ascension; elevation**

Urania *attributes:* celestial globe; compasses [dividers]; crown of twelve stars; globe, especially when it is in a tripod

Uranus *associations:* Hermit [tarot]; L; light blue; seven

urbanity *see* **elegance**

urges jester (repressed unconscious urges)

Uriel *associations:* seventeen; twelve (Uriel and Gabriel jointly) • *attributes:* book; flame held in the hand; scroll

urine dandelion (urination); pot, usually earthen; sap

Ursula, St. maiden in a camp being threatened with an arrow by a soldier; rudely dressed woman holding arrows • *attributes:* cloak lined with ermine;

clock; red Latin Cross; ship; staff with white banner with red cross
usefulness bush; grass (humble usefulness); gull; shoes • *flower language:* dried flax; grass
uselessness bottomless cask (useless labor); skull (the useless nature of earthly things) • *flower language:* diosma; meadowsweet • *see also* **fu-**

tility; worthlessness
usurers *attribute:* fox fur on a fleece
usurpation cuckoo
Usury personified *attribute:* sheep
uterine waters lake
utility *see* **usefulness**
utopia Hanged Man [tarot] (the utopian dream world)

V

vacillation *see* **changeability**
vagabondage *see* **wandering**
vagina *see* **vulva**
Vagrancy personified *attribute:* hare
vagueness *see* **obscurity; uncertainty**
Valentine, St. *attribute:* heart
Valhalla eagle and wolf (the elect part of Valhalla); hill (entrance to Valhalla) • *association:* eight hundred (the number of Odin's warriors at Valhalla)
valor *see* **bravery; courage; pugnacity**
value ascending (a raise in value or worth); crust, piece of bread, sou, straw (something of no value); gold (high value); green eyes (in Elizabethan times, valued for their rarity); light (moral value); offering, sacrifice (giving up something of low value, for something of value on a higher plane); pin (something of value up to the middle of the 18th century, but of no value afterwards); pitcher [vessel] (something of low value); plum (a valuable object or situation); treasure (something of spiritual value); treasure in a cave (value found in the unconscious) • *associations:* excrement (related to gold and with what is highest in value); seven (exceptional value) • *see also* **merit; worth**
vampire garlic (protection from vampires); stake driven through the heart (method of killing a vampire) • *attributes:* bat [animal]; black cape; eyebrows that meet; long canine teeth
vandalism sparrow
vanity comb; cormorant; cosmetics; cymbal; deer; Empress [tarot]; frog;

hoopoe; horse; jackdaw; mouse; peacock; rich robe (worldly pomp and vanity); sieve; skeleton; smoke; turkey; wood pigeon • *art:* overturned cup • *flower language:* Venus' looking glass • *see also* **self-love**
Vanity personified *attributes:* jewels; mirror; purse
vapidness *see* **emptiness**
variation X (a variable quantity)
variety Gorgon (the infinite forms in which creation is manifested); marigolds mixed with red flowers (varying course of life); mundi rose; sycamore • *flower language:* China aster • *see also* **diversity**
vegetation weaving as a feminine activity • *association:* green • *vegetation goddesses:* spindle (attribute)
vendetta black hand; wolfsbane • *see also* **revenge**
venereal disease burning; sweat
venery *see* **sex; wantonness**
vengeance *see* **punishment; revenge; vendetta**
Venice [Italy] *emblem:* lion with wings
Venice [Italy] personified *attributes:* lion with wings; sword with two lions
venture *see* **adventure**
Venus [goddess] lovers under a net, soldier and woman on a couch with his weapon put aside (Venus and Mars) • *associations:* cypress; Friday; goat; goose; lapis lazuli; quince; shell • *attributes:* apple (attribute of both Venus and her handmaidens); bow and arrows; caduceus; chariot drawn by doves or swans; comb; dolphin; girdle [cincture]; eight-pointed star; heather;

mirror; myrtle; putto; red hair; rose [flower]; sturgeon; swallow [bird]; swan; torch; two doves; vase with a flame coming from its mouth • *emblems:* flaming heart; star of the sea (usually seven-pointed); strawberry

Venus [planet] *associations:* C; copper; Friday; green; pale blue; R; six; thumb; V; yellow

veracity *see* **truthfulness**

verbosity *see* **chatter**

vermin cat, magpie, weasel (destroyers of vermin)

vernal equinox *associations:* furze; index finger

Veronica, St. *attributes:* crown of thorns; picture of Christ on a cloth

versatility gull; Ulysses; weather cock, weather vane • *see also* **adaptability**

Vertumnus old woman and naked goddess with cornucopia (Vertumnus and Pomona, respectively)

Vesta *attribute:* lamp

vicariousness scapegoat (vicarious atonement)

vice ape; Babylon; cicada (restraint of vice and lasciviousness); clothes (concealment of reality, truth, nakedness, vice, etc.); dice; harpy; plague; toad • *Elizabethan England:* Bermuda (the underworld district; the brothel district) • *flower language:* darnel; ray grass • *see also* **lasciviousness**

Vice personified *attributes:* chains; mask; pipe [music]; playing cards; tambourine

viciousness crocodile; hornet; horse without any white parts; mantis (female viciousness); swine; wasp • *see also* **cruelty; ferocity**

victims fish swimming into a whale's mouth (unsuspecting souls trapped by the Devil); gull; jester (victim of sacrifice); nightingale (the tragic victim); rabbit; turtle dove; wood pigeon (victim of the cuckoo)

victory Ascension Day; banner; basket with flowers or fruit; beech; blue ribbon (first place in a contest); bonfire; broom [for sweeping]; Chariot [tarot] (progress and victory); club [bat] (victory through destruction); coronation; dancing; dove with olive branch; dragon underfoot, slain, bound, or chained (paganism or sin overcome); elephant with trunk held up; fern leaf (victory over death); flag;

flower; garland of fennel (crown of a victorious gladiator); griffin; hands clasped and raised over the head; helmet with a crest; index and middle finger forming a vee; index finger upraised indicating the number one (sports victory); laurel (victory, especially in the spiritual sense); legs; lion; medal; mountain peak; myrtle; oak wreath (victory on the seas); olive branch; palm tree; pine; panther skin (victory over base desires); poplar; Punch and Judy (the anti-hero overcoming learning, domesticity, death, and the Devil); rhinoceros; purple fillet (victory in sports); tabret (the ecstasy of victory); thumb up; torch; triskele; Virgin Mary with a serpent underfoot (victory of the seed of woman; Mary's victory over sin); whip; white stone; wings; wreath • *associations:* elephant (military victory); green (victory over the flesh; victory over the vicissitudes of life) • *attribute:* scepter tipped with an eagle (victorious general) • *flower language:* mistletoe (I surmount all obstacles) • *heraldry:* goat (victorious warrior); palm tree (after 1500, victory, especially military); raven; red (victorious power); silver • *kabala:* seven • *Orient:* dragonfly • *Rome:* parsley (victory in sports) • *victory over death:* broken handcuffs (death and sin overcome); crown (as the attribute of a martyr); urn with a lid on it (the supreme enlightenment which triumphs over birth and death); white flag with a red cross • *see also* **conquest; subjugation; triumph**

Victory personified woman reclining on weapons • *attributes:* ball; crown of laurel; eagle; lion; palm tree; pomegranate

vigilance badger; blackbird; cherub; crane [bird]; dog; eyelids; goose; griffin (eternal vigilance); hare; hawk; Hermit [tarot] (solitary vigilance); lamp; lighthouse; lion (Middle Ages); maniple; menhir; owl; pheasant; rabbit; rooster; soldier; stars; stork; torch; tower; violet [flower]; weasel; window • *association:* N • *China:* dragon • *Egypt:* Sphinx (power and vigilance) • *flower language:* dame violet • *heraldry:* beaver; cat; crane [bird] (usually has a stone in its mouth); dog; fish; goose;

greyhound; griffin; hare; martlet; owl; serpent • *see also* **wakefulness**
vigor *see* **energy**
vileness *see* **filth**
villainy *see* **evil**
Vincent DePaul, St. *attributes:* children; infant in a cradle
Vincent Ferrer, St. *attributes:* captives; cardinal's hat; pulpit; trumpet
Vincent of Saragossa, St. *attributes:* dalmatic; demon in chains; garment of palm leaves; grapes; gridiron (occasionally); millstone; raven; ship; two crows; whip
violence bear; gun (violence; threat of violence); hawk; red hand; russet [cloth]; tiger (violent desires); whirlwind; white heather (protection against acts of violence); wine • *association:* eight (corresponds to violent passions and abnormal tendencies); • *flower language:* Near East tulip • *heraldry:* key • *see also* **brutality; force**
violet [color] *association:* nine • *heraldry:* purple (occasional substitute for violet)
vipers *flower language:* lavender (associated with the asp that killed Cleopatra, also with the English viper)
Virgil *attribute:* crown of laurel
Virgin Mary Ark of the Covenant; bee (the virginity of Mary); bluebottle (the modesty of the Virgin Mary); bower; burning bush; carnation; ciborium (the womb of the Virgin Mary); eagle (the Virgin Mary leading people to true light); Eve (the inversion of the Virgin Mary); flowers in a field (the Virgin Mary and the church); font (the immaculate womb of the Virgin Mary); garland of roses (rosary of the Virgin Mary); golden house; orb with a snake around it at the feet of the Virgin Mary (her role as the second Eve); sealed book; sealed fountain; sealed well; thornless rose; tower; Virgin Mary holding an apple (Mary as the new Eve); walled or closed garden; white hare at the Virgin Mary's feet (her triumph over lust) • *associations:* blue; ladybug (especially in the Middle Ages); pelican (once thought to be proof of virgin birth); shell; white • *attributes:* almond; asphodel; aureole (normally only used for members of the Trinity, occasionally used for the Virgin Mary); bowl; bramble; bruised

serpent (the Virgin Mary's victory over sin); bunch of keys; camphor; cincture; cinnamon; circular nimbus; crown of stars, especially with lilies; cyclamen; cypress of Zion; daisy; distaff (the Virgin Mary at the Annunciation); fennel; flowering almond; flowering rod; fruit; girdle [cincture]; gold or white aureole; hyacinth [flower]; iris [flower]; ivory; ivory tower; lily; lily of the valley; lizard; lozenge [shape]; mandrake; marigold; mint [plant]; musk; myrrh; myrtle; oak; orange [fruit]; orchard of pomegranates; palm tree; palm, cypress, and olive trees together; peach; pear (occasional attribute); pearl; pitcher [vessel] with dish and two fish; pomegranate; Rod of Jesse; rose [flower]; scepter tipped with a fleur-di-lys; spotless mirror; spotless towel; starry crown, sometimes also with lilies (the Virgin Mary, usually at the Immaculate Conception); sun and the moon together; turreted castle or gate; unicorn; urn, vase (especially of gold or silver with a white lily in it); white flower • *emblems:* A.M. [ave Maria], M, or M.R. [Maria regina] (printed as a monogram, especially with a crown); balsam; clematis; closed gate; crescent; crescent and star; crocus; five-pointed star; fleur-di-lys; fountain; gillyflower; heart pierced with a sword, sometimes the heart has wings; ivory tower; jasmine; lemon; red and white roses together; sapphire; snowdrop; spikenard with saffron or camphor; star of the sea (usually seven-pointed); strawberry; swan, usually white
Virginia woman stabbed by a soldier before a judge
virginity almond; bar on a female symbol (circle, oval, etc.); bee (the virginity of Mary); bell; buds; cherry; closed gate; closed windowless room; daisy; Diana; flower; glass; golden cup; honey; knot; lamp; lily; maiden; mirror; moon; myrtle; padlock; pelican (once thought to be proof of virgin birth); salamander; seal [stamp]; snood; snow; tower; veil; walled or closed garden • *associations:* shell (virgin birth); silver; six • *attributes:* belt; fibula [buckle]; girdle [cincture]; long, flowing hair; white garment; white veil • *folklore:* elephant (an elephant would not kill a virgin); unicorn (it was so wary, it

could only be captured by a virgin) •
emblem: swan, usually white • *heraldry:*
Melusina • *see also* **maidens; purity**
**Virgins, the Five Wise and Five
Foolish** five candles lit, with five candles unlit (the Five Wise Virgins and
the Five Foolish Virgins, respectively);
ten maidens with lamps • *associations:*
five; ten
Virgo personified *attributes:* harpy;
vase
Virgo [zodiac] virgin • *associations:*
brown; F; hazel; J; mercury; Mercury
[planet]; morning glory; O [letter]; pale
gray; peridot; sapphire; yellow-green;
zircon
virility acorn; fibula [clasp or buckle]
(restricted virility); head; horn [ani-
mal]; lion; pine; red knight; tamed lion
(subjugation of virility); victorious lion
(exaltation of virility) • *associations:*
red; right hand • *see also* **masculinity;
men**
virtue ailanthus (virtue growing out
of, but untainted by, sin); beauty; bee
(the Christian's zeal in acquiring virtue); belt; Cato (moral virtue); cedar;
cherry tree (masculine virtue); cicada
(restraint of vice and lasciviousness);
cube (the solidity and persistence of
virtue); flower; garland of roses (reward of virtue); golden hair; jade; lavender [plant]; light; mint [plant]; oak;
peach (the silence of virtue); shield;
violet [flower] (true virtue); Virgin
Mary (virtuous womanhood); white
robe; white stone; wings; woman in
linen (a virtuous woman, as opposed
to a loose woman dressed in silk) • *associations:* gold; scarlet (general virtue
and merit) • *China:* five bats [animals]
(the blessings of longevity, wealth,
health, virtue, and a natural death) •
flower language: mint [plant] • *heraldry:*
gannet (one who subsists on virtue and
merit without material help); gold;
martlet (subsisting on virtue and
merit); star • *portrait painting:* ermine
(alludes to the subject's virtue) • *see
also* **goodness; morality;
righteousness**
virtues nun (higher virtues); Hanged
Man [tarot] (power derived from
charity, wisdom, fidelity, and other
higher virtues); winged animals (the
sublimation of that animal's specific
virtues) • *association:* right side (higher

virtues) • *Christianity:* four (the Four
Cardinal Virtues: prudence, justice,
temperance, and fortitude); seven (the
Seven Virtues: faith, hope, charity,
temperance, prudence, fortitude, and
justice); seven women (the Seven Virtues personified—their attribute is a
book); three (the Three Theological
Virtues: faith, hope, and charity) •
flower language: sage [herb] (domestic
virtues) • *see also* **qualities**
Virtues [angels] angel holding a lily
or red roses
vision *see* **eyesight**
visions *association:* toadstools (ecstatic
visions)
visitors *China:* magpie (foretoken of
a visitor)
vitality bloodstone; full, thick head of
hair; half-opened buds; heat; horseshoe
(associated with a horse's vitality and
sexual potency); houseleek; gall (seat
of vitality); Pan (vitality of base
forces); sulfur (vital heat) • *associations:*
K; Leo (vital forces) • *see also* **energy;
libido**
vivacity hematite • *flower language:*
houseleek
voice hands raised and open (voice
and song); thunder (voice of the supreme deity) • *China:* swallow [bird]
(woman's voice)
volubility *see* **chatter**
voluptuousness *see* **sensuality**
voracity carp; dog; lamprey; swine •
Egypt: crocodile • *flower language:* lupin
• *see also* **greed; hunger; rapacity**
voting black bean, black stone (a
negative vote); white bean, white stone
(a positive vote)
voyages albatross (long sea voyages);
Castor and Pollux (safety at sea) • *see
also* **travel**
Vulcan blacksmith, especially when
depicted forging weapons • *association:*
cuckolds • *attributes:* anvil; chariot
drawn by dogs; crutch; forge; hammer;
helmet; limping; moon; weapons in a
blacksmith's shop
vulgarity *flower language:* African
marigold (vulgar mind)
vulnerability heel; sleep (vulnerability
to evil); sword hanging overhead
(vulnerability to fate) • *flower language:*
passion flower; wax plant
vulva apple; apricot; basket; bay [to-
pography]; beaver; brook; buskin; cat;

chasuble; conch shell; cup; Cupid's quiver; diamond [shape]; door; fig, especially when opened; fish; flower; garden; garden gate [labia]; gate; goblet; Gordian knot; hand with thumb and forefinger touching; hole; horseshoe; keyhole; labyrinth; lozenge [shape]; navel; orchid; oval; peach; precipice; quiver for arrows, but also may stand for the phallus as it contains shooting arrows [semen]; rabbit; reed; rhomb; ring; rose [flower]; scabbard; shell; shoes; sluice gate; spinning wheel; thimble; throat; tunnel; zero • *euphemisms:* lap [anatomy]; navel; pit [topography] • *phallus and vulva:* bell; flagpole with a ball on the end; maypole (the phallic reproductive powers of nature together with the vulva-circle regulation of time and motion); Q; well with trees • *see also* **clitoris**

waiting *flower language:* red columbine (anxious and waiting)

wakefulness almond; nightingale pinching (return to wakefulness or reality) • *see also* **vigilance**

Wales *emblems:* daffodil; harp (usually Ireland, sometimes Wales); leek; three feathers, usually ostrich feathers (Wales; the Prince of Wales)

wandering goat; gypsy; mushroom; sheep (straying); swallow [bird] (wandering spirit) • *see also* **travelers**

wantonness breasts thrust forward; butterfly; colt; cosmetics; dolphin (youth's pleasant wantonness); east wind; gillyflower; hare; heifer; hobbyhorse; jay (even though it is generally a male figure); kitten; light heels (promiscuity); long fingernails; oily or wet palm of the hand; parsley; pinching; popinjay; rush [plant]; Salome; satyr; silk clothes; Sirius; swallow [bird] • *association:* Babylon • *see also* **courtesans; mistresses; prostitutes; seduction; sensuality; sex**

Wantonness personified *attribute:* sparrow

war Abbadon (evil wars); arrow; axe (primitive warfare); bird of prey flying from left to right before a battle (foretoken of defeat); black flag on a submarine (success in battle); blood; blue rose (martial honor); bow [archery]; broom [plant]; cannon; carp; Castor and Pollux (power in battle); chariot; chess; closed gate; crossed swords; dancing; dog; dragon's teeth; drum (call to war); eagle's scream; fire; gadfly [insect]; gladiolus (readiness for battle); hawk (war monger); horse; horseman on a red horse (war as a punishment from God); iron; javelin, lance (martial readiness); metal; ram [sheep] with its pugnacity emphasized; red horse; Sirius; smoke; spear; steel; stick dance; sword; thunder; Trojan; trumpet; turning one's girdle or cincture (preparation for battle); wolf; yarrow • *American Indians:* hatchet; tomahawk • *associations:* eagle (war deities); K (martial qualities); Mars [god and planet]; metal musical instruments; mulberry tree, especially the juice; Pentagon [building]; Q (martial qualities); red; thorn • *China:* red clouds (warfare and calamity) • *flower language:* blue-flowered or Greek valerian; grass-leaved goose foot, especially when the stems alone are presented (I declare war against you); Indian cress, nasturtium (war trophy); York and Lancaster roses together • *foretokens of war:* aurora borealis; comet; eclipse of the sun; soldiers on horseback in the sky; thunder • *heraldry:* tent (readiness for war or battle) • *see also* **warriors**

wardens *attribute:* key

warmth cactus; ember; reptile (lack of human warmth); south; south wind; wool • *association:* Phoenix [bird] • *flower language:* cactus; peppermint;

red and white roses together (warmth of heart); spearmint (warmth of sentiment); spotted arum • *see also* **heat**

warning bell; bonfire; drum; golden plover (warns sheep of approaching danger); index finger upraised; threshold monsters, such as lions, dragons, etc., at an entrance to a holy place (warning against profanation); red flag; siren [mechanical]; skull and crossbones; thunder (divine warning) • *flower language:* burdock, red balsam (don't touch me); hand flower tree; plum blossoms (keep your promises); rhododendron; rose bay [oleander]; saffron (beware of excess) • *see also* **danger; threat**

warriors amputation of thumbs and great toes (incapacitation of a warrior); archer (a soldier of the lower classes); firefly (a ghost of the dead, especially a dead warrior); salamander (a soldier who survives a battle); sistrum; sparrowhawk (brave warrior); wolf • *associations:* eight hundred (the number of Odin's warriors in Valhalla); garland of fennel (crown of a victorious gladiator); musical instruments of metal • *attributes:* anvil; armor, banner (warrior saints); gold necklace (foreign soldiers in the Roman army); horse; one sandal; silver necklace (citizen soldiers in the Roman army); spear; sword; woman with one breast exposed (female warrior) • *heraldry:* centaur (eminence in battle); fess; gauntlet (challenge; readiness for combat); goat (a victorious warrior); leopard (a valiant warrior who has engaged in hazardous undertakings); lion; manticore; tent (readiness for war or battle) • *see also* **the military; war**

Washington, George *attribute:* hatchet and cherry tree

wasteland cactus

watchfulness *see also* **vigilance**

water alder blossoms; aquatic plants (creation from primordial waters); axe and trident (fire and water, respectively); dolphin; hazel wand (said to find water); horned serpent; lake (uterine waters); Leviathan (waters of Chaos); moon (regulator of water and rain); turquoise [gemstone] (water and earth); two pillars of Enoch (the brick pillar is proof against fire, the stone pillar is proof against water); un-

dine (the perilous nature of water) • *associations:* crystal; green, in pagan rites; griffin with a ball underfoot (supporter of a water goddess); Monday (according to the Bible, the waters were divided on Monday); N; scales [biology]; shell • *Christianity:* hart (the faithful partaking of the waters of life) • *emblem:* triangle with the apex down • *Orient:* dragon

Water personified river god with urn • *attribute:* dolphin

wavering *see* **ambivalence**

waves [water] zigzag (waves of the sea)

the Way *Gnosticism:* eagle atop a ladder

weakness Adam (the weak, sinful side of man); amputation, maiming (weakness or defect in the soul—taking revenge for the act shows that some vestige of moral strength remains); bulrush (lack of stamina); calf; cedar (occasionally, God's power to weaken the strong); dragonfly; Friday (fecklessness); grasshopper; hemlock; reed; tear [weeping]; Vulcan (a weak, materialistic, and corrupt soul); worm • *associations:* forty-two; left hand • *flower language:* moschatel; musk plant • *Greece:* ball (fecklessness) • *see also* **frailty; impotence**

wealth amethyst; animal fat; bacon; bee; cake, white bread (food of the rich); castle (heavenly wealth); conch shell; crooked little finger (you will die rich); cushion; diamond [gemstone] (dignity and wealth, especially royal); filled bowl; fleece (closely guarded wealth); genie issuing from a lamp (a magic source of wealth); gold (worldly wealth); golden chain; hand with money; ivory; metal; morning (freshness of wealth); necklace; nuts (hidden riches); oil; ox; palace; park; pearl; peony; peppermint; sunflower (false riches); woolsack • *associations:* eight; marriage on a Monday; seven • *attributes:* golden sandals; sandals (especially in ancient art) • *China:* fish; five bats [animals] (the blessings of longevity, wealth, health, virtue, and a natural death) • *flower language:* corn [maize]; garden ranunculus (you are rich in attractions); kingcup (desire for riches); polyanthus (pride of riches) • *heraldry:* cherry tree; ship (merchant

riches) • *kabala:* ten • *see also* **prosperity**
weaning wormwood
weapons arrow (a spiritual weapon); knife (a base, secret weapon, the inversion of the sword, which is an heroic weapon); lance (an earthly weapon as opposed to the spiritual implications of the sword); scythe (weapon of peasants); sword (a spiritual weapon); tailor (a bad shot with a weapon); thunderbolt (weapon of the supreme deity); tooth (primitive weapon); tusk (an offensive weapon) • *association:* steel • *royal weapons:* club [bat]; double-headed axe; lance; mace; spear (in ancient times); staff; whip
weariness *see* **fatigue**
weaving *associations:* Athena; distaff.
weddings *see* **marriage**
Wednesday Born on a Wednesday, sour and sad (or, full of woe); Wednesday's child is merry and glad; once considered the best day to get married on • *associations:* Gemini; Mercury [god]; Woden; works of science
weeping *see* **tears [weeping]**
welcome hands clasped in a handshake (on a tombstone: farewell and welcome) • *flower language:* American starwort (welcome to a stranger) • *see also* **friendliness**
well-being *see* **prosperity**
Wencelas, St. *attribute:* eagle
werewolves *attribute:* eyebrows that meet (Norse)
West [US] *emblems:* American Indian; sagebrush; ten-gallon hat; windmill
whale *association:* octopus
whalers and whaling *emblem:* harpoon
Wheel of Fortune *association:* S • *emblem:* eight-pointed star • *see also* **destiny; fate; fortune**
Wheel of Fortune [tarot] *associations:* I [letter]; J
Wheel of Life sphere
Whig Party [Great Britain] *association:* blue
whipping branch [plant]; spread-eagle body position (especially associated with flogging); willow switch • *see also* **scourging**
whirlpool counterclockwise spiral
white *association:* spring [season] (occasionally) • *China:* odd numbers (association)

White Goddess *attribute:* hooked nose
white magic clockwise swastika
wholeness bracelet; cone (psychic wholeness); fountain; globe; hermaphrodite; Janus; orchestra (activity of the corporate whole); Pleiades; ring; Sagittarius (the complete man in both animal and spiritual nature) • *associations:* four; Neptune [planet]; seven; ten (wholeness; totality of the universe); twelve • *see also* **completion; ending; unity**
whorehouse nunnery (Elizabethan euphemism)
whores *see* **prostitutes**
wickedness centaur with a bow and arrow (the fiery darts of the wicked); hedgehog; House of God [tarot]; leaven; mosquito; Pandora, Pandora's box (wicked temptations of mankind); rod • *folklore:* eleven (the number of hours of sleep needed by wicked people) • *see also* **evil; villainy**
Widow of Sarepta *attribute:* cruse of oil
widowhood Artemesia (a widow's devotion to her husband's memory); woman placing a coin in a chest (the widow's mite) • *flower language:* sweet scabious; sweet sultan (when the flower is alone) • *heraldry:* lozenge [shape]
wife *see* **wives**
Wild Man *attribute:* club [bat] (the "wild man" of medieval European painting)
wilderness *Christianity:* monk offering a stone to Jesus Christ (the Devil tempting Christ in the wilderness) • *Judaism:* hut (a reminder of the time in the wilderness)
wildness claw; cutting reins (freedom to go wild); doe; falcon; full, thick head of hair; hawk (a wild and intractable woman); lion; ocean (untameable wildness); ogre (prehuman savage life); Pandora, Pandora's box (wild tendencies of imagination); Titan (a wild and untameable force of nature) • *association:* red (primitive wildness) • *see also* **ferocity**
wiles *see* **deceit**
Wilfred, St. *attribute:* ship with a staff
wiliness *see* **cunning**
will bow [archery]; bow with arrows (action as a means of effecting the

will); dog; fear, terror (lack of intellectual will); heart (will power); Hermit [tarot] (the successful union of personal and cosmic will); island (consciousness and will as refuge from the unconscious; the synthesis of consciousness and will); Jupiter [god]; Magic [tarot] (the union of personal and divine will); music; Prometheus (the will to resist oppression); reins; sun; weapons (will directed to a certain end) • *associations:* club suit [playing cards]; Leo; one; Mercury [planet] (free will); Pluto [planet] (the will to exercise power); thumb • *divine will:* earth [soil]; rudder; Magic [tarot] (the union of personal and divine will); shofar (obedience to divine will); Wheel of Fortune [tarot] • *emblem:* cabbage (the self-willed) • *Judaism:* one (the power and will of the universe)

willfulness *association:* seven (willful and unexpected action)

William of Aquitaine, St. soldier receiving monk's habit from an abbot

wind bag; bagpipe; bird; falcon; fan; feather; flute; goose; labyrinth; manticore (attribute of Sirocco personified); sails; vulture • *art:* lips • *association:* eight (the directions of the winds) • *Egypt:* lion with four wings (the south wind) • *wind deities:* see-saw (attribute) • *see also* **air**

winding sheet *see* **burial**

window eyes (window to the outer world)

wine grapes; vinegar (poor man's wine)

wings wings of skin (the higher qualities of wings perverted)

winter cormorant; evening; goose; holly (mid-winter); hyssop; ice; laurel; night; north; north wind; spade [shovel]; wolf • *association:* starling (mid-winter) • *China:* even numbers (association); plum tree (emblem); tortoise • *emblems:* goat with a spiral tail (occasionally); salamander • *flower language:* guelder rose; snowball (winter of age) • *winter solstice:* I [letter], little finger (associations)

wisdom Adam; agate (acquired wisdom); ant; ass; Athena; banana; bat [animal]; beaver; bee; book; breasts; broom [for sweeping]; burnt stick (wisdom and death); centaur; chalice;

chrysolite; cocoa tree; coconut; confetti; coot; crystal; dabchick (a seeker of the wisdom of the deeps); dandelion; divorce (the apparent or delusive separation of love from wisdom); dove; dragon; east; egg surrounded by a serpent (the eternal germ of life encircled by creative wisdom); elephant; father; finger in the mouth, occasionally the thumb; fish; fishing (seeking wisdom; searching for deeper wisdom); flame; flowing or full robe; forehead; fountain; frankincense; fruit; golden carriage (spiritual qualities allied with wisdom); golden fleece, occasionally a white fleece; golden hair; grapes (the spiritual nature of love and wisdom); gray hair; griffin with a ball underfoot (enlightenment protecting wisdom); hand flat on the heart; Hanged Man [tarot] (power derived from charity, wisdom, fidelity, and other higher virtues); hazel; head; head that is severed; helmet; Hermit [tarot]; hind [deer]; honey (wisdom; spiritual wisdom); hyacinth [flower]; ibis; jasper; jet [mineral]; Juno; key of gold (philosophical wisdom); lark; light; linen; lizard; locust [insect]; Magic [tarot] (occult wisdom); manger (wisdom arising from ignorance); milk; mirror; mother; mountain; mulberry tree; myrrh (natural good and wisdom); Nestor; nuts (hidden wisdom); olive branch; owl; pearl (esoteric wisdom); persimmon; Phrygia; pool [water]; prostitute (the soul seeking satisfaction instead of wisdom); rabbit; raven; rice; riches (wisdom, especially when a gift from deities or fairies); roebuck; rudder; salmon; salt; scroll; seraph; serpent (wisdom; wisdom of the deep); serpent with head erect (human wisdom); shepherd (guardian of ancient wisdom); sieve; sleep; Solomon (wisdom combined with weakness); Solomon's ring (wisdom and power); Solon; Sophia (wisdom of the universe); sorcerer (a wise old man); Sphinx (arcane wisdom); stick; sturgeon; swan; sycamore; ten maidens with lamps (the Five Wise Virgins and the Five Foolish Virgins); thrush; Tigris River; toad; tooth; topaz; tree (wisdom, sometimes divine); tuna; tunny; two griffins (wisdom and enlightenment); Virgil (worldly wisdom); virgin;

wall; walnut (hidden wisdom); wheat; white bread; white rose (inspired wisdom); wine; wood; Yggdrasil • *associations:* black; bright yellow (divine wisdom and glory); light complexion; orange (passion tempered by earthly wisdom); orange-yellow (divine wisdom or goodness); purple; red face (applies to Caucasians only); ring finger; S; seven; seventy-two (a ritual number involving solar increase and lunar wisdom); six; white (consummate wisdom) • *China:* wild pear tree (wise administration) • *heraldry:* ash tree (source of wisdom); helmet; helmet surmounted by a wolf's head (courage supplanted by astuteness); palm tree; silver; spider • *divine wisdom:* aspalathus (the wisdom of the Lord); butter (divine love and wisdom); flaming pillar or tree trunk (the God of light and wisdom); galbanum; gold; hearing (reception of divine wisdom); linen; pentagon (heavenly wisdom); tree (wisdom, sometimes divine) • *see also* **esoterica; knowledge; learning; omniscience**

Wisdom personified Athena • *attributes:* breastplate mounted on a pole; gooseberry; olive branch; owl

wishing Cockaigne (ridicule of poetic bliss or wishful thinking); foxglove; siren [mythology] or harpist (death wish); sweet basil (good wishes) • *flower language:* coronella (may success crown your wishes); foxglove • *see also* **aspiration; hope; longing**

wit haberdasher (a person of small wit); Punch and Judy (contagious humor and common sense overcoming all obstacles); rabbit (witty trickery); salt; whetstone • *flower language:* meadow lychnis; ragged robin; southernwood (bantering); wild sorrel (ill-timed wit) • *heraldry:* fox (sagacity or wit used in one's own defense); owl (acute wit) • *see also* **cleverness; frivolity; intellect; sagacity**

witchcraft bat [animal]; beetle; cauldron; mare; mistletoe; nightshade; Satan; whisper • *associations:* bryony; cherry stones; Lapland; menstrual blood • *emblem:* inverted five-pointed star • *flower language:* enchanter's nightshade • *see also* **enchantment; magic; magic spells; sorcery**

witches animal without a tail (may

be a witch in animal form); bearded woman; birch (charm against witches); broom [for sweeping] (witch's steed); crossroads (meeting place of demons, witches, etc.); ferns (hated by witches and evil spirits); keyhole (place for the entrance of witches, demons, etc., which could be guarded by filling it up or leaving an iron key in it); midnight (the witches' hour); red butterfly (a witch); rowan (protection against witches, but also used by them) • *associations:* elder tree; goat; hare; hedgehog; owl; pumpkin; red moon (activity of witches); toad • *attributes:* black cat; double pupils; gloves

withdrawal *see* **retirement**

witness stone; torch (Christian witness)

wives cistern (a wife who must be guarded to be kept pure); hematite (wifehood); hind [deer] (one's own wife); pond • *China:* parrot (warning to wives to be faithful to their husbands) • *Germany:* wimple • *Rome:* slender fillet (a lawfully wedded wife) • *see also* **housewives; marriage; widowhood**

Woden *association:* Wednesday • *emblem:* raven

woes *see* **trouble**

wolves *association:* Mars

womb amphora; ark; cauldron; cave; ciborium (the womb of the Virgin Mary); coffer; furnace; kettle; night; Noah's ark; oven; pomegranate; ship; tomb; vase • *associations:* black; pot, usually earthen (the womb; nature's inexhaustible womb); potter; U; zero *return to the womb:* bath, especially a warm bath; boat (the womb or cradle rediscovered); floating; swan

women apricot; azalea; bat [animal] (a woman between 80 and 90 years of age); bird in a cage (a kept woman); carnation (female love); cherry blossoms (feminine beauty); china (an attractive woman); Circe (feminine wiles); crescent (womanhood); crescent on an outhouse door (use reserved for females); distaff (woman; the domestic role of women); dolphin; fish; flower; fountain; goose (a woman 50 to 60 years of age); guinea hen (a low woman); hawk (a wild and intractable woman); heifer (a young woman); Helen (the instinctive and emotional aspects of woman); hen (a woman 40 to 50 years old); High Priestess [tarot]; lamia (evil woman); magpie (a woman 20 to 30 years old); ocean; peahen (a woman 30 to 40 years of age); reed; sarcophagus; siren [mythology] (a treacherous woman; the base forces in woman); skirt; snare (a strange woman); Virgin Mary with a serpent underfoot (victory of the seed of woman); vulture (a woman 60 to 70 years of age); wall; wisteria (the gentleness and devotion of womanhood) • *associations:* Athena (spinning, weaving, and other women's crafts); green; shell; timbrel • *attribute:* twisted belt (a woman in love) • *China:* azalea; jasmine blossom (emblem); swallow [bird] (woman's voice) • *emblems:* cherry tree; petticoat • *flower language:* carnation, carnation pink (woman's love); orchis (a belle) • *Germany:* fillet (an unmarried woman); wimple (a married woman) • *heraldry:* diamond [shape] (the escutcheon of women); green; lozenge [shape] (an unmarried woman); panther (a beautiful woman, normally tender, but fierce in defense of her children) • *Judaism:* long flowing hair (attribute of single women) • *single women (associations):* fillet (Germany); green stockings (in the Middle Ages, worn at weddings by older unmarried sisters of the bride); long flowing hair (Judaism); lozenge [shape] (heraldry) • *virtuous women:* linen clothes (attribute); Virgin Mary (virtuous womanhood) • *see also* **courtesans; female principle; the female; girls; maidens; mistresses; motherhood; promiscuity; prostitutes; wantonness; wives**

Wonders of the World   *associations:* seven; ten

woods *see* **forest**

woodsmen *see* **foresters**

the word bursting pomegranate (fertility of the word); Empress [tarot]; leaven; light; lizard; oar; sword; thunderbolt (the word piercing the darkness); • *association:* lips • *heraldry:* unicorn • *the creative word:* mouth; scepter (the creative power of the word) • *Egypt:* mace [weapon] • *the word of God:* analogion; Bible; honey; lamp, especially an oil lamp; lighthouse; manna; pulpit; stag; tablet; unicorn; white

horse, especially with a rider • *association:* L

words black and white (the printed word); dart (evil words); drum (communication, especially of word or tradition); gall (poison words); three feathers (good thought, word, and deed) • *association:* W

work bottomless cask, sand (useless labor); brooch, clothes (may indicate the wearer's trade); ditch digger, swineherd (low work); hammer (manual labor); key (a task to be performed and the means for carrying it out); mattock; mule (a faithful worker); ox; partridge (the hopelessness of worldly endeavor); plow; Saturday's child works hard for a living; shovel; spider web (fine work); sweat; wheelbarrow; wine press (patient or solitary labor or suffering); wormwood (bitter labor); yoke; zodiac (the dignity of labor) • *associations:* four, V (hard work); M • *Christianity:* maniple (good works); recessional in church (Christians going forth to work in the world); work in a vineyard (work of Christians for God) • *heraldry:* fusil; spider • *see also* **diligence; industry; tasks**

works *days related to works:* Sunday (light); Monday (divination); Tuesday (wrath); Wednesday (science); Thursday (politics; religion); Friday (love); Saturday (mourning) • *see also* **tasks**

Work [Toil] personified *attribute:* yoke

world ascending stairs (longing for a higher world); clouds, mist (the intermediate world between the formal and non-formal); eclipse of the sun (omen of the end of the world); eyes; garden; globe; goblet filled with liquid (the non-formal world of possibilities); Gordian knot; head; labyrinth; Mount Ararat, threshing floor (world navel); orange [fruit]; orb; orb with a snake around it (sin encircling the world); oyster; sickle (end of the world); sigma, sigmoid (communication between worlds); sphere; stairs (connection between worlds); tent; theater (this world and the next; the world of phenomena); threshold (reconciliation and separation of two worlds, such as sacred and profane, life and death, etc.); thunderbolt (the action of the higher world upon the lower); triangle with the apex up (the urge to escape from this world to the Origin); U (world pot); veil (renunciation of the world); whale; World [tarot] (the totality of the manifest world as a reflection of permanent creative activity); zigzag (the material world) • *associations:* seven, ten (wonders of the world); nine (the three worlds: corporal, intellectual, spiritual) • *Christianity:* orb with a cross (Christian dominion of the world; recognition of God's ultimate dominion over the world); recessional in church (Christians going forth to work in the world); yoke (Jesus Christ bearing the world's sins) • *emblem:* six-pointed star (the action of the higher world upon the lower) • *entrance to another world:* alcove; crystal ball; door; gate; key; mirror • *retreat from the world:* cottage; ivory tower; lodge; Shangri-La • *world axis:* axle tree; I [letter]; mast; maypole; menhir; mountain; nails [for wood]; navel; oak; parasol; phallus; pillar; Pole Star; Q; rod; scepter; spear; spindle; spire; staff; stairs, especially when surmounted by a fleur-di-lys, cross, star, or angel; stem; stick; string; thread; tower

World [tarot] *association:* W

worldliness apple (earthly desires indulgence in earthly desires); asceticism (voluntary abandonment of worldly activities in preparation for renewed life on a higher spiritual plane); ashes (the lower mind); Babylon; belly (the physical side of man); blindness (mentality immersed in the concerns of the lower life); bridle (worldly interests and cares); bubble (emptiness of material existence); Castor and Pollux (the dual worldly and spiritual nature of all things); chains (the attachment of the mind to the lower world); cicada (worldly grandeur; evanescent worldly glory); cincture (contempt for the world); Death [tarot] (abandonment of earthly desires); Gomorrah; ibis; ivory tower (retreat from worldliness); nymph (worldly pleasure); partridge (the hopelessness of worldly endeavor); person in chains (man enslaved by sin or his earthly desires); narcissus [flower] (the triumph of divine love over worldliness); penance (aspiration which implies discontent with the worldly conditions to which one is

bound for a time); Reynard the Fox; rich robe (worldly pomp and vanity); Sodom; tonsure (rejection of the temporal); Virgil (worldly wisdom) • *associations:* brown (renunciation of the world); scarlet; white (detachment from the world) • *heraldry:* orange [color] (worldly ambition) • *worldly things:* coins at the feet of an old man (renunciation of worldly things); globe being kicked (disdain for worldly things); gold (worldly wealth); nuditas temporalis (contempt for worldly things; lack of worldly things); overturned bowl, cup, pitcher (the emptiness of worldly things, especially in still life painting); serpent (the evil inherent in worldly things); sewing; spindle • *see also* **matter**

worry *see* **anxiety**

worship altar; angel holding a censer (heavenly adoration); Ark of the Covenant (Jewish worship); Beelzebub (the worship of false gods); harp (worship in heaven); hill (place of worship and meditation); idol (outward observances regarded as true spiritual exercises); kiss (idol worship); prostitute (worshipper of idols); sunflower; tambourine (bacchanalian worship); trumpet (call to worship) • *flower language:* American cowslip (you are my angel, my divinity) • *Old Testament worship:* Ark of the Covenant; laver of brass; seven-branched menorah; tabernacle in a tent; table with shewbread • *see also* **adoration; eucharist; God; meditation; prayer**

worth ascending (a raise in value or worth); coriander (hidden worth); salt; Victory personified (implies spiritual worth) • *flower language:* alyssum (worth beyond beauty); coriander (hidden worth); fennel (worthy of all praise); full white rose (I am worthy of you); pink convolvulus (worth sustained by judicious and tender affection); woodruff (modest worth) • *see also* **merit; value**

worthlessness ashes; blackberry; chaff; coal [mineral]; coot; copper; cress; dung; egg shell; gooseberry; pin (something of value up to the middle of the 18th century, afterwards, something of no value); pitcher • *see also* **usefulness**

wounds rags (a wound to the soul— the particular garment that is in rags gives a more precise meaning to this); red knight; yarrow (treatment for wounds) • *association:* five, pentagram (the five wounds of Jesus Christ) • *flower language:* European sweet briar (I wound to heal)

wrath tiger • *association:* Tuesday (works of wrath) • *divine wrath:* angel holding a flaming sword; angel sheathing sword (God's wrath turned aside); cedar (occasionally, God's power to weaken the strong); earthquake (omen of divine anger); fire and brimstone [sulfur]; horde of grasshoppers or locusts; khamsin; plague; press [tool]; scroll; smoke (anger and wrath of God); thunderbolt; wine press • *see also* **anger; punishment**

Wrath personified *attributes:* dagger; lion; sword

wretchedness *see* **misery**

writers *attributes:* book; inkhorn; laurel (in portraiture); scroll; writing pen • *see also* **literature**

writing black and white together (the printed word)

X–Y

X *association:* six

Y *association:* seven

yang principle *China:* goose; red; rooster; tree peony

year holly (the second half of the year); zodiac**yearning** *see* **longing**

yellow *association:* six

yes *see* **approval**

Yggdrasil ash tree; squirrel (messenger of Yggdrasil) • *association:* eagle

yin principle *China:* yellow

yoke scapular (the yoke of Jesus Christ) • *association:* five (the Five Yoke of Oxen)

Yom Kippur *see* **Atonement, Day of**

York, House of *emblem:* red rose

youth Adonis [mythology] (youthful beauty); Africa; April; beryl (everlasting youth); billy goat (a boy 10 to 20 years of age); buds; bull (a man 20 to 30 years of age); calf (a boy up to 20 years of age); cicada (eternal youth); dabchick (a girl 10 to 20 years of age); daisy; dawn; dew; Endymion (youthful beauty); foxglove; freckles (youth, especially bucolic); kettle (restorer of lost youth); lilac [plant]; morning; Narcissus (death of youth); Phoenix [bird] (eternal youth); primrose; rosy cheeks; Shangri-La (eternal youth); spring [season]; summer; sun; tennis ball (youthfulness); wine (youth and eternal life) • *associations:* eagle; green; pink [color]; south • *flower language:* almond (the impetuousness of youth); cowslip (early joys, particularly youthful); primrose (early youth); red catchfly (youthful love); red rosebud (you are young and beautiful); white lilac (youthful innocence) • *heraldry:* rose [flower]

Youth personified *attributes:* dolphin (steed of Youth personified); eagle

Z

Z *association:* eight

Zadkiel *attribute:* knife, especially a sacrificial knife

zeal bee (the zeal of the Christian in acquiring virtue); cymbal (religious ardor); elder tree; fir; fire (spiritual

enlightenment and zeal); flaming
heart, flaming sword (intense zeal);
hare (Christian zeal); ruby; seraph;
torch • *associations:* red; scarlet • *flower
language:* elder tree • *heraldry:* flint
(zeal to serve) • *see also* **passion**
Zebulum *association:* ship in a harbor
Zechariah *associations:* four chariots;
four horns; measuring with a line; red
horse; stone full of eyes; walled city;
winged scroll • *attribute:* ass
Zeno, St. *attribute:* crozier with a fish
dangling from it
Zenobius, St. *attributes:* dead child;
elm tree in leaf; fleur-di-lys on a halo
or book; flowering tree
Zepaniah *association:* Jerusalem with
a sword above it
Zephyr *attribute:* cornucopia
zero Fool [tarot] (absolute zero, from
which all proceeds and all returns) •
association: Pluto [planet]
zest *see* **enthusiasm**
Zeus *see* **Jupiter [god]**
Zion temple on a hill (the spiritual
Zion)
zodiac serpent in a circle, biting its
own tail; starred girdle [cincture];
twelve stringed lyre; wheel • *days
related to the zodiac:* Monday (Cancer); Tuesday (Scorpio); Wednesday
(Gemini); Thursday (Sagittarius);
Friday (Taurus); Saturday (Capricorn)